American History

Through the Eyes of Modern Chaos Theory

Where We Were - Where We Are Going

American History

Through the Eyes of Modern Chaos Theory

Burton P. Fabricand

ISBN 978-0-557-15668-9

Designed by Marc Remmen

AMERICAN HISTORY THROUGH THE EYES OF MODERN CHAOS THEORY

TABLE OF CONTENTS

AMERICAN HISTORY THROUGH THE EYES OF MODERN CHAOS THEORY

Where We Were – Where We Are Going

INTRODUCTION

No government is ever perfect. One of the chief virtues of a democracy, however, is that its defects are always visible and under democratic processes can be pointed out and corrected.

Harry S. Truman

The point of view of this history is that of modern chaos theory, a rather recent development that imposes severe limitations on the notion future predictability in the social sciences, not to mention the physical, biological and environmental sciences. When taken into account, there emerges a picture of American history very different from today's conventional ideas. The trees, so to speak, are the same, but the forest is changed. It is the aim of this book to reinterpret America's rise to "Power, Consequence, and Grandeur" in light of these findings.

What unfolds, it must be stressed, is a history they don't want us to know about. Who are they? Why, none other than those active, vigilant and politically adept power groups that pipe money from our pockets into theirs via the United States Treasury. It is a history they wish to hold confidential lest that copious flow of funds be disrupted. It's not that these "benefactors of humanity" lack noble intentions. Not at all. But, as noted by Adam Smith, there are no persons more dangerous than those who presume to do good with other people's money. We have arrived at so exalted a standard of living that many of us fail to see, and do not wish to see, how much harm is now being done. So be it. But for those of us concerned about America's future, let us see if we can ferret out the abuses attending our imperfect government and, before it is too late, point the way toward correcting them.

CHAPTER I

OUR FATHER WHO ERST IN LONDON DWELLETH

Beauty is in the eye of the beholder
Margaret Hungerford, *Molly Bawn*

'Beauty is Truth/ Truth Beauty'
John Keats, *Ode to a Grecian Urn*

Truth, like beauty, is in the eye of the beholder
Burton P. Fabricand, The *Science of Winning*

George William Frederick was born important. More important, even, than anyone in the year 1738 could possibly have imagined. As the eldest son of Frederick Louis, Prince of Wales, and the German princess Augusta of Saxe-Gotha, he was destined to rule what was arguably the world's most powerful nation. And rule absolutely, if Augusta had her way. For, from boyhood on, she had reared young George to "Be a King!", to restore to England the enlightened despotism enjoyed by all other European monarchies. To do so, she well knew, could prove a formidable task. It presumed a King's divine right to carry out God's will "on earth, as it is in heaven." It meant recouping the King's rightful powers usurped from the throne in the Glorious Revolution of 1688-1689. And, most assuredly, it threatened a greedy political establishment gorging itself on the fruits of graft and corruption. No matter, if England were to be rescued from democratic anarchy, it had to be done. Only then could George govern above faction and influence, the acknowledged father of all his people whose sole concern is their welfare. Only then could he exercise his supreme authority to correct social abuses, alleviate suffering and ensure "the greatest happiness of the greatest number." Only then could he purge the country of violence, oppression and immorality. A Kingdom of Righteousness, a model for all the world to emulate – that's what her George would make of England!

Ah, how noble the intentions! They almost always are. We all want to do good, don't we? But fulfilling noble intentions in the real world is fraught with difficulty and the danger of doing not good but evil. Reality, you see, is not nearly as simple-minded as so many of us project it to be. Our mind's eye captures but few of its many fragments, bits and pieces we put together to create some semblance of the whole. "The slings and arrows of outrageous fortune" lurk just beyond our view, ever ready to ambush our fondest dreams and turn them into nightmares. Good, evil, whatever, who knows what the future holds in store when so much of reality is shrouded in mystery? *But Mousie, thou art no thy lane,/ In proving foresight may be vain;/ The best-laid schemes o' mice an' men/ Gang aft agley,/ An' lea'e us nought but grief an' pain,/ For promis'd joy!* (Robbie Burns, *To a Mouse*).

To what extent does reality correspond to what I think is reality? There's the human problem. It has intrigued philosophers at least since the time of Socrates, and it lies at the heart of literature's great comedies and tragedies wherein unpredictable futures await archetypal characters. It is not at all like the fake problems we solve in school, where some teacher's vision of reality is authoritatively impressed on the raw clay of our brains. Hardly! In the classroom we get the "facts," and from these certain conclusions supposedly follow in a strict "logical" manner. A correct geometrical order prevails, each step dictated by the previous one until the "truth" stands revealed. How glorious the real world would be if it worked as neatly as that! How straightforward for each of us to "reason" our way to a rich, happy and secure existence, to heaven right here on earth. But, of course, it isn't that easy. What is easy is to confuse noble intentions with knowledge and wisdom. And it is oh so easy to imagine some mighty father out there who can realize our Utopian dreams for us, one who knows the formula for doing good. From time immemorial, this elitist theme has been packaged and repackaged into endless variations. Look, first and foremost, to that masterly consolidation into one Supreme Being of all the gods and goddesses and demons and spirits of pagan faiths, the "Only True God" worshiped by Christians, Jews and Moslems. Then to the earthly heads of state to whom He presumably extends His heavenly powers. And, finally, to the philosopher-kings of Plato's *Republic* who commune with Ultimate Truth and the Supreme Good, and whose offspring have evolved into the Illuminati of socialist and Marxist persuasion. All profess to find "truth" in random patterns of experience and, thereby, to prophesy and overcome the pitfalls on the "steep and thorny way to heaven." "What is truth?" wise Pontius Pilate slyly asks of Jesus in the *Gospel According to St. John* (18:38). Jesus does not answer, but it is a question we must and shall address later. For now, though, let us turn our attention back to young George and see how he coped with the inscrutable course of coming events.

The premature death of his father in 1751 was followed in 1760 by that of his grandfather, King George II, and our hero ascended to the throne as George III, King of Great Britain and Ireland, at the tender age of 22. All England enthusiastically acclaimed the young and handsome new king, the first George from the German House of Hannover to be born and raised in England. Vigorous, virtuous, intelligent, sober and pious, he embodied all the attributes of the ideal monarch. "Born and educated in this country, I glory in the name of Briton," he could declare in his opening speech to Parliament. And, indeed, there was much to glory. Her burgeoning economy had placed England on the verge of world supremacy in commerce, industry and finance. A growing and increasingly affluent middle class dominated a population of some nine million souls. No country anywhere could match the English standard of living and the freedom from political oppression possessed by its citizens. Nowhere did there prevail equality of opportunity for so many, nowhere such an enormity of private savings for financing new industry and expanding the old, for conducting research and development, and for promoting the new inventions and processes spawned by the industrial revolution. Prosperity was robust and expanding. And, as always when affluence abounds, art, architecture, literature, engineering and science flourished. Schools, libraries, museums, universities, theaters and concert halls arose on a scale never before seen. The names of Adam, Arkwright, Boswell, Brindley, Burns, Cook, Darby, Defoe, Fielding, Gainsborough, Garrick, Gibbon, Goldsmith, Halley, Handel, Hooke, Hume, Johnson, Locke, Newton, Pepys, Pope, Reynolds, Smith, Swift, Watt, Wedgwood, Wilkinson and Wren punctuate English and world history.

Such was the glory of England in the eighteenth century. There were miseries, to be sure, the same that afflict all societies – the inevitable dislocation of farm and factory workers by new labor-saving inventions and machines, city slums, and the poverty-ridden minority on the dole. But the most serious hangover from the past arose from war, what was known as the Seven Years' War in Europe and the French and Indian War in America.

The war had begun in 1756 during the reign of George II, who by this time took no active interest in the affairs of state. In the ensuing vacuum, British policy-making had devolved onto the leading Member of Parliament, William Pitt, whose objective was the seizure of the French colonies in North America and India and the obliteration of France as a threat to English supremacy. By 1760, most of the colonies had been taken, and Frederick the Great, King of Prussia and England's ally in the great European power struggle, was ably prosecuting the land war against a French-Austrian-Russian alliance. George III, however, opposed the War. He abhorred the slaughter of innocent subjects caught up in the political machinations of their infallible rulers. And he deplored the way war stunted economic growth by diverting a country's resources into wasteful military production. But most of all he worried incessantly about the ever mounting taxes and government borrowings needed to finance the carnage. And his view now prevailed, for he had quickly learned how to use his funds and powers of patronage to buy all the Parliamentary votes needed in his bid for sole power. In opposition to Pitt, he concluded a pact with France and thereby hastened the War to its conclusion in 1763, to the great joy and relief of an exhausted Europe. The return of peace lessened the need for military expenditures and freed up money for industrial production and expansion, enabling England's economic growth to resume its heady pace. One wartime legacy remained, however, an astronomical (for the time) government debt of £160 million. It was to become crucially significant. With taxes high and lenders loathe to supply credit to a government steeped in debt, our new king found himself restricted in his ability to fund his beneficent operations. What to do? Raising taxes ever higher on a population already disgruntled by years of wartime deprivations seemed a particularly dangerous way to go. King George was much smarter than his French counterparts who became so enamored of tax increases that they literally lost their heads over them. And he was all too aware of another English king, Charles I, who had suffered the same fate for the same reason a hundred years earlier. Looking around, he spied his prosperous and untaxed American colonies, and lo and behold, he knew what to do. Why not tax them to help rid England of her budget deficits. Why shouldn't they pay their fair share for the benefits bestowed on them by the British victory in the French and Indian War? And those to accrue in the future? What could be simpler? Or fairer? Or safer, since the colonists were an ocean away? Later, we shall meet other leaders with the same naive `conception of the real world. Invariably, the consequences are the same – raising taxes raises government debts, usually in ways unforeseeable. *But Mousie* . . . .

What ensued is too well known to recount in detail. Early Americans showed little enthusiasm for promoting the general welfare as seen by the great minds in London, England. They were sure they could do more good with their money by spending it themselves. Freedom from taxation, after all, was one of the primary reasons they had emigrated from Europe in the first place. Taxes to them symbolized government oppression and once sown, they well knew, could grow and multiply like weeds. It had happened in Spain and Holland, where crippling imposts had strangled commerce and industry to such an extent that those one-time superpowers had been reduced to an also-ran status. It was happening in England where even a constitutional government could ignore the "Rights of Englishmen" and impose onerous taxes the payment of which was enforced by savage punishments. What's more, they insisted, the manufacturing, trade and monetary restrictions imposed on the colonial economy for the homeland's benefit more than compensated for any taxes they might have paid. No, enough was enough. The time had come to stop the developing oppression before it endangered both their freedoms and their rapid economic growth. And so, unlike 20th-century Americans who wimpishly swallowed steady doses of huge tax increases in promoting the general welfare as seen by the great minds in Washington, D.C., they resisted. They dodged, avoided and evaded taxes at every turn, to such an extent that paying taxes became decidedly un-American. They boycotted British manufactures, destroyed British imports, smuggled foreign goods, and in a veritable orgy of law-breaking, created out of secession not the chaos most expected, but a free and independent new nation that would in the next century become the greatest the world had ever known. And, in so doing, they rendered unto George III, the cause of it all, his extra added importance. The Declaration of Independence compelled George to obey Mummy and "Be a King!" He had the power, he knew the Truth and the Good, and he was carrying out God's will. Law and order, it had to be upheld. The British Empire, it had to be preserved. And so, despite recommendations from William Pitt and Adam Smith (whom we shall meet later) and many others to grant the colonies their independence, he decided on war. The wanton mayhem and bloodshed so rife in Europe spread once again to America's shores and persisted for eight long and unexpectedly grim years. Not until 1783 did the tax revolt known as the American Revolution finally end. And, of course, the debt grew worse with each passing year. So unmanageable did it become that the King, perhaps inspired by desperation, called to power an unbelievably wise young man of 24, a disciple of Adam Smith and the son of William Pitt. William Pitt the Younger took over as Prime Minister in 1784 facing a dangerously unbalanced budget and a government debt totaling £250 million. He promptly ended almost all taxes on manufacturers to encourage production, drastically reduced customs duties on a large number of imports to discourage smuggling – a tax on tea, as an example, dropped from 119% to 12½% of value – and sharply reduced government expenditures through improved auditing procedures. And, as a result, tax revenues jumped to such an extent that budget deficits vanished in four booming years of economic expansion. Had the younger Pitt been around in 1776, America may still have been one with Britain. As it turned out, the British people never again tolerated in any ruler, benign or otherwise, the power once exercised by King George III. And, for fear of him, the new American nation eschewed a strong central government until well into the 20th century, until 1913, by which time his menacing figure had been all but forgotten and the country had grown unimaginably rich.

CHAPTER II

OUT OF CHAOS

The scientist is astonished to notice how sublime order emerges from what appeared to be chaos.

Albert Einstein

Bob Noyce was born unimportant. Outwardly, there was little to distinguish his birth from the four million others that occurred in the land in 1927. Certainly, no "Star of Burlington" appeared over his small home town in Iowa to guide the elite to his manger. Yet, for reasons we humans may never know, this birth was unique, for it helped start an avalanche of random events that led to the information revolution of the late 20th century. "Among the three or four million cradles now rocking in the land," noted Mark Twain, "are some which this nation would preserve for ages as sacred things, if we could know which ones they are."

I met Bob when he joined my research group at the old Philco Corporation in Philadelphia in the early 1950s. He was fresh out of the Massachusetts Institute of Technology with a Ph.D. in physical electronics. The recent invention of the transistor by William Shockley, John Bardeen and Walter Brattain of the Bell Telephone Laboratories had awakened everybody to the prospect of enormous advances in electronics, and many companies were sponsoring research and development programs aimed at improving established products and creating new ones. Bob had everything; he was attractive, knowledgeable, bright, clever, quick-witted, courteous, well-spoken, and politically nimble. He seemed to the corporate manner born. His outstanding qualities did not go unrecognized and he advanced rapidly at Philco – until he accepted a job offer from Shockley, who by now had left Bell Labs and was heading up the Shockley Semiconductor division of Beckman Instruments, a very successful high technology firm. So in debt was Bob from the costs of a college education that I lent him $500 to help move his family to California.

Once there, he set to work developing some of Shockley's esoteric ideas. Now there is no denying Shockley's greatness – he was brilliant, imaginative and a Nobel Prize winner. But he was also a bit of an eccentric. He worked from 4 A.M. to noon, and then would spend the rest of the day sailing and thinking. And so it happened that while he was away, his boys did play. Independently of Shockley, Noyce and his fellow workers managed to produce a diffused-base silicon transistor, one of the notable advances of the era. They wanted to go into immediate production, but Shockley vetoed the idea on the grounds that a comparatively mundane device such as this would soon invite severe competition. Even a luminary like Shockley could ill foresee the magnitude of coming developments. They went to Arnold Beckman, the chairman, who sided with Shockley. Disappointed and frustrated, they decided to go into business for themselves. But how? They had in hand something new and promising, yes, but it was only a laboratory prototype. The operation they had in mind went far beyond their meager financial resources. Furthermore, they possessed neither the production nor the marketing expertise necessary to capitalize on their new device. Were there people around willing to risk their money in backing such a venture?

Crucial to the winning ways of America is the small investor pursuing his or her own best interests in an environment free from government interference. In a stochastic process reminiscent of the condensation of water molecules on atmospheric dust particles to form raindrops and the agglomeration of galactic chaff to form stars and planets, capital accumulates about individuals in varying degrees as a result of their labor and circumstances. What a person does with excess monies, profits, savings – call it what you must – depends on the framework in which he or she operates. In a collectivist society, an individual's wishes are neither respected nor trusted, and private wealth is taxed away to be spent supposedly more wisely by politicians and bureaucrats. In a free society, on the other hand, everyone is encouraged to amass to the greatest extent possible those financial and real assets desired and use them as one chooses. Who gets to spend the money? There's the basic difference between capitalism and socialism.

Dubbed the "Traitorous Eight," Noyce and his group had little hope of obtaining government money for their enterprise – Shockley had much too much influence within the scientific and political establishments for that. But, fortunately for Noyce and all of us, America has long had in place a private capital market system that spells opportunity for just such fledgling entrepreneurs. An introduction to the Wall Street investment banking firm of Hayden, Stone gave Noyce his chance. It is one of the jobs of investment bankers, or underwriters as they are sometimes called, to funnel private savings into what they deem are worthy businesses needing money, usually through stock purchases by the investing public. The risks are very high for start-up ventures such as this – maybe one in ten works out – but when successful, the rewards can be substantial. Noyce's investment banker found a private donor in the Fairchild Camera & Instrument Company, a small firm trying to establish a foothold in high technology. Fairchild put up $1.25 million to finance a new division called Fairchild Semiconductor, and Noyce and his coworkers went to work. That was in 1957. On a visit to what is now known as Silicon Valley in the fall of that year, I accompanied Bob to an empty new building he had just purchased for the manufacturing operation. One year later, I again visited the same plant and saw it brimming over with production facilities for the new silicon transistor. Bob told me that the semiconductor division would show its first profit that month, an amazing performance for a brand new operation. Unfortunately for me, the significance of this surprising information – what in later years would be labeled "privileged" or "inside" information – for forecasting stock market behavior was at the time far beyond my understanding and, I should add, that of economists and the investment community as a whole. Within three years, Fairchild Semiconductor sales exceeded $100 million, dwarfing those of the parent company the stock of which jumped from $25 to over $500 a share. But the story is just beginning.

In 1961, Noyce patented a semiconductor device that contained several transistors on a single silicon wafer. (Independently of Noyce, Jack Kilby of Texas Instruments did the same). This electronic marvel was the forerunner of the microprocessor, the computer-on-a chip that was to revolutionize the computer and electronics industries in the coming decades. All through the 60's, extraordinarily sophisticated techniques were developed to pack more and more electronic components on a chip. But Noyce was unhappy. He felt that progress was snail-paced and wanted to devote much more money and effort to research and development. On this point, he came into increasing conflict with Fairchild's top management. Again, he and his group decided to begin anew. In a hugely successful initial public offering, he and his colleagues launched the Intel Corporation, which in 1971 pioneered the first microprocessor. Its inceptive use as a central logic chip in computers has since spread to hundreds of thousands of other products from microwave ovens and digital watches to automobiles. It is the key element in making possible today's information age, and Intel has become far and away the dominant factor in the semiconductor industry. Needless to say, Noyce became a deservedly rich young man. On 13 February 1983, he was inducted into the National Inventors Hall of Fame, joining forty-four other members including Thomas A. Edison, Henry Ford and Charles Goodyear.

Bob Noyce died in 1990, his name virtually unknown outside semiconductor circles. We learn in school the glorified history of one political ne'er-do-well after another, but how many of us know anything about those truly responsible for our high standard of living, men of vision like John D. Rockefeller, Andrew Carnegie, Alexander Graham Bell and Robert Noyce. They are among the unforeseen few who rose from the cradle to enrich the lives of millions. They and others like them belong to an exceptional group of ambitious, innovative, courageous and resourceful entrepreneurs who, by wresting order out of chaos, manage to produce the affordable goods and services upon which our society relies. Not all were as successful, and many were the failures. There is no way of foretelling the many possible outcomes. But what all these swashbucklers had in common was the freedom to try, and try and try again if necessary. And freedom is what America, more than any other country, supplies in abundance. Coping with chaos through individual freedom and initiative rather than through the planning-the-unplannable antics of a big central government, that is the secret of America's wondrous wealth. The Intel story is but one of thousands that made America great. Almost all would be inconceivable under virtuous public servants practicing the social and economic equivalents of alchemy and astrology. Were that the way to go, Soviet Russia, with her multitude of five-year plans, would almost certainly have become the greatest country in the world. As it turned out, the country with the least government became the greatest by far, and that country is, of course, the United States of America.

How "sublime order" springs forth spontaneously and unpredictably "from what appeared to be chaos" is the subject of much of today's exciting new physics. The wind and water patterns in the atmosphere and oceans, storm systems, plate tectonics, nations like America, businesses such as Intel, the consumer and financial markets that secure our future needs, you, me, life itself, all are examples of self-organized states of being that arise out of chaos, what I shall call "chaons." They are complex, robust systems capable of resisting deconstructing future shocks. All demand a constant inflow of energy to maintain their chaonic status, including in our human case the three-meal-a-day requirement. Truly they are miracles, and we shall learn about them in the next chapter. The implications for each of us are far-reaching, and as yet vastly under-appreciated in our increasingly collectivist societies.

CHAPTER III

CHAOS, CHAONS, AND PREDICTING THE FUTURE

The gods did not reveal from the beginning

All things to us; but in the course of time

Through seeking, men find that which is the better.

But as for certain truth, no man has known it.

Nor will he know it, neither of the gods,

Nor yet of all the things of which I speak.

And even if he were to utter the final truth,

He himself would not know it.

For all is a woven web of guesses.

Xenophanes

"Why is it so damned hard to predict the weather?" asked meteorologist Edward N. Lorenz in 1963. "Why, indeed?" many of us respond whenever the weather so often takes an unexpected turn for better or worse. What is it about this daily occurrence, this most commonplace topic of conversation, that baffles us so? Is it some irreparable chink in the heady notion of future predictability so coveted by humankind in all the millennia since Creation? Does it threaten our belief in a harmonious, rational world in which we can foresee the full consequences of our many noble initiatives? Might controlling our destinies be nothing but an idle dream? Must the random cruelties of God and man be forever with us? Or is it perhaps merely a minor annoyance that we shall one day exorcise from our thoughts?

Lorenz set out to find answers. And, in so doing, he gave birth to a new and exciting picture of our universe painted with the fresh brush strokes of modern chaos theory. It is a picture that transcends logic, one in which older ideas of natural law and truth no longer suffice. It is a picture of eternity unbound, a reality wherein an unyielding fate no longer prescribes a clockwork future from now until the end of time. No, no, not at all. There is plenty of room for surprises and a more humanistic approach is called for. We must think in terms of free will as opposed to predestination and of each individual's drive toward self-fulfillment. We must think in terms of many potential futures and of God throwing dice, albeit loaded ones, to fix the one future that actually occurs. We must think in terms of risk and reward and the probabilities of future events. In sum, we can take delight in a world where choice abounds and anything is possible, where we are free to exploit a cornucopia of random opportunities in pursuing "that which is the better." And, just possibly, that is the way God ordained it. Maybe He created us to assist Him in a war against Chaos, the first god in many religions. Maybe we play a crucial role in His future campaign, one whose outcome even He cannot foresee. Why in the world would He bother with the likes of us if He could do without us?

Before proceeding, let me digress briefly on the meaning of chaos. Technically, it is a hard term to define. So, for present purposes, let's just say that we have order when the future is predictable and chaos when it is not. Tomorrow's sunrise is an example of order, the roll of dice an example of chaos. You might think of chaos as the opposite of fate.

Predicting the future! That's the key to combating chaos. Doing it best has set our species apart from all others and won for us dominance of planet Earth. Doing it better than the competition in our everyday quests for fame and fortune separates winners from losers. And doing it best on an international level has taken America from modest colonial beginnings to the greatest nation on earth in a very short span of years. Humankind has dreamed of it since Creation, and the methods employed to do so have been legion. Think of fortune tellers, crystal balls, tarot cards, mazusahs, black cats, broken mirrors, animal entrails, human and animal sacrifices, oracles, dreams, etc., etc., etc. The marketplace, however, quickly disposes of false claims, and none but one need concern us here. That one is the latest and most successful attempt to read the future, and it is what the science of physics is all about. Let us begin our study of chaos by trying to understand the reasons behind the great successes of physics and, at the same time, discover its limitations.

How does physics work? Suppose we begin by looking backward to 1967 and the Apollo 8 mission to the moon. Astronauts Frank Borman, James A. Lovell Jr., and William A. Anders are in earth orbit and about to risk their lives on the predictive power of Isaac Newton's Laws of Motion. Round and round they go, one orbit, two orbits, three orbits, all the while the computers here on earth busily solving and re-solving Newton's equations of motion to obtain available flight paths, checking and double-checking the many mathematical calculations and, most importantly, computing the future consequences of measurement errors in the spacecraft's initial coordinates, its position and velocity. Finally, at some point in time and space, the astronauts ignite their rocket engine briefly and blast off into a pre-calculated trajectory which, they believe, will lead them to a future rendezvous with the moon 250,000 miles away. Any miscalculation or coordinate error, or possibly a deficiency in the Laws of Motion, could doom them to an eternity in space. All went well, fortunately, and this first manned voyage to an extraterrestrial orb concluded successfully. Magic? Truth? Some of both? Whatever, but certainly one of the innumerable triumphs of Newtonian physics!

Our space voyage epitomizes the doctrine of determinism: The present gives birth to one unique future, and that future is knowable through the application of established laws. So ordered and predictable was the Newtonian world picture that the great French scientist and mathematician, Pierre Simon de Laplace (1749-1827), could imagine his famous superman, who, given the present position and momentum of every particle in the universe, could compute the entire course of world history, past and future. This scientific ideal, so imaginatively developed in physics, exerted enormous influence on the social sciences where workers like philosopher Karl Marx, economist John Maynard Keynes, and psychiatrist Sigmund Freud hoped for comparable progress by exploiting the same thought procedures. Alas, it was not to be, for the results have been disconcertingly dismal. And the cause is not hard to fathom. Viewed in the light of modern chaos theory, the world is, apparently, much more chaotic than anybody has heretofore contemplated.

All through the era of determinism, people were well aware of unpredictably chaotic phenomena. Popular games of chance, for example, demonstrate a clear absence of determinism. The roll of a pair of dice begets not one but eleven possible futures, any whole number from "2" to "12." The spin of an American roulette wheel begets 38 possible futures, all whole numbers from "0" to "36" plus "00." But we need not confine ourselves to mere gambling games. Suppose we select a group of 100 pregnant women and ask for the number of boys to be born to them. Now we have 101 possible futures, any number from zero to 100 boys. And more if we allow for multiple births. A much greater multiplicity of futures afflicts the important problem of turbulence, which affects weather forecasting and airplane flights. But even more startling is a discovery made more than one hundred years ago by Henri Poincaré (1854-1912), another great French scientist and mathematician, who found chaos where it wasn't supposed to be, in the seemingly well-ordered motions of the heavenly bodies. It was a startling revelation, a challenge to all science and physics in particular. So fundamental a limitation on human predictability had not previously surfaced in Newtonian physics and it shocked Poincaré profoundly. "So bizarre that I cannot bear to contemplate them" was how Poincaré described his discoveries and their chaotic consequences. Nor did most other scientists deign to contemplate them. Chaos was decidedly out of fashion. Nobody wanted to hear of any shortcomings in the power of pure reason to reveal "the truth, the whole truth, and nothing but the truth." Albert Einstein's remark, "God does not play dice," well summarized the prevailing attitude of the time. Or, as put more poetically by Scottish physicist James Clerk Maxwell, the architect of the electromagnetic theory, *Naught happens by Chance/ But by Fate*.

And so, with the quantum and relativity theories lighting the way to the exciting scientific advances of the 20th century, Poincaré's "curiosity" remained conveniently ignored. Seventy years were to pass before Poincaré's nightmare surfaced once again, this time in Lorenz's atmospheric research, and many more years before chaos emerged at the forefront of knowledge. Chaos, we now believe, predominates in our universe. Since Lorenz's discovery, all realistic models of environmental, economic and social behavior contain it. It is the rule rather than the exception, and the great successes of determinism are limited to a small part of the real world. That "small part of the real world," I should quickly note, has been responsible for most of our wonderful technology.

How does chaos arise? Let us return to the Apollo 8 mission and the blast-off point from earth orbit. That was the start of our journey into the future, and a precise knowledge of the beginning condition is crucial to Newtonian determinism. The spacecraft's position and velocity at the time of ignition must be accurately measured and inserted into the Laws of Motion. Only then is it possible to compute a unique moon trajectory. Fortunately for the astronauts, a small error in these measurements produces only a small shift in the computed trajectory, and this small shift can be neutralized by a mid-course correction. Here, then, is where the magic lies. Using Newton's evolution equations and a determination of just three observables, the position and velocity of the spacecraft at some instant of time, we can generate an infinite set of positional coordinates and velocities that define with great precision its future trajectory.

Chaos enters the picture when the future behavior of a system exhibits a hypersensitive dependence on those beginning conditions. Tiny differences here, even those unobservable by human standards, can generate wildly different futures and limit predictability. We might think of the straw that broke the camel's back and how many straws can be added before that happens. The difference in weight load on the camel before and after that last straw is infinitesimal. Yet the future following the next-to-last straw is very different from that following the last straw. In the same manner, small and overlooked errors in starting conditions may lead to great and unforeseen consequences whenever chaos is present. *"For want of a nail ."*

Similarly with rolling dice and spinning roulette wheels. No matter how carefully we try to control and specify the initial conditions, there is still too much uncertainty, and we find the outcomes as chaotic as ever. Matters are a bit better when it comes to weather forecasting. Numerous daily balloon launchings and weather satellites now provide the mandatory initial data on atmospheric temperatures, pressures and air movements. These measurements, when entered into Newton's Laws of Motion and processed with high-powered computers, yield evolution equations that produce valid forecasts for a few days more or less. Sooner or later, however, turbulence arises and vitiates them. It is much like the stream of smoke from a steadily held cigarette. At first, the flow is smooth and predictable. But, after a short time, it breaks up into unpredictably chaotic patterns.

On a longer time scale, chaos limits our predictions of planetary movements in the solar system to five or ten million years and even less for Mars. That means we cannot predict with certainty what our solar system will be like that far in the future or what it was like that far in the past. Because five or ten million years is but a microsecond in the four and a half billion year history of the solar system, our ignorance of events is enormous. Mars exhibits a shining example of the chaos that exists in planetary orbits. The planet shows distinct evidence of liquid water flow in the long distant past, indicating perhaps that its orbit once approached the sun much more closely than it does now. As I write this in July of 2006, Poincaré's nightmare is surfacing once again. In August, Mars and earth will have their closest encounter in the last

5000 years. Astronomers know little about earlier encounters because the orbit of Mars is unstable and cannot be pinpointed over longer stretches of time. As for the future, it may only be said that such a close encounter will probably not occur for at least another 60,000 years. The problem here lies with the strongly perturbing gravitational attraction of a third body, Jupiter, which introduces chaos into the equations of motion. Jupiter also perturbs orbits in the asteroid belt chaotically, and that prevents the formation of a planet where one might be expected. Of more importance to us earth dwellers, Jupiter's presence makes it impossible to predict when the earth will again collide with an asteroid as has happened many times in the past. That the earth's orbit and obliquity have remained relatively stable for more than four billion years, as evidenced by the presence of liquid water and life forms over that period, is truly a miracle. The odds against such stability are astronomical. Could it be that God fights Chaos by creating a universe on a cosmic scale hoping to get just one planet on which life can evolve? Certainly, the SETI (Search for Extraterrestrial Intelligence) program has found no evidence of intelligent life in any of the nearby star systems.

When we look at the so-called "social sciences," the picture is more turbulent. Time evolutions here are notoriously complex and even limited predictability is highly questionable. Why this should be is not hard to trace. Chaos dominates human relations because we live and learn. Our expectations of future events, our desires and our behavioral incentives are ever changing, and we are never the same system twice. Mathematically speaking, stationary probability distributions and linear equations rarely approximate reality. Moreover, the specification of initial conditions both for us and our institutions, a goal of historical studies, may be humanly impossible. Is it any wonder, then, that the methods of physics have not worked in this area? Even Laplace's superman would find himself confounded by the inscrutable ways of human beings and unable to foresee the chaotic consequences of our nobly-intentioned endeavors.

But let us return to Edward Lorenz and his worries about the weather. Lorenz was well aware that the laws of Newtonian physics were supposed to govern the behavior of planets and space probes and most other phenomena in our macroscopic world. Why, therefore, shouldn't they apply to the atmosphere? Knowing that a realistic treatment of the real-world atmosphere was far beyond the day's (and today's) scientific and mathematical capabilities, he analyzed a highly simplified atmospheric model and proceeded to predict its future behavior. But, first, as always, initial values had to be inserted into the equations of motion, the equivalent of temperature, pressure and wind speeds. For the computer calculations, he used numbers precise to 3 decimal places, 6.174 for example. More places seemed superfluous since atmospheric measurements are not made with nearly such precision. One day, in order to check the computer's consistency, he decided to repeat the computations and check the predictions for some arbitrarily chosen two-month time period. Accordingly, he stopped the computer and typed in the equivalent final values of temperature, pressure and wind speed as spewed out by the computer at the end of the previous time period. These numbers, the same ones used by the computer originally, would again serve as the initial conditions for the repeat sample. There was a slight difference. Whereas the computer had printed out the end numbers to 6 decimal places, Lorenz, in order to speed up matters, had rounded them off to 3 places before restarting the computer. With little to do for the next hour, he went out for what was to become a very famous coffee break. For upon his return, he could scarcely believe his eyes so unexpected were the results. During his absence, the computer had again simulated the same two months of weather. Fine and good. But the weather pattern now put out by the computer differed wildly from that obtained previously. What had happened? Was there some kind of computer malfunction? Had he made a copying error? A typing error? No, it was none of these. Lorenz finally traced the discrepancy to his rounding-off procedure. The computer's original prediction for the period had been based on initial conditions good to 6 decimal places, 6.174122 using our example. But Lorenz had rounded these numbers off to 3 decimal places, to 6.174 for the repeat computations. The difference between 6.174122 and 6.174 C is tiny and neither Lorenz nor anybody else could have expected a few parts in a million to matter much insofar as future predictions were concerned. But matter it did, and in a big way. Such hypersensitivity to initial conditions was entirely unprecedented. Only Poincaré before him had any inkling of such chaotic complexity and so drastic a limitation on human predictive powers. How many decimal places are necessary before consistent predictions can be obtained, Lorenz wondered? Ten? Twenty? A hundred? Is any finite number sufficient? As of today, nobody knows. And, given the errors inherent in all human measurements, how can we ever be sure of the "true" values of any initial conditions?

Lorenz pictured his discovery in terms of the "butterfly effect": The flapping of a butterfly's wings produces only minute pressure disturbances in the atmosphere, but it may suffice to change the weather at distant locations from what it would otherwise have been. Or, as he introduced it in the alliterative title of a 1966 speech to the American Association for the Advancement of Science: "Can the Flapping of a Butterfly's Wings in Brazil Produce a Tornado in Texas?" As with the rolling dice, future prediction depends on knowing initial conditions with godlike accuracy, and even that may not be sufficient. Although highly simplified, Lorenz's model revealed a complexity that defied his attempts at forecasting. Can we even guess as to what the real atmosphere may be like?

Are we at an impasse? Is the future a random variable, to be decided by God throwing dice? Is it forever closed to the vision of mere mortals? These questions are not easy to answer. But we must note, after all, that a great deal of order does abound in our world. And it abounds not only in the old Newtonian picture but also in those remarkable chaons that I have already mentioned. These self-organized, robust structures circumvent determinism and bring a new type of order to the universe. Their random exploration and exploitation of all potential futures begets, in the words of biologist J. B. S. Haldane, a "universe that is not only queerer than we suppose, but queerer than we *can* suppose." Every creation, in reality, is a chaon. And even though unpredictable from first principles, we can certainly observe the conditions under which chaons may arise and possibly exploit the rich variety of behaviors they display. It is as if we live in a turbulent ocean of virtual chaons from which real ones emerge fortuitously.

We are already familiar with the emergence of the Intel chaon from the apparent chaos of a free market society. Now let me illustrate with an example from inanimate nature, what is known as the Bénard cell. This simple system may be viewed as a comprehensible first step toward understanding modern chaos theory, what the hydrogen atom was to the quantum theory and the solar system to Newton's theory of gravitation. A study of its behavior and its relationship to other real-world systems rewards us with many insights into the nature of chaos and prepares us for our later study of free markets.

The Bénard cell may be pictured as a boxed arrangement of two parallel plates separated by a fluid, say water or air. Of interest is the fluid's future behavior when we change its environment by raising the temperature of one plate with respect to the other. Even though this is naught but a laboratory setup, we should note a distant similarity to atmospheric dynamics and plate tectonics, both of which deal with fluid flows under a temperature difference, or gradient as scientists call it.

Offhand, we would not expect extraordinary behavior from a system as mundane as the Bénard cell. And at first that seems to be the case. If the fluid is heated by raising the temperature of the bottom plate with respect to the top plate, everything remains in equilibrium; nothing seems to happen other than heat conduction from bottom to top. On a microscopic level, the molecules of fluid jiggle more vigorously about their equilibrium positions as the temperature is raised, but the cell is void of visible motion and structure throughout. That part of the fluid warmed by the bottom plate attempts to rise but is held in place by viscous forces. Nothing surprising so far. But suddenly, at some critical temperature characteristic of this particular cell, a spontaneous long-range order appears where there was none before. The fluid between the two plates begins to flow in a pattern of *adjacent* clockwise and counterclockwise cylindrical rolls or whirls. A chaonic state has emerged in the form of a self-organized rotational structure that balances heat energy intake against dissipation. Note that the chaon does not appear until the cell is driven sufficiently far from its initial equilibrium state of uniform temperature. Only then can it draw from the surroundings the energy needed for the whirls to subsist. As the temperature is raised still further, a mosaic of highly structured but ever changing patterns appears. In this regime, cyclic and chaotic motions coexist and vie for dominance. Finally, at another still higher transition temperature, all patterns vanish and full turbulence sets in. There are no cycles, no repetition of patterns.

Our cell has more surprises for us. At the crucial moment of the first transition, two possible futures become available to it, a phenomenon known as *bifurcation*. If we pick any small volume of fluid, our cell must choose for it either a clockwise or a counterclockwise flowing roll. And, since neighboring rolls flow oppositely, that fixes the circulation in all other rolls. The choice is unpredictable; we never know from one experiment to the next what it will be. Some "last-straw" fluctuation, a "butterfly" at the transition temperature, decides between the two future states. Once made, however, our cell tends to stabilize itself in its new state for as long as the required temperature difference is maintained. As the temperature is raised still further, many more structures with varying degrees of stability become available. And, to complicate matters even more, spontaneous and unpredictable jumps from one state to another become possible – fluid flow in the rolls may reverse at irregular intervals. Here in the multiplicity of possible futures lies the richness and promise of chaos. As simple a system as it is, the Bénard cell teaches us to watch out for surprises and big events, for abrupt changes in space and time and the emergence of dissipative self-organized structures in systems driven far from equilibrium.

We have in the Bénard cell an example of a real-world system self-organizing into a chaon under the influence of an external parameter, the temperature gradient between the plates. From a beginning without form or motion (the equilibrium state), it evolves to long-range order, to structured rolls, to shifting patterns, and finally to full turbulence. If we reverse the procedure by starting with a high temperature difference between the plates, we would observe our chaon emerging from turbulence. No matter from which direction we approach our chaon, the transition is nothing short of miraculous. Based on naïve probability considerations, it would be just about impossible for so many trillions of randomly moving molecules to self-organize into a structure of such long-range order. Perhaps that is why the Biblical writers, having no knowledge of chaons, could think of Creation only in terms of divine intervention when they wrote (Genesis 1:1,2): *In the beginning, God created the heaven and the earth. And the earth was without form, and void; and darkness was upon the face of the deep.* We should also note a parallel with the Big Bang theory wherein the laws of physics as we know them today emerged when our expanding universe cooled to some critical temperature. And perhaps they will change yet again at some lower temperature.

With the Bénard cell in mind, let us examine some of the roles played by chaons both in our inanimate and animate worlds. That part of the earth's atmosphere nearest the ground, known as the troposphere, may be looked on as a giant Bénard cell, heated from below by water and earth and cooled from above by the colder air of the stratosphere. Just as in our laboratory Bénard cell, rolls of flowing air set up large-scale wind circulations known as Hadley cells. The first occurs in tropical regions. Hot air rises at the equator and flows in the upper atmosphere toward the cold polar regions. At about 30° latitude, the polar flowing air divides in two. One part descends and re-circulates back to the equator as the trade winds or easterlies. The trades actually come from the northeast in the northern hemisphere and the southeast in the southern hemisphere rather than directly from the poles because of the earth's rotation and what is known as the Coriolis effect. In the upper atmosphere, the flow continues poleward and becomes the jet stream. In the temperate zone, another Hadley cell dominates, a mirror image of the first. Here, the surface winds are the prevailing westerlies. Finally, in the polar regions, a third Hadley cell with an air circulation similar to that in the tropics manifests itself. The prevailing surface winds here are the polar easterlies.

Plate tectonics has its origin in another temperature gradient, that in the mantle between the earth's crust and hot core. As in the atmosphere, huge counterflowing rolls exist. Hot magma rises, splits into two oppositely flowing currents at the surface, and then falls back to the core. The horizontal parts of the flows produce sea floor spreading and continental drift. In the core itself, still another temperature gradient between its solid center and outer layers most likely generates similar patterns of motion. These are not stable over geologic periods of time. A probable butterfly effect causes the core to change state about every 500,000 years and flip the magnetic poles of the earth from north to south and vice versa.

The large-scale chaons of the atmosphere and mantle have access to an almost unlimited supply of energy, the former from the sun and the latter from radioactivity, and thus persist indefinitely. However, in order to learn more about the birth and death of a chaon, let us look at a short-lived one. Hurricanes in the northern hemisphere are born in an oceanic band at low latitudes during the months from June to December. That is when and where the physical environment provides the four conditions necessary for their emergence: (1) The sun, which is directly overhead at the zenith, heats the sea water to its highest yearly temperature, about 30 C (86 F), down to a depth of a few hundred feet. This pool of hot water provides the life energy for our incipient chaon. (2) Horizontal wind velocities vary little from the ocean surface to the stratosphere (what is called small vertical wind shear), so that high winds aloft do not decapitate a storm's superstructure. (3) The air temperature falls steadily with altitude (there are no inversion layers) allowing parcels of hot and humid air to rise unobstructed to 30,000 feet or more. And (4) the band of low latitudes is far enough from the equator (about 300 miles or more) for the Coriolis effect to kick in and impart a vortex motion to the air about some center. Although all these environmental conditions must necessarily attend a hurricane's birth, they in themselves are not sufficient to bring it about. As in the Bénard cell, the air-ocean system must be driven sufficiently far from equilibrium before our potential chaon can be actuated. A "butterfly" in the form of a random fluctuation in water or air temperature, air pressure, wind currents, humidity, or some combination of these is required to trigger the system. Fortunately, that is a low probability event and it does not happen very often. Otherwise, given the huge surface area of the earth's tropical oceans, there would be far more hurricanes than the 80 or 90 that occur on a yearly average throughout the world. Once triggered, however, the countless numbers of randomly moving air and water molecules quickly self-organize into some hurricane state. This being a very complex system, many futures are open to it. Any chaon from a well-formed vortex to a large, sloppy, cloud-covered sprawl may take shape and endure until its energy supply is cut off, when the hurricane encounters cool water or land.

In the animate world, too, chaons generate spontaneously and unpredictably when the right conditions materialize. In all likelihood, life began in chance clusters of large organic molecules. When triggered by external environmental forces (lightning or heat, for example), some of these clusters self-organized into complex cell-like structures that could carry on the chain of chemical reactions known as metabolism. Again, as with our inanimate examples, so many trillions of atoms and molecules are involved that the chances of such occurrences would appear to be near zero. But that is not the case when far-from-equilibrium chaonic states are available. When and where favorable conditions existed, these robust structures took on a life of their own. They secured their energy needs by feeding off the surroundings and persisted in their self-organized living states until death, at which time their atoms and molecules disintegrated back into a formless equilibrium, into the primal dust from whence they came. We and all other living organisms follow the same course.

An omniscient God could, I suppose, program all His creations for survival by anticipating every random cruelty that a hostile environment might inflict on them. He chose, however, not to do it that way. Instead, He uses a self-perpetuating scheme of ongoing, random mutations to populate all ecological niches with the widest possible variety of life forms. Those chaons that adapt to the prevailing conditions survive and propagate, their numbers regulated by the prodding forces of the environment. Those that fail to achieve stability fade into oblivion. Species come and species go as this dynamic process wrests order from chaos by selecting from the multitude the few winners. We call it "evolution."

Chaos plays a similar role in protecting us from disease-bearing bacteria and viruses. Once again, it is conceivable that the immune system could have been so programmed to repel not only all existing invaders but all future mutations as well. But nature chose otherwise. The body's response to invasion is to change state and generate a wondrous assortment of randomly shaped molecules. The attachment of just one of them to an invader earmarks it for destruction by white cells and signals the body to manufacture prodigious quantities of that one unique molecule. When the threat is removed, production ceases and the body returns to its original state. The use of chaos is primary not only in the origin of winning species but also in their preservation from random attack.

Out of chaos created, in chaos living. That is how our earliest ancestors perceived the world, and their view is not too different from that put forth by today's chaos theory. As we do now, they combated chaos by exploring as best they could every worldly nook and cranny seeking "that which is the better." Most performed about average, which meant survival with plenty to spare. But an unforeseen few broke new paths. They were the great ones, those who advanced the arts and crafts, discovered new worlds, invented technological marvels, created new systems of thought and built innovative businesses. Each success contributed fresh information to our race's store of knowledge. Each enhanced the production and marketing of the necessities and niceties of life and raised the standard of living. All erupted as "butterflys," as random events in space and time. These self-organizing transformations from chaos to chaons, from disorder to order, constitute the essence of what is known as Adam Smith's "invisible hand," the principle set forth in his runaway best seller of 1776, *An Inquiry into the Nature and Causes of the Wealth of Nations*. This book exerted a profound influence on our Founding Fathers and through them on the future history of America. Its basic idea is simply this: The greatest wealth and prosperity emerges, as if "guided by an invisible hand," when and where all individuals have a maximum of freedom to decide upon and pursue their own best interests. Or, if I may put it in our terms, the *chaon of greatest prosperity emerges from the chaos of maximum freedom*. Here, in this embodiment of modern chaos theory, we have the basis of both democracy and capitalism, the underlying concept that forever links them together in bonds of holy matrimony. It is a picture of free, randomly motivated individuals self-organizing, like the randomly moving air molecules of the atmosphere, not into hurricanes but into a myriad of social orders each trying to stabilize the shifting sands of the future and promote the well-being of all.

Human beings, according to Smith, possess an instinctive and organic drive toward self-betterment. "The natural effort of every individual to better his own condition ... is so powerful a principle, that it is alone, and without any assistance, not only capable of carrying on the society to wealth and prosperity, but of surmounting a hundred impertinent obstructions with which the folly of human laws too often incumbers its operations." That such an instinct might be driven by motives of vanity and acquisitiveness and power matters not in the least, Smith believed. Allowed to follow their natural urges, people create for themselves, *without even consciously willing it*, a richer, more educated and freer society. Doing best for oneself motivates everyone to act far more often for the betterment of humankind than to its detriment. Clearly, Smith rejected orthodox notions of guilt and sin as irrelevant. Who, after all, can predict the consequences good or bad of one's actions? But, he noted, self-interest demands that we treat others as ourselves, a "truth" first put forth by the German philosopher, Samuel Pufendorf (1632-1694). Plundering and murdering others for their possessions lies far off the best path to self-betterment, which is why social orders come into existence in the first place. However, no social order can legislate wealth and those that try suffer from self-delusion. The best of them simply get out of the way and allow the marketplace to do its work. Or, as the great jockey Eddie Arcaro put it, "The best jockey hinders the horse the least." Here then is the "invisible hand" at its most subtle, the sophisticated alternative to absolute rule by a benign dictator or an elitist oligarchy. Under its guidance, it becomes the job of politicians to promote the least government possible, which is of course contrary to their selfish interests. Nowhere, as we shall see, was the soil more fertile for Smith's ideas than in early America.

Matters, it would seem, have turned almost full cycle. We moderns now regard the world much like our earliest ancestors, one dominated by chaos. With a difference, however, for now we perceive a new type of order inherent in the very nature of things. It arises whenever a real chaon emerges at random from a vast substratum of virtual ones. Never shall we be able to pinpoint their occurrences. To establish the conditions most favorable for their emergence, that is all we can hope to do. Does God Himself play it that way? Is our reality naught but His laboratory in which He creates trillions of galaxies and stars and planets hoping to get just one earthly chaon on which life can evolve? Does He evolve multitudes of species and individuals in an exhaustive search for the exceptional few who may somehow contribute to what He apparently seeks? Does He have in mind some superchaon to supplant us when we are no longer of any use to Him? Will He in the far distant future attain His unimaginable goal?

CHAPTER IV

A BAKE SALE

Money is the symbol of duty, it is the sacrament of having done for mankind that which mankind wanted. Mankind may not be a very good judge, but there is no better.

Samuel Butler, *Erewhon*

"Mom," Tad says at dinner one evening, "my history class is planning a three-day tour of Washington during Easter vacation."

"That's wonderful," Mom replies, "but where will you get the money?"

"We've thought of that," Tad rejoins enthusiastically. "The class is going to sponsor a bake sale. That'll help finance the trip."

"My son, the capitalist," sighs Mom. "I suppose you want me to bake some of my Scottish shortbread and apple pies."

"Oh, Mom, would you? We'll make such big profits we'll go first class."

"Why, Tad, that would be wonderful. But I wish you wouldn't use that word 'profits.' It's so obscene and it's not politically correct."

At this, Dad puts down his knife and fork and leans over to his wife. "I wish you teachers would stop brainwashing the youngsters with all that liberal twaddle," he remarks. "Look what it's doing to our daughter. We spend all this money on her college education and what does she become - a vegetarian Marxist. You wouldn't be able to do any baking whatsoever without using some of our savings – er, profits, if I dare use the word - to buy the ingredients. Tad and his classmates are simply a group of people channeling their energies and resources toward achieving a common goal beyond the means of any one of them. That's capitalism, and I see nothing wrong with it." "There are better ways of doing such things. And I hope you're not comparing our Tad to those robber barons running the big corporations, are you?" Mom retorts, her voice taking on an edge.

"Robber barons, eh? That's a cheap journalistic shot coined by a leftist ignoramus who couldn't understand but certainly took advantage of America's high standard of living. Just like Tad, your robber barons try to do the best they can for themselves and their companies. And in so doing, they turn out the high quality, affordable products we all need and rely on, like our car and our television set and our home."

"And gouging the public into poverty with their greed."

"I don't think they are any more greedy than you or Tad or I."

"You just don't understand, do you?" Mom snaps. "The difference is that Tad has good intentions and they don't."

"Oho," retorts Dad, "what do we have here, another P.C.-square? Politically correct except when personally concerned, I mean. Look, I really don't care about the intentions of men like Rockefeller or Carnegie or Ford. Sure, they enriched themselves. Why not? But they enriched the whole country a million fold more by making oil, steel and cars accessible to all. Without them, we couldn't possibly have the wonderfully high standard of living we all enjoy in America. Don't you think it possible that doing best for yourself does best for everybody? That's Adam Smith's philosophy."

"I know all about Adam Smith. I used to see his program on television all the time and he never said anything like that. You're just talking anarchy."

"For your information, the real Adam Smith lived over two hundred years ago. And I can well understand why you I-squares don't want to know about his free market ideas. It's so politically incorrect these days. You'd rather put your faith in some Maximum Leader who plans and regulates everything. Well, just look at the results in your communist and socialist countries. There's where you find anarchy because their I-square politicians can't foresee how terribly wrong noble intentions can go. They may have balls, but they sure aren't crystal."

"Hey, Pop!" Tad whoops at this. "That's a great line. I'm going to use it on Mr. Fouresse, my history teacher in school. He's from nowhere."

"Tad, you will do no such thing. Your father is talking nonsense and I won't sit here and listen to him."

"Pop, what's an I-square?"

"Shhh. Don't let your mother hear. It stands for intellectual idiot – smart, smart, smart, and so very, very stupid. It's what Irving Kristol's mother used to say about his Marxist friends. He's a conservative author and columnist. It's for people who have no idea of how much they don't know."

"That's Mr. Fouresse, all right. He's always so cocksure about what's going to happen."

At this point, we had better take our leave of this ongoing domestic spat. The bake sale, however, epitomizes the beginnings of capitalism. Tad and his fellow students are politically free to decide upon and pursue their own best interests (no government approval or authorization is required). They have access to savings (the ingredients and equipment supplied by Tad's parents) which enables them to get started. They have the know-how to make a desirable product (through Tad's mother who evidently makes superior shortbread and apple pies). And they have the organization (through the students) to market the products. Hopefully, they will be rewarded for their time and effort. Who knows? This fledgling operation may blossom in time into a mighty multinational chaon such as the Kellogg or Heinz companies, supplying a vast variety of food products to millions worldwide. Multiply this chaon thousands upon thousands of times and we come to Adam Smith and his "invisible hand," the subtle alternative to blunderbuss rule by elitist know-it-alls. Today's chaos theory lends encouragement and guidance to those of us who wish to apply Adam Smith's ideas toward achieving "the greatest happiness of the greatest number."

Nowhere were people more adept at bake sales than in the Italian city-states of a thousand years ago. That is, they were especially good at pooling their resources and channeling them into business ventures. Fueled by an ever-growing reservoir of savings, groups of merchants and craftsmen and other small investors self-organized into efficient and profitable partnerships. They built tall ships, stocked them with expensive cargoes of Italian manufacture, and sent astute captains abroad to trade their goods for foreign merchandise and gold on a favorable basis. They set up minimal governments attentive to their commercial and industrial interests, and they fought off envious kings and nobles seeking to grab the mounting wealth. Equality of opportunity, not equality of reward, was the pervasive feature of their society. When their ships came in, investors could become rich. When they didn't, they could be ruined. There were all degrees of success and failure. But for the city-states, the expectation was for good fortune, and it created a very wealthy middle class. It was a good fortune rooted in the spend-save decisions of individual investors, all free to decide how to get the most for their money.

So prosperous did the city-states become that they were able to initiate and finance the great cultural flowering of the Italian Renaissance. The Serene Republic of Venice forms the backdrop to Shakespeare's tragedy *Othello*, but Shakespeare was more interested in the petty jealousies of a minor general than in the stupendous creative forces of individual initiative and human freedom that transformed Venice into a commercial and artistic colossus for over 600 years. The 13th century saw the unfolding of a similar development in northern Europe with the formation of the Hanseatic League. Richard Wagner's opera *Die Meistersinger von Nürnberg* celebrates the manifold contributions to the arts made by the "bourgeoisie," a disparaging word leveled at the rising middle class by an envious and parasitic nobility. Today, former Hanseatic cities like Gdansk and Riga are restoring their former beauty after years of degradation under a Marxist elite.

The power and prosperity of the city-states waxed for several hundred years and then gradually waned with the advent of a new and more powerful political entity, the national state. In England, Holland, France and Spain, nationalism welded to aggressive business enterprises augmented unity and vigor at home and expanded trade routes and privileges abroad to a far greater extent than was possible for amorphous and factious unions of city-states. The bake sale, too, took on heightened sophistication as it evolved into a modern capital market. Shares denoting fractional ownership of industrial and commercial organizations were parceled out to people willing to risk their present savings for possible future rewards. Investors received, in other words, a piece of the action proportional to their investment. In time, those shares became transferable from one person to another, and we find stock markets springing up to facilitate the exchange and allocation of funds to new and old businesses. In a later chapter, we shall investigate the stock market's crucial role in financing the American dream.

England and Holland were at the forefront of those nations that vigorously promoted commerce and industry and the unregulated allocation of savings by individuals, and these nations realized the highest standards of living for their citizens. At the same time, their governments held public spending and taxes within tolerable limits. Lagging behind were France, Spain, Austria and Russia, where spendthrift monarchs squandered their people's lives and savings on their own versions of doing good – wars, special interests (especially their own), and bureaucracies. In France, the aggressions and excesses of one king after another kept the country continually on the verge of bankruptcy. The ever higher taxes levied on an increasingly disgruntled populace bled the people dry and severely limited the amount of money available for productive investment. Jean-Baptiste Colbert, finance minister to "Sun King" Louis XIV and master craftsman of nefarious schemes to defraud the taxpayer, was incessantly charged with "so plucking the goose as to produce the largest quantity of feathers with the least possible amount of squealing." Much the same occurred in Spain despite all the gold and silver she received from her exploitation of the New World. The value of that treasure horde never amounted to more than a small part of the huge taxes levied at home, and, to make matters worse, it encouraged profligate borrowing from foreign creditors. Adding to her troubles was the expulsion of Jews and Moslems, which deprived the country of many of her most productive citizens. Nevertheless, war and taxes and human folly notwithstanding, free markets were able to deliver with the resources left to them a millennium of spectacular gains in freedom and abundance. Industry, commerce, science and the arts flourished as never before. The standard of living advanced dramatically from peak to ever higher peak, so much so that millions of people found themselves living better than the kings of yore. So impressive were the results that even Karl Marx, the chief critic of capitalism, could pay glowing tribute to its colossal productive power, to "wonders far surpassing Egyptian pyramids, Roman aqueducts and Gothic cathedrals."

Such was the miraculous progress in living standards that Adam Smith sought to document and explain in The *Wealth of Nations*. In vain did he search for the great benign dictators who might be responsible for creating the enormous wealth. In vain did he ferret out a single one of Plato's philosopher-kings who could exercise the Highest Reason to achieve the Supreme Good. Knowing what we know now, how does anybody reason with chaos? What Smith found instead was in complete accord with Charles Maurice Talleyrand's observation that "We should be terrorized if we knew by what small men we are governed." While fantasizing themselves as godlike beings doing good, these pip-squeak "benefactors of humanity" have wrought on societies havoc and grief beyond description, folly beyond human comprehension. The highly ordered production and distribution systems that created the wealth arose in spite of them, not because of them. How could they or anybody else possibly comprehend the complexity of such structures? Those responsible for the great advances almost always were unknowns who rose to the occasion by happenstance. Those responsible for the lesser advances we rarely hear about. No, naught but the "invisible hand" made sense to Smith – let many have the freedom to try and an unknown few will point the way. Any big government, even of the noblest intentions, must with overwhelming probability fail. And when that happens, that government doesn't just disappear. It continues to grow and build on its own failures, becoming in the process more and more tyrannical ... until the beheadings.

Smith, along with most early economists, regarded the apparent chaos of the market economy with awe. They could only marvel at how free markets cause prosperity, how its mélange of workers, households and businesses, acting without visible coordination and guided mainly by self-interest, could produce such extraordinarily beneficial results. It is truly a chaon in our sense, what we now call the "efficient market," and our understanding of it is little better today. How unfortunate that this free market miracle inspires so few of us! Today's message, to the contrary, is quite the opposite. From childhood on, our teachers and news media engage us in a never-ending crusade against capitalism. They brainwash us into believing that every problem is the fault of free markets, and it is the responsibility of government to fix it. Too much freedom! That's the root cause of all our troubles. Better to give Talleyrand's "small men by whom we are governed" all the power and money they think they need to do good. It's the old story of the supposedly clairvoyant benign dictator versus "the invisible hand." The choice of one or the other of these conflicting views of reality is constantly before us. Wherein lies the truth?

CHAPTER V

QUESTIONS AND ANSWERS

He knows nothing; and he thinks he knows everything. That points clearly to a political career.
George Bernard Shaw, *Major Barbara*

A great deal of intelligence can be invested in ignorance when the need for illusion is great.
Saul Bellow

Political power grows out of the barrel of a gun.
Chairman Mao

"If I had my way, I would try every politician in the world, and then shoot them!" The speaker was a portly Englishman, the president of a large company who happened to be in Budapest at the time.

I was taken aback for a second or two, but then I heard myself responding: "Hear! Hear! But how about trying them afterwards?"

I had just finished delivering a talk on the symmetry of free markets at the Hungarian Academy of Sciences in Budapest, and this provocative comment actuated a spirited discussion of government's role in the marketplace. The year was 1991, and Hungary had but recently emerged from Communist domination following the demise of the Soviet empire. Earlier, I had written a paper entitled *Symmetry in Free Markets* and its publication in a Pergamon Press book, *Symmetry 2 - Unifying Human Understanding* (edited by Istvan Hargittai, 1989) had led to an invitation to address the Academy.

"I would just like to point out that you Americans had to do just that to free yourselves from British oppression," our guest continued. "Unfortunately, in your war of independence you shot their representatives, the poor soldiers and sailors, not the politicians themselves. If you want liberty, which is the basis of the symmetry Professor Fabricand is talking about, you must sooner or later be prepared to shoot or the politicians will take it away from you. They are always trying."

"I couldn't agree more," I replied. "'All government, after all, is against freedom.' That is a quote from a great American journalist, H. L. Mencken. The business of politicians is to create more and more government and make more and more laws. That government is best which governs most – that is their motto. And why not? Most politicians are lawyers, and every new law gives them more work and more money. They simply take care of themselves at our expense. Of course, they clothe it all in the noblest of intentions."

"'The more laws it has, the worse the state,'" responded my newfound sympathizer, quoting the Roman historian Tacitus.

"And the more the unintended consequences," I added. "There is another quote I should mention by someone named Bernard Savrin. It is written on a plaque hanging at the Canterbury School in New Milford CT where I live: 'The law often permits what honor forbids.' And, I might add, what the law permits all too often turns into tyranny."

"Are you an anarchist?" The question came from a former president of the Academy, a distinguished chemist and, I had been told, an ardent Marxist.

"Well, I've been called that before. So, I brought along some dictionary definitions of anarchy to discuss. The first is 'anarchy is the absence of government.' I think you might agree with that. But, tell me, hasn't Hungary suffered under too much government over the past 30 years? And weren't you far worse off under it than you were before?"

My questioner was silent for a moment. Finally, he answered in muted tones. "When the Russians invaded in 1956, we had no choice but to give Marxism a chance. I myself made a deep study of the theory and I wrote many papers on it. But now, I must confess that it doesn't work. None of its predictions have proven right. It has been a terrible disappointment to me."

That revelation raised some eyebrows.

"As far as I am concerned, it is big government that doesn't work," I responded. "And to me, Marxism and big government are synonymous. They are both characterized by bureaucrats and regulators who are very sure they know how to make the world work properly. The bigger the government, the less the freedom and the greater the chaos – that's how I see it. May I ask you how much government you have now that the Russians are gone? Or, first, how many seats are there in that beautiful Parliament building of yours?"

"386."

I was astonished. "That's a very large number for a country of just ten million people. To give you a comparison, America has 535 for a population of 250 million and that, I believe, is far too many. It will be interesting to see how a free Hungary is able to support all those wonderful politicians. But, more importantly, how much of your gross domestic product is spent by government as opposed to individual citizens?"

"I would say about 60%."

"No, no, much more," came a chorus of dissenting voices.

"I certainly can believe that," I agreed. "Russia, for example, now has an income tax that rises to 60% for very low incomes, and there is a value added tax of 28% on top of that. In Yugoslavia, where I have just come from, it is 71% plus a value-added-tax. And I understand you have a 70% income tax here. Do you realize that today's governments are trying to confiscate more from the people than the Communists ever did? Black markets and tax evasion must be rampant. The untaxed underground economy was the only thing that kept Russia going for as long as it did, and I would bet it's going strong here. It seems to me that your politicians have discovered what ours did long ago: It's easier to get the people's money with income-tax laws and Gestapo-like tax collection agencies than with guns."

"Do you equate government with entropy?" came another question. "You seem to believe that the more government there is, the greater the disorder. Or, if I may put it in another way, does the free market generate a state of lower entropy and higher order?"

"That is a wonderful analogy," I replied. "And that is exactly what I believe. I see many expressions of disbelief on your faces. So, let me ask you another question. A few years ago, my wife and I took a train tour to Mexico's spectacular Copper Canyon. As we crossed the border between America and Mexico, a question sprung into my mind which I put to you now: How does it come about that an arbitrarily drawn political line separates extreme wealth on one side from extreme poverty on the other? My traveling companions could not provide any answers, and I wonder if anyone here can."

There was only a baffled silence. Questions like that are rarely encountered in the history books. "Let me give you my opinion," I continued. "When the American colonists gained their independence from England, they did something that no other country ever did. They adopted the very unfashionable policy of having almost no central government and no taxes. Centralization and concentration of power, in their eyes, invariably led to tyranny. Most people believed that only chaos could result from so little political control. Yet, just one hundred years later, America became by far the largest producer of goods and services in the world. You must admit that this could not have happened without a very high degree of social order. Mexico, on the contrary, has experienced one tyrannical government after another, and the people have been taxed into poverty. Most of their money finds its way into the politicians' pockets to be spent inefficiently and squandered. The border between East and West Germany provides another example. Now, let me ask: How much government involvement was there in the American miracle? Or, what percentage of gross domestic product was spent by government during America's explosive growth period during the 19th century?"

Again, silence.

I held up the index finger of my right hand to many gasps of disbelief. I smiled. "Yes, indeed. About 1% or less. In other words, the nation that achieved the highest ever standard of living did it with almost zero government. If I may, I would now like to redefine terms and say that 'anarchy is the presence of government.' Or, if I may quote that first and greatest economist Adam Smith: 'That government is best which governs least.'"

"But what you are describing is a state of lawlessness. We have all heard about your Wild West and the crime in your cities?"

"True enough," I responded. "But the Wild West was not nearly as wild as it's made out to be. Most families were able to live out their lives as normally there as anywhere else. And that is more than I can say for Europe. To me, they were crimes of the highest magnitude when your big governments sent millions of young men to their deaths in one useless war after another. And as for crime in our American cities, most of that was caused by a government that brought us prohibition in 1919. Have you heard of prohibition? Those idiotic politicians of ours tried to stop the drinking of alcoholic beverages in America, including the wine and beer which make life so much more enjoyable for so many of us. I can see from your expressions that many of you think I am joking. Well, I can assure you I am not. It actually happened. And, of course, the American people rebelled. They hadn't lost their taste for the good things of life. The market was still there, but now it had to be supplied by illegal means, just like in your black market. A whole new class of entrepreneurs arose – they were called 'bootleggers' – and they had to set their own standards of behavior because they operated outside the law. As a result, we got gang wars, violence, high crime rates and, as any half-wit might expect, lots more drinking. Talk about chaos – there it was, and all created by government. You may have heard of Al Capone. He was the most famous of the bootleggers and he saw himself purely as a businessman serving the public. And that's how I see him. The real criminals were the politicians who created him. Maybe, for all the killing they caused, we should follow the suggestion of our British guest."

I could see him beaming.

"There is one more point I would like to bring out," I continued. "It concerns the free market's lightning-fast reaction time to change. The day – the day mind you – the day prohibition went into effect, our underworld economy was ready to act. Under the leadership of Al Capone's boss and mastermind of the whole bootlegging operation, Johnny Torrio, the distribution and marketing of alcoholic beverages began in earnest. Years before, Torrio had understood what prohibition was going to do and had planned accordingly. The politicians were far behind the times, their usual position. When you think about it, it's obvious why they have no idea as to what's happening in the rest of the country. They sit in Washington or Budapest or wherever thinking of things to legislate. They drag in all sorts of experts to testify, and, all of a sudden, they themselves become overnight experts on everything. In the meantime, the world is moving on much faster than they and their expert witnesses can ever hope to understand. Then they pass one bad law after another trying to fix a situation that has long since been corrected by the marketplace. Life changes but laws, especially spending laws, are embedded in concrete. To make matters worse, our lawmakers invariably implement the new laws by creating expensive new agencies staffed by guess who? Right. Their political cronies or the expert witnesses themselves along with their colleagues and students. These incipient bureaucrats insinuate themselves into the very bowels of government and get paid handsomely for their bad advice. In the case of prohibition, the answer was to spend huge amounts of money employing law-enforcement agents to fight rampant illegal drinking. Of course, it didn't work. Not only did the bootleggers get very rich, but so did many politicians and agents who took big payoffs to look the other way. The same thing went on in China in the years preceding the Opium Wars of the 1840s. The Emperor in his infinite wisdom had forbidden Chinese exports. That did not sit very well with the British, who found their sources of tea and silk cut off. So, what happened? English ship captains bought opium in India and bartered it surreptitiously in China for tea and silk. They would sail along the Chinese coast stopping every now and then to negotiate the exchange with local politicians. Not only did the opium trade make great fortunes for many British families, but the Chinese politicians got even richer, to the tune of hundreds of millions of pounds. And every once in a while, those wonderful civil servants would stage a huge drug bust to show the Emperor that they were doing something about "foreign mud," as it was called. The same shenanigans go on today with drugs. And one more thing I should tell you about. The same politicians who brought us prohibition also gave us those two *Communist Manifesto* items, central banking and the income tax, both in 1913. We in America were unbelievably lucky to have grown so rich before those two monstrosities made their appearance."

"I am a humanist. And I cannot believe all this scientific garbage you talk about. You seem to have no human values whatsoever, no social responsibility. Where is your compassion for the children, the aged, the poor and the needy? What about health and education? Would you throw us all on the mercies of a savage free-market economy? As far as I am concerned, markets don't work and these problems can be solved only by government. Ordinary citizens cannot be trusted to make the right decisions. And, if I may, I'll conclude by saying you scientists are not the benefactors of humanity you think you are. You have created a very inhuman world for the rest of us and you don't know how to manage it. Under Marxism, at least, everybody is equal and there are neither poor nor rich."

"I am so glad you spoke up," I responded, "because I am truly puzzled by the way you humanists now think. In the nineteenth century, you objected to the scientific doctrine of determinism on the grounds that it exposed free will as an illusion. And I think you were absolutely right, then. But look at what's happened today. Most of you are Marxists or socialists or communists because you believe big governments can make everything right. You seem to think that noble intentions are all you need and, furthermore, they are exclusive to humanists. But your thinking is deeply flawed. Why? Because all those 'isms' of yours assume a deterministic world in which the future is predictable by an elite class of intellectuals. In what must be the triumph of hope over experience, you always expect a Marxist messiah to come along and make government work. But it never happens. You have done a complete about-face and I think you insult the future with your certitudes. You scientists here could not even openly practice the quantum theory in your work under Communist rule; it was outlawed because there is no place for probability in Marx's deterministic world. The real world, however, is much more chaotic than you suppose, and nobody is smart enough to know what consequences may follow an action no matter how small or how nobly intentioned. That's why benign dictators almost always become oppressive tyrants. We must think in terms of probability and expectations, and because Karl Marx and Plato knew nothing about such sophisticated developments, they are highly irrelevant in today's chaotic world. We should never forget that old sixteenth century proverb, 'The road to hell is paved with good intentions.' And as for scientists corrupting the human race, we all do our thing and who can tell where the chips may fall.

"I see that it is time to stop talking. So let me conclude with an old fable about "The Little Red Hen": Once upon a time there was a little red hen who scratched about the bare barnyard in which she lived looking for food. She managed to uncover a few grains of wheat at which point she called to her neighbors and said, 'If we plant this wheat, we can have bread to eat and we will not have to go hungry. Who will help me plant it?'

'Not I,' said the cow.

'Not I,' said the duck.

'Not I,' said the pig.

'Not I,' said the goose.

'Then I will,' said the little red hen. And she did. The wheat grew tall and ripened into golden grain. 'Who will help me reap the wheat?' asked the little red hen.

'Not I,' said the duck.

'Out of my classification,' said the pig.

'I'd lose my seniority,' said the cow.

'My unemployment compensation would be terminated,' said the goose.

'Then I will,' said the little red hen, and she did.

At last it came time to bake the bread. 'Who will help me bake bread?' asked the little red hen.

'That would be overtime for me,' said the cow.

'I'd lose my welfare benefits,' said the duck.

'I'm dropping out,' said the pig.

'If I'm to be the only helper, that's discrimination,' said the goose.

'Then I will,' said the little red hen.

She baked five loaves and held them up for her neighbors to see. They all wanted some and, in fact, demanded their fair share. But the little red hen said, 'No, I can eat the five loaves myself.'

'Excess profits,' mooed the cow.

'Capitalist leech,' quacked the duck.

'Equal rights,' honked the goose.

'Robber baron,' oinked the pig.

And they painted UNFAIR on picket signs and marched round and round the little red hen, shouting obscenities.

And then the politician came. He said to the little red hen, 'You must not be greedy. You must share the bread.'

'But I earned the bread,' said the little red hen.

'Exactly,' said the politician. 'That is the wonderful free enterprise system in action. Anyone in the barnyard can earn as much as he or she wants. But under our modern government regulations, the productive workers must divide their product with the idle. It is the law and you should be most grateful to share the bread.'

The little red hen smiled resignedly. 'If it is the law,' she clucked, 'I shall be most grateful to obey it and share the bread. Yes, yes, I am most grateful.' But her neighbors always wondered why she never again baked any bread. And so it was that they all lived hungrily ever after.

"Thank you for this opportunity to present my ideas, and I wish you the best of luck with your new government."

CHAPTER VI

NOWHERE BUT IN AMERICA

If I were a young man and of heroic stature, I would go to America.

Horace Walpole, English author

The end of the Revolutionary War in 1783 saw Americans zealously guarding their newly gained freedom from government. Having experienced firsthand the oxymoron of enlightened despotism imposed on them by George III and his royal henchmen, they were determined not to let it happen again. A minimum of government and a maximum of freedom were uppermost in their minds. To most "informed" observers that spelled chaos, a chaos that failed to materialize. On the contrary, exactly the opposite occurred. Economic growth in the former colonies surged as the nation's merchants could now trade freely throughout the world and businessmen could operate without British prohibitions. In February of 1784, less than one year after the Treaty of Paris ended the War, the *Empress of China* sailed from New York to Canton, China, carrying a cargo of 242 casks of American ginseng (reputed in the Orient to have marvelous Viagara-like powers), furs, lead, wine, tar, and Spanish silver dollars (the pieces-of-eight in Robert Louis Stevenson's *Treasure Island*) and opened up a hugely profitable trade with the Far East. She returned in May of the following year with a cargo of precious silks, teas, fans, umbrellas, window blinds and porcelains – goods all actively sought by prosperous American consumers. By 1810, America had assumed a position second only to England in trade with China. Such trade had been forbidden to the colonies under British rule. The furniture industry, an excellent indicator of the general level of prosperity and one of the few untouched by British trade restrictions during the colonial period, boomed. In Boston, Newport, Portsmouth, Salem, New York, Philadelphia, Charleston and many other places, skilled craftsmen produced a wide variety of high quality household pieces that served a rapidly expanding market. The coal mining, iron forging and woolen goods industries flourished; stage coach routes and state-chartered private enterprises for building bridges and turnpikes proliferated. Benjamin Franklin, early in 1787, could declare that the country was, on the whole, so prosperous that there was every reason for profound thanksgiving. Prosperity, he contended, was widespread and obvious. Never before was the farmer paid better prices for his products, never was the value of his lands so high, nowhere in Europe were the laboring poor so well paid, fed, or clothed. In corroboration, we should note that the merchants and manufacturers of New York and New England, already lobbying the new Constitutional government for protection in 1789, complained that "their countrymen have been deluded by an appearance of plenty; by the profusion of foreign articles which has deluged the country." The fact that all these imports had to be paid for in hard money or trade did not serve to enlighten them. But George Washington understood. He pointed with pride to the number of American ships threading the seven seas, to his inaugural suit made of woolen cloth in Hartford CT the quality of which "exceeds my expectations," to the number of shoes produced in one Massachusetts town and nails in another as being "incredible." And soon after his inauguration, he wrote to his beloved "adopted son" Lafayette of plentiful crops, of "great prices" paid for American grain in Europe, of a rate of exchange "much in our favor," of money flooding into the Treasury from duties on extensive imports of European goods, and of our flourishing "trade to the East Indies."

What centralized authority there remained after the Revolution existed under the "Articles of Confederation and Perpetual Union," which had been ratified in 1781 by the states. This first governance of what would become the United States of America had its nascence in September of 1774 with the 1st "Continental" Congress. That association of delegates had convened in Philadelphia to adopt a "Declaration of Rights and Grievances" and submit it to King George for his consideration. It was at this meeting that Patrick Henry (1736-1799) set the tone for the Congresses to come with his bold rhetoric: "The distinction between Virginians, Pennsylvanians, New Yorkers and New Englanders are no more. I am not a Virginian, but an American."

When the petition was summarily rejected, a 2nd Continental Congress convened on 10 May 1775, soon after "the shot heard round the world" had been fired at Lexington and Concord. This 2nd Congress established an armed force commanded by George Washington, instituted relations with foreign countries, and authorized the issuance of a paper money called "Continentals" that would pay for most of the coming war's costs. A committee headed by Thomas Jefferson drafted the Declaration of Independence and another chaired by John Dickinson (1732-1808) submitted the first draft of the Articles of Confederation to the Congress on 12 July 1776.

The 3rd Continental Congress convened on 20 December 1776 to prosecute the Revolutionary War. It also modified and finalized the Articles of Confederation and submitted the new governance to the States for ratification. It was finally approved on 17 March 1781. Under its terms, America became a league of 13 sovereign states, somewhat like the German and Italian city-states. Article I of the Articles baptized the new nation as "The United States of America." The legislative body was a unicameral Congress which, having little taxing power, could not do much harm. The Congress could only ask for voluntary contributions from the states to pay its bills and these were not often granted. Most people saw little need to build up a federal bureaucracy to do jobs that were well handled by the states. One member of the Congress was appointed annually to serve a one-year term in an executive capacity with the title, "President of the United States in Congress Assembled." What the Congress could do was to act as a national judiciary in disputes between states and conduct diplomacy. It could also, with the consent of nine or more states, enter into treaties, wage war, emit bills (paper money) and borrow money on the credit of the United States. It passed the Ordinance of 1787 which required the states to relinquish to the central government their conflicting claims on the lands north and west of the Ohio River and east of the Mississippi River. Known as the Northwest Territories, the region had been ceded to the new nation under the terms of the Treaty of Paris. The Ordinance banned slavery in the Territories and set the procedure by which subsequent western territories were admitted into statehood. The Congress also established a decimal system for the currency based on the dollar some 200 years before the British got around to doing it. In all likelihood, the majority of Americans were well satisfied with a national government that had developed a liberal and far-sighted land policy and had faithfully administered its responsibilities without encroaching at all upon the liberties of its citizens.

Of significance in the Articles of Confederation was its attempt to ward off the seemingly endless series of violent tax revolts that beset most European nations. To ensure popular acceptance, any bill dealing with monetary matters required a supermajority of nine states (each voting as a block) before it could become law: "The United States in Congress assembled shall never ... coin money, nor regulate the value thereof, nor ascertain the sums and expences necessary for the defence and welfare of the United States, or any of them, nor emit bills [paper money], nor borrow money on the credit of the United States, nor appropriate money ... unless nine states assent to the same ..." (Article IX). The Founding Fathers debated a three-quarter stricture on spending and taxing powers at the coming Constitutional Convention but then opted for a simple majority vote in the new Congress *plus* what they called "tax uniformity." Future violations of that stricture were to beset the new American nation with a series of tax revolts.

Also deserving of emphasis is the full designation of the agreement between the states, the "Articles of Confederation and Perpetual Union." In Article XIII, the *Union shall be perpetual* appears, and the word perpetual is reinforced by other references to the full title further on. The authors of the Articles obviously wished to preclude the possibility of secession by the states. Such language is conspicuously absent from the Constitution, a point I shall take up later. The prosperity seen by Franklin and Washington in the years after ratification of the Articles of Confederation stands at odds with the gloomy picture painted by later statist historians (are there any other, asks Charles Adams?) of the social and economic conditions prevailing at the time. These devotees of autocratic government love to portray its absence during the years from 1783 to 1789 just prior to the adoption of the Constitution as "the critical period," a time of "chaos" and dissolving social order. But it would seem more likely that their so-called "critical period" was rooted in nothing more than their fancies for the blunderbuss policies of a benign dictator. Just as it has for the illuminati of all ages, the subtle movements of Adam Smith's "invisible hand" completely escaped their jaundiced eyes. But not those of George Washington whose first inaugural speech reveals a deep insight into world chaos: "No people can be bound to acknowledge and adore the *invisible hand*, which conducts the affairs of men, more than the people of the United States [italics mine]. Every step, by which they have advanced to the character of an independent nation, seems to have been distinguished by some token of providential agency." Quite clearly, Washington recognized the random sequence of events leading to the American chaon as deriving from a maximum of individual freedom and not from the dictates of some "godlike mind." His subsequent renunciation of the absolute power within his grasp foreclosed the possibility of an American monarchy or any type of enlightened despotism. Either might well have destroyed that freedom from government so indispensable for the great progress that was to come. How different America would have been had he chosen otherwise! "If he does that, he will be the greatest man in the world!" exclaimed George III when informed of Washington's intention to retire to Mount Vernon after the War. How many *pomposos* of any age, so driven by the glory of their own magnificences, would turn down the chance to "Be a King!"? "The moderation and virtue of a single character probably prevented this revolution from being closed, as most others have been, by a subversion of that liberty it was intended to establish." Could anyone have written it better than Thomas Jefferson?

The great progress of the former colonies was hardly surprising to Adam Smith. In The *Wealth of Nations*, he had predicted just that: "Such has hitherto been the rapid progress of that country in wealth, population, and improvement, that in the course of *little more than a century*, perhaps, the produce of American [taxation] might exceed British taxation [italics mine]. The seat of empire would then naturally remove itself to that part of the empire which contributed most to the general defence and support of the whole." "From shopkeepers, tradesmen, and attornies, they [the Americans] are become statesmen and legislators, and are employed in contriving a new form of government for an extensive empire, which, they flatter themselves, will become, and which, indeed, seems very likely to become, the greatest and most formidable that ever was in the world." And he recommended that the colonies be granted their independence forthwith if they so desired. "By thus parting good friends, the natural affection of the colonists to the mother country would quickly revive. It might dispose them ... to favor us in war as well as in trade, and, instead of turbulent and factious subjects, to become our most faithful ... and generous allies." Very rarely do we encounter such foresight in the social sciences. Unbelievably, Adam Smith had anticipated the American chaon.

And so too had John Adams, who was to become our second President. As early as 1756, he discerned what we would now term the "butterfly effect" in political science. Noting that some years back England had lost a small number of inconspicuous citizens to an untamed wilderness in a new world, he wrote that "This apparently trivial incident may transfer the great seat of [power] into America." Most of the other Founding Fathers, guided as they were by their own personal antipathy toward elitism, felt the same. A phrase from Virgil's *Eclogues* appears on the Great Seal of the United States and conveys their high expectations: *Novus Ordo Seclorum* ("a new age now begins"). A great nation was the goal, one that would ultimately rise to "Power, Consequence and Grandeur", in the words of Robert Morris, widely regarded as the financier of the Revolution. His establishment of the first commercial bank in Philadelphia in 1782, the Bank of North America, provided a depository for foreign loans from France and Holland and a specie backed paper currency.

The Americans "are employed in contriving a new form of government," so wrote Adam Smith. And indeed they were! They were doing something unheard of, something that no other nation before or since has done. They were ridding themselves of a costly and oppressive autocracy and replacing it with almost no government at all and very little in the way of taxes. It was so unlike the French who guillotined their tax-happy rulers only to replace them with the likes of a bloodthirsty Citizen Robespierre and a war-crazed, self-appointed new emperor named Napoleon. Or the Russians who shot the Tsar and fell prey to Comrades Lenin and Stalin. Or the Chinese who dispatched the Kuomintang and got the murderous Chairman Mao. Or the Germans who traded their democracy for Nazism and the monstrous Adolph Hitler. Or the new nations of Africa who rid themselves of colonial rule only to get an Idi Amin and a whole zoo of self-aggrandizing dictators. Or our Latin American neighbors to the south who supplanted their European oppressors with even more ruthless native tyrants. Nowhere but in America was a George Washington to be found. Even today, most of the world endures unnecessarily low standards of living brought on by parasitic political establishments relatively huge by American standards. Although inspired by the American Revolution, the unfortunate people in none of these nations learned the essential lesson. They completely failed to comprehend the anti-government bias that had ingrained itself into the American spirit and is best proclaimed by Adam Smith's maxim, "That government is best which governs least", or as echoed later by Henry David Thoreau, "That government is best which governs not at all."

The years after the Revolution and before the Constitution were indeed "a critical period," but hardly in the sense implied by later historians. The times were critical because Americans were engaged in a crucial experiment, one that would decide between modern capitalism and the ancient philosophy of elitism. Justifiably skeptical of "great minds," the former colonists had chosen Adam Smith's "invisible hand" to "run" the country. That noblest of intentions, "the greatest happiness of the greatest number," was to be achieved through the illusory chaos of maximum freedom for each and every individual. It was not to be entrusted to the de facto chaos of Maximum Leader in the form of a king, a benign dictator, or Greek oligarchy. The decision shaped American society for generations to come. It was the gamble of the millennium, and it paid off with a nation whose standard of living is by far the highest ever achieved. We shall shortly consider the practical implications of the "invisible hand," all of which were soon to be embodied in the new Constitution.

CHAPTER VII

HOW TO CREATE A MONSTER:
THE DETERMINISM-ELITISM-TYRANNY
CONNECTION

Let experience be our guide. Reason will lead us astray.

John Dickinson, Delegate to the First Continental Congress (1774) and the Constitutional Convention (1787), author of *Letters from a Farmer in Pennsylvania*

One day when I called on him [Richard Wagner], I found him burning with passion for Hegel's Phenomenology, which he was just studying, and which, he told me with typical extravagance, was the best book ever printed. To prove it he read me a passage which had particularly impressed him. Since I did not entirely follow it, I asked him to read it again, upon which neither of us could understand it. He read it a third time and then a fourth, until in the end both of us looked at one another and burst out laughing. And that was the end of Phenomenology.

Friedrich Pecht, artist friend of Wagner.

    The unprecedented political restraint exercised by the young American nation was and still is incomprehensible to elitists indoctrinated from childhood into Princess Augusta's "Be a King!" dictum. What this nobly-intentioned caste of personages advocates, simply stated, is rule by illuminati, a select group of superior people to whom we must relinquish control over our lives. Its most eloquent statement is recorded with great literary skill in Plato's misleadingly entitled dialogue, The *Republic*. Herein is envisioned the first state-sponsored Utopia, a society ruled by an elite class of philosopher-kings. Their eyes fixed on immutable First Principles, these exalted beings harmonize with the very structure of the universe. Their minds honed to the Highest Reason, they command both a unique access to Truth and Beauty and a monopoly of Virtue. Their psyches attuned to Ultimate Wisdom, they lead the just State to the Supreme Good and administer the citizenry's lives accordingly. A geometrically precise social order prevails: The philosopher-king rules, the warrior fights, and the worker enjoys the fruits of his labor, each social class happily performing the function to which it is assigned. Democracy, because it makes no attempt to connect political power with any special qualifications of intellect, is doomed to failure. The free market, because it champions self-interest and equality of opportunity, is morally inferior to a society of equal reward. Equality as handed down by philosopher-kings is preferable to human freedom.

How sad to contemplate the generations of young minds so wretchedly misprogrammed by such antiquated, naïve and unsubstantiated tripe! How nauseating to encounter older minds so brainwashed! Plato's dictatorship of the elite is a utopia for philosopher-kings, no doubt. They make the laws, administer the laws, interpret the laws, and, if today's lawmakers are any example, they exempt themselves from the laws and profit mightily from them. And if perchance their Highest Reason should lead the State into tyranny, they have an armed warrior class to protect them from the "happy" and unarmed workers who support it all with their taxes. "Of course I'm for gun control," said one politician to another. "We can't have armed taxpayers, can we?" Confiscation of private arms, I might note, is the first action undertaken by all oppressive governments upon assuming power. The Revolutionary War, we should never forget, began in earnest when American Minutemen thwarted a British attempt to seize the military stores at Lexington and Concord. Fortunately for us, early Americans not only insisted on retaining their arms but were quick to use them in defense of their liberty.

In the deterministic world of elitism, the supremacy of human reason in pursuing utopian goals might go unquestioned. Only the finest thinkers, a Sherlock Holmes, for example, or better yet, members of the legal profession who tailor governments to their own unjust enrichment, would then be chosen as ruling philosopher-kings. English philosopher Jeremy Bentham's proposal to grant government all the power it needs to secure the "greatest happiness of the greatest number" would be the way to go. I think that we might all accept this notion *if*, and it is a very big if, the world were like a high school geometry class and free of chaos. But, as most of us know, it is not. And if it is not, not even a philosopher-king can see what happens next; the Highest Reason is irrelevant in a chaotic world. Because there are so many more ways of doing evil than good, any one government or person, no matter what the intentions, is likely to become tyrannical if given sufficient power. Benign dictators invariably believe in their power to do good, but they are in no respect different from the monster in Mary Shelley's *Frankenstein* or Lennie in John Steinbeck's *Of Mice and Men*, characters who also know not the consequences of their actions. Chaos trumps reason and sooner or later brings about what may be called the determinism-elitism-tyranny connection. Here is the philosophic fallacy underlying Plato's anti-republic and its elitist derivatives, socialism, communism, Marxism and fascism. Adam Smith's "invisible hand," on the other hand, allows us to adapt to and exploit the indeterminacy of chaos by affording each of us a maximum of freedom to overcome adversity and find "that which is the better." And if and when a better way is found, it can then be turned to the greatest good for all. A remarkably similar type of social behavior manifests itself in an ant colony. Workers sent out from the nest forage randomly for food. And when a discovery is made by one ant, a signal to congregate on paths leading to that food source goes out to all other ants. One successful ant has shown the way to all the others.

For more than two thousand years, intellectuals have extolled the primacy of reason as a guide to all human behavior and virtue. So pervasive are their elitist ideas in today's world that it behooves me to take a brief look back and assess anew the authors of it all, that holy trinity of Greek antiquity, Socrates, Plato and Aristotle. Only now I shall do it with due regard to two areas in which most intellectuals past and present display abysmal ignorance – modern finance and modern chaos. Trying to understand the nature of reality without a command of these two disciplines, as so many are wont to do, is like trying to understand the nature of an elephant without the benefit of sight and sound. The wisest man of his day in the opinion of the Delphic Oracle, Socrates (470-399 B.C.) roamed the free market agora discussing truth, knowledge, virtue and justice with any willing protagonist. "I know that I know nothing," he would protest with supreme irony after exposing others' intellectual pretensions. But his actions belied his outward humility. His fanatic belief in elitism permeates the pages of The *Republic* and he conspired unceasingly with like-minded young men to overthrow the Athenian democracy, until condemned to death for treason in one of those historical episodes cloaked in obfuscation by later historians. Never once in his long life did he recognize the agora's central role in financing the glory of ancient Greece. Never once did he perceive the freedoms of a democratic society as the source of Athenian power. Adam Smith's "invisible hand" did not make the scene for another 2,000 years, it is true. But, even so, the Greek populace well understood the worth of democracy and the free market, concepts far beyond the ken of Socrates.

Socrates' student, Plato, lays out in The *Republic the* consummate education of a philosopher-king. One might expect such a paragon of learning to recognize TRUTH when it rears up and slaps him in the face. Yet, Plato, and his learned student, Aristotle, rejected the very modern atomic theory of matter of Democritus (c460-c370 B.C.) in favor of the air-earth-fire-and water "truth" of Empedocles (c490-c430 B.C.). And they rejected the heliocentric picture of the solar system in favor of the geocentric "truth" in which the earth remains stationary at the very center of the universe. They could hardly have been further removed from the accepted models of today's thinking. But these are merely "scientific" matters, and Plato and his disciples disdained science as incapable of revealing "truth." Scientists dealt only with hypotheses and models of reality, while he, Plato, concerned himself with absolute values and the "only true reality." So let us note that he flopped miserably on two separate occasions when invited to apply his elitist principles to governing the very prosperous Greek city of Syracusa on the island of Sicily. His "higher knowledge" of the social sciences proved sorely inadequate when coping with the sordid details of everyday living. Like so many megalomaniacs today, he presumed himself capable of managing the production and distribution of goods and services more efficiently than the free market agora with its supposedly illiterate mob of merchants, artisans, farmers, and traders. Apologies and excuses notwithstanding, the hard nosed public of western societies has rightfully held in contempt out-of-touch-with-reality intellectuals ever since. "Any mental activity is easy," counseled novelist Marcel Proust, "if it need not take reality into account."

Despite their inherent flaws and fallacies and downright foolishness in many respects, the voluminous Greek writings exerted enormous influence on future medieval scholars when re-introduced into Europe by the Arabs. Partly because their manuscripts survived intact and those of most others did not and partly because their erudition and scope exceeded anything ever seen before, Plato and Aristotle were venerated as apostles of a self-evident body of truths handed down from antiquity. Their authority went untested and unquestioned. "The older the truthier," seemed to be the guiding slogan. There were inconsistencies with the Judeo-Christian Bible, but those were resolved when St. Thomas Aquinas integrated Aristotelian teachings into Catholic theology, errors and all. That set the stage for the determinism-elitism-tyranny connection. Thus, when Giordano Bruno proposed the idea of many individual realities and questioned the Platonic concept of absolute truth, he was in effect challenging Catholic doctrine. For his efforts, this farseeing man was burned at the stake. When Galileo disputed Aristotle's teachings on the geocentric model of the heavens, he too was attacking Church dogma. "The Bible tells people how to go to heaven – not how the heavens go," he opined, but he was very lucky to escape Bruno's fate. The Protestant Reformation provided a partial release from the obvious fallacies that had found their way into the Church. And the Church itself countered with reforms putting doctrine more in conformity with ever changing versions of reality.

Nowhere has the determinism-elitism-tyranny connection been more insidious than in Marxist doctrine and its applications to twentieth century politics. In country after country, leaders have foisted Marxism on the people as the solution to all their problems despite the abundance of evidence testifying to capitalist successes and Marxist failures. Marxism has become an effective vehicle for the tyrannical control of the many by small political elites throughout the world. Only where a highly armed warrior class holds an unarmed citizenry in sway does it continue in existence. We try to limit its spread. But, even in our Western democracies, Marxist termites crawl into the tax and legal structures and eat away at our substance and our freedom. This brand of elitism, like all the others, promises utopia somewhere down the road. But just what is it that people are buying?

Karl Marx (1818-1883) was a reasonably sensitive and erudite man well versed in the deterministic learning of his day. While aware of capitalism's great contributions, he asserts (in *Das Kapital*) that the working class (proletariat) is not getting its fair share of the spoils. Because businessmen (bourgeoisie) prosper by exploiting workers, the rich can only get richer and the poor poorer. The antagonisms arising from this dichotomy of interests must beget a class struggle in which the proletariat is destined "to wrest, by degrees, all capital from the bourgeoisie, to centralize all instruments of production in the hands of the State." Only then can the State "increase the total of productive forces as rapidly as possible." Because everybody shares equally in the greater material wealth, class distinctions would thus gradually disappear and even the State would "wither away" for lack of anything to do. This scenario of what Marx called "dialectical materialism" is foreordained, rooted as it is in the "self-evident truths" of the underlying assumptions and its irrefutable logic. It appears that Marx and his mentor, the German philosopher Georg Hegel (1770-1831), applied some simplistic physics to complex social systems. Because natural forces can under suitable conditions produce and separate material opposites from each other (the hot and cold air masses of the atmosphere, for example), they reasoned that sooner or later these must mix and approach their original equilibrium state (the same temperature). In general, according to Hegel, "thesis" and its opposite "antithesis" must interpenetrate to produce a unity called "synthesis." Marx extended Hegel's reasoning to social classes: Capitalism begets rich and poor and these must inexorably coalesce to produce equal wealth for all. But the analogy is faulty: Atmospheric air masses do not mix easily (think of the cold and warm fronts that come through with regularity) and the laws governing the behavior of air molecules retain little significance for human behavior. And, of course, neither Marx nor Hegel knew anything about probability theory or chaos. Self-organization into ordered chaonic states remained a concept far beyond them. It took the greater minds of Adam Smith and George Washington to appreciate the limits of reason when applied to human affairs.

Let us picture what Marx is saying. Under capitalism, private businesses can expand a nation's production only to a certain upper limit. There results some total amount of goods and services called the Gross Domestic Product. I shall call it the "Pie". According to Marx, the capitalist Pie can never be large enough to reward the proletariat sufficiently for its labor. Only by taking the means of production out of private hands and placing them under State control can the Pie be significantly enlarged. Marx seems not to have fallen for the fatuous notion, so in vogue today, that a Robin Hood-type redistribution of wealth from rich to poor can in itself materially benefit the poor. If we Americans, by far the wealthiest group of people in the world, were forced to donate our worldly riches to the other 6 billion souls on the planet, we would all be equal and as poor as everyone else. Marx's goal, a bountiful and equal slice of the Pie for each and every individual, was predicated on a much larger Pie.

Marx's noble intention of better living through bigger government has found worldwide support among intellectuals, have-nots and revolutionaries, Lenin's "useful idiots" who fervently believe that their "superior" knowledge qualifies them for their "rightful" place at the head of society. But hard questions arose and demanded answers: Who is the "State"? Since a "State" cannot run anything, some politically appointed bureaucrat must mastermind the enlargement of the Pie. Who is it to be? When does the State step in, after capitalism has shot its bolt or beforehand? Considerable debate centered on the timing. How is State takeover to be achieved? Confiscating private property is apt to cause much bloodshed and the destruction of plant and equipment. Should the process be revolutionary or evolutionary?

Marxism got its chance when the Communist Party emerged as the dominant force in post-tsarist Russia. Vladimir Lenin and his two lieutenants, Josef Stalin and Leon Trotsky, became the new philosopher-kings and the *Communist Manifesto the* new Bible. They began carrying out its dictates immediately. Published in 1848 by Marx and Engels, this rather poorly written, demagogic ("WORKERS OF THE WORLD, UNITE") pamphlet sets forth a program based on ten "truths." Designed to bring about equality through elitist regulation, it does nothing so much as enhance the power, privilege and wealth of politicians at the expense of individual liberty. Every one of its implications had been rejected earlier by America's Founding Fathers in their deliberations on the Constitution. The *Manifesto* begins with the expropriation of private property – land, businesses, factories and the means of transportation. It then proceeds to a heavy progressive income tax, abolition of inheritance, centralization of all credit in a central bank owned and run by the State with no private competition tolerated, "free" education for all children in public schools, and, finally, equal liability assumed by adults and children alike to labor at whatever activity the State directs. What's left is a minimum of freedom.

The new philosopher-kings fared no better than Plato, for the results have been abominable. How many millions were massacred to establish a classless Russian Utopia somewhere down the road nobody knows. What we do know is that Communism lasted for seventy years at the end of which time the Russian people lived on a level far below that of most other Western countries. All the blood and terror and brutality apparently went for naught.

What else could have been expected? For Marxist philosophy has faulty underpinnings – neither its assumptions nor its predictions show much correlation with reality. It is ponderously deterministic, creaky, old-fashioned and so alien to human nature that it remains a potent force only in countries where highly armed elitist minorities brutally suppress the great majority. It shows in the terribly low production efficiencies and it shows in the people's faces. There is no room for the exploitation of the richness and randomness of chaos and no understanding of chaons. Communist theorists even suppressed the quantum theory because of its repudiation of determinism. In a poignant description of the city of Prague, Czechoslovakia, under its Communist regime, Manuela Hoelterhoff depicts regimented life everywhere: "Prague is without the bustling people that make cities come alive. There's no pulse here, no heartbeat, only the pallid blip-blip emitted by a planned economy" (*The Wall Street Journal*, Oct. 15, 1982).

Marx completely misunderstood the nature of capitalism's great productive power. As so many do, he thought of it in terms of giant corporations effortlessly and endlessly producing a huge quantity and variety of goodies. Even if that were so – and you have to wonder about the simpletons who entertain such fancies – he forgot about or was ignorant of the fact that more than half the gross domestic product of capitalist nations is produced by small business. That sector of any free economy is responsible for the creation of almost all the new jobs and product innovations that contribute so richly to the quality of life. To repudiate the entrepreneurs running these productive businesses, let alone think that politicians and bureaucrats or anyone else can duplicate their achievements by means of centralized planning, is asinine. Sniffing out investment opportunities in new products and services demands people with flair, with business talent, and most importantly, with their own money and careers on the line. Public servants do not possess these essential qualities. Imagine, if you can, an Intel Corporation founded and run by government bureaucrats.

The *Communist Manifesto's* promulgation of a central bank to control a nation's credit and money has found favor in almost all of today's political establishments. The subject being rather involved, I shall reserve until later a full discussion of its implications. Suffice it to say here that the incorporation of this benign dictatorship oxymoron into modern governments has caused untold mischief and suffering throughout the world.

Lastly, Marx was forced to use naïve and far-fetched arguments to explain what he considered to be the exploitation of the working class. In his self-serving analysis of the raw data, the great improvements in proletarian living standards under capitalism somehow escaped his jaundiced eye. As a consequence, his prediction of class conflicts in the United States and other capitalist nations was far off the mark. His vast erudition is exceeded only by the stupidity of his predictions. Despite its deficiencies, Marxism remains popular on American campuses. There it is taught not as history or economics or as an example of George Orwell's "Big Brother" (which would properly recount its failures) but as a sophomoric moral code, a path to secular salvation, and a doctrinaire analysis of failed democracy and collapsed capitalism. Somehow, capitalism's supposed exploitation of the masses gets transferred to the exploitation of both animals and environment, and we thus have vegetarianism and "green" movements rampant among students and faculty alike. Such views are shared by many intellectuals in the news media, in politics, in academe, even in big business and religious hierarchies, anywhere where special interest groups might benefit from the ministrations of a "Big Daddy" government. The list of horrors that is the *Communist Manifesto* makes little impression upon these elitists. Nor do they appear to have any appreciation of what life might be like under maximum regulation. It is indeed fortunate that Marxism's appeal in America has been limited to a politically correct small minority, those "smart-smart-smart-stupid" people who think-think-think while failing utterly to comprehend the futility of logic in a chaotic world.

Several years ago, when Russia was still under the Communist regime, my wife and I were touring the Hermitage museum in St. Petersburg, then known as Leningrad. We stayed close to our guide, a lovely authoritative young woman who spoke English without the trace of an accent. She had begun learning the language at 5, she told us. It being a national holiday, every entrance to the museum was jammed with shoddily dressed sightseers, and it looked as if we could spend hours just waiting in line. We reckoned without our guide, however. Time and again, with a disdainful wave of her hand, she shooed the masses back. Never were there any complaints as we passed through. A few instances of this arrogant display induced my wife to mention how very embarrassing her performance was. To which our guide replied, her eyes flashing: "You are our guests. They will do as they are told!" Under Communism, the frightening ramifications of that statement extend to all aspects of regulated life — to the home, to the workplace, to the children. Manners and courtesy? Who needs them in regimented societies? Why else do they wane as societies become less free and, as a consequence, less efficient?

How well one does in a society of regimented "equality" depends not on the judgment of the marketplace but on one's connections with the bureaucratic hierarchy. This aspect of a regulated society surfaced convincingly on a tour of Varna, Bulgaria, a resort city on the Black Sea reserved for the Communist elite. A tall, handsome young man acted as our guide. At one point, as we were walking along a street lined with beautiful old mansions built long before Communism made its debut in Bulgaria, our guide remarked: "Some day, I will have a house on this street." "Oh," I commented, quizzically, "you were telling us just now that everybody is equal here." He gave me that stone-faced look affected by all WE-KNOW-THE-ONLY-

TRUE-TRUTH fanatics when confronted with an unwelcome observation. "Oh, I see," I continued brazenly, "some of you are more equal than others." It would seem that the privileged political classes of a Communist society, unlike the masses, enjoy a full measure of material comforts.

"It's a lot of fun to win," commented Brian Halla, chairman of the National Semiconductor Corporation, in a letter to shareholders on his company's remarkable comeback from adversity. And of course it is. Could there be a more appropriate answer to what inspires people to better themselves? But the only winners under socialism's dictum of "equal" reward are the politicians and their henchmen. Everyone else "will do as they are told." America's Founding Fathers understood this hostility toward entrepreneurship all too well, acquainted as they were with the blunderbuss policies of enlightened despotism and the monsters it could call forth. Their thoughts went in exactly the opposite direction, to Adam Smith's "invisible hand" and maximum freedom for all, to an unregulated, free-market economy as the producer of the greatest wealth. Theirs was a world of "life, liberty, and the pursuit of happiness", not political control. They would have wholeheartedly agreed with H. L. Mencken's remark that I quoted earlier: "All government is, after all, against freedom." Our American Constitution rests squarely on this premise.

CHAPTER VIII

HOW THE CHAON OF GREATEST PROSPERITY EMERGES FROM THE CHAOS OF MAXIMUM FREEDOM I

THE

NORMAL

LAW OF ERROR

STANDS OUT IN THE

EXPERIENCE OF MANKIND

AS ONE OF THE BROADEST

GENERALIZATIONS OF NATURAL

PHILOSOPHY + IT SERVES AS THE

GUIDING INSTRUMENT IN RESEARCHES

IN THE PHYSICAL AND SOCIAL SCIENCES AND

IN MEDICINE AGRICULTURE AND ENGINEERING +

IT IS AN INDISPENSABLE TOOL FOR THE ANALYSIS AND THE

INTERPRETATION OF THE BASIC DATA OBTAINED BY
OBSERVATION AND EXPERIMENT

Statistician W. J. Youden

   Imagine yourself playing this game. Draw a line on the ground 200 paces long and stand at its midpoint. Now flip a coin. If it comes up heads, take one step to the right. If it comes up tails, take one step to the left. Repeat after each step. Where will you be, say, after 100 flips? Or, if we think of playing the game in two dimensions, it may be pictured as the drunkard's walk: A very inebriated woman lets go of a lamppost and lurches randomly in all directions. How far from the lamppost will she be after 100 steps?

This is the problem of the random walk, first solved more than three hundred years ago by Swiss mathematician Ames Bernoulli (1654-1705). Its importance derives from the fact that many natural phenomena seem to behave in just such a manner. Brownian motion, discovered in 1827 by the Scottish botanist, Robert Brown, is perhaps the most celebrated example. Brown noted that microscopically small particles of matter – bits of pollen or glass or rock, for example – jiggle unceasingly along erratic, zigzag paths when suspended in water. All efforts to understand this phenomenon of perpetual motion failed, and not until 1905 did an explanation come forth. Then it was that Albert Einstein (1879-1955) likened Brownian motion to a random walk and was able to predict the probable future positions of the particles in a statistical sense. That is, he could calculate the *number* of particles to be found at any given distance from their starting points at some future time, but not where any single designated particle would be. Einstein pictured the Brownian particles as randomly bombarded by the much tinier water molecules. Every so often, an imbalance in the number of molecular "kicks" on the relatively massive particle displaces it an observable distance and starts it on a random walk into the future. Einstein's work not only provided a description of vitally important diffusion processes, but offered as well the most convincing proof up to that time of the existence of atoms and molecules.

Unbeknownst to Einstein, however, his remarkable research had been anticipated five years earlier in 1900 by Louis Bachelier (1870-1946), a student of Poincaré at the Sorbonne in Paris. Unbelievably, Bachelier had derived many of the same results, not for Brownian motion, but for the fluctuations in stock prices on the Paris stock exchange over a period of time. The problem here was how far from its starting price would a stock be displaced after some given time? Bachelier pictured random imbalances in the buy and sell decisions of investors as the cause of the observed price fluctuations. He, like Einstein and his Brownian particles, could accurately predict the number of stocks that would show a given price change after some elapsed time, but not how any one stock would perform. His random walk model of the stock market, now widely accepted, was offered as a doctoral thesis in mathematics and later published in *La Theorie de la Speculation* (Paris: Gauthier-Villars, 1900). Most mathematicians and scientists, however, looked askance at the subject matter and ignored his work. Their attitude weighed heavily against this great man's just claim to fame and position.

Our two examples pose searching questions about reality. Is the world, from the atoms and molecules of which it is composed to the affairs of human beings, at the mercy of chaotically fluctuating forces whose application is ultimately decided by the flip of a coin? Do human intelligence and ability count for naught? How closely does this game of chance mimic real-world happenings? "What is truth?" Earlier we encountered another example of the random walk when asking for the number of male babies to be born to our group of pregnant women. Simply by replacing the steps to the right and left with baby boys and girls, the random walk emerges. We might think too of a life insurance company that knows accurately the number of people who will die at some given age but cannot pinpoint any one person. And we have already traced the sequences of random steps that led to the Intel Corporation and American independence. The quote from George Washington's intuitively perceptive inaugural address bears repeating: "No people can be bound to acknowledge and adore the invisible hand, which conducts the affairs of men, more than the people of the United States. Every step, by which they have advanced to the character of an independent nation, seems to have been distinguished by some token of providential agency." In complex worldly phenomena such as these, we have little idea of the step by step probabilities of future happenings. On the other hand, long periods of product research and development have led to the more predictable sequences that go into the manufacture of our cars and television sets. Many other examples will suggest themselves. But first let us clarify the complexities of the random walk and its real-world manifestations by joining a group of 100 people playing roulette. This is an example of a *money market*, one in which people risk money to make more money. Lest you consider games of chance frivolous in nature, let me remind you that such activities have played a vital role in the development of mathematics, physics and statistics. And the knowledge of elementary probability theory they impart is essential for an understanding of free markets. To cope adequately with reality, we must think in terms of future probabilities, not certainties. Might this be why so many "intellectuals," lacking this prerequisite, despise capitalism and turn to simplistic, deterministic Marxism as their philosophy of choice? We moderns, however, must couch our future predictions in terms of probability, and in what follows we shall learn a useful bit about the subject. It might be helpful to keep in mind your personal wealth as of today and what it might be one year from now as a result of the many decisions under uncertainty you will be called on to make.

For simplicity's sake, our 100 players will be constrained to wagering $1 on either black or red. And we shall ignore the non-black, non-red numbers of "0" and "00" that casinos employ to shift the odds in their favor. If we play with an ideal roulette wheel, there is a fifty-fifty chance (a 50% probability) of betting correctly on black or red. A correct call yields a profit of $1, an incorrect call the loss of $1. How much will each of us have, I ask, after 100 spins of the wheel if each of us starts with a capital of $100? The final amounts, as you can well imagine, may vary considerably. It is possible for a very lucky player to end up with $200 (100 correct calls) and a very unlucky one with nothing (100 wrong calls). Most of us, however, will do about average, which in this case means ending up with an amount at or near our $100 starting capital. Clearly, what we have here is just the random walk in one dimension, not measured in steps but in dollars. We can picture each member of our group traveling along 100-step paths leading to many possible futures with every step accompanied by a decision under uncertainty. Each spin of the wheel causes our original $100 to fluctuate up or down in $1 amounts. All in all, there are 101 possible end results, every even amount from $0 to $200. The one hundred decisions give rise to an astronomical number of different 100-step paths, more than a thousand million trillion trillion or a 1 followed by 30 zeros. (A trillion is a 1 followed by 12 zeros). To illustrate,there is one path leading to a final capital of $200 (a person following that path must make 100 correct guesses) and one path leading to $0 (100 wrong guesses). These two are the only smooth or *linear* paths. The possible paths to the other final capitals increase enormously in number and they kink chaotically. To end up with a capital of $198, for example, a person must make 99 correct guesses and 1 wrong guess. Since the one wrong guess can occur on any one of the 100 steps, there are 100 different paths leading to $198, all with one kink. The same is true for an ending capital of $2 (99 wrong guesses and 1 right guess). For a final capital of $196 (98 correct guesses and 2 wrong guesses), there are 4950 possible paths with two kinks each, for $194 (97 correct guesses and 3 wrong guesses), 161700 paths, etc. The greatest number of paths (on the order of 1 followed by 29 zeros or 8% of the total) occurs at an ending capital of $100 (50 correct and 50 wrong guesses), just where we all began. In statistics, that is called the "expectation" or the "average".

What must be stressed at this point is that our game is one of equal opportunity. We would all like to choose the one path leading to $200. But each of the more than 100000000000000000000000000000 other paths is just as likely to occur, and there is only an infinitesimal chance of traveling along that one path to $200. Not even an Einstein can use his great reasoning powers to foresee the best path to follow. And that is exactly what is meant by real-world chaos – the future is as unknown to the smartest as it is to the dumbest amongst us. When confronting a chaotic situation, all of us are equal. In our roulette model, 95% of all possible paths lead to a final capital between $90 (45 wins, 55 losses and a $10 overall loss) and $110 (55 wins, 45 losses and a $10 overall profit), and it is in this range that ninety-five of us will most likely end up. The luckiest among us (2½% or "2½" of us) will win $10 or more and increase their starting capital to $110 or more, and the unluckiest among us (again 2½%) will lose $10 or more and end up with $90 or less. But where any single individual finishes, nobody can predict with any degree of certainty. We can only say that each of us has a 95% probability of doing about average (a final capital between $90 and $110), a 2½% probability of doing better than average and a 2½% of doing worse than average. On the next 100 spins of the wheel, the percentages stay the same but where any one individual ends up is again unpredictable. Previous gains do not by any means guarantee future successes.

If we graph the *number* of possible paths against each final capital, there emerges the histogram known as the bell shaped curve, the symbol of randomness. In technical parlance, it is referred to as the "normal" or "Gaussian" distribution, or the normal law of error, and *it is the distinguishing feature of equal opportunity markets.* The average occurs at the peak of the curve (where the greatest number of paths terminates) while the spread of the curve gives an idea of the uncertainty involved. In an equal reward game, there is no spread – every path ends up at the same fated future. In another way of looking at it, equal opportunity markets are symmetric in that all participants are *indistinguishable* insofar as their expectations of future performance are concerned. In exactly the same way, a sphere possesses a symmetry because its reflection in a plane mirror is indistinguishable from the original. Similar results obtain for a group of 200 pregnant women. With a 95% probability, between 90 and 110 boys will be born to any group of 200 women, neglecting the possibility of multiple births. In a capitalist equal-opportunity society, most people find themselves near average, the so-called middle class. That is where the greatest wealth resides, and, as we shall see, that is the area targeted by the income tax. The relatively few rich inhabit the right wing of the curve, the relatively few poor the left wing.

If you remember, we started our roulette game with the Marxist ideal of equal wealth for all – all players began with the same capital – and we ended up with an unequal distribution of assets as displayed by the bell-shaped curve. We should now understand why it is that *equality of opportunity and equality of reward are mutually exclusive*. You can't have both when chance rules. Marx and Engels considered unequal rewards a "problem" and their "solution," as we have seen, was to have an all-powerful elite equalize the rewards by taking the profits from the winners and redistributing them to the losers. They are the role models for most of today's "benefactors-of-humanity" politicians. Our Founding Fathers, on the other hand, went to extraordinary lengths to protect "sacred and inviolable" private property from government forfeiture and a possibly overbearing majority. They most certainly did not wish to embark the country on the yellow brick road leading to the Emerald City where dwelt that great benign dictator, the fakir known as the Wizard of Oz.

Using our roulette model, we can understand the significance of human freedom when trying to resolve a chaotic problem, one not susceptible to a reasonable solution. As we all know, there are many more ways of doing something wrong than doing something right. So, suppose we equate the "correct" ways of achieving some goal with the 2½% of the paths that end up at a final capital of $110 or more. If that be the case and equal opportunity exists for all, then any one person – a government official, for example – hoping to do something right has very little chance of doing so. But if everybody has the freedom to try, 2½% of us will find the way and the rest of us can then follow.

Suppose we switch for the moment to our personal wealth and how it may fare over the next year as each of us makes one decision under uncertainty after another. The number of possible paths and outcomes now dwarfs those in our roulette example, but we as a whole can still expect to do about average. In the United States where there exists a nearly equal-opportunity society and the government's tax "take" in the past has not been exorbitant, we have an incentive in the form of higher income to produce more from year to year. As a result, the rewards at the ends of all paths increase and the standard of living goes up. The whole bell-shaped curve shifts to the right, toward greater personal wealth. Or, as phrased by Jack Kemp, "A rising tide raises all ships". There will of course be a disparity of incomes. In fact, a graph plotting the *number* of people against income yields something similar to the bell-shaped curve with today's average (what we call the "middle class") at about $40,000 per annum. One year's performance, however, holds no guarantee of future results; the next 100 spins of the roulette wheel, for example, will find many of the previous winners in the losing column and vice versa. Only a negligible few can hope to become millionaires on the basis of a chance progression of wins from year to year. Still, the actual distribution of incomes is not bell-shaped: There are more above-average incomes in America than can be expected on the basis of chance. Many people, it would seem, are able to outwit the averages. An understanding of this asymmetry is important. To see how it may come about, let us "take reality into account" and play our roulette game in a real-world casino.

Once there, we immediately confront a seemingly obvious but unappreciated fact common to all gambling and investment activities: *Only people have money!* Roulette tables do not have any. Horses do not have any. Neither do investment instruments like stocks and bonds have any. Winning, therefore, means getting other people's money. We want their money. They want our money. And they are not about to give theirs away easily. They know the "truth" just as well as we do. Anyone deciding to compete in one or more of these gambling or financial markets will face, I assure you, unremittingly fierce competition from the smartest of people.

From whom do we hope to win money at the casino? Why, from the casino owners, of course. They are in business, and to stay in business they must offer a product that the public wants at a price the public is willing to pay. That price must enable them to recover operating costs *and* get a fair return on their investment. And it must also be competitive with that of other casinos if they hope to attract customers. As we have played it thus far, the roulette game does not suffice for their purposes. Most players will end up near break even and the profits from the losers will go to the winners, leaving nothing for the house. To ensure the needed revenue, casinos add two extra numbers to the wheel in American roulette, the "0" and "00". These are neither red nor black, and a red or black bet loses if the ball comes to rest on either of them. The bell-shaped curve is now shifted to the left because most paths to the future end up at a capital of $94.70 rather than $100. Far fewer paths lead to a profit. Thus, our group can expect to have only one or two winners after a hundred spins of the wheel and nobody can know who they will be. The expectation is not break even but a loss of $5.30, or 5.3% of the total $100 bet. That is the percentage of our money that goes to the house. If you decide to play roulette in a casino, it is the cost to you of having fun. Through hard experience, casino owners have discovered the 5.3% "take" to be best for business. It is not too high to discourage patrons from playing roulette, and it is high enough for an adequate return on their investment. The 5.3% casino "take," I should note, is a far cry from the confiscatory 50% and more that government monopolies take from their lottery and numbers rackets. And, on top of that, they take another 50% of what's left in income taxes! Only politicians can get away with such scams.

We have in the roulette money market an excellent example of a free or voluntary market. Casinos offer the game to any and all comers irrespective of race, religion, intelligence or wealth. For their customers, they provide hospitality, entertainment and, most importantly, an environment in which the game can be played in an orderly fashion. In this sense, casinos act much like a form of limited government. Within the rules established by the casino, all patrons are equal. They are free to employ any system that may help them to win, free to keep and do what they like with their winnings, and, in short, try their damnedest to beat the averages. No philosopher-king is there to confiscate profits or tell players what they may or may not do. No benign dictator is there to take and spend their money for them. If there were, who would bother to play? But with money as the prize and everyone free to act in his/her own best interests, we may rest assured that many very smart people will access all possible information to win. On the other hand, the casino owners are quite aware of the opportunity they are offering. They have assessed the risks and have decided to pit their knowledge and their money against the world. And here is the key point: They do not expect anyone to develop a surprisingly new system of play that could turn the game into a losing proposition and jeopardize their investment. To them, all market participants are *indistinguishable* insofar as their expectation of loss is concerned; nobody can have an expectation of profit when playing roulette. The basis of their belief is in what I call "conservation of information" – *there is* no information available that gives to any one individual an *advantage over any other*. Such information, if and when it exists, is called "privileged information." Those markets in which conservation of information holds are called "efficient," and if such be the case intelligence and ability do count for naught. Or, as I might put it, we are all equal when dealing with a chaotic situation.

Questions arise: Is it possible to know something the casino professionals do not? Does there exist privileged information that enables its possessor to do better than average in the roulette market? Is the market efficient? Suppose, for example, that one member of our group spots a bias in the roulette wheel indicating that red is more likely to come up than black. After all, mechanical devices are to some degree imperfectly constructed and a bias is quite likely. If valid, the finding places our hero above the crowd, or, as a scientist would say, in a far-from-equilibrium situation. He has discovered probabilities that approximate the "truth" better than those of anybody else. Because of his new knowledge, he can anticipate better-than-average performance by betting solely on red. From the vantage point of his simple red-betting system, the paths leading to future gains outnumber those leading to a loss. Sooner or later, of course, equilibrium in the form of equality of opportunity will be restored. Once they learn about the bias, the casino operators will take steps to neutralize that threat to their operations. During the interim, however, privileged information has opened a window of opportunity for those relatively few people who learn of its existence. It distorts the bell-shaped curve and violates our conservation law of information.

In the language of chaos, privileged information has changed the probabilities and driven the market far from its equilibrium state of equal opportunity. A chaon has been triggered, what in our example is a simple strategy for doing better at roulette. Steps into the future do not proceed randomly now but follow an ordered pattern, an algorithm: Follow each bet on red with another bet on red. That is how to choose the "correct" paths. As always, this chaon must arise spontaneously and unpredictably or it will arise not at all. The casino operators would see to that.

On the basis of all evidence to date, the roulette market is "efficient." The casinos have offered the game to all comers for hundreds of years and continue to do so with no hint of bankruptcy. In The *Eudaemonic Pie: Or Why Would Anyone Play Roulette without a Computer in His Shoe* (Boston:Houghton Mifflin, 1985), Thomas Bass recounts how a group of physicists tried to apply their knowledge of computers and Newton's Laws of Motion to make a fortune at roulette. Their intelligence and ability notwithstanding, the attempt failed and our conclusion remains. The casino managers know the "truth" as revealed in the historical record and "breaking the bank" is highly improbable. That has not always been the case for other games.

In the 1960s, mathematician Edward O. Thorp discovered a profitable system for playing blackjack and published it in his book, *Beat the Dealer* (New York: Vintage, What he found was a faulty assignment of probabilities to the game's future outcomes. The casino model on which those probabilities had been based assumed a constant deck of 52 cards and made no allowance for the diminution of the deck as the game progressed. With new probabilities calculated for a diminishing deck, Thorp was able to devise strategies that put him on paths leading to capital appreciation in what was previously a losing game. He had triggered a chaon.

Armed with his newfound knowledge, Thorp proceeded to put his chaon to the test. Card dealers, who at first scoffed at the surprisingly lucky newcomer, became by degrees increasingly bewildered and frustrated. Their consternation mounted as funds drained from their coffers. Finally, Thorp was barred from playing in one casino after another. Disguises and changes of venue no longer sufficed once dealers caught on to the style of play. But the respite was short-lived. People invariably flow to where the money is and with the publication of Thorp's book, hordes of newly expert blackjack players descended on the gambling palaces seeking quick fortunes. It was as if Thorp had placed an information time bomb everywhere blackjack was played, one that threatened the very existence of casinos. By now, the house experts understood that Thorp had exploited a deficiency in their knowledge of blackjack "truth" and they frantically sought a remedy. First, they changed the rules of play to ensure a losing expectation for the players based on the new probabilities. But under the altered rules, play at the blackjack tables fell off sharply, obliging a return to the old ones. Next, they made it more difficult for players to "case" the deck, a prerequisite for profitable operations, by employing multiple decks dealt from a shoe and more frequent shuffling. Finally, system players were vigorously excluded or taken care of by nimble-fingered dealers. Needless to say, the window of opportunity was closed and this modern day gold rush effectively detoured. Once incorporated into the public store of knowledge, privileged information loses its status and becomes commonplace and ineffective. In our chaotic real world, staying above the crowd is indeed difficult because knowledge feeds back and, sooner or later, the competition will learn and react. When that happens, a chaon dies and the chaos of equal opportunity is restored. Free markets sponge up information with unbelievable rapidity in most cases.

Are other free markets efficient? Do there exist illuminati, economists and politicians, for example, who can divine "truth" in the historical records and thereby forecast future trends better than the rest of us? Are there godlike fortune tellers whose crystal balls can guide us to heaven on earth? These questions become of the utmost urgency when we take up the consumer and financial markets that make up a nation's economy and the government's role in it. First, however, let us prepare ourselves by looking at a prototype of all free markets, one that is far more complex than those heretofore considered but one in which risk and reward can be treated with simple analysis. Elitists take note! This money market offers "superior" people a seemingly unparalleled opportunity for riches by matching them, not against expert casino operators, but against a motley crowd of "inferiors."

On 1 November 1938, there took place an event that stirred the imagination of our whole Depression-ridden nation. It was the "race of the century," a match (beautifully described in Laura Hillenbrand's book *Seabiscuit*) between two great thoroughbreds, Seabiscuit and War Admiral, running for a nominal winner-take-all purse of $15,000 at the Pimlico Race Track in Baltimore MD. For two minutes, millions from President Franklin Delano Roosevelt on down, held their breath as they listened to the call on the radio. Forty thousand people at trackside risked $76,811 of their hard-earned money trying to make more money by betting on either

Seabiscuit or War Admiral. Seabiscuit, a rags-to-riches wonder, was the sentimental favorite, but most money was bet on classy War Admiral, triple-crown winner and undisputed champion. Of the total amount bet, $55,235 (72%) was on War Admiral and only $21,576 (28%) on Seabiscuit. These were relatively large amounts at the time because, as we shall learn, a third of the nation's money had self-destructed during the Great Depression.

That this "pari-mutuel" money market is an ideal laboratory for the study of free market mechanisms under institutional conditions was first recognized in my book, *Horse Sense A New and Rigorous Application of Mathematical Methods for Successful Betting at the Track* (New York: David McKay, 1965). What we have here is a microcosm of society struggling as best it can to solve its own unique set of problems. Thousands of diverse individuals, all with easy access to enormous amounts of historical information, are trying to see what the future holds in store. Their problem is everybody's – to evaluate the risks and rewards associated with the possible future outcomes of an event, in this instance a horse race. For our match race there are but two possible futures, a War Admiral win or a Seabiscuit win. Judged by the percentages of money bet on the two horses, the racing public forecast a 72% probability for a War Admiral win and, consequently, a 28% probability for a Seabiscuit win. These are the numbers that quantify the risks involved in choosing one of the two possible futures. The public's underlying assumption is this: If the race were to be run many times in the future under the same starting conditions (insofar as they can be known within errors of measurement and judgment), War Admiral would win 72 times in every hundred races, Seabiscuit 28 times. Note that these probabilities in general may vary from 0% when the public thinks that some horse has no chance to win (no money is bet on it) to 100% when the public thinks that some horse is certain to win (all the money is bet on it). It is much like the weatherman forecasting a 72% chance of sunshine tomorrow versus a 28% chance of rain. In both cases, these numbers are beforehand estimates, based on past experience, of the true and unknown probabilities.

The possible rewards for those betting on the race are given by the "odds" (the *profit* to be expected on a winning wager for each dollar bet). A War Admiral win would have netted his backers a 25¢ profit for every dollar bet (odds of one to - four or a $1 profit for every $4 bet). Seabiscuit's win, on the other hand, netted his backers a $2.20 profit for every dollar bet (odds of 2.20-to-one). Where does this reward money come from? Certainly not from Seabiscuit or War Admiral. They don't have any money! The payoff, therefore, must come from the pari-mutuel pool of $76,811. It is a simple matter of *loser pays*, in this case, the people who bet on War Admiral. Here is where the pari-mutuel market differs from the other markets we have thus far considered. In the casino market, it is the operators who set the future probabilities and rewards as they see them and they are the ones who guarantee the winners their money. In the pari-mutuel market, on the contrary, the race track operators have no direct financial interest in the outcomes of races. They merely pool all the money bet and take a certain percentage off the top (for this race, 10%) to pay costs and taxes and net a fair return on their investment. The remaining money goes to those who backed the winner. For our match race, $69,130 remained in the pool after the 10% "take." Subtracting the $21,756 staked on

Seabiscuit leaves $47,554 of the losers' money to be returned as a profit to the winners, or $2.20 for every dollar bet. Of course, the winners also get back their original $21,576.

Although unexpected, Seabiscuit's win still had a 28% chance of occurring according to the betting public. That was a lot higher and more reasonable than the near zero win probability assigned to Seabiscuit by the handicapping experts of the news media – less than 5% of them backed the winner. Is the pari-mutuel market efficient, one of equal opportunity for all bettors? Is a chaon in the form of a profitable betting system possible?

To answer these questions, let us suppose that some bettor at that Pimlico meeting placed 100 $1 win bets on horses starting at dollar odds of $2.20 (those horses on which 28% of the win pool money is placed). How would he or she have fared? If the public's probability equals the true probability, there would be an average *loss* of $10.40 (28 wins each worth $2.20 for a gain of $61.60 versus 72 losses of $1 each) and, with a 95% probability, the losses would range between $5 and $16 for each 100-race sample. There will of course be fluctuations, both good and bad betting days, but over time the averages will assert themselves. Note that the average loss of $10.40 is 10.4% of starting capital. However, it would equal the track's "take" of 10% exactly if payoffs were made to the nearest penny rather than to the nearest nickel or dime. A $2.20 pari-mutuel payoff could in reality be anything from $2.21 to $2.29, with the track pocketing the pennies as an extra take known as "breakage." A similar calculation for any other win probability reveals the same result: A 10% average loss can be expected over any 100-race sample *if the public's probability estimates closely approximate the true probabilities*. And, if that is so, both Einstein and the village idiot are *pari-mutuelly indistinguishable* insofar as their expectations are concerned.

Suppose, on the other hand, that some person (like mathematician Thorp, for example) had been able to handicap the historical data and divine a different "truth" from that of the crowd, that Seabiscuit had a 50% chance of winning rather than the public's 28% chance. Over a hundred races of this sort, our expert could then expect 50 wins, the same as in the roulette example we considered earlier. But because each win now pays $2.20 rather than $1, the average *profit* on the $100 starting capital would be $60 (50 wins each with a gain of $2.20 versus 50 losses of $1 each). And with 95% probability, the profit would fall between $44 and $76, an extraordinarily high return on the $100 investment.

How close are the true probabilities to the public's perception of them? Can anyone hope to calculate win probabilities more accurately than the "mobocracy" at the race track? These are the questions to be answered by all bettors trying to pick the winner of a horse race. Of course, few people look at it in this way. Most assume that one horse is, to use a deterministic phrase, "going to win," and somehow or other they must discover the one so fated. Their methods of selection vary greatly: Some play hunches or tips, some look for "inside information", some use intuition, some select blindly, some pray to God, some invoke superstitious practices, some follow the selections of experts, and some discover "truth" in a deep analysis of past performances. Whatever, each bettor somehow discovers his or her own unique "truth" as represented by the horse chosen to win. Put it all together and you get the public's probability estimates. How close to the "only true truth" are these? Let me just say that anyone trying to produce better ones will soon find, as did *Mousie*, "that foresight may be vain." Why? Because the public is unsurpassed in its ability to set accurate win probabilities. Somehow, as if guided by Adam Smith's invisible hand, the *thousands of truths held by thousands of randomly betting individuals*, each pursuing his/her own best interest by risking his/her own money, *clash*, interact and modify one another into a final consensus that forecasts future probabilities better than those of any single *individual*. Can there be a better example of democracy in action? Is there a physical law of human behavior being exhibited here?

Racing aficionados, as all others, find public superiority hard to swallow – until it is drilled into them by steady betting losses. After all, it is argued, the betting public as a whole does not represent an intellectually superior cross section of society. Shouldn't people with highly developed reasoning powers, physicists or economists or lawyers, perhaps, be better able to analyze historical information and predict future results more accurately? And shouldn't the same apply to expert handicappers using modern computer programs? If so, there should be no limit to the amount of money these "superior" people might win. But emotional fixations aside, all is to no avail. Analyses of hundreds of thousands of races from 1955 to the present have left no doubt as to the public's superiority in setting win probabilities. When, for example, the public assigns a 10% win probability to a large sample of thoroughbreds, we can be sure that 10% of those horses will win, although we cannot pinpoint the winners. The pari-mutuel market, therefore, is a superb example of an efficient market, and all bettors have the same expectation – the loss of the track's "take." The takes today are so large – 15% to 20% – that over a hundred race sample, very, very few paths lead to a profit, far fewer than in our roulette example.

Rarely these days do we hear about free markets other than in pejorative terms. Lacking the rudimentary knowledge of expectations and probabilities required for an understanding of such markets, most teachers, politicians and media mavens are unable to assimilate the efficient market concept. It is so much easier for them to spout forth on benign dictators and "Big Daddy" governments à la Plato and Marx, innocents who had nary an inkling of modern probability theory. Even the "expert" reviewer of *Horse Sense* in *Sports Illustrated* (June 1965) found my confirmation of public superiority so emotionally difficult to grasp that he missed completely the efficient markets concept. But is it not the basic assumption of our democracy that we as a national group know more than any one of us? And doesn't the old saw "You can't beat the horses" imply that "You can't beat all the other bettors," and, furthermore, that the public discounts all relevant information before the race? How exhilarating for those Adam Smith disciples among us to find statistically valid evidence, a rara avis in the social sciences, confirming public superiority!

Interestingly, many psychologists and psychiatrists picked up on this idea of public superiority and references to my book appeared in many of their journals. Some even use it professionally. They believe that if unfounded notions of superiority can be expunged, if fantasies of a world beholden to "the greater glory of me" can be exorcised, their patients' minds stand a good chance of being cleansed. I wonder if Hercules in the Augean stables had a more difficult clean-up job. How can all those inflated egos we meet every day possibly accept such a denial of their exalted status? Only mature people are wise enough to know and admit to what they don't know, and only they can accept the efficient market concept without qualification.

In another way of looking at it, the pari-mutuel market may be regarded as a poll in which people risk their money on the horse they think most likely to succeed. Similar polls in which people bet money on their choices in Presidential elections exist in Iowa and Ireland. And these polls, like the pari-mutuel polls, have proven amazingly accurate, far more so than those "too-close-to-call" polls so well publicized in the news media.

Can the horses be beaten? Believe it or not, there once was a time when it could be done. When pari-mutuel betting was first introduced in America, the race track "take" amounted to a reasonable 10%, the same as in our Sea Biscuit-War Admiral example. Astute bettors quickly discovered a chaon: Bet only on the favorite as shown at the close of betting. Following this algorithm produced a *profit* of one or two percent of the amount bet over time. As explained in my book *Horse Sense* (1965), favorable late-breaking information unknown to the general public often attaches to favorites and makes them underbet. This chaon persisted until World War II when the takes were raised "temporarily" to 15% or more. Today, the market digests information much too quickly and the bias has disappeared altogether.

The question, however, is particularly apropos because it relates to efficient markets in general. If there exists no formula to do better than the public in the pari-mutuel market, what can be said about other markets that may or not be efficient, the stock and consumer markets, for example? How can these much more complex markets be "beaten" when the pari-mutuel market cannot? What can be said about all those stock market gurus who purport to "beat the market"? And the economists who try to predict and control those so-called "business cycles"? And all those government officials who intervene in free markets trying to make them work better? And, finally, what are we to make of those godlike "designated gamblers" known as central bankers who try to regulate a country's economy? What qualifies any of them to try and do good? And with our money?

CHAPTER IX

HOW THE CHAON OF MAXIMUM PROSPERITY EMERGES FROM THE CHAOS OF MAXIMUM FREEDOM II

Speculation ... is the self-adjustment of society to the probable. Its value is well-known as a means of avoiding or mitigating catastrophes, equalizing prices and providing for periods of want. It is true that the success of the strong induces imitation by the weak, and that incompetent persons bring themselves to ruin by undertaking to speculate in their turn. But legislatures and courts generally have recognized that the natural evolutions of a complex society are to be touched only with a very cautious hand ...

Oliver Wendell Holmes

Let us carry over our ideas to a similar but more vital entity, another free market in which public superiority asserts itself. As an allocator of savings in a capitalist economy, the stock market's crucial role in the development of the American chaon can hardly be overstated. It is, as we shall see, the preferred channel for directing flows of private savings into the creation and expansion of a nation's physical wealth, its means of production. As such, it sensitively reflects developments in all other consumer and financial markets the totality of which is a nation's economy. Here is a ready market that brings together corporations needing money and people willing to risk it for possible future rewards. The initial public stock offering that gave birth to the Intel Corporation is an apropos example. A buyer of stock in some company expects a return, from price appreciation and dividends (cash payments out of profits made to stockholders), greater than that available elsewhere. A seller of stock expects to do better either in another stock or in some other investment instrument. What investors are trying to do through the aggregate of their investment decisions is to fix a price for each stock that adequately reflects the risks involved in securing a good return on the investment. With each passing moment, the risks are assessed and reassessed in the light of any late-breaking information that arises, and market prices fluctuate with each revelation. The thoughts of the investing public concerning the prospects of the many businesses upon which our society relies are mirrored in the market quotations on the financial pages of the daily newspapers. These are the numbers that quantify the collective opinion of millions of decision-makers who at every moment must buy or not buy, sell or not sell. They take into account all possible futures and their related probabilities as seen by the investment community. What fantastic complexity, what unfathomable, immeasurable forces underlie this market! How remindful are its price fluctuations to the particle displacements in Brownian motion where molecular kicks substitute for buy-sell imbalances!

Deep questions of predictability must be answered. Is the investing public, like its counterpart in the pari-mutuel market, able to forecast accurately the future probabilities of stock prices? Do market trends reflect the prospects and health of the nation's economy? Is the market "efficient"? If the answer to all these questions is "yes," the invisible hand is operating in fine fashion. The expectation of gain is then the same for all investors and conservation of information reigns supreme. The probabilities of future events are discounted by stock prices which are set with due regard to both the short-term and long-term health of both business and nation. Fairer prices are not to be expected, and any government intervention in this form of savings allocation can only lessen market efficiency. After all, what qualifications can our public servants possess other than noble intentions if no superior knowledge exists? On the other hand, if stock prices are perversely or randomly related to the future prospects of businesses, the stock market then becomes the equivalent of pure gambling and its effectiveness in promoting the general welfare is nil.

In the years since Bachelier's seminal research, a huge body of research has poured forth that largely confirms his random-walk model of the stock market. We may look on a stock purchase as opening a path to some return on investment, just as the first red-black bet in our roulette game. At every step along the way to some final capital when the stock is sold, a decision to sell or not sell must be made. And just as in roulette, these paths will exhibit chaotic ups and downs in capital. A plot of the number of stocks versus their investment returns from any large randomly selected sample fits the bell-shaped curve quite closely and indicates an average return of almost 10% per year compounded annually. That has been the expectation for blind or random investments in the stock market from 1926 to the present as determined from exhaustive samplings of stock price movements. It is a higher expectation than could have been obtained in any other form of investment over that period. Of course, the possibility of huge price fluctuations may yield anything from a complete loss of capital to thousand-fold gains. But, overall, there can be little doubt that the investing public is an excellent forecaster of future stock market trends and has been well rewarded by common stock investments. No system of investment based on *historical* (as opposed to *privileged*) information has been shown to beat the public record in this efficient market. The multitude of books that purport to do so fail in every case to include adequate statistical tests. "They're much worse than the books on horse racing," author and handicapper Tom Ainslie once told me after perusing what was available on the stock market. Winners and losers there will always be, and we tend to adulate the former and neglect the latter. But the past is no harbinger of future performance and today's winners can just as easily turn into tomorrow's losers.

The New York Times reported confirming evidence of public superiority on 16 August 1967: "A member of the Senate Banking Committee sought to prove today that it is possible to pick a portfolio of stocks that would do better than most mutual funds simply by throwing darts at the New York Stock Exchange list. Senator Thomas J. McIntyre, Democrat of New Hampshire, reported to the committee that he had done just that, and gotten better investment results than the average of even the most growth-oriented mutual funds. A hypothetical $10,000 investment made 10 years ago in the Senator's dart-selected stocks would be worth $25,300 now." The results, which did not include reinvestment of dividends, were a bit better than those achieved over the period by thirty-five growth category mutual funds. Senator McIntyre tried his experiment, he told the committee, after fund managers had disputed testimony given earlier by two noted economists, Paul A. Samuelson of the Massachusetts Institute of Technology and Henry C. Wallich of Yale University, that a random selection of stocks would yield investment results as good or better than those achieved by the funds. The great popularity of index funds that merely try to match the averages attests strongly to the public's superiority in evaluating stocks.

Close analyses of stock price changes over many years, however, have revealed consistent deviations from randomness in that too many better-than-average returns distort the right wing of the bell-shaped curve. In particular, there is a disproportionate number of outlandishly profitable investments, called "outliers," that fall far outside the curve. Some people, it would seem, are more equal than others when it comes to investing. That circumstance, we should now understand, indicates the presence of an inefficiency in the market and the possible emergence of a chaon. In 1969, I published *Beating the Street* (New York: David McKay, 1969), the importance of which was not recognized for many years. In it, I pointed out that the asymmetry of the bell-shaped curve could be traced to privileged information in the form of suddenly changed expectations in corporate earnings estimates. In the absence of privileged information, the market is a random walk and must be regarded as efficient – all investors have the same expectation no matter which stock they buy. However, privileged information generates surprises or "shocks" – unforeseeable, unreasonable, low probability events that constitute the "slings and arrows of outrageous fortune" – and these alter expectations "irrationally," as economists would say. When a corporation reports *surprisingly* favorable news, expectations of its future earnings will in all likelihood jump. During the short time it takes for the market to adjust fully to such surprises, such news is privileged. The relatively few investors who buy quickly are able to gain the advantage and realize better-than-average investment returns. These are the returns that distort the bell-shaped curve. My book publicized this window of opportunity and, amazingly, it remained open for twenty long years during which time many thousands of my readers invested with considerable pleasure and profit.

In my book, I focused on unexpectedly good earnings as reported in the financial press because of easy availability and suitability for statistical analysis. Surprises such as these, we shall come to understand, signal wealth creation. Let me illustrate with an example from *Beating the Street*. On 15 July 1964, after the close of the market, the Westinghouse Electric Corporation (no longer an independent entity) reported earnings for the second quarter sharply higher than those for the first quarter. The announcement caught Wall Street unawares. Everybody had been expecting a continuing decline in earnings from a company that had not kept up with the competition, and no immediate turnaround was envisioned. Even The *New York Times* financial writer who reported the news remarked about the surprisingly higher earnings.

The next morning, I and many other knowledgeable investors lined up to buy Westinghouse shares causing the opening to be delayed until buy and sell orders could be matched. It finally opened for trading on a huge (for those days) block of 35,000 shares, up a dollar from the previous day's close of 31 ¼, and continued to rise for the next year, more than doubling in price. What had happened? The surprising earnings upswing jolted the market out of equilibrium and caused investors to revise sharply upward their future earnings estimates for Westinghouse. Something good was obviously happening at the company and when expectations go up, so do stock prices as a rule. Surprise and confusion were again the key to this chaon. Those people who bought while the late-breaking information was still privileged reaped substantial benefits. Their money paths all pointed to Westinghouse. Much credit must go to Westinghouse's officers for keeping close-mouthed about the earnings report before its public release. And much credit must also go to them for restoring Westinghouse's premier status and adding to America's wealth a first-rate line of electrical products.

Clearly, the market of the 1960s did not react with dispatch to changes in earnings forecasts. But, as I have indicated, nothing ever stays the same when people get involved. My system of stock selection based on surprising earnings reports was adopted (without acknowledgment, I might add) by most investment services, professional fund managers and serious investors. Even the financial news media finally caught on. Although the *Wall Street Journal* and The *New York Times* deigned not to review *Beating the Street* in 1969, the *Library Journal* praised the book highly and it appeared in most libraries across the country. "Better-than-expected" and "worse-than-expected" earnings now feature today's financial pages. One cannot read or hear about an earnings announcement without reference to a forecast by a consensus of analysts. Never is it explicitly stated, however, that the whole idea is based on an efficient stock market, that current stock prices furnish the best possible estimate of future probabilities. Without changed expectations, stocks would simply execute random walks about the market averages. Not until the late 1980s and 1990s (and for reasons I shall discuss in the next chapter) did the investment community embrace the relationship between revisions of earnings estimates and stock price movements, and when it finally did, the chaon died. So quick is the market's reaction today to earnings both in advance and after announcements that it is all but impossible to take advantage of apparent surprises. As I mentioned above, a free market acts like a sponge in soaking up new information.

The correlation between better-than-expected corporate earnings and rising stock prices is noteworthy. An upside earnings surprise suggests the emergence of a chaon in the form of an improved company. Whether the chaon results from innovative new products and services, unexpected discoveries of resources, or enhanced efficiencies of production and distribution, it signals greater profit expectations and higher stock prices. The company's goods and services are augmenting the nation's standard of living in a manner approved by the consuming public. That is the essence of wealth creation. And if our country's high standard of living is any indication, stockholders, workers and the nation benefit in the best possible way.

Thousands of such upside earnings alerts mark a strongly growing and prosperous economy. The greater the number of these (why not call them miracles?), the greater will be a nation's prosperity, the higher the stock averages and the higher the standard of living. The greatest prosperity occurs when conditions are most favorable for chaon creation. And that means a society of maximum individual freedom and minimal government, a society that affords ample opportunity and reward for those rare and unforeseen individuals who are able to perceive and correct market inefficiencies. That is how all of America's great companies began. People must be free to find and travel those unpredictable paths that lead "to that which is the better." The above-average rewards that accrue to the owners (stockholders) of growth companies are exceeded only by those that accrue to the nation as a whole in the form of a rich variety of innovative and affordable goods and services.

Corporations and their stocks connect intimately with all the financial and consumer markets that make up a nation's economy. A rising stock market portends prosperity because increased demand for their products leads most companies to higher profits and higher wages. A falling stock market portends depression; the demand for goods and services declines, profits wither and workers lose their jobs. There have been and will be times in this chaotic situation when stocks go up and down without forecasting the state of the economy and times when it does. Other factors such as taxes, interest rates and international news events can cause significant fluctuations. But, on the whole, is there any better judge of future trends? Since no one of us knows more than all of us, the stock market is surely the best indicator of things to come. A happy stock market signifies a happy country.

Stagnant nations, on the other hand, are beset with inefficient companies having inadequate returns on investment. To stay in business, these must be government subsidized and that means high taxes and political decisions as to which companies to support. The historical record of such socialist practices is dismal.

Finally, let us imagine what a random-walk society, one in which equal opportunity for all exists, might be like? First of all, wealth will tend to be distributed according to the bell-shaped curve distorted slightly to the right. There will be a few rich, a few poor, but most people will find themselves in the middle class near the central maximum. No more favorable distribution consistent with the highest possible standard of living for all has ever manifested itself. People are free to find "that which is the better" and at every step into the future decide and pursue their own best interests. By so doing, they are "led by an invisible hand" to promote the "public interest," whatever that may be, in the best possible way. Random decisions occur by the trillions and move money unpredictably from one pocket to another. Free consumer and financial markets dominate the economy and wring order out of chaos. "I have never known much good done by those who affected to trade for the public good. It is an affectation, indeed, not very common among merchants, and very few words need be employed in dissuading them from it," wrote Adam Smith. The economy itself can be likened to the surface of the tropical ocean, calm and smooth except for the unforeseeable and unavoidable appearance of infrequent disturbances which, if left to themselves, disappear rapidly. There are no politically invasive income taxes to redistribute earnings; only highly visible consumption taxes are available to support a limited government. There is no central bank to disturb free-market equilibrium and few if any governmental regulatory agencies to mandate our responses to unpredictable futures. After all, other than noble intentions, what qualifies our public servants to interfere? Chaons emerge frequently and skew the bell-shaped income curve to the right, causing society's average wealth to rise steadily. There is no catalogue of horrors emanating from "what the law permits" to trash our freedoms and destroy efficiency. As a consequence, fewer lawyers and accountants and bureaucrats exist "to harass our People and eat out their Substance." With minimal government and few laws, a society of honor prevails; a handshake is the equivalent of a contract. Does it sound like paradise? Yet that is what America achieved during the first one hundred fifty years of her existence as she created the greatest good for all out of the narrow self-interests of each and every individual. "The inherent vice of capitalism is the unequal sharing of the blessings," wrote Winston Churchill. "The inherent blessing of socialism is the equal sharing of the miseries."

CHAPTER X

THE EMPEROR'S NEW MONEY

There is no art which one government sooner learns from another than how to drain money from the pockets of the people.

Adam Smith "The Wealth of Nations"

DOUBLES THE MONEY WITHIN THREE MONTHS: 50 PER CENT INTEREST PAID IN 45 DAYS BY PONZI – HAS THOUSANDS OF INVESTORS

Headline of *Boston Post* column, 24 July 1920

No man's life, liberty, or property is safe while the legislature is in session.

Mark Twain

William and Mary had a problem, one common to all spendthrift politicians yesterday and today: How do you wangle money from the people without letting them know about it? A half century of strife and civil war had left England with a depleted Treasury, and the new royals could not find the funds to carry on William's longstanding campaign against another aggressive and spendthrift politician, "Sun King" Louis XIV of France. The Glorious Revolution of 1688 had exiled Catholic-leaning King James II, the son of William I, to France and established as joint rulers William, stadholder of the United Provinces of the Netherlands, and Mary, James' Protestant daughter. However, on their ascension to the throne in 1689, King William III and Queen Mary II had committed themselves not only to the English Bill of Rights but to Parliamentary control of both the finances and the army. And Members of Parliament, fearing another in an apparently endless succession of tax revolts, were not about to accommodate the Crown in its demands for money. The fate of William I reminded them all too well of the consequences of some "last-straw" tax increase. Borrowing, then, remained as the only path to getting the people's money. In the past, such dealings had been carried out through London's goldsmiths who would buy government IOU's and redistribute them to private buyers. But a suspension of debt repayments by William II in 1672 had generated a wave of bankruptcies among them and now, to the Crown's horror, they balked at granting his successors any further monies.

Unable to tax and unable to borrow, the political elite cast about for some innovative new scheme to help them finance their noble intentions. It was supplied by William Paterson (1658-1719). The son of a farmer in Catholic Scotland, he had escaped arrest for his Presbyterian beliefs by fleeing to a relative's home in Bristol, England. A job with a London trading firm led him to the West Indies where he acquired a vast knowledge of trading routes and markets, much of it from pirates, it was rumored. In any event, by 1690 he had become a well-established London merchant with a reputation for financial wizardry. His cunning solution to the government's fiscal dilemma was inspired by the success of the Amsterdam Wisselbank eighty years earlier and won out over many other proposals. It would later be taken up by Alexander Hamilton as his model for the Bank of the United States, by Karl Marx in the *Communist Manifesto*, and by all modern governments.

Boiled down to essentials, Paterson perpetrated on people everywhere the beginnings of central banking and a permanent national debt. He proposed the creation of a "Bank of England," privately capitalized at £1.2 million in gold and silver or the equivalent, and a "Fund for Perpetual Interest." The Bank was to be structured as a private "joint-stock" company, one with transferable shares. Given the great suspicions of its lawmakers harbored by the English populace at the time, a government-owned bank would probably not have been tolerated. In Paterson's plan, the "Bank" functioned as the government's depository and administered its financial dealings. The "Fund," for its part, raised money through the issuance of government bonds and notes, these to be underwritten (bought) in competitive bidding by the Bank, the East India Company and some large insurance firms. This newly printed government paper could then be held for interest income or parceled out to small investors at a premium (profit). We have at this time the genesis of giant investment banking houses with a vested interest in huge national debts. "Merchants of debt" like London's Baring Bank, the Rothschild Banks of Europe and many of today's Wall Street firms would come to profit mightily from unlimited government spending. And, as we shall see, play significant roles in world affairs.

In addition to serving as the government's banker, the Bank of England was empowered to accept deposits from private sources and issue up to £1.2 million of its own notes (convertible on demand into specie). This newly created money could then be made available for interest-bearing loans to businesses and private individuals. In short, it assumed under its government sponsorship and its relatively huge specie reserves many aspects of a modern monopolistic central bank. Its central banking powers, however, were still embryonic, limited as they were by the restriction on note issue. Not until a hundred years later when William Pitt the Younger drove it to financing the French Revolutionary and Napoleonic Wars would it become a full-scale central bank in the modern sense, able to buy unlimited amounts of government debt through unrestricted note issues.

On 21 June 1694, the corporate books of the Bank of England were opened for stock purchases at Mercers Chapell, London. The first entry for £10,000 (the maximum permitted) was recorded in the names of William and Mary. 1,267 others quickly bought in, including William Paterson and the most influential of politicians and businessmen. Backing for the Bank at the highest levels of business and government was thereby assured. We now see Paterson's scheme shining forth in all its brilliance. Not only did it provide politicians with the money they wanted without the necessity of tax increases or direct public borrowing, it redistributed wealth to the wealthy by providing enormous dividends to the Bank's well-heeled stockholders. Central banks of the future, including our own Federal Reserve System, would follow the same plan. What about the nine million English people who were excluded from sharing in the Bank's profits? Why, their taxes would guarantee both the Bank's profits and the dividends paid out to the favored few.

In return for granting a Royal Charter, the government borrowed the Bank's entire capital of £1.2 million sterling in the form of expendable Bank notes collateralized by the deposit of specie and IOU's (government bonds) in the Bank's vaults. At 8% interest (£96,000 per year) plus a management fee of £4,000 per year, the proceeds to the Bank from this source alone totaled £100,000 per year, this amount to be paid ultimately through tax collections. In addition to these revenues, the Bank derived substantially more interest income from the £1.2 million of its own notes it printed up and loaned out to credit worthy private borrowers. That brought the total amount of Bank of England notes floating around the economy to £2.4 million, less than half of which was backed by specie. But because withdrawals and deposits normally balanced out on any given day and because the Bank acted as the depository for government revenues (on which it paid no interest), it could easily handle all demands for specie redemption of its notes. And because few so demanded, the notes circulated as a common currency at full face value. It was at this time that the concept of imaginary or fiat money emerged, money that could assume many forms, possess no intrinsic value and still be accepted as legal tender. Said Paterson: "The bank hath benefit of interest on all moneys which it creates out of nothing."

If politicians spent their newly created money efficiently, the economy would create equivalent amounts of goods and services and prices would remain stable. Unfortunately, that rarely happens because public spending is all too often wasteful and excessive. When such is the case, too much money then chases too few goods and services, and we then have the inflation plague that central banking has inflicted on all nations. Of course, politicians place the blame on "greedy" businessmen, never on their own profligacy. Again and again, they and their central banker cohorts try to resolve the inflation problem by penalizing private spending with price controls and high interest rates while government spending continues untouched and unabated. In the eyes of our public servants, cutting their own spending power is unthinkable. How much better to saddle the nation with reduced economic growth, unemployment, depression, and even war!

So successful was Paterson's scheme that Parliament found the urge to spend other people's money more irresistible than ever, and with nary a hint of a homeland tax revolt. With that threat removed and the Bank's capital ever increasing from loan interest and loan repayments, "The Fund" was permitted to issue more and more bonds with the government receiving in return more and more expendable bank notes. As a result, spending in excess of tax revenues zoomed up the British national debt from £12 million during the reign of William and Mary to £850 million by 1815, and the Bank's profits went up accordingly. The money created was squandered for the most part on wars, on colonies, on political pork-barreling, and on a South Seas Bubble scam that has relevance for present-day America. Remarkably, the English free market could still produce a steadily increasing amount of goods and services that raised the British standard of living considerably. But what this introduction of central banking cost in terms of lost production has never been calculated. The effects lay hidden in the inflationary prices paid by consumers for goods and services and the higher than necessary costs of capital needed to start up and modernize new and old businesses. What is easily comprehended, however, is how much higher their standard of living might have been had the English people been able to emulate their American colonists and spend more of their own money! There would have been no need for pillaging the colonies, and England would surely have grown into the world colossus that Adam Smith foresaw for America.

The unintended consequences of Paterson's scheme began to unravel in short order. By 1710, the national debt and the interest payments thereon were beginning to assume mountainous proportions relative to tax receipts, and politicians were once again casting about for some means of dealing with it. A partial solution was proposed by Tory Party leader Robert Harley and Londoners John Caswall and John Blunt. It was a twist on Paterson's Bank of England scheme. Hoping to build a financial institution on a par with that Bank, they offered to assume £9.47 million of the government's outstanding short-term war debts (the part that Parliament had not yet funded with specific taxes), the money to be raised by an initial public stock offering in what was to be known as the South Seas Company. In return, the government would guarantee an annual interest rate of 6% on the debt sold to the Company, a good deal less and much more manageable than the 8% or more paid on current short-term public debt. In addition, the Company would receive for its services monopolistic trading privileges with the islands of the South Seas and the rich Spanish colonies in the New World.

Parliament, anxious to lessen the debt burden and inspired by numerous bribes, chartered the Company in 1711. The exchange offer proved very successful, 97% of the debt being converted into easily tradable Company stock at par value (£100). The ongoing war with Spain at the time seemed to matter not at all given the government's implied backing for the Company and the mammoth riches to be derived from the New World once the war terminated. Then, too, something else was in the air − the seizure of the Spanish colonies in the Americas.

The Treaty of Utrecht (1713) ended hostilities with Spain for a time. It also ended Louis XIV's ambition to annex Spain and her vast colonial empire by placing the Dauphin Philip of Anjou on the Spanish throne. Under the terms laid down by the Treaty, England obtained Gibraltar but was given very limited trading privileges with the Spanish colonies. The South Seas Company was allowed but one ship a year to transport 4800 slaves to the colonies and one ship for general trade, hardly enough to make much money. The Company's first ship sailed in

1717, but most of the profit went to venal Spanish officials. In 1718, the latter confiscated all the Company's ships and assets in Spanish ports. Throughout this period, naval skirmishes were ongoing as foreign pirates and privateers sought to prey on the New World's riches being conveyed back to Spain. Of significance was the capture in 1716 of the heavily armed English privateer *Stanhope* by a small Spanish frigate commanded by Don Blas de Lezo (1688-1744), an incident that caused great embarrassment in England. It revealed the soon-to-be "mistress of the seas" as not yet ready to take on the Spanish navy. A one-armed, one-eyed, one-legged man of indomitable spirit, Don Blas became a figure to be reckoned with. For the next fifteen years he waged a vigorous campaign against piracy on the high seas and was personally responsible for the seizure of six English and six Dutch ships carrying millions in cargo. His historical importance would come in 1741 when he almost single-handedly ended all English hopes for the conquest of the Spanish colonies.

In January of 1720, South Seas Company stock was selling for £130, a reasonable value considering the steady stream of earnings derived from the 6% interest received on the government debt it held. But confidence in the Company's prospects rose steadily as its ties to the government grew ever closer. The first governor of the Company had been Robert Harley, the Chancellor of the Exchequer. He was succeeded in 1714 by the Prince of Wales and in 1718 by King George I himself. In 1719, in response to a government debt that had grown ever more outlandish, the Company's directors conjured up an ambitious new plan of action. They offered to assume more than half (£31 million) of the entire national debt in a voluntary exchange for newly issued Company stock at prices to be determined. For the privilege of so doing, the Company would make a lump-sum payment of £3 million to the government. When the Bank of England submitted a counterbid, the payment was upped to £7.5 million, and it was accompanied by £1.3 million in bribes to Members of Parliament and the King's mistress, the Duchess of Kendal. For a perspective on these monetary amounts, a middle class family at the time could live very comfortably on £200 a year.

In March of 1720 and after considerable debate, Parliament awarded the debt assumption to the South Seas Company at an annual interest rate of 5%, again saving the government much in debt servicing. The conversion of debt into stock proved an immediate success; over 80% was converted into Company stock at £130 per share and up. By the end of March, the price of the stock had jumped to £380. If the Company had stopped with the debt assumption, there may not have been a problem. But the temptation to issue unauthorized shares and feed them into the marketplace proved irresistible. The initial £1.3 million in bribes had been paid in just such unauthorized stock, not in cash.

To keep the share price rising in the face of repeated issues of stock, the directors brought into active play what today we would call a "Ponzi" or chain-letter scheme, the central figure of which was probably the Company's treasurer, Robert Knight. Current purchasers of shares were promised huge dividends, 50% of their stock value and up, these to be paid by a new generation of buyers rushing in to buy freshly issued stock. The new investors received in turn large dividends that were once again paid by the shares bought by a still newer generation of investors. And on and on it went. To facilitate share purchases, an installment plan enabled investors to buy on margin. A share purchased at £300, for example, could be paid in five installments of £60 each. Complementing this initiative, the Company publicized its cash position as so strong that it could lend money to investors collateralized on their stock holdings, money that could then be used to buy more stock. Throughout, a steady stream of accompanying press releases publicized the limitless growth potential of the Company and the incredible prosperity lying just ahead. Even Jonathan Swift of *Gulliver's Travels* fame and Daniel Defoe of *Robinson Crusoe* fame contributed articles to the newspapers extolling the Company's prospects. By early June, the stock price was over £500.

The government, as if it hadn't done enough, then added another of its contributions to the madness. The success of the Company had naturally attracted imitators in the form of hundreds of other "joint-stock" companies that arose to feed on the speculative frenzy. Sensing a liquidity squeeze, the Company's directors inveigled Parliament to pass on 11 June the so-called "Bubble Act" which banned the formation of all joint-stock companies not having a royal charter. This piece of legislation probably retarded economic development for years to come. But the price of South Seas stock jumped, peaking finally at over £1000.

Throughout the summer the price bubble deflated, gradually at first and then at an accelerating pace. Losses mounted as investors experienced ever increasing difficulty in meeting installment payments on already purchased stock and, having exhausted their cash holdings, in buying new shares. Even Isaac Newton was caught up: "I can calculate the motions of the heavenly bodies," he lamented after losing £20,000, "but not the madness of people." When the stock price dropped to £400 in early September, the politicians summoned the Bank of England to the rescue. The Bank was pressured to sell South Seas bonds, the money raised to be used for retiring the Company's shares. The stock price rallied to £500 on the news and then collapsed to £135 when a run on the Bank forced it to renege on its agreement and suspend specie redemption of its notes. Thousands of fortunes evaporated, both great and small, and bankruptcy listings in the *London Gazette* recorded an all-time high. King George I hastened back to London from Hannover and recalled Parliament to investigate charges of fraud and corruption against the Company's directors. Robert Knight, who had absconded to the continent, was arrested and jailed in Antwerp. The King publicly called for his extradition, but the Duchess of Kendal secretly assured foreign officials that His Majesty would be most grateful if Knight and his secrets remained abroad. Knight was released and lived in exile for twenty years before receiving a royal pardon.

The South Seas Bubble ultimately ran its course of bankruptcies. The Company continued in operation for another twenty-five years, during which time it enslaved 34,000 Africans and transported them to the Spanish colonies. A mortality rate of about 15% on the Atlantic crossing made its operations relatively efficient compared to most other slave traders. Its main function, however, was managing its part of the government debt.

But English aspirations in the Caribbean had yet to be played out. A naval incident of 1731 provided sufficient justification for the assault on the Spanish colonies. The English brig *Rebecca*, under the command of one Captain Jenkins, was boarded by Spanish coastguardsmen near Havana. According to Jenkins, he was accused of smuggling and when he protested, his ear was sliced off. Testifying before the House of Commons seven years later, in 1738, he offered in evidence for the dastardly act his well-preserved ear pickled in brine. Nothing more was needed. Despite the opposition of de facto prime minister Robert Walpole, Parliament declared war on Spain in what became known as the War of Jenkins' Ear. Hostilities began with Admiral Edward Vernon's capture of the lightly defended city of Portobelo on the northern coast of Panama in 1739. The action was greeted with wild acclaim and jubilation by an English populace mesmerized by the wealth that would soon be theirs. Vernon was lionized; commemorative medals struck in his likeness exceeded those for any other person or event in the eighteenth century. Since first coming to the Caribbean in 1708 as a ship captain, he had risen steadily in rank, to commodore in 1720 and, as the projected campaign for the Spanish colonies escalated in importance, to Commander-in-Chief of all His Majesty's ships in the West Indies. In 1741, he led a force larger than the Spanish Armada – upwards of 150 ships and thirty thousand men – in an attack on Cartagena, jewel of the Spanish Crown and the principal seaport and staging area for the trans-shipment to Spain of gold, silver and precious stones. Another squadron under Admiral George Anson was dispatched to the Pacific Ocean where it would target the Spanish colonies in Chile and Peru and then, if all went well, join up with Vernon for the capture of Panama City. Serving under Admiral Vernon was Lawrence Washington, half brother of George, who named the Washington estate at Mount Vernon in honor of his commanding officer.

So confident of victory was the British military that some commemorative medals of the time depicted the Spanish commander Don Blas (a two-legged version) kneeling before Vernon in token of surrender. It did seem like a foregone conclusion even though Don Blas was not taken lightly. What few naval vessels Spain had in the Caribbean at the time could not hope to cope with the Royal Navy, and Don Blas had at most 6,000 men under his command. But the Spanish had spent two hundred years turning Cartagena into an impregnable fortress, and the armada could not punch through to the harbor. Forced into a land operation, Vernon disembarked his forces east of the city where they faced ferocious opposition. Pinned down and unable to advance, the troops succumbed to the agonizing abdominal pains of yellow fever and dysentery, to convulsive heatstroke, and (the lucky ones) to Spanish bayonets, bullets and artillery. After weeks of stalemate, Vernon was forced to withdraw with the loss of ten thousand men and seventy ships. Almost expunged from English history, the Cartagena disaster was spun into a great victory when Vernon received a Westminster Abbey burial. The whereabouts of Don Blas' remains are unknown to this day.

The lesson should be clear. Raising money is not a problem for absolute monarchs or benign dictators. Such personages command the entire wealth of a nation for as long as they keep their heads. It just becomes more difficult with the advent of representative government. Ergo, the introduction of central banking, and then, in 1799 in England, the new-fangled income tax to "pluck the goose so as to get the greatest amount of feathers with the least amount of squealing." Did it matter that the Bank of England performed its duties so poorly that sinister Jewish conspiracies were often served up as scapegoats to deflect any ill-feeling toward the Crown? Did it matter that it posed a terrible drag on the economy? Or that it prevented an alternative chaonic structure based on free banking from forming? Or that it failed miserably in its efforts to maintain monetary stability and the value of the currency? How would that £200 average middle class income of 1720 compare with the £30,000 in the England of today? The difference for the most part represents money created over and above what could have been raised in taxes. It is, therefore, stealth money literally stolen from the people's pockets for financing the "overriding needs" of politicians. But the most frightening part of all is that so much of the money was squandered on war. No matter how you look at it, big government kills. *And over time the killing correlates closely with the increase in inflationary living costs.*

For England, the immediate consequence of all that easy money was a hundred years of incessant war that sent hundreds of thousands of young men to their deaths. In the 119-year period from the establishment of the Bank of England to Waterloo in 1814, England spent fifty-six years at war and the rest of the time preparing for war. Indeed, the "Fund for Perpetual Interest" became a "Fund for Perpetual War." Jenkins's Ear was followed by the War of the Austrian Succession (1740-48) and the Seven Years' War (1756-63) as the French colonies became the objects of desire, the American Revolutionary War (1776-1783) to preserve the empire, the French Revolutionary Wars (1792-1802) to protect the crowned heads of Europe, and the Napoleonic Wars (1803-1814) in which self-preservation became the one legitimate issue. It was all made possible by capital that, if not squandered on killing, could have been used for private economic development. How unfortunate for Britain that the Bank of England began operations *before the* advent of the Industrial Revolution!

Guided only by Adam Smith's "invisible hand," America surpassed England economically one hundred years after independence. Except for the Civil War period, there was insignificant government spending (a paltry 1% of gross domestic product) to ride herd on the economy. Not until 1913, by which time our production dwarfed that of any other nation, did we get a costly central bank (the Federal Reserve System) whose only real purpose is to provide limitless amounts of money for politicians to squander. Nor did we get a permanent income tax until that same year. Nor a government-sponsored, generation-stealing, actuarially unsound Ponzi scheme until social security was foisted on us in the 1930s. Nor did we, except for our Civil War, get involved in any large-scale war or generation-mauling Depression until after 1913. Again, "some token of providential agency" appeared to be on watch during the strong growth years of our republic.

CHAPTER XI

WHO ORDERED ECONOMISTS?

They are our economists, and you cannot imagine how much harm they can do.

Mikhail Gorbachev responding to a question about the identity of a motley group of stragglers following a May Day military parade in Red Square

The Federal Reserve possesses the legal power to create as many dollars as it pleases, any time it pleases, and for any reason it pleases.

Llewellyn H. Rockwell, Jr.

I should like to say to Milton and Anna: Regarding the Great Depression. You're right, we did it. We're very sorry. But thanks to you, we won't do it again.

Fred Bernanke, Chairman of the Federal Reserve Board in a speech honoring Milton Friedman on his 80th birthday

Not even wrong!

Comment by Nobel Prize-winning physicist Wolfgang Pauli after attending a lecture on nuclear physics

The crop never came up to my expectations but then I never expected it would.

Maine potato farmer

It is well enough that the people of this nation do not understand our banking and monetary system for, if they did, I believe there would be a revolution before tomorrow morning.

Henry Ford

"Why is it so damned hard to predict the economic weather?" ask many of us appalled by the consistently dismal predictions of economic "science." Why, indeed? And the answer is the same as Edward Lorenz's for atmospheric weather: Chaos! It shows up in all realistic models of the economy. Which means that economists face the same chaotic conditions as weathermen. Their predictions, consequently, are highly questionable and, furthermore, any action they and their political cohorts may take to correct or regulate some perceived economic ill will in all probability make things worse. That is the story of most panics and depressions in our country's history, as we shall discover later. The goals as usual are noble, to smooth out "business cycles" and achieve a full employment, cycleless and non-inflationary growth prosperity. Of course, that is exactly what America achieved to an extraordinarily high degree in the 19th and early 20th centuries, an era marked by Adam Smith's efficient markets economy and relatively little government interference. But somewhere along the way we deluded ourselves into thinking that economists can do better. And to help them achieve their noble goals, we have entrusted them with enormous power over our money. It behooves us, therefore, to take a critical look at their methods before we learn too late "how much harm they can do." As has happened all too often in the past, the road to hell is paved with government money.

To forecast the future, economists emulate physicists in employing mathematical models to simulate the economy. Their basic evolutionary tool is a second order *linear* difference equation, solutions of which, they hope, will enumerate the possible trajectories of economic performance into the future and help them choose the "correct" path to a stable prosperity. The procedure is much like that on our moon voyage where the spacecraft's future was to be determined through an application of Newton's Laws of Motion. Only now, economic parameters are of concern. What, for example, will the nation's total output of goods and services – what is known as the *gross domestic product* – amount to six months, a year or five years from now? How high the inflation rate, the unemployment rate, the money supply? But, unfortunately for them, economists have not been blessed with the linear reality studied by physicists. Their mathematical equations apply only to a fictional world in which history evolves on a smooth, unkinky path into the future, one devoid of "shocks." Their models, therefore, are naïve and irrelevant, of the "Not even wrong!" variety, and hardly capable even of predicting tomorrow's date. The "business cycles" of boom and bust that they attempt to explain and foresee are not cycles at all since no two are ever the same. In common with the shifting patterns of the Bénard cell, those aperiodic wiggles displaying economic behavior have all the earmarks of chaos, but on a longer time scale. Herein lies the great dilemma faced by economists. Their linear equations lack realistic content; they can neither reproduce world chaos nor predict the emergence of chaons. As a result, they cannot "linearize" their way to the future. Nevertheless, to hold on to predictability, economists have long ignored abrupt changes in expectations. Bringing expectations into the picture implies an absence of determinism, and economists along with most philosophers of the past wanted no part of that. Herein lies the reason behind their belated recognition of the relation between non-linear earnings surprises and future stock prices pointed out in my book *Beating the Street*. Yet, such shocks as the Westinghouse report and the Intel phenomenon "happen all the time" in free markets, and these are the events that drive our economy from peak to ever higher peak. By modeling reality with non-linear equations, as many now try to do, they may conjure up better theories but then face that bugaboo of chaos, a hypersensitive dependence on initial conditions. Economics is cursed with imprecise measurements ("soft numbers," as they are called) so that specifying those initial conditions and forecasting unique futures are hopeless tasks. Not even Laplace's superman can be of any help to them. Nancy Reagan, the wife of our 40th President, believed in astrologers; we believe in economists. The main difference is that economists are far more expensive.

In pursuit of their "impossible dream," economists along with their banker allies have guided government policy away from free markets and toward ever more regulation of the private economy. Most of them, following John Maynard Keynes, see public spending as preferable to private spending, especially during economic downturns. Politicians never object because government intervention in the economy gives them more of our money to spend, and money is power. Bankers never object because it relieves them of many of the competitive conditions associated with free markets. Economists never object because it opens up an enormity of job opportunities for them. And, best of all, the public does not object because, as Henry Ford understood, it has little idea of how much of its money politicians get to spend for them.

Michael Gorbachev's observation at the head of this chapter demands to be amplified and bellowed forth. Let us do so by undertaking a probe of that most powerful of our regulatory bodies, the Federal Reserve Board. Because this institution seems to have acquired an above-criticism sacrosanct status in today's America, let me start by pointing out two opposed characters who understood very well how central banking squeezes money out of the people's pockets and into those of politicians: Karl Marx, who established it as a key plank in the *Communist Manifesto*, and President John F. Kennedy who undertook the first steps to abolish it.

We can all agree at the start that our national government needs money to carry out its duties. From where should it come? Taxes, you say? True enough. But politicians decided long ago that taxes hardly sufficed to accommodate their irresponsible spending habits. And to raise them could at some point become dangerous. Beyond some "last straw," the public might object and roll out the guillotines, as happened during the French Revolution. Where can money safely be found when the tax receipts run out? Simple enough. Just borrow it. Have Treasury's Bureau of Engraving and Printing print up lots of IOU's in the form of interest-bearing bonds and notes and market them to the public through large investment banking firms, which of course profit handsomely from such underwritings. But even that proved insufficient to satisfy the insatiable demands of our spendthrift lawmakers because only a too limited amount of that kind of paper could be sold without disrupting the credit markets. And so it was that in 1913, bankers and economists conjured up the Federal Reserve System, a monetary printing press that furnished politicians with all the extra money they thought they needed without worrying about public approval. It followed the scheme devised by William Paterson in 1690 for the Bank of England and would be taken up by Alexander Hamilton in 1790 for his proposed 1st Bank of the United States. Politicians, bankers and economists were ecstatic. With the creation of the Federal Reserve System, they thought that the struggle to perfect a sensible, conservative monetary system was over. The dollar would be stable and there would be a cessation of economic panics and bank failures. Everywhere in the world, money of whatever kind would now be exchangeable, without pretense or delay, into gold. Silver was for dinner ware, silver-plating and photography. America, the greatest country in the world, had now come on board and accepted a permanent national debt. She now had an instrument for creating all the money her politicians needed for doing good. "Ah, humbug!" as Charles Dickens would say.

How does the Federal Reserve System work? It all begins with Congress drawing up a federal budget for the next fiscal year detailing expected tax revenues and expenditures. Appropriation bills are then passed authorizing spending for budgetary line items. These include among other things defense, social security payments, interest on government indebtedness, agricultural and business subsidies, research grants, bridges and roads to nowhere, salaries and pensions for hundreds of thousands of "public servants" who think they know how to make free markets work more efficiently, etc., etc., etc. Now, if Congress appropriates more than can be gleaned from tax collections and debt issues, as almost always happens, how does Treasury foot the bill? No problem, now. Why, just send some lackey truckin' down the street to the Federal Reserve Building. There, he or she adds to the national debt by depositing with the Federal Reserve all the bonds and notes necessary to cover expenditures and in return receives freshly printed, spendable paper, what we call Federal Reserve notes. It's called "monetizing the debt." Of course, because millions or billions in spendable paper is much too great an inconvenience to handle, Treasury simply writes government checks on its FED deposits. Everybody is then happy. The politicians are happy because they get all the money they can squander without having to raise taxes; the credit markets are happy in not having too many bonds and notes to digest; the bankers are happy because the FED can provide them with succoring loans of last resort should poor business practices get them into trouble; the economists are happy because the FED is their top employer; and the public is happy in not having to face higher taxes. Better yet, few bother to ask why the government never seems to run out of money.

But look at what has happened. An abundance of new Federal Reserve notes created out of nothing now floats around the economy. That would be fine if, and again it is a very big if, government spending were efficient. That is, if the new money circulating added an equal dollar amount of goods and services to the gross domestic product. Dollar prices on average would then remain stable. If not, everything costs more because too many paper dollars begin chasing too few goods and services. The Fed then becomes an engine for the inflationary financing of political spending. And that is exactly the accommodation that politicians desire!

The Federal Reserve Act of 1913 says nothing about defrauding the public of its money without raising highly visible taxes. It simply charges the new agency with providing an "elastic currency." That means stabilizing prices by matching the value of the Federal Reserve notes it prints to gross domestic product. The problem here is that no economist knows how to accomplish this noble goal. Suppose we look at the dollar's value before and after 1913 in order to see just how successful our central bank has been in stabilizing prices. This is knowledge of a kind that economists and politicians like to keep confidential, and why it is that free markets are anathema to most of them.

From the year of the Constitution's adoption in 1789 until 1913, an era of free markets and mostly free banking, the purchasing power of the dollar actually *increased*. According to a consumer price index (CPI) maintained by the U. S. Department of Labor, a 1913 dollar could buy a larger basket of representative goods and services than a 1789 dollar. In other words, prices *fell* over that long period of time. We had a combination of enormous economic growth plus price deflation, a general lowering of prices. Inflation? There wasn't any, except during times of government war spending. This despite explosive gains in the standard of living that transformed America from a lowly colonial status into the greatest country in the world by far. This despite the devastations of a Civil War that far exceeded those of all subsequent wars combined. And this despite the emergence of extraordinarily efficient "evil monopolies," such as John D. Rockefeller's Standard Oil Company and Andrew Carnegie's United States Steel Corporation, businesses that supposedly could raise prices at will. Free markets and free banking, in other words, were extremely efficient in matching the money supply to a meteoric expansion in goods and services. The attitude of economists toward this happy growth period is pointedly summed up by Milton Friedman and Anna Schwartz in their epic A *Monetary History of the United States (1867-1960)*: "And their coincidence [deflation and growth] casts serious doubt on the validity of the now widely held view that secular price deflation and rapid economic growth are incompatible."

In stark contrast, what has developed since 1913 is an inflation hardly to be believed. If we accept the findings of the economists at the Labor Department, it takes *twenty* of today's dollars, as represented by Federal Reserve notes, to buy what one dollar could have bought in 1913. During the last ninety-five years, our dollar has depreciated by 95% in value! Or, putting it in another way, most of the money created since 1913 has been far in excess of what was needed to increase the production of the goods and services that enhance our quality of life. Is the dollar, we must ask, heading down the path followed by the coinage of the Roman Empire, toward "dollar zero," at which point it will buy nothing?

Let us try to pin down some specifics. In 1913, the gross domestic product (GDP) is estimated to have amounted to $50 billion as compared to, say, $50 million at most in 1789. These figures are very rough estimates since GDP was not even defined until the 1930s and, of course, not measured. If anywhere near the mark, however, the period from 1789 to 1913 produced a thousand-fold increase in GDP, a growth rate amounting to a spectacularly exuberant 16% per year compounded annually. That is even more than China's growth today. The American population over the same period increased 25 times, from 4 million to 100 million. Since the dollar's value actually increased, that indicates more than a 40-fold jump in the standard of living (as measured by the GDP per capita). And because our society was one of nearly equal opportunity, income distribution undoubtedly followed the bell-shaped curve and shifted sharply to the right, "raising all ships." Almost everybody became far richer in 1913 than anyone in 1789, not to mention the rest of the world.

Now what has happened since 1913? Today in 2006, GDP is about $12 *trillion* figured in today's dollars. In terms of the dollar's 1913 value, however, that amounts to a much lesser figure of approximately $600 billion, one-twentieth of today's nominal GDP. In other words, our economy produced $550 billion more in goods and services than in 1913 (about twelve times more) as measured by a constant dollar. Because our population has increased three-fold since then – from 100 million to 300 million people – our standard of living in constant dollar terms has improved roughly four-fold. The bell-shaped curve of income distribution again shifted sharply to the right although not nearly as much percentage wise as previously. But these figures also indicate that more than *11 trillion* of today's dollars are being spent inefficiently. By whom? Why, by "tax-consumers," people who are receiving dollars in one way or another and who are not contributing to GDP. These are the non-producers. Their parasitic spending has driven up prices to today's inflated levels. The conclusion is inescapable: Central banking enables politicians to subsidize non-producers with money "created out of nothing" and embeds inflation into the economy. *It is simply taxation without representation.* Just imagine how much higher our standard of living might become if that extra $11 trillion were spent efficiently on new products and services. Also inescapable is how high the inflation rate may become if the number of non-producers continues on its strong upward trend.

Just as I was writing this chapter, my wife inadvertently expressed in everyday terms how great our dollar's devaluation has been. Admonishing me for my delay in paying a dental bill, she remarked, "Why don't you just put a 3¢ stamp on this letter and mail it with a check." She had obviously reverted to her teenage years in the 1940s when first class postage required only a 3¢ stamp rather than the 41¢ of today. But it illustrates the point – for the same service, we are now paying almost fourteen times more. In contrast, the postage rate on pre-paid letters dropped from 5¢ to 3¢ in 1851 and to 2¢ in 1885. One source of that $11 trillion of inefficient spending was pointed out in a *Wall Street Journal* editorial, 15 August 2006: In 2005 our government's civilian workers received an average salary of $106,579, twice as much as the $53,289 paid to private sector workers. In 1950 the salaries were at parity. It works out to an excess of at least $100 billion a year if we place the number of federal employees at two million and assume they are worth their pay. In addition, these workers have much more advantageous pension and medical benefits than the average American. And let us not forget the excessively high numbers of overpaid state and local government employees. As youngsters in Rome were advised during the final years of the Empire: "Work for government, young man. The pay is higher and the work easier." What else can be expected from unbusiness-minded politicians trying to manage a tenured bureaucracy with other people's money?

A second source of inefficiency is associated with America's trial lawyers. According to the authors of *Jackpot Justice: The True Cost of America's Tort System* by Lawrence J. McQuillan and

Hovannes Abramyan, the total cost of our tort system amounts to an astounding $865 *billion* per year. This constitutes an annual "tort tax" on a family of four of $9,827, and it does nothing but transfer wealth from productive businesses and people to those less productive. Included are what the authors call the "static" costs of litigation – damage awards, plaintiff attorneys' fees, defense costs, administrative costs, and the "deadweight" costs from product liability cases, medical malpractice litigation and class action lawsuits. Added to these are the "dynamic" costs – the impact of lowered research and development spending because of money diverted to legal matters, the extra expense of defensive medicine and the related rise in health-care spending as doctors seek to protect themselves from law suits, and the consequent loss of output from sickly workers arising from reduced access to health care. Not only is our tort system out of control, its cancerous growth can only metastasize as more and more youngsters pour out of law schools.

A third source of inefficiency arises from what are called "earmarks." These are hidden expenditures, add-ons to appropriation bills unrelated to the main subject. We can see how abusive earmarks have become by examining the federal government's spending bill for fiscal 2007. It contains 15,818 earmarks totaling $40.8 billion, up from 4,146 and $20.4 billion in 1994. Just imagine! *That amounts on average to more than $76 million and 29 earmarks per Congressman.* No wonder politicians campaign so unrelentingly for Congressional seats. Rest assured that most if not all of this money would be better spent privately by you and me.

Nowhere to be found is there a cost-benefit analysis of the Federal Reserve or the thirteen Departments of government and the hundreds of agencies associated with them. Nor is there an accounting of all the inefficiencies heaped on the economy by subsidies, grants and regulatory mandates without end. Our politicians and non-elected government bureaucrats promulgate thousands of pages of binding legislation, a deluge of vaguely worded rules and regulations that straitjacket a free economy and prevent the emergence of chaos. The *United States Code*, which contains an accumulating mass of all federal statutes, takes up over 56,000 single-spaced pages in 47 volumes, as of 1994. A large part of it is devoted to the Internal Revenue Code. An annotated version, which attempts to bring order out of chaos, has 230 hardcover volumes and 36 paperback supplements. Regulatory law conjured up by non-elected administrators takes up more than 207 volumes and 135,000 pages in the *Code of Federal Regulation*. The *Federal Register*, which updates federal regulations daily, overflowed with 68,000 pages in 250 volumes. Federal law is further augmented by more than 2,756 volumes of judicial precedent. And then there are the states with their own laws, regulations and judicial precedents. Little of value would be lost and much gained if most of these volumes simply self-destructed leaving, as James Madison expressed it, "the mass of powers in other hands." Such a mass of legalities invites arbitrariness, abuse, corruption and circumvention, especially by lawyers, accountants, bureaucrats and the politicians themselves, and the disruptive effects sooner or later bring on chaos at the expense of our honor and freedoms. Breaking the law has become tantamount to survival for thousands of small businesses. For every law passed and regulation instituted, a little more freedom is lost. Honorable business people must resort to all kinds of subterfuges – loopholes in and end runs around the tax code – to remain in business.

There are so many laws, so many rules and regulations, so many complexities and so many interpretations that even lawyers do not know what the law is. And when law becomes ambiguous and unpredictable, honor flies out the window. We get violation after violation of our basic "unalienable rights" – crime without intent, retroactive liability, self-incrimination, asset forfeiture without due process, violation of the attorney-client privacy, delegation of legislative powers to unelected officials, impediments to a vigorous and vocal defense of our freedoms, and the manufacturing of evidence by ambitious prosecutors.

Let me insert here a word about retirees. Those that put aside some of their working income for their old age are not to be included among the non-producers. Their savings, at least those invested in income-producing instruments of the private economy such as stocks or bonds or bank accounts, get handled in a myriad of unpredictably productive ways. That is in sharp contrast to social security savings which accumulate in a "General Fund" and are then lumped together with all other tax receipts to be spent most inefficiently by politicians. There is no "locked box" containing these savings, only promises to redeem retirees out of future tax revenues. This massive Ponzi scheme is no different from that of the South Seas Company: Collect social security taxes from the present generation of workers (the new buyers of stock) with promises of great future benefits, then hand over the money to the present generation of retirees (the older buyers of stock), etc., etc., etc. The system will work only so long as *real* GDP (the one measured in constant dollars) expands at a rate that at least keeps up with a growing population.

To "paper" over the abject failure of our central bank to stabilize the currency, economists promulgate the fiction that economic growth must be contained to check inflation. And that is the job of the Fed's Chairman, an all-powerful Wizard of Oz-type fakir appointed by the President, and his rubber-stamp Federal Open Market Committee. At regular intervals, the Chairman retires to a back room to consult his crystal balls or read tea leaves or perform voodoo rites or see what the latest econometric model of reality has to say. Rumor has it that he even undertakes secret missions to Greece to consult with the Delphic Oracle. In any event, he finally decides whether economic growth is "overexuberant," "underexuberant," or "normal." If "overexuberant," he orders the sale of government bonds, notes and bills in the Fed's possession in what is known as an "open market operation." As I shall later explain, that pulls money out of the private economy, in effect causing money to self-destruct. Interest rates (the costs of money) rise as the supply of money contracts and that stifles private spending, especially for houses and new plant and equipment. If carried too far, it may also cause plummeting stock prices, bank closures and failed businesses. Public sector spending, however, remains unaffected. It goes along on its merrily inefficient way untouched since government can afford almost any interest rate increase when borrowing money from the Fed. "Leaning against the wind" is what the economists call it. "Socking it to the public" is what it really is. The obvious solution to the inflation problem is to cut inefficient government spending in favor of efficient private spending. But, of course, the Fed was given no power to curb Congressional exuberance.

If the Chairman overreacts and raises interest rates past the "last straw," as happened during the "great contraction" of the money supply in the Depression years 1929-32, too much private money self-destructs and we get economic breakdowns. Because of the Fed, however, federal spending can proceed as if nothing were happening in the private economy. It can increase even as tax receipts fall. That happened in 1932 when President Franklin Delano Roosevelt "saved" capitalism from itself through what is called "deficit spending," a recommendation of economist John Maynard Keynes for getting out of the Depression. As we now know, Roosevelt lengthened that government-created Depression into the 1940s by squandering the money on a host of inefficient "New Deal" agencies. As posed by H. L. Mencken, "The New Deal began, like the Salvation Army, by promising to save humanity. It ended, again like the Salvation Army, by running flophouses and disturbing the peace."

If the Chairman's decision is for "normality," he will decree no change in interest rates. And if for "underexuberant," he will try to increase private spending and lower interest rates by buying government debt in the open market with freshly printed money. He is in reality the nation's "designated gambler," and a non-elected one at that, with our money at stake. Again, may I say, how very fortunate we were to have gotten a central bank *after* our industrial revolution, not before like most European countries! "The statesman, who should attempt to direct private people in what manner they ought to employ their capitals, would not only load himself with a most unnecessary attention, but assume an authority which could safely be trusted, not only to no single person, but to no council or senate whatever, and which would nowhere be so dangerous as in the hands of a man who had folly and presumption enough to fancy himself fit to exercise it" (from Adam Smith in The *Wealth of Nations*).

Of course, inflation and depressions are never blamed on politicians and their wasteful spending habits. Taking their cue from the Roman emperor Diocletian (who reigned from 284-305 A.D.), most writers accuse greedy and unscrupulous businesspeople for these disasters. In the preamble to the Edict of 301, one of the first attempts to contain inflation with wage and price controls, Diocletian writes: " ...Avarice boundless and frenzied, with no consideration for humankind, multiplies its spreading grasp like wildfire, not by years or months or days but every hour and minute. If self-restraint could curb its excesses or if the general welfare could tolerate the rank license which wickedly lacerates it daily, there might be place for turning a blind eye and keeping silent till public suffering should temper the abominable and pitiable cruelty. But since the unrestrained madness of lust will take no thought for the common welfare, since only necessity, not their own wish, can check the seething and torrential avarice of all, and since the impoverished victims have been forced to an awareness of their wretched state – in view of this situation we who are protectors of humankind have resolved that justice should intervene as arbiter so that the remedies we provide may effect the general improvement which mankind has long hoped for cut could never itself attain...

"So abandoned is the passion for gain that men in the business actually try to control wind and weather by the movement of the stars and wickedly abhor the rains which make fields fertile, for the abundance which favorable weather brings they calculate as a loss... Men with enough wealth to satisfy whole nations try to capture smaller fortunes and strive after ruinous percentages; concern for humanity in general persuades us to set a limit to the avarice of such men…"

What a case study in psychological projection! Nowhere does Diocletian mention the profligate government spending that had plagued the Empire for two hundred years prior to his reign, nowhere the debased coinage used to defray budget deficits. Because paper or "fiat" money did not exist in those days, the Roman treasury could finance government extravagance only by minting more and more coins containing less and less silver until they were merely pieces of base metal encased in a thin veneer of precious metal. The markets, however, were hardly fooled. Business people and farmers simply raised prices; the less the silver in the coins, the more coins they demanded for their products and services. Guess where the same shenanigans took place recently. In the United States of America in 1964! That was when our government removed silver from the coinage because face values fell below the value of the silver contained in the coins. And it is again happening today! The value of copper and zinc in the lowly penny now exceeds 1¢, and the pure copper pennies minted before 1982 are worth more than 2¢; furthermore, the value of the nickel is more than 7¢. And, of course, our government now threatens to make illegal the act of melting down these coins. Will the day come, we must wonder, when the value of the paper in the one dollar Federal Reserve note exceeds one dollar?

To enforce the Edict, Diocletian authorized a huge new and costly tax-collecting bureaucracy which proceeded to persecute, execute and exile those businesspeople and farmers accused of violations. He even fractioned the Empire into four parts, each with its own emperor, to enforce price and tax compliance more efficiently. And that did nothing but greatly increase government spending as the emperors in the three new sections of the Empire attempted to build up their capitol cities to rival the magnificence of Rome. But nothing, not even the death penalty, availed to stop the inflation. With the incentive for honest labor drastically curtailed, huge numbers of provincials became non-producers and chose to live as exiles and outlaws rather than support the burdens of civil society. Famine and ruinous losses in production spread throughout the Empire. Writes Edward Gibbon in The *Decline and Fall of the Roman Empire*: "From this period to the extinction of the Empire, it would be easy to deduce an uninterrupted series of clamors and complaints. According to his religion and situation, each writer chooses either Diocletian, or Constantine, or Valens, or Theodosius as the object of his invectives, but they unanimously agree in representing the burden of the public impositions, and particularly the land-tax and capitation, as the intolerable and increasing grievance of their own times." The number of those receiving from government approached and then exceeded those contributing to government. Loyalty, patriotism, and the will to defend the Empire dissipated steadily. Not one hundred years after Diocletian, "barbarian" infiltrations from the north were not to be beaten back again. How ever more frightening the parallels with 21st century America become, even to the "barbarian" attacks not from the north this time but from the east!

We have in Washington a most powerful institution trying to do good by regulating the money supply. But with economic theory woefully inadequate for the job of taming chaos, it must with overwhelming probability fail. And when it fails, the country as a whole suffers. The evil consequences, however, are spread over the whole population, and the time scale of events can be in years or decades or even centuries. The lesson was all too clear to President Kennedy, as it was to President Abraham Lincoln during the Civil War period: If the government can issue debt-and interest-encumbered paper in the form of bonds to raise money, why couldn't it simply issue a debt- and interest-free currency for the same purpose? On 4 June 1963, Kennedy took the first step toward abolishing the Federal Reserve by signing Executive Order #11,110. That directive authorized the U. S. Treasury "to issue silver certificates against any silver bullion, silver, or standard silver dollars in the Treasury." In other words, the certificates could be redeemed for silver at the option of the bearer. Silver certificates had first been issued in 1878 in exchange for silver dollars. They became the major type of circulating currency until abolished by Congress in 1963, when the silver backing of the $1 notes had increased in value to $1.29 and there was a run on Treasury silver. To replace the certificates, the Fed was empowered to issue $1 and $2 Federal Reserve notes with no backing. A first issue of the new "Kennedy bills" amounting to more than four billion dollars began circulating in denominations of $2, $5, $10 and $20 and these were debt-free and interest-free. No recourse to the FED printing press was required. Federal Reserve notes, as I have noted, are issued against government IOU's deposited at the FED. These IOU's add to the national debt and require the payment of interest. To whom? Why, to nobody else but the FED itself. Yes, indeed! We the people are paying interest on our pocket cash and bank deposits to service the FED. Oh, yes, the Kennedy bills were withdrawn from circulation by President Lyndon Johnson immediately after Kennedy's assassination.

The Federal Reserve System derives further revenues from the interest on loans to commercial banks and various fees charged for routine operations such as check clearing and fund transfers. Any operational profits realized on its gigantic $3 billion budget are remitted back to Treasury, but only after its huge overhead expenditures are satisfied and only after its stockholders are rewarded with their annual 6% dividends. Stockholders? Dividends? Most people are unaware of the fact that the FED is a private corporation, incorporated in the state of Delaware, and that its twelve Federal Reserve Banks – each one more opulent than the next – are owned by large commercial banks. The President appoints its chairman and seven of the sixteen members (governors) of the Federal Reserve Board, its ruling body. The stockholders choose the rest. In theory, the Board is independent of a popularly elected President.

From the FED's 1995 annual report, we see that it realized net income of $23.9 billion, which makes it one of the most profitable of world companies. Of this amount, $23.4 billion went back to the Treasury, $283 million stayed with the FED, and $232 million was paid out in dividends. These billions of dollars are naught but a hidden tax on the citizenry, a tax that in the past has wreaked tremendous harm on the nation.

Our national debt has ballooned by a worrisome *six trillion* dollars since 1963. That has not been too much of a problem as yet. But if government spending continues growing on its present course outpacing the private economy, a time of "dollar zero" must come. The dollar's value relative to foreign currencies and especially to gold will tell the story. "As is clear … the stock of money shows larger fluctuations after 1914 than before 1914 and this is true even if the large wartime [World War I] increases in the stock of money are excluded. The blind, undesigned, and quasi-automatic working of the gold standard turned out to produce a greater measure of predictability and regularity – perhaps because its discipline was impersonal and inescapable – than did deliberate and conscious control exercised with institutional arrangements intended to promote monetary stability. Here is a striking example of forces operating beneath the surface" (from A *Monetary History of the United States 1867-1960* by Milton Friedman and Anna Schwartz). The Friedman-Schwartz analysis clearly reveals a monetary chaon, a "sublime" ordering of the money supply out of the apparent chaos of a free market. And it also reveals incisively the ill-fated scam perpetrated on us by our monetary "experts."

"The Federal Reserve Board … has cheated the government of the United States and the people of the United States out of enough money to pay the national debt several times over." This is a quote from a speech delivered by Congressman Louis T. McFadden of Pennsylvania, as recorded in the Congressional Record of 1934, and we are now in a position to understand what he was talking about. The present government debt approximates $9 trillion and is represented by bonds and short term notes. Assuming a rate of 5%, the interest cost to the taxpayer is $450 billion per year. Added to this amount are the lucrative commissions charged by Wall Street's "merchants of debt" in marketing and redeeming the debt. And because of all the easy money made available by the Fed, politicians find the temptation to spend other people's money more irresistible than ever. Put it all together and we have the $11 trillion of inefficient spending in the GDP calculated above. Kennedy's Executive Order #11,110 was his opening salvo in an attempt to get rid of the agency making it all possible.

The Fed today employs nearly 20,000 people! It started with 300. Why so many now, who knows? Many of them are high-priced economists performing research of dubious value. In league with these bureaucrats are hordes of politicians, judges, scholars, reformers, lawyers, media mavins and social scientists, all Marxist fossils convinced they can improve on free markets, and at the same time dipping into the public trough. The pomposity of their numerous pronouncements is exceeded only by the stupidity of their forecasts. Ordinarily, free markets quickly perceive the pervasive twaddle heaped on them for what it is and ignore it. But not when the authority of law is invoked to enforce it. Should it not be patently clear by now that private, unregulated risk-taking – in effect, spending – by millions of individuals in free markets, as in the pari-mutuel and stock markets, drives us to the best of all possible futures – an unpredictable chaon emerging out of apparent chaos!

CHAPTER XII

TOWARD A CONSTITUTION

The old order changeth, yielding place to new.

Tennyson

A government big enough to give you everything you want is big enough to take from you everything you have.

Gerald Ford

The military aspect of the American Revolution ended in 1783 with the signing of the Treaty of Paris, but it left the quest for maximum freedom and minimal government still short of its goal. Outwardly, there seemed little need for any major changes in American governance under the Articles of Confederation. Most Americans, among them a large debtor class of small farmers and such luminaries as Thomas Jefferson, Samuel Adams, Patrick Henry and James Monroe, believed that the American experiment was progressing well and needed little fixing. These anti-Federalists, as they came to be known, saw no need to risk the freedoms so recently won by establishing another strong central government. What more could be done that the states couldn't do for themselves, they asked? There was no monarchy to support; state militias handled matters of internal security very efficiently; and with the Atlantic Ocean providing a natural defense bastion against external aggressors, military spending could be kept to a minimum.

Others, however, saw things differently. Yes, the new nation had freed itself from the shackles of British oppression. But now it was the machinations of local politicians that posed the supreme threat to maximum freedom. Past colonial practices of "leveling democracy," what today goes under the name of socialism, had been resurrected in many states and were encroaching upon "life, liberty and the pursuit of happiness." The Marxist-Robin Hood syndrome of stealing from productive people and giving it to the non-productive was too much in evidence. But suppose we let Adam Smith describe chaotic government at work.

"The paper currencies of North America consisted, *not in bank notes payable to the bearer on demand* [italics mine], but in a government paper, of which the payment was not exigible [redeemable] till several years after it was issued: And though the colony governments paid no interest to the holders of this paper, they declared it to be, and in fact rendered it, a legal tender of payment for the full value for which it was issued. But allowing the colony security to be perfectly good, a hundred pounds payable fifteen years hence, for example, in a country where interest is at six per cent, is worth little more than forty pounds ready money [present value]. To oblige a creditor, therefore, to accept of this as full payment for a debt of a hundred pounds actually paid down in ready money, was an act of such violent injustice, as has scarce, perhaps, been attempted by the government of any other country which pretended to be free. It bears the evident marks of having originally been … a scheme of fraudulent debtors to cheat their creditors. The government of Pennsylvania, indeed, pretended, upon their first emission of paper money, in 1722, to render their paper of equal value with gold and silver, by enacting penalties against all those who made any difference in the price of their goods when they sold them for a colony paper, and when they sold them for gold and silver … A positive law may render a shilling a legal tender for a guinea [21 shillings]; because it may direct the courts of justice to discharge the debtor who has made that tender. But no positive law can oblige a person who sells goods, and who is at liberty to sell or not to sell, as he pleases, to accept of a shilling as equivalent to a guinea in the price of them. Notwithstanding any regulation of this kind, it appeared by the course of exchange with Great Britain, that a hundred pounds sterling [of colonial paper] was occasionally considered as equivalent, in some of the colonies, to a hundred and thirty pounds [of British currency], and in others to so great a sum as eleven hundred pounds [British] currency; this difference in the value arising from the difference in the quantity of paper emitted in the different colonies, and in the distance and probability of the term of its final discharge and redemption. … No law, therefore, could be more equitable than the act of parliament [the Currency Act of 1764], so unjustly complained of in the colonies, which declared that no paper currency to be emitted there in time coming, should be a legal tender of payment."

Does 1 = 2 or 3 or 10 or 130 or 1100? Or anything the law says it is? And is such mathematics to be used by politicians to confiscate private property? Or to impair the validity of contractually agreed on payments? Talk about chaos and anarchy! There it was, and all created by governments in a country that "pretended to be free." Few businesses could have survived had they fully complied with such ill-gotten stay and legal tender laws. And it pays to bear in mind that Pennsylvania was always more moderate in its emissions of paper money than the other colonies. State governors were little more than tools of irresponsible, directly elected state legislatures that pursued "leveling" policies to subsidize a large class of subsistence farmers. The state courts had no jurisdiction beyond enforcing whatever laws the legislatures passed. In retrospect, we can understand why the British Parliament banned such practices. And, believe it or not, the farm "problem" is still with us today! In 2001, net farm cash income was a record $59.5 billion *one-third of which came from the federal government.* Which means of course that farmers got almost $20 billion of our tax money in subsidies to augment the $40 billion income they netted from market prices. How nice it is to jump income by 50% from government handouts! The rest of us, of course, must pay for it through higher taxes and higher food prices.

Note my italics above in the quote from Adam Smith, *not in bank notes payable to the bearer on demand*. Paper money is not inherently bad. On the contrary, when redeemable on demand at present value, great advantages derive from its use in the conduct of business. Then as now, it proved much more convenient, safer and cheaper to circulate a "proper" amount of paper as a proxy for cumbersome gold and silver bars, coins, or whatever could be bartered. That was so even though colonial and state governments issued paper in excess of what was required. Adam Smith again describes the goings-on: "It is convenient for the Americans … to save as much as possible the expence of so costly an instrument of commerce as gold and silver, and rather to employ that part of their surplus produce which would be necessary for purchasing those metals, in purchasing the instruments of trade, the materials of clothing, several parts of household furniture, and the iron-work necessary for building and extending their settlements and plantations; in purchasing not dead stock [gold and silver], but active and productive stock. The colony governments find it for their interest to supply the people with such a quantity of paper money as is fully sufficient and *generally more than sufficient* [italics mine] for transacting their domestic business. Some of these governments, that of Pennsylvania particularly, derive a revenue from lending this paper money to their subjects at an interest of so much per cent. Others, like that of Massachusett's Bay, advance upon extraordinary emergencies a paper-money of this kind for defraying the public expence, and afterwards, when it suits the conveniency of the colony, redeem it at the depreciated value to which it gradually falls. In 1747 that colony paid, in this manner, the greater part of its public debts, with the *tenth part* [italics mine] of the money for which its bills had been granted [publicly expended]. It suits the conveniency of the planters to save the expence of employing gold and silver money in their domestic transactions; and it suits the conveniency of the colony governments to supply them with a medium, which, *though attended with some very considerable disadvantages*, enables them to save that expence [italics mine]. The redundancy [proliferation] of paper money necessarily banishes gold and silver from the domestic transactions of the colonies, for the same reason that it has banished those metals from the greater part of the domestic transactions in Scotland; and in both countries *it is not the poverty, but the enterprizing and projecting spirit of the people* [italics mine] …which has occasioned this redundancy of paper money."

Benjamin Franklin was even more enthusiastic in his endorsement of paper money, his opinion published as early as 1727 in a "Modest Enquiry into the Nature and Necessity of a Paper Currency." Asked by English bankers to account for the great prosperity of the American colonies, he replied: "That is simple. In the colonies, we issue our own money. It is called Colonial Script. We issue it in proper proportion to the demands of trade and industry to make the product pass easily from the producers to the consumers. In this manner, creating for ourselves our own paper currency, we control its purchasing power, and *we have no interest to pay to no one*" [italics mine].

In response to Franklin, the bankers exerted their influence on Parliament to pass the Currency Act of 1764 making it illegal for the colonies to print their own money. A debt-free currency simply could not be tolerated. If turned loose in England, it would not only end the nation's debt, it would also extinguish the great profits derived from that debt by the wealthy stockholders of the Bank of England and government bond holders, and those privileged classes included the royals. The Act further required the colonists to pay all future taxes in gold or silver. Observed Franklin: "In one year, conditions [in the colonies] were so reversed that the era of prosperity ended, and a depression set in ... . The colonies would gladly have borne the little tax on tea and other matters had it not been that England took away from the colonies their money, which created unemployment and dissatisfaction. The inability of the colonists to get the power to issue their own money permanently out of the hands of George III and the international bankers was the PRIME [sic] reason for the Revolutionary War." There will be much more to say later about the great advantages of an unbacked paper currency, especially in its relation to "international bankers."

It is appalling to note how many historians, who you might think should know better, ascribe the supposed hard times during "the critical period" under the Articles of Confederation to a shortage of specie. But that was hardly the case. As pointed out by Adam Smith and also by Benjamin Franklin, most Americans had little use for the mercantilist idea of hoarding gold and silver. They didn't need it. Their "enterprizing and projecting spirit" was much better served by paper money despite its "very considerable disadvantages." If required for foreign trade, precious metals could always be bought. The flood of European imports alluded to earlier by George Washington and American manufacturers demonstrate this point very clearly. Foreign businessmen demanded payment in hard money or commodities like lumber and iron ore and furs and tobacco and sugar; they were hardly likely to sell their wares for worthless American paper money. By 1786, seven of the thirteen former colonies were again in the money business issuing an excess of paper along with intolerable stay and legal tender laws. Other threats to economic growth had surfaced as well. Those adversely affected or dissatisfied with the Articles of Confederation may be divided into five major groups: They were (1) property owners and creditors seeking relief from the vigorous attacks waged on private capital by local politicians; (2) free-traders opposed to the erection of tariff barriers to shield local businesses from interstate competition, (3) holders of government Revolutionary War debt securities watching their certificates depreciate to the vanishing point, (4) owners of western lands hoping for removal of the Indian threat, and, finally, (5) entrepreneurs looking to promote interstate road and canal projects. Included in one or more of these groups were most delegates to the future Constitutional Convention. But, as is most often the rule in our chaotic world, people working for their own selfish ends achieve the greatest good for all. The Constitution would turn out to be a happy confluence of idealism and self-interest.

Clearly, powerful forces of self-interest were at work, forces truly national in scope. Influential people from New England to Georgia, all "informed by a conscious solidarity of interests," as Woodrow Wilson was to write later, well understood how state legislatures were defrauding them of their assets and depriving them of what English philosopher John Locke had termed "life, liberty, and estate." For them, *too much government at the state level had overwhelmed too little at the national level.* A redress in that balance was mandatory and would lead, they believed, not only to a new governance but to much *less* government overall.

A seemingly inconsequential dispute between Maryland and Virginia over fishing rights in the Potomac River provided the "butterfly." It instigated the Virginia legislature to summon delegates from other states to a meeting where common problems could be discussed, particularly those relating to interstate commerce and rival claims to western lands. There resulted the Annapolis Convention of 1786. Because only five states responded – there seemed little interest in tinkering with prosperity - the conferees accomplished little other than to propose a subsequent convention to be held in Philadelphia the following May. Its purpose, as stated by delegate Alexander Hamilton in carefully veiled language, was "to devise such further provisions as shall appear to them necessary to render the constitution of the federal government adequate to the exigencies of the Union." On 21 February 1787, the Continental Congress voted to convene a constitutional convention.

In view of the poor attendance at Annapolis, not much was expected. But in the intervening year, a developing crisis changed matters dramatically and galvanized the new nation into action. The state of Massachusetts, in an effort to redeem its Revolutionary War debts, levied a tax on land. Several thousand New England farmers, their property threatened with foreclosure for failure to pay the tax, rebelled. They stopped court proceedings in Springfield and Worcester that would have deprived them of their farms and then marched on the weapons arsenal at Springfield. Most were small subsistence farmers who had paid for their land and tools either with borrowed money or with debt certificates issued by the Continental Congress for war service. Their leader, Daniel Shays, had fought bravely in the Revolution at Lexington and Concord, Bunker Hill and Stony Point. A sword presented to him by Lafayette (and later sold for taxes) attests to his bravery. He commanded a force estimated at twelve to fifteen thousand "desperate debtors" well suited to fighting in what came to be known as "Shays' Rebellion." This was a larger number than Washington had commanded during much of the Revolution and threw the country into turmoil. The Shaysite creed anticipated the *Communist Manifesto* by 75 years in its call for the elimination of private property: "That the property of the United States has been protected from the confiscations of the British by the joint exertions of all, and therefore ought to be the common property of all. And he that attempts opposition to this creed is an enemy to equity and justice and ought to be swept from off the face of the earth."

A few cannon shots sufficed to turn back the attack on the Springfield arsenal and a *privately* financed militia from Boston under General Benjamin Lincoln scattered the remnants of the rebel force. Despite the dire forebodings, the rebellion was over almost before it began. Shaysites were not ready to stake their lives on a creed that failed to arouse any sympathetic vibrations in the rest of America. The new nation had spoken, and it was not willing to forsake equality of opportunity for socialistic equality of reward. As for the rebels themselves, they sought and obtained some redress at the ballot box and most were pardoned.

The move toward a strengthened central government now gathered momentum. On 25 May 1787 there convened at the State House in Philadelphia fifty-five delegates from all the states except Rhode Island, many of whom had been involved in drawing up their State constitutions. Among the more renowned participants were George Washington, James

Madison and George Mason from Virginia, Alexander Hamilton from New York, Benjamin Franklin, Gouverneur Morris, Robert Morris and James Wilson from Pennsylvania, John Dickinson from Delaware, and Roger Sherman from Connecticut. Fully understanding the limits of reason in a largely chaotic world, this extraordinarily brilliant group of men followed the lead of George Washington and rejected out of hand the ancient philosophy of elitism. They well understood how the wisest and purest of men, even those with the exalted title of "philosopher-king," could mutate into monsters who knew not the consequences of their actions but thought they did. They also rejected any form of government dominated by an all-powerful legislature that could attack property rights with impunity. No, creating the greatest prosperity through a maximum of freedom and a minimum of government à la Adam Smith – that was their noble intention. And, somehow or other, that is what they hoped to achieve at this Constitutional Convention.

CHAPTER XIII

THE CONSTITUTION: A PRESCRIPTION FOR MAXIMUM FREEDOM AND MINIMAL GOVERNMENT

It is not the powers they conferred upon the government, but the powers that they prohibited to the government which makes the Constitution a charter of liberty.

Journalist Frank I. Cobb

In Malaya, superstition has it that the orangutan is really human, but that she remains silent to avoid paying taxes. Which is frightfully clever of the orangutan. The rest of us less clever beings seem to require at least some government and its concomitant taxation to get along. And that brings us face-to-face with any number of very difficult problems that worry the orangutan not at all. What purposes do governments at the federal, state and local levels serve and how much of each of them do we need? What taxes should be collected to support them? Who should pay and how much? How much debt should be allowed? And who is to make the ultimate decisions on taxing, spending and borrowing? These questions are of vital and ongoing import to any civilization, and they are the ones that confronted the delegates to the Constitutional Convention.

The preamble to the Constitution sets forth the lofty goals of the Founding Fathers: *We, the People of the United States in order to form a more perfect Union, establish Justice, insure domestic Tranquility, provide for the common Defense, promote the general Welfare, and secure the blessings of Liberty to ourselves and our Posterity do ordain and establish this Constitution for the United States of America.* As always, we have the noble intentions. But marrying public strength to a maximum of individual freedom so as to fulfill those aims? Therein lay the problem.

The Fathers were not operating in a vacuum. They were the beneficiaries of a centuries-long struggle to attain a system of justice known as the "Rights of Englishmen," best summarized in William Blackstone's best seller both in England and America, his *Commentaries on the Laws of England* (1765). Unlike the Ten Commandments, the Rights were neither carved in stone nor handed down from above. Rather, they were very human achievements fought for by those that believed in them. Based on personal liberty and "sacred and inviolable" private property, these are the principles that tend to shield every British citizen from the tyranny of enlightened despots and arbitrary government power. *They define freedom.* They are the rights referred to in the Declaration of Independence and it is the purpose of government not to endow these rights but to secure them: *We hold these Truths to be self-evident, that all Men are created equal, that they are* endowed by their Creator with certain unalienable Rights, *that among these are Life, Liberty, and the Pursuit of Happiness – That* to secure these Rights, *Governments are instituted among Men, deriving their just Powers from the Consent of the Governed, that whenever any Form of Government becomes destructive of these Ends, it is the Right of the People to alter or to abolish it …*

Due process, no crime without intent, habeas corpus, the presumption of innocence, no self-incrimination, no ex post facto laws, no taxes without Parliamentary consent, no quartering of soldiers upon the citizenry, no martial law in time of peace, the right to counsel, client-attorney privilege, the right to confront one's accusers, and the duty of prosecutors to serve truth and not their aspirations – these are what make up the "Rights of Englishmen." As anterior to law, they constrain government's use of the law as a weapon for oppression, i.e. inequality before the law. All are indispensable if we are to have a maximum of freedom and a minimum of government, the necessary condition for the effective operation of the "invisible hand." And all are either explicit or implicit in the Constitution. The one weak point, I might note at this point, is the last. In aspiring for higher office, many prosecutors are prone to circumventing our Rights with twisted interpretations of the law. Their behavior in today's America is fast becoming a menace to our freedoms and economic growth.

The "Rights of Englishmen" are diametrically opposed to the law as handed down by the Roman emperor Justinian I (483-565) in *Corpus Juris Civilis.* Published in numerous editions, this body of law survived the collapse of the Roman Empire and became the ultimate model and inspiration for the legal system of nearly every European nation. Its basic assumption is that the "command of the King has the force of law." Or, as phrased by France's Louis XIV, "It is legal because I wish it." What we have here, of course, is a body of law issuing from an above-the-law benign dictator who possesses unlimited powers to try his hand at doing good. In England, however, matters evolved along a different path. In the ninth century, Alfred the Great (849-899) issued his own code of common law, reformed the administration of justice and pointed it toward equality before the law for all persons irrespective of means, wealth and position. The movement continued with the Magna Carta of 1215, which denied the King absolute power and subjected him to the "law of the land." In 1628 followed the Petition of Right which allowed the King to be petitioned and criticized for allegedly wrong actions, and which also denied the taxing power to the King without Parliamentary consent. And the movement culminated in the triumph of parliamentary power over royal absolutism in the Glorious Revolution of 1688-1689 and the accompanying British Bill of Rights. Wrote Blackstone: "The true liberty of the subject consists not so much in the gracious behavior, as in the limited power, of the sovereign." Well before most other countries, England had abolished the "divine right of kings" doctrine.

Equality before the law regardless of class or status – on this premise rests the beauty and significance of the Rights of Englishmen. Economic and political differences among people certainly exist, but as far as their Rights are concerned, one person is legally indistinguishable from the next. Everyone shares in and benefits from the legal security provided. And none more so than the rich and famous and out-of-favor government officials. Violations of life, liberty and property can skewer the most powerful when not properly safeguarded for all classes. The mock trials in Stalinist Russia that resulted in the execution of thousands of Party workers are a bloody sample of the consequences when and where the Rights are either nonexistent or overridden. Marxists in particular find reconciliation of the Rights with the "truths" of the *Communist Manifesto* very difficult indeed.

Even in a republic, as the Fathers were well aware, brutal violations of "unalienable Rights" are likely to occur when subject to the overriding needs of politicians. To finance a war against Cassius and Brutus, the assassins of Julius Caesar, Antony, Octavian and Lepidus formed the second Roman triumvirate and singled out one hundred senators and more than 2000 rich men of distinction for forfeiture of their wealth. Most were executed for "conspiracy." Among those killed was Cicero, orator, philosopher and perhaps the greatest Latin writer of history, because in his speeches he had dared to criticize Antony for his scandalous behavior and improper handling of Roman affairs. It hardly mattered that Cicero was friend, adviser and mentor to Octavian, the future Augustus and first emperor of Rome.

Equality before the law, and that includes tax law, is what makes capitalism possible. Freed from the worry of arbitrary abuses of government power, Englishmen could direct their creative energies to the "universal, continual, and uninterrupted effort to better their own condition," quoting Adam Smith once again. It is that "equal and impartial administration of justice which renders the rights of the meanest British subject respectable to the greatest, and which, *by securing to every man the fruits of his own industry, gives the greatest and most effectual encouragement to every sort of industry*" [italics mine]. "It is this effort, protected by law and allowed by liberty to exert itself in the manner that is most advantageous, which has maintained the progress of England towards opulence and improvement in almost all former times, and which, it is to be hoped, will do so in all future times." "Consumers and manufacture[r]s can seldom flourish long in any state which does not enjoy a regular administration of justice, in which the people do not feel themselves secure in the possession of their property, in which the faith of contracts is not supported by law, and in which the authority of the state is not supposed to be regularly employed in enforcing the payment of debts from all those able to pay. Commerce and manufactures, in short, can seldom flourish in any state in which there is not a certain degree of confidence in the justice of government." Of especial importance is the "faith of contracts" phrase. In a society built on a division of labor, individuals with limited and specialized skills can combine or exchange labor and material resources for personal gain only through the medium of meticulously upheld contracts shielded from force and fraud.

With Adam Smith's "invisible hand" serving as its philosophic foundation, the Founding Fathers erected the monumental edifice of the American Constitution, assuredly one of the most influential of historical documents. In just a preamble and seven articles they put forth a tightly woven model of minimal government and maximum freedom. Although they endowed the federal government with well-defined positive powers, they structured it so as to break the force of majority rule whenever the Rights of Englishmen were at stake. And they made the Constitution a "charter of liberty" by denying to government any powers that could render our "unalienable Rights" hostage to the "overriding needs" of government. Neither what Thomas Jefferson referred to as the "elective despotism" of the majority nor the dictatorship of a minority was to be tolerated.

The language of the Constitution is cold, severe and formal. It betrays none of the emotions that vibrate through the French Constitution of 1791 and the *Communist Manifesto* of 1848. Nor does it expose the motives behind its adoption and the evils it was supposed to exorcise. Yet it cannot be read without sensing the paramount importance of the individual as against the government. The most profound statement of its antecedents is to be found in The *Federalist*, a series of 85 essays that exposes in clear, illuminative prose the political and economic philosophies of the Founders. Written by Alexander Hamilton, James Madison and John Jay in support of ratification of the Constitution by the states, they were widely published in the *New York Packet* and many other newspapers. I shall have frequent opportunity to quote from them.

The Fathers created their own Holy Trinity, a government of three independent branches coexisting as one. Article I, Section 1 of the Constitution follows immediately on the preamble and establishes in one sentence the legislative branch: "*All* legislative Powers herein granted shall be vested in a Congress of the United States, which shall consist of a Senate and House of Representatives" [italics mine]. Article II, Section 1 establishes the executive branch: "The Executive power shall be vested in a President of the United States." And Article III, Section 1, perhaps their most controversial contribution to political science, the judicial branch: "The judicial Power of the United States shall be vested in one Supreme Court and in such inferior Courts as the Congress may from Time to Time ordain and establish." In these three brief statements, the Fathers set up a governmental structure of three independent branches and at the same time interposed among them a clear separation of powers. The French philosopher, Charles Louis de Secondat Montesquieu, had proposed just such a balance in 1690 to keep government minimal.

Note the word *All* at the beginning of Article I, Section 1. Little though it may be, it introduces a sophisticated system of checks and balances that, it was hoped, would forestall the possibility of any one branch exceeding its constitutional limits and assuming excessive power unto itself. For what it does is to deny legislative powers to the executive and judicial branches. The Fathers well understood the tyranny that could result when the independence of the branches was undermined, especially with George III's usurpation of legislative powers very fresh in their minds. They could only be appalled at the behavior of today's lawmakers who foist onto the executive branch both the legislative and judicial powers needed to administer and adjudicate their labyrinthine legislation. Wrote Madison in The *Federalist* (No. 47): The *accumulation of all powers, legislative, executive, and judiciary, in the same hands, whether of one, a few, or many, and whether hereditary, self-appointed, or elective, may justly be pronounced the very definition of tyranny.* And the very definition of a benign dictator!

Take a look at your income tax return. It smacks of the very tyranny that arises from just such a consolidation of powers. The Internal Revenue Service, part of the executive branch's Treasury Department, promulgates a tax code that has the force of law, takes upon itself Congress' Constitutional obligation to collect the booty, judges every taxpayer for? How were 20compliance with the Code's three and a half million words and thousands of pages of convoluted rules and regulations that defy interpretation, violates habeas corpus by assessing penalties and seizing private property for "non-compliance," violates the original Constitution's stricture on the apportionment of direct taxes and, in the process, terrifies almost everyone who pays taxes. There is in theory the right of appeal in tax court from an IRS ruling, but for the average taxpayer the money and time loss is to say the least unpardonable, not to mention the indignity and psychological strain involved in such proceedings. "A power over a man's subsistence," wrote Hamilton in The *Federalist* (No. 79), "amounts to a power over his will." Who could doubt Hamilton after coping with a maze of income tax forms every April 15thth century Americans ever duped into accepting this clear violation of Constitutional intent? How were they finagled into giving politicians all the money they wanted so that it could be squandered on a cataclysmic World War I and a ridiculous prohibition amendment among other tragedies?

In 1888 the German government imposed an income tax on her citizens. So draconian was the impost that it horrified even the politicians of other European countries who were thinking of raising money along similar lines. Once accepted by the German people, however, it was but a short step to totalitarian Nazism. The Enabling Act of 1933 required the Reichstag, the legislative branch of the German government, to "delegate" its legislative powers to Chancellor Adolf Hitler's executive branch: "In addition to the procedure for the passage of legislation outlined in the Constitution, the *Reich Cabinet is also authorized to enact Laws* [italics mine]… The national laws enacted by the Reich Cabinet may deviate from the Constitution … The national laws enacted by the Reich Cabinet shall be prepared by the Chancellor and published in the official gazette. They come into effect, unless otherwise specified, upon the day following their publication." Our Internal Revenue code has all the earmarks of that Enabling Act. When all powers, executive, legislative and judicial accumulate in the same hands, you get an Adolf Hitler and an Internal Revenue Service. Need more be said?

In light of the "leveling democracy" policies pursued by the state legislatures, the legislative branch was singled out for special consideration in the Constitution. In any power struggle between the branches of government, the Fathers thought, Congress was likely to win out. The House of Representatives, being elected directly by the people, might be easily influenced by a possibly overbearing majority of the electorate. The property and rights of society's most productive workers could then be sacrificed at the national level. That the Fathers were determined not to let happen. They knew instinctively what we discovered in our analysis of chaos, that an unequal distribution of assets is inevitable in a free society and from it arises many different classes with a whole spectrum of contending interests. Competition among these multifold interests, they expected, would serve naturally to dampen the dominance of any one class and bring about the most equitable distribution of wealth. Any political meddling was to be discouraged; it could only be detrimental to maximum freedom and greatest prosperity. And, in general, that is how matters progressed – until the 20th century saw the Constitution warped into a "living, evolving" document that encouraged political intervention into social and economic affairs.

To provide a check on legislative powers and forestall an excess of law making, the Fathers designed a deliberately cumbersome apparatus for the passage of legislation. Before it could become a law, a bill had first to secure approval of both the House of Representatives and the Senate. It was then subjected to executive control. Article I, Section 7 gives the President veto power over any bill passed by the Congress, to be countermanded only if passed by at least a two-thirds vote when reconsidered by both Houses. Quoting that staunchest of advocates of a strong central government, Alexander Hamilton in The *Federalist* (No.73): "It may perhaps be said that the power of preventing bad laws includes that of preventing good ones… But this objective will have little weight with those who can properly estimate the mischiefs of that inconstancy and mutability in the laws which form the greatest blemish in the character and genius of our governments. They will consider every institution calculated to restrain the excess of law-making, and to keep things in the same state in which they happen to be at any given period, as more likely to do good than harm. The *injury which may possibly be done by defeating a few good laws will be amply compensated by the advantage of preventing a number of bad ones*" [italics mine]. How Hamilton would have decried the legislative diarrhea that passes for lawmaking today!

Hamilton's warning displays the amazing insight held by the Founding Fathers into modern chaos theory. They understood all too well how what we now term "butterflys" could magnify into national disasters when too much power is concentrated in too few hands. Only by limiting lawmaking at the national level as much as possible could widespread harm be averted.

In addition to the executive's veto power over legislation, the Fathers raised the possibility of judicial control. Article III, Section 1 states that "The judicial power shall extend to all cases, in law and equity, arising under this Constitution, the laws of the United States, and treaties made, or which shall be made, under their authority …" The meaning of this anomalous statement aroused continuing controversy in the years to follow. Does it authorize an appointed judiciary to abrogate statutes it deems unconstitutional, statutes passed and approved by a popularly elected Congress and President sworn to uphold the Constitution? Does the judiciary have the sole power to do so? Is the federal government, through its own appointed courts, to determine unilaterally the limits of its own powers? In The *Federalist* (No.78), Hamilton wrote ambiguously on this point: "The complete independence of the courts of justice is peculiarly essential in a *limited* Constitution [italics mine]. By a limited Constitution, I understand one which contains certain exceptions to the legislative authority, such, for instance, as that it should pass no bills of attainder, no ex post facto laws, and the like. Limitations of this kind can be preserved in practice in no other way than through the medium of the courts of justice whose duty it must be to declare all acts contrary to the manifest tenor of the Constitution void." I must insert at this point that today's courts overlook with impunity even the specific prohibitions on ex post facto laws and bills of attainder. Hamilton continues: "In a monarchy, it [the judiciary] is an excellent barrier to the despotism of the prince; in a republic, it is no less an excellent barrier to the encroachments and oppressions of the representative body [Congress]... If, then, the courts of justice are to be considered as the *bulwarks of a limited Constitution against legislative encroachments* [italics mine], this consideration will afford a strong argument for the permanent tenure of judicial offices since nothing will contribute so much as this to that independent spirit in the judges which must be essential to the faithful performance of so arduous a duty ..." Hamilton favored judicial control, it would seem, only as long as the courts were "bulwarks of a limited Constitution." Writing further in The *Federalist* (No. 80), he limits judicial review to the "mere necessity of *uniformity* in the interpretation of the national laws" [italics mine]. Note again the Constitutional phrase above: "The judicial power shall extend to all cases, in law and equity ... ." The penchant of today's judges to legislate and tax from the bench would have shaken Hamilton to the core. A sharply contrasting view of judicial control, imbued with an amazing foreknowledge of the corruption existing in today's legal practices, comes from one Amos Singeltary of Massachusetts: "These lawyers, and men of learning, and monied men, that talk so finely, and gloss over matters so smoothly, to make us poor illiterate people swallow down the pills, expect to get into Congress themselves: they expect to be the managers of the Constitution, and get all the power and the money into their own hands, and then they will swallow up all of us little folks, like the great Leviathan."

Judging by the lack of a clear Constitutional statement, there must surely have been grave reservations in the minds of the Framers as to the extent of judicial powers. And it made them hesitate. Entrusting the people's "unalienable Rights" to the interpretive preconceptions of a coven of lawyers themselves part of the federal establishment should give anybody reason to pause. It was almost as if they could foresee the perverted interpretations to be placed on their handiwork by future do-gooders under the spell of alien ideologies. To read the Constitution in accordance with the Fathers' views, we must constantly keep in mind the initial conditions for chaon emergence, a maximum of individual freedom and a minimum of government. It is much too easy to say along with Humpty Dumpty: "When I use a word, it means just what I choose it to mean − neither more nor less." Or, in the words of Felix Frankfurter, one of a plethora of smart-smart-smart-stupid Supreme Court justices to come, "The Constitution is what the Court says it is." Sounds like Louis IV promulgating "It is legal because I wish it." Such is the fix of mind that demolishes the courts as "bulwarks of a limited Constitution" and establishes them instead as bastions of a big, "do-good" central government. Such is the fix of mind that trashes our "unalienable Rights" whenever the justices find an overriding "public interest" at stake. Instead of the wisdom of the Founding Fathers, we have the simple-minded noble intentions of their much inferior successors.

A prime example of distorted "reasoning" arises in the Constitutional phrase "promote the general welfare" (Article I, Section 8, Clause 1 and the Preamble) which today is twisted far from its original intent. To Socrates, Plato, Marx, Bentham and most modern politicians, it means the "benign dictator" oxymoron wherein politicians get all the power and money they think they need to achieve "the greatest happiness of the greatest number." For Adam Smith and the Founding Fathers, on the contrary, promoting the general welfare comes about only when government maximizes freedom and governs least. Problems associated with the Constitutional interpretation of judicial powers were to persist until 1865. And then it took the slaughter of 620,000 young men and 50,000 civilians to settle the issue, for many of us, in a very unsatisfactory manner.

The Constitution as a "charter of liberty" denies to government those powers most likely to deprive the citizenry of its "unalienable Rights." Uppermost in the Fathers' minds was taxation, the basis of all other powers, and it was the first one treated. Maximum freedom and minimal government, the Fathers well knew, meant minimal taxes. The Revolution had not been fought so that Americans, like most Europeans, could be saddled with heavy taxes for the support of some spendthrift national government. Safeguarding the people's money and property was their first priority. The weight of taxes borne by the English people at the time filled George Washington "with astonishment hardly to be conceived." He would, he wrote, have "absolutely disbelieved" had he not read it in the leading English agricultural journal. And English taxes were far less than those of most other European countries. The tax burden of present-day Americans would be for Washington and all the Founding Fathers akin to insanity.

Article I, Section 2, Clause 3 states: "Representatives (*and direct Taxes*) shall be *apportioned* among the several States which may be included within this Union, according to their respective Numbers, (which shall be determined by adding to the whole Number of free Persons ... three-fifths of all other Persons)" [italics mine]. A direct tax is one levied on a person's body, income or property and paid by that person directly to the government. According to this provision, such taxes could be imposed only in an amount proportional to the population of the states, as is the case with the number of Representatives in Congress. In other words, if a state like New York has ten times as many people as Georgia, it would be expected to pay ten times more in taxes, but no more. That New Yorkers might be more than ten times richer than Georgians matters not at all. The apportionment provision (plus the uniformity requirement in Section 8) was intended to prohibit Congress from inflicting the "leveling democracy" syndrome on a national scale; no single person or group of persons could be singled out for confiscatory or favorable tax treatment. Sixty years later, the *Communist Manifesto* would promulgate the progressive income tax, and non-apportioned taxes have ever since been the way taken by most of today's "enlightened" nations. Everybody is equal before the law, they say, but not when money is involved.

The Fathers' fear of direct taxes received renewed emphasis when this prohibition was reiterated in Article I, Section 9, Clause 4: "No Capitation [head tax], or other direct, Tax shall be laid, unless in Proportion to the Census or Enumeration herein before directed to be taken." Interestingly, the apportionment clause of the Constitution was not repealed by the 16th Amendment of 1913 that inflicted the permanent income tax on America. That Amendment, therefore, is in fundamental conflict with the original document.

Civilization's greatest thinkers from Cicero to Montesquieu, Hume and Smith had warned of the tyranny associated with permanent, direct taxes and that these were to be avoided except during the direst of emergencies. Apportionment and uniformity, the Fathers hoped, would subject such taxes to popular approval by making everybody liable for them. Without these conditions, such taxes jeopardize the "Rights of Englishmen" by pitting the huge resources of the State against any individual of choice. And when money is involved, freedoms are easily overlooked. In the latter days of the Roman Empire, a highly unpopular head tax reached levels that forced fathers and mothers to kill their children rather than have them counted by ubiquitous tax collectors. As protests mounted to calamitous proportions, a steadily increasing number of citizens discovered that "life, liberty and the pursuit of happiness" were better found with the "barbarians" from the north rather than with the Emperor in Rome. And let us remember at this point that our system of law is based on the "Rights of Englishmen," which in turn derives from the "barbarian" Angles, Saxons and Jutes, not from the supposedly more civilized Romans.

Obviously, popular approval of direct taxes was the Fathers' intention. Fresh in their minds was the "ship money" tax resurrected in 1635 by King Charles I to finance his profligate spending. Dating from 1007, this ancient tax had formerly been levied directly on individuals living in seaport towns for defensive purposes, the building and outfitting of naval ships. Although forbidden to do so by the Petition of Right in 1628, Charles unilaterally extended its reach to all of Britain. Government officials appeared in every parish to make out lists of landowners and the proportionate amounts each was to contribute to the farce. Everyone knew the tax had nothing to do with ships and there was a great amount of grumbling. When one John Hampden, a cousin of Oliver Cromwell, claimed that the tax put the entire property of the country at the King's disposal and refused to pay, sycophantic judges ignored the Petition of Right and upheld the tax. Other Englishmen protested with their feet, flocking to America in such numbers that the Crown instituted restrictions on emigration. Whatever else it did, this forerunner of the income tax demonstrated once again the effectiveness of direct taxes in getting the people's money into government coffers. It also demonstrated what can happen to politicians when a "last-straw" tax is enacted. Fourteen years later, the King was beheaded for his tax policies. Fortunately for the progress of America toward world supremacy, the Constitution effectively blocked a permanent direct tax until the ratification of the income tax amendment in 1913. This direct tax on income undermined the very concept of limited government as envisioned by the Founding Fathers. And it raised fundamental Constitutional questions still unresolved and still ignored by the tax-supported non-entities comprising the Supreme Court. I will have much more to say about it when we come to later history.

In The *Federalist* (No. 10), Hamilton sets forth the great advantages of indirect consumption taxes as opposed to possibly ruinous direct taxes: "Imposts, excises, and, in general, all duties upon articles of consumption, may be compared to a fluid, which will, in time find its level with the means of paying them. The amount to be contributed by each citizen will in a degree be at his own option, and can be regulated by an attention to his resources. The rich may be extravagant, the poor can be frugal, and private oppression may always be avoided by a judicious selection of objects proper for such impositions." "It is a signal advantage of taxes on articles of consumption that they contain in their own nature a security against excess. They prescribe their own limit, which cannot be exceeded without defeating the end proposal, that is, an extension of revenue." "If duties are too high, they lessen consumption, the collection is eluded, and the product to the Treasury is not so great as when they are confined within proper and moderate bounds. *This forms a complete barrier against any material oppression of the citizen by taxes of this class*, and is itself a natural limitation of the power of imposing them" [italics mine].

Hamilton was elaborating on a quote from the great Scottish philosopher, David Hume (1711-1776): "A duty upon commodities checks itself, and a prince will soon find that an increase of the impost is no increase of his revenue. It is not easy, therefore, for a people to be altogether ruined by such taxes." Unfortunately, today's lawmakers have counteracted this type of public limitation on their revenue by adopting progressive income taxes and central banking. These self-anointed prophets, who cannot forecast the future behavior of even a simple pendulum, think they can prophecy the consequences of their actions on complex social and economic systems. Taking their cue from Plato, George III, Charles I and Karl Marx, they consider themselves the nonpareil managers of the people's affairs. After all, dear reader, don't these "small men by whom we are governed" know how to spend our money better than we do?

In order to assure popular approval of taxes, the Articles of Confederation had required approval by nine of the states before any spending bill could be passed. By thus containing government spending, taxes could be kept sufficiently low to avoid uprisings. Guided by this provision, the Fathers first considered a 75% Congressional plurality rather than a simple majority vote for the passage of appropriation bills. But after a thorough investigation of European tax systems, and especially the numerous and violent tax revolts that recurred with alarming frequency, they decided that inequity in tax laws was the major cause of tax troubles, and they opted for a majority vote *plus* uniformity. This was the device adopted by the Convention to thwart what Madison called "schemes of oppression" by a Congressional super majority. In The *Federalist* (No. 36), Hamilton had minimized the danger of tax oppression by pointing to the Constitutional command that taxes "shall be UNIFORM [sic] throughout the United States." The full and basic meaning of UNIFORM he emphasized by its capitalization. How right the Fathers were in their deliberations burst forth in grisly detail just a few years hence. During the French Revolution, everyone associated with tax inequity and tax collection was beheaded – the bureaucrats at the French tax bureau, the king and queen, the nobility, the politicians, the clergy and all others who had not been required to pay taxes. Even the great French chemist, Antoine Lavoisier (1743-1794), the discoverer of oxygen, was beheaded because he moonlighted as a tax collector. Unfortunately for America, uniformity did not work. Although fine in theory, violations of it were to become major factors in future tax rebellions, including the Civil War. And the killing was immense.

Another limitation on taxing powers was set forth in Article I, Section 7: "All bills for raising revenues shall originate in the House of Representatives; but the Senate may propose or concur with amendments as on other bills." Under the new Constitution, Representatives were elected directly by the people, unlike Senators who were chosen by state legislatures. Popular approval of taxes was thereby mandated because at the time only taxpayers could vote. Today, that limitation is fast disappearing as the number of non-taxpayers approaches and threatens to exceed the number of taxpayers.

Article I, Section 8, Clause 1 of the Constitution details the tax powers of the federal government: "The Congress shall have Power To lay and collect Taxes, Duties, Imposts, and Excises, to pay the Debts and provide for the common Defence and general Welfare of the United States; but all Duties, Imposts, and Excises shall be uniform throughout the United States." An excise is a tax imposed on a happening, such as the sale of a product or service. It is not imposed on property. Here we must note once again that it is the obligation of the legislative branch to collect taxes, not the executive branch. Our present system of collecting income and other taxes is, therefore, decidedly unconstitutional. Also, under the "uniform" requirement, no single person or group can be singled out for discriminatory tax payments or favorable treatment. In other words, everybody must be equal before the law and that includes tax law! Finally, appropriations from tax monies must be strictly limited. They cannot, for example, be constitutionally used for local or anti-"general Welfare" pork barrel schemes. Of course, all these restrictions on government powers have long since been dumped by the wayside.

The phrase "three-fifths of all other Persons" in Article I, Section 2 brings up the ugly question of slavery for the first time. It referred to a slave population that had been denied the Rights of Englishmen. By counting three-fifths of the slaves in the determination of Representatives and direct taxes, we have the first of many compromises to come between North and South. Northerners did not want slaves fully counted lest they be outvoted in Congress by southern Representatives. And southerners did not want them counted if apportioned direct taxes were ever levied. There will be more to say about slavery later. But let me at this point insert two passages from The *Wealth of Nations* (page 365): "The experience of all ages and nations, I believe, demonstrates that the work done by slaves, though it appears to cost only their maintenance, is in the end the dearest of any [work done by freemen]. A person who can acquire no property, can have no other interest but to eat as much, and to labour as little as possible. Whatever work he does beyond what is sufficient to purchase his own maintenance, can be squeezed out of him by violence only, and not by any interest of his own." "The pride of man makes him love to domineer, and nothing mortifies him so much as to be obliged to condescend to persuade his inferiors. Wherever the law allows it, therefore, he will generally prefer the service of slaves to that of freemen." Madison, who owned slaves but hated slavery, believed it an outmoded and inefficient institution that would die out naturally or eventually be abolished. He pointed repeatedly to a ten-acre farm owned by one Richard Rush just outside Philadelphia that brought in more money than his own 2000-acre property worked by slaves. How unfortunate it was that the Founding Fathers were unable to agree with Adam Smith on the specific issue of slavery as it applied to African-Americans! They certainly understood, as Karl Marx did not, that the incentive to better oneself applied generally to all other workers.

Article I, Section 8 goes on to list the specific powers granted to Congress. These are known as "enumerated powers" and I shall take them up as later situations demand. But let me note here that the Constitution drastically limits the size of government by granting to government these powers and no others. The intent, obviously, was to leave as little as possible up to the discretion of those in power. Not granted were any powers that could infringe on the "Rights of Englishmen" – freedom of speech, freedom of assembly, freedom of religion, freedom of the press, and the freedom to keep and bear arms. Most Federalists of the time thought the later addition of the Bill of Rights unnecessary and irrelevant because the Constitutional doctrine of enumerated powers authorized no laws that could abrogate our "unalienable Rights" and civil liberties. Hamilton in The *Federalist* (No. 84) argues: "I go further and affirm that bills of rights … are not only unnecessary in the proposed Constitution, but would even be dangerous. They would contain various exceptions to powers not granted, and, on this very account, would afford a colorable pretext to claim more than were granted. For why declare that things shall not be done which there is no power to do? Why, for instance, should it be said that the liberty of the press shall not be restrained when no power is given by which restrictions may be imposed? … The Constitution ought not to be charged with the absurdity of providing against the abuses of an authority which was not given …" Hamilton, as leader of the soon-to-arise Federalist Party, would come to reject "enumerated powers" while an opposition Democratic-Republican Party headed by Jefferson would embrace the doctrine.

As a further limitation on Congressional lawmakers, all powers granted specifically to the national government are subject to the general conditions set forth in Article I, Section 9, Clauses 2 and 3. These clauses apply to all laws and seek to thwart egregious violations of "unalienable Rights." Clause 2 states: "The Privilege of the Writ of *Habeas Corpus* shall not be suspended, unless when in Cases of Rebellion or Invasion the public Safety requires it." In other words, as a protection against illegal imprisonment for an alleged crime under any law, a person must be brought before a judge or court for an assessment of the charges. And Clause 3: "No Bill of Attainder or *ex post facto* Law shall be passed." A bill of attainder transfers judicial power to the legislative branch by allowing the legislature to determine a person's guilt or innocence in cases involving treason or felony. An *ex post facto* law is one that can be applied retroactively. We shall come to see, unfortunately, that violations of this Clause have been blandly ignored by the courts.

Article I, Section 10 denies certain powers to the states. Right at this point is where the chaos issuing from state governments was reduced to a level below that which existed under the Articles of Confederation. Clause 1 states: "No State shall … make anything but gold and silver coin a tender in Payment of Debts; pass any Bill of Attainder, ex post facto Law, or *Law impairing the Obligation of Contracts* …" [italics mine]. This crucially important clause singles out the sanctity of contracts in a free society built on a division of labor. Because all of us possess but limited and specialized skills, we must secure the necessities and niceties of life by negotiating with others the exchange of labor and resources for mutual gain. And we must be shielded from force and fraud when so doing. In particular, this clause prevents the negation of contracts by the stay and legal tender laws legislated by the states under their "leveling democracy" practices.

Clause 2 establishes the new nation as a huge free trade zone devoid of interstate tariffs: "No State shall, without the Consent of the Congress, lay any Imposts or Duties on Imports and Exports, except what may be absolutely necessary for executing its inspection Laws …" In conjunction with Article I, Section 8, Clause 3 ("The Congress shall have the Power To regulate Commerce with foreign Nations, and among the several States …"), this "commerce" clause abolished trade barriers and consolidated under one federally administered code a maze of state-mandated shipping regulations.

Writing in The *Federalist* (No.11), Hamilton sounds very much like Adam Smith in extolling the advantages of free trade: "An UNRESTRAINED [sic] intercourse between the States themselves will advance the trade of each by an interchange of their respective productions, not only for the supply of reciprocal wants at home, but for exportation to foreign markets. The veins of commerce in every part will be replenished and will acquire additional motion and vigor from a free circulation of the commodities of every part. Commercial enterprise will have much greater scope from the diversity in the productions of different States." And in (No. 22): "The interfering and unneighborly regulations [tariffs] of some States, contrary to the true Spirit of the Union, have in different instances, given just cause of umbrage and complaint to others, and it is to be feared that examples of this nature if not restrained by national control, would be multiplied and extended till they became not less serious sources of animosity and discord than injurious impediments to the intercourse between the different parts of the Confederacy. The commerce of the German empire is in continued trammels from the multiplicity of the duties which the several princes and states exact upon the merchandises passing through their territories, by means of which the fine streams and navigable rivers with which Germany is so happily watered are rendered almost useless. Though the genius of the people of this country might never permit this description to be strictly applicable to us, yet we may reasonably expect, from the gradual conflict of State regulations, that the citizens of each would at length come to be considered and treated by the others in no better light than that of foreigners and aliens." We should note Hamilton's use of the word "Confederacy" rather than Union in this excerpt.

From the point of view of "enumerated powers," politicians are constrained "by the silence of the Constitution" from pursuing their version of the "public interest." Absent extra-Constitutional governmental intrusion into private and business affairs, freedom is assured. And when freedom is assured, Adam Smith's "invisible hand" can then take care of providing "the greatest happiness of the greatest number." Quite clearly, that was the Fathers' intent. Listen to Madison speaking against a protective tariff in a speech to the 1st Congress: "I own myself the friend to a very free system of commerce, and hold it as a truth, that commercial shackles are generally unjust, oppressive, and impolitic; it is also a truth, that *if industry and labor are left to take their own course, they will generally be directed to those objects which are the most productive, and this in a more certain and direct manner than the wisdom of the most enlightened legislature could point out*" [italics mine]. We have here the essence of Adam Smith's "invisible hand."

Despite Hamilton's assurances of superfluity, a Bill of Rights was appended to the Constitution. It stands as an uneasy compromise between the Federalists and anti-Federalists, those in favor and those against the Constitution. Passed by Congress on 25 September 1789 and submitted to the states for approval, the Bill of Rights became part of the Constitution on 15 December 1791 when ratified by three-fourths of the states. There can be little doubt that the Founding Fathers, having grown up under English common law, revered their English heritage and intended to incorporate fully into the new government the Rights of Englishmen. On this point everyone was in agreement. Where they differed was on the necessity of amending the Constitution.

Most Federalists wanted the Constitution as originally drafted in Philadelphia left as is. They believed, as argued by Hamilton above in The *Federalist* (No. 84), that its limited and enumerated powers prevented the government from threatening the "unalienable Rights" of the citizenry. Any listing of those rights might imply a government's prerogative to regulate and usurp those not mentioned and could cast doubt on the "doctrine of enumerated powers" itself.

Many anti-Federalists, on the other hand, hoped to destroy the Constitution altogether and return the nation to the Articles of Confederation. They were not at all convinced that the new and experimental Constitution would serve the best interests of the nation. At the very least, they were unwilling to leave the protection of the Rights of Englishmen to mere inference. George Mason, whose "Declaration of Rights" for the state of Virginia had so influenced the writing of the Declaration of Independence, refused to sign off on the Constitution because of its lack of clear intent in this regard. He was supported by Thomas Jefferson and Patrick Henry who also demanded a specific statement of rights. To counter their objections and ensure ratification by nine (three-quarters) of the states, Madison promised a Bill of Rights and promptly introduced it into the 1st Congress assembled under the Constitution in 1789. Of the more than one hundred proposed amendments submitted by the States, twelve received the required two-thirds vote in Congress and were sent back to the states for approval. Ten of these received the required three-quarters vote by the states and became our Bill of Rights. As Madison had intended from the beginning, the ten amendments in no way altered the governmental structure set in place by the Constitution. They supposedly no more than clarified the limits of power and responsibilities of the new national government.

Politicians are only human. Like Charles I and George III and all other philosopher-kings, they lust for power supposedly to do good. But the nobility of their goals is surpassed only by their ignorance of the consequences. Fortunately for the future of America, such power was not theirs to exercise. "Let no more be said about confidence in men," wrote Jefferson, "but bind them down from mischief with the chains of the Constitution." And in the hands of Jefferson, Madison, Monroe, Jackson and most other Presidents of the 19th century, the Constitution did just that. That its proscriptions worked so well enabled the new nation to avoid the chronic disease of "leftwandering" that was the ruination of so many other nascent republics. As the Fathers knew, "enumerated powers" implies limited government and a maximum of individual freedom, just the condition required for the emergence of the American chaon. Americans, more so than any other of the world's peoples, were free to decide, free to spend, free to create, free to invest, free to discover, free to implement, and free to amass all the real and financial assets they desired. A decidedly unfashionable policy it may have been, but it produced a nation that was to become, in the words of Adam Smith, "the greatest and most formidable that ever was in the world."

CHAPTER XIV

OF DEBTS, DUTIES, AND TAXES: THE INVISIBLE HAND VERSUS THE BENIGN DICTATOR

Money is coined liberty.

Fyodor Dostoevsky, "House of the Dead"

To do good is noble. But to teach others to do good is more noble – and much easier.

Mark Twain

America's gamble on minimal government, begun with the Articles of Confederation, continued under the Constitution. And make no mistake, for a gamble it was, and one generally recognized as such. It could hardly have been an oversight that the Constitution itself makes no mention of the union of states as a permanent entity. If it had, it would never have been adopted. The Founders and the states they represented were well aware of the risks attendant to a strengthened central government and the possibly oppressive consequences it might engender. In any event, the states played it cautiously. The legislatures of New York, Rhode Island and Virginia, when ratifying the Constitution, specifically reserved the right to take back the powers granted to the federal government if matters did not work out, and the other states did so by implication. "It is safe to say," wrote statesman and author Henry Cabot Lodge (1850-1924) in his book, *Life of Webster*, "that there is not a man in the country, from Washington and Hamilton to Clinton and Mason, who did not regard the new system as an experiment from which each and every State had a right to peaceably withdraw." It was a view held by most until the Civil War was to prove them wrong. It is surely significant that no Confederate leader was ever brought to trial for treason, a trial that could have brought forth a verdict on the constitutionality of secession.

When in 1788 New Hampshire became the ninth state to ratify, the venerable Continental Congress declared the Constitution in effect and endorsed the first federal elections for the House of Representatives. On 4 March 1789, the 1st Congress convened at Federal Hall in New York City. Comprised of 65 Representatives and 26 Senators, it began the long and costly process of fleshing out the new government. With a robust prosperity carrying over from

Articles of Confederation days, circumstances could hardly have been more favorable: harvests were bountiful; lumber, iron goods, furs and tobacco were in demand at home and abroad, and there was almost no government involvement in financial and commercial affairs. The American chaon was working out most favorably. So smoothly went the work of the 1st Congress that Jefferson could only express his amazement at finding that "the opposition to our new Constitution has almost totally disappeared." There were many procedural details to attend to: the election of a Speaker and Clerk for the House of Representatives, a Senator *pro tempore* and Secretary for the Senate, establishing rules of order, validating the credentials of all the new Representatives and Senators, administering oaths of office, the establishment of executive departments, the creation of the Supreme Court and other inferior courts, confirming Presidential appointments, protocol, and the certification of the Electoral College election of George Washington as President and John Adams as Vice-President. But the primary order of business was funding the new government. And according to Article I, Section 7, Clause 1: "All bills for raising revenue shall originate in the House of Representatives; but the Senate may propose or concur with amendments as on other bills." The House quickly decided that the least oppressive tax was a duty on imports. No politician wished to risk a tax revolt and possibly his head at the very birth of the new nation. There followed a long and arduous debate on what to tax and how much. Of great concern to the 1st Congress was the Constitutional requirement of uniformity, that the duties imposed would bear equally on all parts of the country. Smuggling and the protection of American commercial and business interests from foreign competition also came in for considerable discussion. What finally emerged was "A bill for laying a duty on goods, wares, and merchandises, imported into the United States." And in the end none of wrangling mattered because nobody could take offense at the small duties imposed (5% ad valorem in most cases). In practical terms, considering the wide geographical extent of the country and its diversity of interests, only by keeping duties (and government spending) negligibly small compared to the private economy could uniformity have been approached and smuggling contained. Regrettably, this maxim was to be forgotten over succeeding decades. Capitulating to pressure from Northern industrial interests, Congress would soon impose ever higher tariffs on importations, to a point at which the agrarian South felt threatened with impoverishment. This massive violation of the "uniform" clause was to become the major cause of the Civil War.

Enter once again Alexander Hamilton, now in power as the newly appointed Secretary of the Treasury. In short order, he issues a *Report on Public Credit*, a proposal for a monopolistic government-sponsored bank, a proposal for a non-uniform excise tax, a *Report on Manufactures*, and a conjuring up of a government-blessed Society for Establishing Useful Manufactures (SEUM). "To be ruled by a busybody is more than human nature can bear," was how English historian Thomas Babington Macaulay characterized power-lusting politicians, and in Hamilton America got a busybody *extraordinaire*. Almost everything he proposed did nothing so much as involve politicians and bureaucrats in private affairs and retard America's astounding growth. A stout supporter of "enumerated powers" before taking office, he is about to switch allegiance and introduce the first Humpty-Dumpty construction of the Constitution, the so-called doctrine of "implied powers." This he defines as follows in his *Report on Public Credit*: "If the end [the noble goal of a proposed act of Congress] be clearly comprehended within any of the specified powers, and *if the measure have an obvious relation to that end* [italics mine], and is not forbidden by any particular provision of the Constitution, it may safely be deemed to come within the compass of the national authority." Or, putting that mouthful into plain English, the end justifies the means. Or, paraphrasing Louis XIV, "it's legal because it's noble." But let us not be misled by Hamilton's language. "Implied powers" implies the oxymoron of benign dictatorship; reinterpret the Constitution so as to bequeath to politicians all the power they think they need to do good. That is what Hamilton is really saying. As newborn "chaosticians," we can surely recognize the fallacy in Hamilton's line of reasoning: A law that has an obvious relation to what it hopes to achieve is a rare event in a world dominated by chaos. There is a chaotic gap between noble intentions and general welfare, and those means to some desired end lead all too often to tyrannical consequences. Hamilton's report is the first of many future initiatives to create a big central government unbound "from mischief by the chains of the Constitution." And so it seems to be whenever men attain power.

In his *Report on Public Credit*, Hamilton proposes his idea of a sound fiscal policy that will *ensure the survival and prosperity* of the United States. I stress here that even Hamilton implicitly supports the anti-Federalists in their contention that America was doing very well under the Articles of Confederation and these needed little fixing. Be that as it may, Hamilton favors the funding and assumption by the new government of both the federal and state Revolutionary War debts at full value, not at the existing depreciated market value of ten to twenty cents on the dollar. The total amount, he estimates, would stand at $79 million including interest. This he intends to do by replacing the old debt with new 6% and 3% long-term government bonds, these to become the first major issues of publicly traded securities. "Funding" and "assumption," he believes, will substantially raise the credit rating of the new government enabling it to borrow (and spend) more easily in the future. The power of government "to pay the Debts of the United States" is clearly specified in the Constitution (Article I, Section 8, Clause 1 and Article VI, Clause 1) and no argument need arise on this point. That is so, I suppose, even though Hamilton's assistant, William Duer, had leaked his plans both to politicians and Northern speculators, enabling them to buy up old debt certificates at very discounted prices before the news spread. Wrote a critical Senator William Maclay from Pennsylvania: "Nor have the members [of Congress] themselves kept their hands clean from this dirty work. ... Henceforth, we may consider speculation as a congressional employment." And seventy-five years later, matters hadn't changed much. Mark Twain could still write: "It can probably be proven by facts and figures that there exists no native American criminal class, except Congress."

But Virginia and North Carolina had already redeemed most of their Revolutionary War debt, and other states were in the process of doing so. By 1786, New York, Pennsylvania and Maryland had assumed nearly $9 million of debt securities by exchanging them for new state IOU's. And they were doing so at existing market value. That not only cut the cost of redemption considerably but deprived speculators, who now owned most of the paper, of exorbitant profits. When southern Congressmen balked at funding and assumption, the bill's chances of passage appeared slim. Not until Hamilton had logrolled an agreement with Madison and Jefferson to locate the new nation's capital further to the south on the Potomac River was the bill narrowly passed and signed by Washington. The close vote displayed the first hint of divergence between Northern moneyed interests and Southern planters.

The strong central government now favored by Hamilton required revenues far above those needed under the Articles of Confederation. There were rentals to be paid for the Treasury's new offices on lower Broadway in Manhattan and other government buildings; federal payrolls to be met for Senators, Congressmen, clerks, bookkeepers, auditors, customs collectors, port wardens, a coast guard and military personnel; bills to be met for furniture, lighthouses, beacons and buoys; salaries for the staffers of Treasury, State, and War, three new departments created by Congress; and interest to be paid on the new debt issued under "funding and assumption." Hamilton moved with alacrity. On 4 September 1789, the day after his confirmation as Secretary of the Treasury by the Senate, he negotiated a $50,000 loan from the Bank of New York, established in 1784, and another from the Bank of North America, the first commercial bank in America established in 1781.

Hamilton knew that customs duties could not possibly cover all the burgeoning expenses of the new government. He also knew that levying a general internal tax at the federal level could instigate rebellion or possible secession by the states. To remedy this deficiency, he proposed the chartering of a government-sponsored private bank to be known as the Bank of the United States. Modeled after William Paterson's Bank of England and "Fund for Perpetual Interest," the new monetary arrangement "will be very conducive to the successful conducting of the national finances; will tend to give facility to the obtaining of loans, for the use of the government, in sudden emergencies; and will be productive of considerable advantages to trade and industry in general," according to the preamble of the bill authorizing its establishment. In simple terms, such a bank would provide, as it had in England, Holland and France, the means of financing government through borrowings rather than taxes, operations that avoided taxpayer scrutiny and lessened the chances of a tax revolt. It would as well redistribute the nation's wealth to the wealthy.

But now we have a matter fundamentally different from "funding and assumption" because chartering a bank or any other corporation is not one of the enumerated powers. In fact, a proposal that Congress be empowered to "grant charters of incorporation" had been rejected at the Constitutional Convention. Was the Constitution to be deconstructed from birth by, again quoting from a now forgetful Hamilton in The *Federalist* (No.73), "that inconstancy and mutability in the laws which form the greatest blemish in the character and genius of our governments?" Was it right from the beginning to be transfigured into a document that, as noted by Jefferson, "permitted Congress to take everything under their management which they should deem for the public welfare?"

Hamilton justified the Bank by invoking Article I, Section 8, Clause 18 of the Constitution, what is known as the "sweeping" or "elastic" clause: The *Congress shall have the power to make all laws which shall be necessary and proper for carrying into execution the foregoing* [enumerated] *powers, and all other powers vested by this Constitution in the government of the United States, or in any department or officer thereof.* In his opinion, the clause justified the "implied powers" interpretation of the Constitution as opposed to "enumerated powers." But his view was vehemently opposed by both Federalists and anti-Federalists alike, including Madison, Jefferson, Benjamin Franklin, Patrick Henry and newly Congress, *"it is a grant of particular powers only, leaving the general mass* [of powers] *in other hands.* So it had been understood by its friends and its foes, and so it was to be interpreted" [italics mine]. Madison knew his English, which is more than I can say about many of today's lawmakers, judges, lawyers and journalists. "When men give power, they know not what they give," cautioned Patrick Henry. And Jefferson, chiming in against the Bank after making known his position to Washington: "That it was a fact, as certainly known as that he and I were then conversing, that particular members of the legislature, while those laws [funding and assumption] were on the carpet, had feathered their nests with paper, had then voted for the laws, and constantly since lent all the energy of their talents and instrumentality of their offices to the establishment and enlargement of this system [the proposed Bank]. That they had chained it about our necks for a great length of time [the Bank was to be chartered for twenty years], and, in order to keep the game in their hands, had from time to time aided in making such legislative constructions of the Constitution as made it a very different thing from what the people thought they had submitted to. That they had now brought forward a proposition far beyond every one ever yet advanced, and to which the eyes of many were turned as the decision which was to let us know whether we live under a limited or an unlimited government." appointed Attorney-General Edmund Randolph, all of whom concurred in the belief that implied powers were inadmissible. To Madison, such a use of the "necessary and proper" clause established an unwarranted and dangerous precedent. In The *Federalist* (No. 41), he points out that the powers granted to Congress in Section 8 are contained in a single sentence, its eighteen paragraphs separated by semicolons. Such usage of punctuation clearly identifies the lead power granted in the Constitution – "To … provide for the … general Welfare of the United States" – as a general power subject to the specific powers immediately following: "It is not a general grant, out of which particular powers are excepted," Madison goes on to say in a speech to the 1st

The fallacy inherent in "implied powers" shows clearly in the Bank issue. It is not at all like establishing a customs service (also not mentioned in the Constitution) to collect tariff revenues or an army to provide for the "common defence," for example. Repeating Hamilton's summation: "If the end [the noble goal of a proposed act of Congress] be clearly comprehended within any of the specified powers, and *if the measure have an obvious relation to that end* [italics mine], and is not forbidden by any particular provision of the Constitution, it may safely be deemed to come within the compass of the national authority." Where, we might ask, is the "obvious relation" between the establishment of a huge government-sponsored bank and "the successful conducting of the national finances" or the realization "of considerable advantages to trade and industry in general," or for that matter the nation's goal of "Power, Consequence, and Grandeur." Such a link between hope and reality implies the ability of some person or persons to forecast the economic future with reasoned accuracy and, thereby, to comprehend the consequences of current actions. Such prescience did not exist then, and it does not exist today. All we have here are noble intentions in the pursuit of which the Bank of the United States, like the Bank of England and all other central banks, inflicted great harm on their national economies. "Enumerated powers" sharply delimits the powers of a central government in order to avoid chaotic unpredictability, the consequences of which can be nationwide in scope. Even though unable to cast the idea into words, most Founding Fathers understood instinctively how "butterfly" decisions could magnify into national disasters when too much power is entrusted into too few hands. They relied heavily on experience in granting to the central government just those powers which had in the past proved helpful rather than harmful, "leaving the general mass [of powers] in other hands." In this way, any great harm resulting from apparently insignificant mistakes and minor miscalculations by policy makers would be limited to a single state or to local communities. That is the substance of the objections lodged by Madison, Jefferson and Henry. Only three major central-bank type institutions were available for comparison at the time of the Convention – Amsterdam's Wisselbank, the Bank of England and John Law's bank in early 17th century France – and the chaotic and inflationary consequences resulting from these debacles could hardly inspire confidence in another such scheme.

Congress procrastinated. Not until after Franklin's death in 1790 was Hamilton able to persuade a majority of lawmakers to pass the necessary legislation. Washington, after many weeks of agonizing indecision, sided with Hamilton and signed the authorization bill. The 1st Bank of the United States, America's first "merchant of debt," thus became the initial salvo in a concerted attack on the doctrine of "enumerated powers" and its protective value against chaos.

On 4 July 1791, Presidential appointees opened an office in Philadelphia and conducted by far largest initial public offering ever witnessed up until that time. Subscribers to the Bank's authorized capital of $10 million bought stock priced at $400 per share and paid for it in gold and silver (at least ¼ of the total) and/or that part of the public debt (government bonds) bearing interest at 6%. Initially, "scrip" was sold, each unit giving a buyer the right to purchase 1/16 of a share at $25 per scrip. Twenty percent of the stock had been reserved for the federal government and eighty percent for private individuals. The government paid for its share with government bonds having exempted itself from the "¼" requirement. It immediately borrowed its $2 million back using the same convenient recipe: Print up more IOU's (bonds), deposit them with the Bank and get not stock but spendable bank notes in return. Suddenly, there was an additional $2 million floating around the country to be spent by politicians and bureaucrats rather than by private people. As stated in the preamble to the authorization law, the Bank "will tend to give facility to the obtaining of loans." Facility to whom? Why, the politicians of course! The public nationwide is ultimately liable for both the interest on the bonds held by the Bank and their redemption. A pipeline had been created that channeled money from taxpayer pockets to the Bank's stockholders, a few hundred composed mostly of politicians and rich folk in the northeast who were all too happy to receive the tax-secured 8.4% dividend paid regularly. Small wonder that so many people were upset! The Bank had become the first hallmark of big government, private reward and public risk.

So huge was the demand for scrip that the price surged from $25 to over $300 before falling back to $150, all within days. Much of the buying had been done with specie borrowed from state-chartered banks (there were at the time five large commercial banks) using as collateral the government bonds issued in the "funding and assumption" operation. When the scrip price fell, the banks covered their outstanding paper by dumping the bonds on the market to get back their specie, sending prices into free fall. The Bank's intrusion overwhelmed the financial markets and exacerbated to frightening levels the natural fluctuations to be expected in a random-walk economy. Hamilton now sought to calm the storm. He tried to support prices by buying government bonds in the open market. Such purchases, he hoped, would tend to stabilize as well the prices of the Bank's securities. Like a modern central banker, he had become the nation's "designated gambler" trying to forecast and control economic swings. Prices eventually stabilized, whether due to market forces or Hamilton's puny amount of buying ($150,000 worth of bonds out of almost $80,000,000 outstanding) who knows. Since government bonds never fell below their issue price at par ($100), Hamilton had to pay more for them. He therefore lost money on the transactions since the bonds were redeemable at maturity only at par. All losses, of course, were charged to the nation's taxpayers. The stage had been set. Again and again in the future, and at unpredictable intervals, government intercessions such as this into the financial markets would cause untold mischief, the next to occur just one year later.

And what did the people get for their money? They got what was by far the largest enterprise in America, a government-sponsored Goliath able to control the entire fiscal structure of the country. Right from its beginning, economic carnage beset the new nation. The specie payments demanded for stock in the huge new enterprise depressed deposits in other parts of the country forcing banks to call in loans. These actions – just how we shall soon learn – caused money to self-destruct, leaving an insufficient amount to carry on normal business operations. Suddenly, as described by Thomas Jefferson, "Ships are lying at the wharves, buildings are stopped, capitals are withdrawn from commerce, manufactures, arts, and agriculture to be employed in gambling, and the tide of public prosperity almost unparalleled in any country is arrested in its course …"

Supporters of the Bank touted the monopolistic advantages of this embryonic central bank. As the government's fiscal agent, the Bank could conduct deposit, loan, transfer and payment operations throughout the country. Its notes would be convertible into specie and circulate at full face value much like today's checks and paper dollars. And unlike other bank notes, they could be used to pay taxes, import duties and excises.

But let us not be deceived. These very routine operations could and would be handled in the future far more economically by a free banking system than by a monopolistic, government-sponsored Bank. And, as many Founding Fathers knew, the unintended and harmful consequences of the Bank's monopoly position could easily outweigh any achievements it might claim. Firstly, it opened the door to central government involvement in the money and credit markets, the primary cause of future business panics. Secondly, it had the potential of acting as a monetary printing press for use by politicians whenever public approval of higher taxes was not forthcoming. In its 20-year history, the Bank's loans to government amounted to $13,500,000, a very large sum for the time. It was money that could have been raised through taxes or state-chartered banks only with difficulty if at all. The only justification for such exorbitant borrowing, of course, is the dubious notion that politicians know best how to spend the people's money. Thirdly, it inhibited the opening of competitive regional banks more attuned to local developments than the Philadelphia monolith. As the depository for government funds on which it paid no interest, the 1st Bank held a great competitive advantage over those banks. Specie tended to flow from the West and South to the East leaving behind a trail of debtors unable to meet their obligations. In effect, the Bank's commanding presence and government sponsorship tended to block the emergence of an efficient, free banking chaon. And fourthly, the Bank's stockholders and governors became the de facto regulators of the economy, a "moneyed aristocracy" whose crystal balls enabled them to see into the future and do good – and to severe consequences nationwide whenever misguided policy actions were adopted. We shall come to understand how fortunate it was that America grew strongly despite the harm wreaked by this oligarchy. Just one year after the wild market fluctuations marking the 1st Bank's establishment, there erupted the Panic of 1792, a prototype of the many recessions and depressions to come. (Modern usage has successively euphemized the word "panic" to depression, recession and slowdown.) Here's the situation. We have the 1st Bank sitting astride the country's credit markets with its authorized capital of $10 million, including 20% of the nation's total specie by some accounts. The Bank now proceeds to accept deposits on which it hopes to get an adequate return for its stockholders. To do so, the Bank must negotiate loans to credit worthy customers. As with any banking institution, its main income derives from interest on such loans. In simple terms, suppose the Bank has $100 in gold deposited in its vaults and a customer walks in desiring to borrow $900. If the loan is approved, the customer gives his or her IOU to the Bank and walks out credited with a deposit of $900. The Bank has in effect *created nine hundred dollars of new money*. It now has total deposit liabilities of $1000 that can be withdrawn as bank notes or gold and spent by its depositors. And it has only $100 in total specie to cover them! Economists then ascribe to the Bank a "reserve ratio" of 10%. This is an example of *fractional reserve banking*, and it has increased the amount of money available for spending by an extra $900, *an amount that consists only of bookkeeping entries represented by the new deposit*. In the unlikely event that both the new and original depositors try to redeem all bank notes for gold simultaneously, our Bank would have on its hands a "bank run" and be forced to suspend redemption of its notes. But banks had long since discovered that a reserve ratio of only one or two per cent was more than adequate for daily business purposes since on any given day deposits and redemptions tended to balance each other out. The stated policy of the 1st Bank was to hold an outlandishly high 40% or more specie in reserve as compared to the 10%-25% of most banks at the time. Modern American banks hold reserves of 10% to 15%, and the reserves are *not* gold and silver or any other commodity; they are just more paper in the form of Federal Reserve notes. Clearly, the 1st Bank's reserve policy made loans much too difficult to obtain. Its huge presence in the national economy, therefore, kept money too tight and "last-straw" interest rates too high. As a consequence, the burgeoning loan demand of a vibrantly expanding economy could not be properly met. Borrowing costs were pushed beyond the means of too many people hoping to become productive citizens as farmers, merchants and businessmen. Most farmers and businessmen of the time were all too aware of the Bank's unduly restrictive policies.

A chain reaction may begin when our Bank's depositors spend the notes for personal and business purposes. Sooner or later the notes are deposited either in other banks or the 1st Bank itself. These secondary banks know only that they have more money on deposit; they do not know where it came from. And they attempt to loan it out, issuing new notes in the process. If they do, the amount of money available for spending, the money supply, increases again. Then there are the tertiary banks doing the same, and so on down the line until some minimum reserve requirement is reached. A multiplying factor on the money supply has developed that is contingent on each bank's reserve ratio. Obviously, a small amount of gold can create a huge supply of money, as long as people have confidence in the banking system.

Exactly the opposite happens when the originating loan matures or is called in. Unless that loan is replaced by a new one, the money supply must contract as the lending bank pulls notes out of circulation and loses deposits. (Remember that the IOUs representing the loans had been added to bank deposits). An implosion of the money supply now ensues as all the subsidiary banks in the chain recall loans. What happened in 1792 was a sudden policy reversal by the 1st Bank. After flooding the market with notes during its first year of operation and accepting those of other banks for payments, the Bank called in government and commercial loans and demanded specie redemption of notes from the state banks. Hamilton's expensive programs were mushrooming the federal debt to levels too uncomfortable for acceptance by the 1st Bank's president, Thomas Willing, and the board of directors. Because of its huge presence, most regional banks also had to terminate lending activities so as to maintain reserves at an acceptable level. Suddenly, a lot of money, as represented by those bookkeeping entries, simply vanished and too little flowed in the nation's economic arteries to nourish the business environment. Consumer spending dropped; tariff revenues contracted; payrolls could not be met; many leading merchants and banks went bankrupt; unemployment rose sharply; and the Wall Street market in government bonds plummeted by 20% over a two month period – a very large-for-the-time $3 million loss to holders, more than the total savings of all New Yorkers.

Fortunately, this "Panic of 1792" proved short-lived and America's economic growth resumed quickly. Hard money from strong exports and foreign investments in America's emerging markets quickly dissipated the downturn. Europeans were very much aware of and all too eager to invest in America's great growth potential. Helping to restore confidence were the more orderly markets in bank and government securities established by two dozen brokers on 17 May 1792. The rules of trading they drew up in the shade of a buttonwood tree on Wall Street laid the foundation for what became the New York Stock Exchange in 1817.

By 1795, Hamilton's spending had magnified the government's debt to the point where interest payments on it were climbing toward 55% of total expenditures. Tariff collections, accounting for 90% of federal revenues, could not keep up forcing Hamilton to resort to repeated bank borrowings. To maintain reserves at acceptable levels, the 1st Bank and the state-chartered banks had to keep interest rates high tending to "crowd out" the private sector of the economy. As we have learned, that is the *modus operandi* of all central banks: Throttle down the public's freedom to spend in favor of inefficient government spending.

Banks concentrate money in time and space and make it available for promoting "all the valuable arts of mankind," noted one John Brown, a leading Providence merchant in 1791 (Klebaner, *American Commercial Banking – A History*, Twayne Publishers, 1990). That view was well recognized all over the new nation, as did the need for centering wealth locally lest it drain away to other towns and states. Regional bank formations, as a result, accelerated. There were 5 state-chartered banks when the 1st Bank of the United States opened in 1791. By 1816, the year the 2nd Bank of the United States began operations, there were 246. By 1832, there were almost 400. And when it became clear in 1832 that President Andrew Jackson opposed renewal of the 2nd Bank's charter, the number of state-incorporated and private banks doubled in the short span of five years and doubled again by 1860 to over 1500. The American public well understood that a multiplicity of small banks better served the nation than one huge monopoly.

Hamilton's program also implements an excise tax to help defray the costs of the "funding and assumption" operation and the government's 1st Bank investment. Acting like George III before him, Hamilton looks around for somebody to tax without creating too much of a furor. Having relegated the "doctrine of enumerated powers" to the scrap heap, he is now about to violate two more of the Constitution's strictures – uniformity in taxation and the prohibition on non-apportioned direct taxes. If "implied powers" gives Congress the power to legislate at its pleasure, non-uniformity gives Congress the power to tax at its pleasure. But, as we might now suspect, Hamilton lives to see his noble intentions come to unanticipated ends. The nation gets the first of many tax rebellions, the birth of political parties, the demise of Federalist power in America, the rise to the Presidency of his arch enemy, Thomas Jefferson, and an end to internal taxation at the national level.

Hamilton sets his sights on Western grain farmers, those beyond the Appalachians, many of whom used a large portion of their crop for the distillation of whiskey. Not only did "spirituous liquors" bring higher prices, they were more easily transported over the mountains to eastern markets. Because of the relatively small number of distillers and their lack of political clout, Hamilton recommends an exorbitant 25% excise tax on estimated whiskey production (7 cents per gallon on a market price of 28 cents), the amount to be determined by revenue officers guessing at the total productive capacity of each individual still. The tax placed a heavy burden on frontier farmers engaged in scratching out a living in the face of harsh weather conditions and constant threats from rapacious Indians. Most would have been forced into bankruptcy had they fully complied with such a tax. What made matters worse was a lack of acceptable money with which to pay the taxes since most business in the hinterland was conducted by barter. Also, as noted by Virginia Congressman Jonathan Parker in a prescient speech opposing the bill: "It will let loose a swarm of harpies, who, under the domination of revenue officers, will range through the country, prying into every man's house and affairs, and like a Macedonian phalanx bear down all before them." Did he foresee, perhaps dimly, the future income tax? Rebellion and possible secession worried many other observers.

It looked like easy money, and a tax on "spirituous liquors" became law in 1791 with few Congressional dissenters. Opposition to the tax developed immediately necessitating a new and costly bureaucracy to collect the tax. In what became known as the "Whiskey Rebellion," revenue officers were tarred and feathered, threatened with their lives, and driven out of town, much like the experience of British tax collectors twenty years earlier. Many who paid the tax found their stills destroyed. Sympathetic local juries exonerated tax dodgers and no attempt was made to tax stills in other states. Governor Thomas Mifflin of Pennsylvania, a signer of the Constitution, refused Washington's request to quell the uprising by calling out the militia. Thomas McKean, chief justice of the state supreme court, denied the right of the federal government to use force in Pennsylvania. There were persistent calls for Pennsylvania to secede from the Union, a harbinger of times to come. In 1794, Washington issued a proclamation ordering an end to all resistance by the end of September. Governor Mifflin finally acceded and called out the Pennsylvania militia, but no one reported. In a face-saving move, Washington and Hamilton led a militia of some 13,000 men from four neighboring states into western Pennsylvania and arrested twenty leaders of the revolt, all of whom Washington later pardoned. Little tax money was ever collected and in 1801, President Thomas Jefferson ended *all* internal taxation at the federal level. For the next 113 years, years of unbelievably powerful economic growth, the American government would support itself in the main solely by consumption taxes, the tariff collections.

To western grain farmers, Hamilton had betrayed the Constitution. Where was the uniformity in the whiskey tax? Tobacco farmers were not taxed. Cotton farmers were not taxed, nor were vegetable and dairy farmers. And what about the Constitutional prohibition on direct taxes? Here was a direct tax on personal property, the "spirituous liquor" inventory of each individual farmer, and it was unapportioned. Neither of these questions was answered by a judiciary sworn to uphold the Constitution, and the issue of tax uniformity was to come up again and again in the years to come when Southern planters pressured their states to secede from the Union.

Many historians treat Washington's decisive action in quelling the Whiskey Rebellion as a demonstration of the new central government's power to enforce the law. It was hardly that. What it did demonstrate was that the new government could set aside questions of constitutionality whenever politicians thought they needed money. This revolt was but the first of many to come in which courageous citizens stood up for their Constitutional rights. True, the farmers capitulated in the face of military encounter and out of their love and respect for George Washington. But they achieved their goal, as did Mahatma Gandhi and Martin Luther King later, through what Henry David Thoreau called "civil disobedience" and eventually through the ballot box. Many of their leaders, Albert Gallatin in particular, were to become influential in future administrations.

"When men give power, they know not what they give" had been Patrick Henry's comment on the new and strengthening central government and his insight now came to the fore. Once laid down on parchment, words can be either ignored or subjected to Humpty-Dumpty-type meanings by nobly-intentioned crusaders. Hamilton's "implied powers" doctrine led right from the beginning not only to novel excesses in Constitutional interpretation but to tyrannical legislation just a few years hence. We can only wonder whether the Hamilton of The *Federalist Papers*, the personage who had argued so powerfully for "enumerated powers" and uniformity in taxation, identifies with the power-lusting Hamilton of Treasury fame.

The final part of Hamilton's fiscal program, set forth in his "Report on Manufactures", proposes protective tariffs to shield Northern manufacturers from foreign competition. Again, we have the noble intentions and the presumption that politicians have the foresight to single out those sectors of the private economy worthy of subsidy. As a tax – and make no mistake, a protective tariff is a tax paid by the public in the form of higher prices – it stands in violation of the Constitution's "uniform" clause. Although rejected by the 1st Congress under the leadership of Madison, protectionism was eventually to play the decisive role in dividing the country into opposed Northern and Southern camps. As for SEUM, as we shall see, it ended in disaster for its stockholders.

Hamilton's policies occasioned a deep philosophical split in American thinking out of which arose the first political parties. Was the governing basis of the new nation to be a Constitution of "enumerated powers" and limited government – often called "strict construction" – as championed by Jefferson and Madison and the budding Democratic-Republican Party? Or was it to be one of "implied powers" as advocated by Washington, Hamilton and John Adams, the leaders of the Federalist Party? And once again, America's future course "seems to have been guided by some token of providential agency." For how lucky we were to get a George Washington at the beginning of our republic, and, when he succumbed to the benign dictator syndrome, an Adam Smith messiah in the guise of Thomas Jefferson!

CHAPTER XV

THE TYRANNY OF IMPLIED POWERS
MAKES ITS FIRST APPEARANCE

It is seldom that liberty of any kind is lost all at once. Slavery has so frightful an aspect to men accustomed to freedom that it must steal in upon them by degrees and must disguise itself in a thousand shapes in order to be received.

David Hume: "Of the Liberty of the Press" 1742

"Congress shall make no law …" So begins the first of the ten amendments to the Constitution known as the Bill of Rights. And keeping in mind Hamilton's warning in The *Federalist* (No.73) – "the injury which may possibly be done by defeating a few good laws will be amply compensated by the advantage of preventing a number of bad ones" – maybe the Amendment should have ended right there. But to continue: "Congress shall make no law respecting an establishment of religion, or prohibiting the free exercise thereof; or abridging the freedom of speech, or of the press; or the right of the people peaceably to assemble, and to petition the government for a redress of grievances." The language seems clear and understandable enough, you would think. Yet, less than seven years after the Amendment's ratification by three-fourths of the states, the tyranny feared by so many rears its ugly head. John Adams is now President, having narrowly beaten out Thomas Jefferson in the electoral college vote of 1796. A Federalist-controlled Congress passes and Adams signs into law the Alien and Sedition Acts of 1798. The Alien Act extends the residence time required for immigrants to become citizens from five to fourteen years, and it also authorizes the President to hold and deport aliens at his whim. Section 1 of the Sedition Act restricts freedom of assembly, but it is under Section 2 that the main action transpires: "*And be it farther enacted,* That if any person shall write, print, utter or publish, or cause or procure to be written, printed, uttered or published, or shall knowingly and willingly assist or aid in writing, printing, uttering or publishing any false, scandalous and malicious writing or writings against the government of the United States, or either house of the Congress of the United States, or the President of the United States, with intent to defame the said government, or either house of the said Congress, or the said President, or to bring them, or either of them, into contempt or disrepute; or to excite against them, or either or any of them, the hatred of the good people of the United States, or to stir up sedition within the United States, or to excite any unlawful combinations therein, for opposing or resisting any law of the United States, or any act of the President of the United States, done in pursuance of any such law, or of the powers in vested by the constitution of the United States, or to resist, oppose, or defeat any such law or act, or to aid, encourage or abet any hostile designs of any foreign nation against the United States, their people or government, then such person, being thereof convicted before any court of the United States having jurisdiction thereof, shall be punished by a fine not exceeding two thousand dollars, and by imprisonment not exceeding two years."

Does that read like freedom of speech and freedom of the press? Hardly! It's exactly the tyranny one expects under a dictatorship, a law that criminalizes these freedoms. Under Section 2 of the Sedition Act, twenty-five newspaper editors were jailed and their papers shut down for publishing "false, scandalous and malicious" news and opinion. Included among them was Benjamin Franklin Bache, a grandson of Benjamin Franklin and editor of the Philadelphia *Aurora*, who was charged with writing inflammatory articles libeling President Adams. Like his grandfather, Bache was a strong advocate of "enumerated powers" and in his editorials persistently denounced the Federalist policies of Hamilton and Adams. Unfortunately, this promising Republican leader died of yellow fever at age 29 while awaiting trial.

And how did the Supreme Court react to these egregious violations of the "unalienable Rights" guaranteed to us under the 1st Amendment? It actively supported the Sedition Act and the imprisonment of its violators. Perhaps an English reading test, based on the Constitution, should be administered to all public servants, and that holds true even more so today. In any event, it remained for Jefferson to pardon all those convicted under the Sedition Act when he became President in 1801. Nobody had been prosecuted under the Alien Act.

Two states took great exception to the Alien and Sedition Acts. On 16 November 1798, the Kentucky legislature passed "The Kentucky Resolutions." This beautifully written document, and a similar one approved by the Virginia legislature, puts forth a definitive statement of the "doctrine of enumerated powers" and the right of a state to *nullify* unilaterally any act of the federal government it deems unconstitutional: "…where powers are assumed [by the federal government] which have not been delegated, a nullification of the act is the rightful remedy: that every State has a natural right in cases not within the compact (*casus non fœderus*) [the Constitution] to nullify of their own authority all assumptions of power by others within their limits: that without this right, they would be under the dominion, absolute and unlimited, of whosoever might exercise this right of judgment for them … ." And in the Virginia Resolutions: " …the General Assembly [of Virginia] does solemnly appeal to the like dispositions of the other states, in confidence that they will concur with this commonwealth in declaring, as it does hereby declare, that the acts aforesaid [the Alien and Sedition Acts] are unconstitutional." Clearly, the authors of these Resolutions had no use for tenured, tax-supported judges as guardians of our "unalienable Rights." To them, the judiciary equated with a federal fox guarding the chicken coop of American freedoms. Although given short shrift by most historians, these Resolutions stand with the Declaration of Independence as ringing proclamations of the supremacy of human rights over and above any government's presumption of overriding interests. The author of "The Kentucky Resolutions" remained anonymous until 1821, when it was revealed to be none other than the then Vice-President of the United States, Thomas Jefferson. His fellow Virginian, Congressman James Madison, authored the related version known as "The Virginia Resolutions." Aside from establishing "enumerated powers" as the guiding light of most administrations for the next hundred years, these documents placed nullification squarely on the table. Under "implied powers," almost any goal is certifiable as noble. According to the Federalists, the Alien and Sedition Acts were passed as wartime emergency measures to unify the country and combat espionage, even though no war had been declared and none developed. In one of those chaotic bifurcations so typical of human history, France, our former ally in the Revolutionary War, posed somewhat of a threat. In 1795 John Jay had negotiated a "Treaty of Amity, Commerce and Navigation between His Britannic Majesty and the United States of America, by their President" that resolved many of the unsettled problems arising out of the Treaty of Paris in 1783. But the French, involved in yet another of their innumerable wars with England, regarded Jay's Treaty as discriminatory and a betrayal of their support and friendship. By seizing American ships, French privateers provoked an undeclared naval action that threatened to escalate. Even the possibility of invasion was bruited about. But, to the chagrin of intensely pro-British Federalists led by Hamilton, full-scale war was averted when Adams cosigned with France a commercial treaty known as the "Convention of 1800."

To Jefferson and most Republicans, on the other hand, the Alien and Sedition Acts were intended to shore up a deteriorating Federalist hold on the national government: The Alien Acts sought to delay citizenship and voting rights to immigrants, most of whom became Republicans, while the Sedition Act attempted to squelch steadily mounting criticism of Federalist policies. Edmund Randolph had even gone so far as to assert that Washington had become merely a tool in the hands of Hamilton. And Albert Gallatin (1761-1847), a Jeffersonian Republican who had risen to prominence as a moderating force in the Whiskey Rebellion, was persistently attacking Hamilton's financial policies. An unjustifiably unacknowledged name in early American history, Gallatin had been born into an aristocratic family of Geneva, Switzerland, one year after the coronation of George III in 1760. Upon completion of his education, he refused a commission in the Hessian army and emigrated to America, proclaiming "a love for independence in the freest country of the universe." After seeing action in the Revolutionary War and speculating successfully in frontier land ownership, he settled in western Pennsylvania. Elected to the United States Senate from Pennsylvania in 1794, he immediately demanded a detailed accounting of the government's financial condition. "Funding and assumption" and government spending were piling up debt faster than it could be paid down and Gallatin wanted to know why. The Federalist-controlled Senate responded to Gallatin's charges by expelling him on a technicality, that he had not been a citizen for a sufficient length of time. Gallatin's heavy French accent and Republican sympathies toward France helped matters not at all. But he was elected to the House of Representatives the following year, and his criticism of Hamilton's spending and borrowing operations continued unabated.

Compounding the growing unpopularity of Federalist policies was the laying of a direct tax (constitutionally apportioned on the basis of the 1790 census) on houses, property and slaves in 1798. However, it violated the constitutional restriction on uniformity in its progressive feature wherein larger homes paid more per $100 of value than others. Except for a short period during and after the War of 1812, it was the last peacetime internal tax for some time to come. Intended to raise $2 million for a war that never came, it begat the new nation's second tax revolt known as the Fries Rebellion. Again, opposition to the tax developed in Pennsylvania where that state's share had been set at $237,000. Government assessors trying to evaluate houses and property were seized, assaulted and driven out. A group of citizens led by John Fries, a cooper and auctioneer, freed 19 protesters who had been arrested by a federal marshal and incarcerated in Bethlehem, PA. President Adams, emulating Washington, called out the militia. Fries was arrested and tried for treason in Philadelphia, his trial presided over by Supreme Court Justice Samuel Chase riding circuit. Under the Judiciary Act of 1790, a bottom tier of federal district courts (usually following state boundaries) had been created along with three middle level circuit courts. The latter were composed of a district judge and two Supreme Court justices who traveled to hear cases twice a year.

Chase's court turned the prosecution into a railroad job of unprecedented proportions. Determined to get the maximum penalty, Chase harassed Fries' lawyer, the highly respected and future Secretary of the Treasury Alexander Dallas, out of court and forced the legally inexperienced Fries to defend himself. Chase's charge to the jury allowed no verdict other than death by hanging. Adams' entire cabinet approved of the sentence, as did Alexander Hamilton, but Adams nevertheless pardoned Fries and two other "rebels" two days before the execution. According to the Constitution (Article III, Section 3), "Treason against the United States shall consist *only* [italics mine] in levying war against them, or in adhering to their enemies, giving them aid and comfort." In light of this clause, was a tax protest tantamount to treason, asked Adams? To his great credit, he did not think so.

Chase's behavior was not lost on Jefferson, and it heightened his antipathy toward a tenured judiciary as a protector of the people's rights. Six years later, President Jefferson instigated impeachment proceedings against Chase for dispensing intemperate political remarks from the bench. The House of Representatives impeached but the Senate failed to convict. That led William Rehnquist, a recent chief justice of the Supreme Court, to declare Chase's exoneration a great moment in American judicial history because it assured an independent judiciary. In reality, it meant that no judge can be easily removed from office, whether it be for senility, incompetence, mental illness, intemperate conduct or almost any other reason whatsoever – not a Chase who considered democracy equivalent to "mobocracy" and not a host of today's misfits who render Marxist decisions with abandon, in tax cases most of all.

CHAPTER XVI

THE JEFFERSONIAN LEGACY

A lot of bad government hides behind noble intentions.

Burton P. Fabricand, The *Science of Winning*

The election of 1800 sounded the death knell of the Federalist Party and brought into power a trio of brilliant Republicans, Thomas Jefferson as President, James Madison as Secretary of State, and Albert Gallatin as Secretary of the Treasury. They all believed, as did Adam Smith, that taxation, spending and regulation did nothing so much as sap a nation's productive resources. Their first order of business was, therefore, to stop and reverse the growth of government which, under the "implied powers" policy of the two previous administrations, had generated a huge deficit of $80 million. Freedom from government became the watchword of the new administration as it cut federal expenditures and *abolished* all previously imposed internal taxes under the National Debt Reduction Act of 1802. Once again the elitists were confounded, for the outcome was the same as when William Pitt the Younger cut spending and reduced taxes to erase a large budgetary deficit in England. Economic growth accelerated and customs receipts surged, enabling Gallatin to begin paying down the debt. It was $45 million when he left office in 1812 and *zero* in 1835, this despite the Louisiana Purchase of 1803 and the War of 1812. With the reinstatement of "enumerated powers" as government policy, the Jefferson administration had placed our upstart country back on track to become "the greatest and most formidable that ever was in the world." And Thomas Jefferson to become, perhaps, the greatest of our presidents.

The Louisiana Purchase Treaty of 1803 – the acquisition of much of the land between the Mississippi River and the Rocky Mountains – is but another of those tokens of "providential agency" that seems to have guided America to greatness. Originally a French colonial possession, Louisiana was ceded to Spain in 1763 as a result of France's defeat in the French and Indian War. In a "secret" agreement with Spain, Napoleon had it retroceded to France in 1800 in what he envisioned as a resurrected French empire in the New World with its capital on the Caribbean island of Hispaniola (presently divided between Haiti and the Dominican Republic). Alarmed at the prospect of a French army on our western border, Jefferson instructed his minister to France, Robert R. Livingston, to seek the purchase of New Orleans and West Florida. Napoleon showed little interest at first, but events soon forced a change of mind. A large army sent to retrieve Hispaniola from a slave uprising was ravaged by yellow fever and, with yet another war with England brewing, Napoleon could not afford to pursue his trans-Atlantic dream. In 1803, his foreign minister, Charles Maurice Talleyrand, offered a surprised Livingston all of Louisiana. With the opportune arrival the next day of James Monroe, Jefferson's minister extraordinary, negotiations began in earnest, finally concluding in the Louisiana Purchase Treaty. A price of $15 million was arrived at, $11,250,000 in 6% bonds to be amortized in annual payments of not less than $3 million beginning 15 years after ratification and $3,750,000 in claims by American citizens against France to be assumed by the United States government. Barings Bank of London bought the bonds from Napoleon at a discount, paying 87½¢ on the dollar for them. That gave to Barings an enormous profit. And it gave to Napoleon the ready money to squander on the ongoing war with England and even mount a possible invasion of the British Isles. Patriotism, as we shall learn, matters little when big money is involved.

The Treaty was a diplomatic, political and economic coup for Jefferson. In one fell swoop, it ended the threat of Napoleon on our western border, almost doubled the size of the United States, provided trans-Appalachian farmers with unlimited navigation of the Mississippi River and access to the strategic port of New Orleans for shipping to the east coast and overseas. The acquisition did, however, pose somewhat of a problem for Jefferson in that nothing in the Constitution authorized the government to buy land. Was a Constitutional amendment required, Jefferson wondered? But he quickly decided to approve it. Napoleon, after all, might change his mind. Besides, the Louisiana Purchase was a treaty with a foreign power and, according to Article II, Section 2, Clause 2 of the Constitution, "He [the President] shall have power, by and with the advice and consent of the Senate, to make treaties, provided two thirds of the Senators present concur …" His action was overwhelmingly confirmed by the Senate.

CHAPTER XVII

THE AMERICAN INDUSTRIAL REVOLUTION BEGINS

What is it that confers the noblest delight? What is that which swells a man's breast with pride above that which any other experience can bring to him? Discover! To know that you are walking where none others have walked, that you are beholding what human eye has not seen before, that you are breathing a virgin atmosphere. To give birth to an idea — to discover a great thought — an intellectual nugget, right under the dust of a field that many a brain plow had gone over before. To find a new planet, to invent a new hinge, to find the way to make the lightnings carry your messages. To be the first — that is the idea. To do something, say something, see something, before anybody else — these are the things that confer a pleasure compared with which other pleasures are tame and commonplace, other ecstasies cheap and trivial. Morse, with his first message, brought by his servant, the lightning; Fulton, in that long-drawn century of suspense, when he placed his hand upon the throttle valve and lo, the steamship moved; ... Howe, when the idea shot through his brain that for a hundred and twenty generations the eye had been bored through the wrong end of the needle; Columbus, in the Pinta's shrouds, when he swung his hat above a fabled sea and gazed abroad upon an unknown world! These are the men who have really lived — who have actually comprehended what pleasure is — who have crowded long lifetimes of ecstasy into a single moment.

Mark Twain, The *Innocents Abroad*

Arrestiti, c'e bello!

From the opera *Mefistofele* by Arrigo Boito, the phrase *Stop, it is beautiful!* referring to that single moment in time for which Faust bargains his soul to the Devil.

Bequeathed their Founding Fathers' gift of minimal government and maximal freedom, Americans were ready to adapt to and exploit chaotic reality as never before in finding "that which is the better." Three early "butterflys" ushered in the "Silver Age," a time during which our fledgling nation began its meteoric rise to "Power, Consequence and Grandeur." The first of these seemingly inconsequential events occurred in 1789 when a disguised young foreigner arrived in America seeking his fortune; the second in 1793 when a 30-year old widow with five children and a plantation to look after offered sanctuary to a penniless, unemployed Yale graduate; the third when Benjamin Franklin took a liking to a portrait of him painted by an unknown artist from Lancaster PA.

In 1769, Richard Arkwright (1732-1792) patented his "water frame," a spinning machine operated by flowing water that produced a new type of cotton thread, greatly strengthened and stretched to silky smoothness. It brought to England the first application of power-driven machinery to large-scale manufacturing processes – what we now call the industrial revolution. In partnership with inventor Jedediah Strutt (1726-1797), he built huge mills for the spinning of raw cotton and established the world's first mass-production system. The results were nothing short of spectacular; the production of cotton yarn, previously insignificant compared to that of wool and linen, jumped from a mere half million pounds in 1765 all spun by hand in private homes to 12 million pounds in 1784 all spun by machine. Even more spectacular was the improvement in living standards sparked by the appearance on the market of affordable cotton fabrics. Before Arkwright, most of the populace went about miserably clothed and uncomfortably bedded with animal skins and itchy, coarse, hard-to-wash woolens. Finer fabrics – silks, satins, damasks, brocades and velvets – were far beyond the reach of the average person. Body odors, vermin and filth were the norm for the great majority. People literally stunk. Health standards, as a consequence, were abysmally low, the relationship of cleanliness to disease being far beyond contemporary understanding. The advent of Arkwright's low-cost, smooth-as-silk threads, however, vastly upgraded the social and physical environments. Woven cotton quickly became the fabric of choice for wearing apparel. Comfortably worn next to the skin, washable, durable, absorbent, ironable and abrasive resistant, it made for highly desirable summer wear and was easily layered and napped for winter warmth. When dyed with bright colors and textured in elaborate weaves, it proved suitable as well for fashionable wear. And largely because of cotton, cleanliness became *de rigueur*.

In 1786, King George III knighted Arkwright for his great contributions to the health and wealth of the British Empire. As a result of his work and that of innovators like Kay, Hargreaves, Crompton, Cartwright and many others who remain anonymous, England achieved worldwide dominance in the manufacture of cotton fabrics. The textile industry became the key to England's economic and trade policies. And because it was so very lucrative to both businessmen and politicians alike, they collaborated closely in keeping the industry free of competition from foreign and local upstarts. The American colonies in particular were prohibited under the severest penalties from obtaining or copying English machinery and competing with the homeland monopoly. Of course, as pointed out by Adam Smith, it was the English and American consumers who paid the higher prices necessitated by the government-imposed lack of competition.

It so happened that a 14-year old youngster apprenticed to Strutt gained a thorough familiarity with the machinery and factory system developed by Arkwright. Faced with the upward immobility characteristic of the English business and social structures, Samuel Slater (1768-1835) saw little opportunity to exploit his knowledge. As had many before him, he looked overseas to where a free America beckoned. English law, however, forbid the emigration of textile workers and he was forced to escape disguised as a manual laborer. Once in America, he contracted with manufacturer, philanthropist and eponymous benefactor of Brown University, Moses Brown of Providence, to reproduce Arkwright's mill. This he did from sheer memory, a prodigious feat. Neither by purchase nor by smuggling had anyone beforehand been able to obtain plans or models of English factories. Brown and Slater's first mill opened in Providence in 1790, a second in Pawtucket and America's great textile industry was launched. In 1807 only 15 cotton mills existed in the United States operating only 8000 spindles. Four years later, there were 87 mills and 80,000 spindles, and in another four years, more than 500,000 spindles whirring under the watchful eyes of 76,000 tenders. Once referred to as the father of the American industrial revolution, Samuel Slater is all but forgotten today.

As mentioned above, Alexander Hamilton and his newly appointed assistant Treasury secretary, Tench Coxe, had in 1790 lent their official offices to the founding of SEUM, the "Society for Establishing Useful Manufactures," a business venture that would enjoy the "blessings" of government. Their noble intentions were to promote the industrialization of America and make her independent of European manufactures. The prospectus, probably written by Hamilton, projected the creation of a manufacturing town with investors profiting from the production of a host of manufactures plus the appreciation of the underlying real estate. Because of Hamilton's involvement, an initial public stock offering sold out instantly, enabling the company to raise $500,000 in seed money. Textile production was the first goal since both Hamilton and Coxe were well aware of the role it had played in turning England into the greatest nation on earth. Hamilton negotiated contract after contract with English textile refugees, each one of them claiming the ability to reproduce some aspect of Arkwright's mass production system. In 1791, a mill was erected on the banks of the Passaic River in what was to become Patterson NJ, but troubles arose immediately. William Duer, Hamilton's first assistant Treasury secretary now sitting on the SEUM's board of directors, dipped into its funds for speculative purposes and lost the money. Another Hamilton crony absconded to Pennsylvania with much of what remained. And to the dismay of stockholders, the English textile "experts" hired by Hamilton never fulfilled their claims to get the mill into production. SEUM ultimately came to naught, led as it was by men with no entrepreneurial talent whatsoever. It remained for Adam Smith's invisible hand to choose Moses Brown and Samuel Slater to lead America into the industrial age.

Soon after Slater built his first mill, there occurred the second "butterfly," one consequence of which was to assure the textile industry at home and abroad of an abundant supply of raw material. As a boy on his father's farm in Massachusetts, Eli Whitney (1765-1825) had evidenced unusually creative mechanical skills. He could take apart and reassemble his father's watch, had built a violin to his own design, and for a time was the country's sole maker of ladies hatpins. During the Revolution, he had built a forge, again of his own design, for the manufacture of nails which were then in short supply. A lack of money thwarted his desire for a college education until he was 23, at which time he entered Yale, an unusual practice at the time for anyone not interested in law or theology. Upon graduation in 1792 and with no positions open for a man of his talents, he accepted a tutorial position in South Carolina that fell through. But en route to his prospective job aboard a coastal packet to Savannah, he had the good fortune to meet Catherine Littlefield Greene (1755-1816) who invited him for a stay at her Mulberry Grove rice plantation.

Catherine had been married to Nathanael Greene (1742-1786), America's greatest Revolutionary War general after Washington, the man who had battled that "modern-day Hannibal," Lord Cornwallis, to a standstill in the Carolinas, eventually forcing him to Yorktown and defeat of the British cause in America. Through all the harshest years of the War, Catherine had remained steadfastly at her husband's side and was much revered by the troops for her kindness and hospitality. Having spent most of their personal fortune on supplies for the army, the Greenes had been all too happy to receive Mulberry Grove as a gift from the state of Georgia in recognition of their efforts. During the War, it had belonged to a Tory politician now fled the country.

At Mulberry Grove, Catherine and her neighbors acquainted Eli with the desperate plight of southern planters occasioned by the lack of a money crop. Rice, indigo, corn and wheat had become at best marginally profitable despite, or more probably because of, a slave population that numbered almost a million. Slavery was a declining institution at the time and manumission, the freeing of slaves, was not uncommon. As Adam Smith had pointed out in *The Wealth of Nations*, slave labor is very costly and planters would undoubtedly have been better off had they freed the slaves and paid them wages. Tobacco and sugar were the only cash crops that could afford the expense of slave cultivation. Cotton of the short-staple green seed variety offered promise. It was the only kind that grew well inland, but under existing conditions was little more than a weed. To be of use, its fibers had to be separated from sticky seeds by hand and this was too time-consuming a process for cotton planting to be very profitable.

Whitney analyzed the separation process and within ten days designed a machine to do the job mechanically. His first model of the "gin" (for engine) could do in one hour the full day's work of many laborers. Soon he was producing 50 pounds of cleaned fiber per day, and cotton for the first time appeared to be the bonanza everyone was looking for. An agricultural revolution was in the offing, and neither the South nor the North would ever be the same again.

As we modern chaosticians have come to expect, information in a free market spreads with unbelievable rapidity. Word of Whitney's cotton gin quickly brought thousands of acres throughout the South and West into cultivation to grow what was now no longer a useless weed. The demand for slaves to work the fields soared. Manumission became a forgotten word. Impoverished planters who had little truck with the fine points of law and ethics copied the invention with impunity even though Whitney received a patent for it in 1794. Because of the piracy, a factory in New Haven built by Whitney in partnership with Phineas Miller, Nathanael Greene's former secretary and subsequent plantation manager, took in too few orders and closed. By 1803, more than a million pounds of cotton fiber were being shipped, mostly to England and New England, and its value had risen to almost $10 million from $150,000 in 1793. Cotton production proceeded to double each decade thereafter, and by 1850 America was growing three-quarters of the world's crop. It remained America's largest export until well into the 20th century.

As the man who brought prosperity to the South, Whitney should have made millions, but what money he did earn from his gin (less than $100,000) was squandered on law suits trying to collect royalties on his patent. "An invention can be so valuable as to be worthless to the inventor," he lamented, and never again did he patent any of his numerous innovations. Down this man of genius may have been, but he was far from out. The ramifications of the Whitney "butterfly" were still to play out.

Sometime during the period of legal battles, Whitney conceived of manufacturing durable goods with interchangeable parts. The idea was hardly new. Johannes Gutenberg (1400-1468) had utilized interchangeability in the first movable-type printing press, but he had to fashion the letters with jewel-like precision to make it work. And there was the rub. Interchangeable parts required tight tolerances, and tight tolerances demanded slow, meticulous handiwork by highly skilled craftsmen. Whitney was proposing something different, high quality mass production using unskilled workers operating machines. Although it would take another hundred years of development for his proposal to reach fruition in Henry Ford's remarkably efficient assembly line production of automobiles, Whitney was the far-sighted genius who got things rolling. Once again, "the freest country of the universe" had found the right man in the right place at the right time to advance her cause.

In 1798 Secretary of War James McHenry (of Fort McHenry and *Star-Spangled Banner* fame) proposed the creation of a standing army to forestall a possible invasion. At the time, the French naval action against private American ships, which had been instigated by the Jay Treaty, was threatening to escalate into full-scale war. Congress eventually approved the formation of twelve regiments of regulars and McHenry sought bids from private contractors for 40,000 muskets to equip the new force. It was a tall order because in early America only a handful of skilled machinists were even capable of making a musket. Production from government armories was painstakingly slow, only 1000 muskets having been crafted in the previous three years. Each musket was the sole responsibility of an individual worker who formed and fitted all the pieces from stock to barrel into a final assembled whole. The result was almost a work of art because every gun was unique unto itself. Any broken or lost parts had to be specially made at great expense because of the lack of interchangeability.

Whitney proposed to manufacture 10,000 muskets for delivery in two years at a price of $13.40 each. They would be composed of interchangeable parts and made by unskilled workers. On the surface, the proposal was laughable. He had after all no factory to show, no gunsmith experience, and no craftsmen. And who ever heard of interchangeable parts? From anyone other than Whitney, the proposal would have been dismissed out of hand. But even though little money resulted from his invention of the cotton gin, his reputation as its inventor was such that McHenry granted him the contract. In this regard, he undoubtedly had the backing of

Vice-President Thomas Jefferson who learned about the concept when minister to France in 1785. Jefferson had visited the shop of one Honoré Le Blanc, a gunsmith making muskets with handcrafted parts of such precision that they could be interchanged. He never forgot the experience and Whitney always had his full support.

The contract at $134,000 was the largest ever granted up until that time. To get started, Whitney raised $30,000 from New Haven investors and $10,000 from a bank. At the end of the first year, he was just getting into production – an amazing feat for so short a time – but had produced only 500 muskets. There seemed an infinite number of problems to contend with – material shortages, worker training, a lack of precise gauges, and new and innovative machine tools that had to be built and tested. The key to Whitney's project was his invention of the milling machine, a tool that replaced the chisel and enabled an unskilled machinist to cut metal into any desired shape much as a dressmaker uses a scissors to cut fabric on a template.

To alleviate concern about his "slow" progress, Whitney in 1801 staged a demonstration in Washington before a select group of government officials including President John Adams, President-elect Thomas Jefferson, McHenry and a number of military officers. From a pile of parts for ten muskets, Whitney invited his audience to select pieces at random. To their amazement, he then proceeded to reconstruct working muskets from them. Although the parts for the demonstration may have been secretly handcrafted, the future of manufacturing was clearly indicated. Fortunately, by this time the crisis with France was over and the pressure to produce was off. It took Whitney another eight years to fulfill the contract, but in 1811 he took an order for 15,000 muskets and delivered them in two years, just in time for use in the War of 1812.

Eli Whitney finally achieved fortune as well as fame, but what he contributed to the wealth of America was incalculably more. Unfortunately, his cotton gin also reinvigorated the institution of slavery and its harmful future consequences. As for Catherine Littlefield Greene, she sold Mulberry Grove to pay off debts incurred in financing Whitney and Phineas Miller in their business partnership, married Miller, and spent her final years on Cumberland Island off the Georgia coast where she and Nathanael had bought property long before. Mulberry Grove was burned to the ground during the Civil War by General Sherman on his march to the sea.

The third of our fluttering "butterflys" revolutionized transportation worldwide. Like Eli Whitney, Robert Fulton (1765-1815) was born on a farm and, like Whitney, displayed great mechanical aptitude at a young age. But more than that, he showed artistic talent and helped support his widowed mother by painting store signs for local merchants. It was his dream to follow in the footsteps of Benjamin West, the American expatriate artist who had risen to fame in London, even to president of the Royal Academy, a society founded by George III for the establishment of an art school and an annual exhibition devoted to the works of living painters. With few job opportunities available in Lancaster, the 17-year old Fulton left home for Philadelphia where a family friend had recommended him to Jeremiah Andrews, a silversmith who taught him to make necklaces, rings, belt buckles and other pieces of fine jewelry. All his spare time, however, was devoted to enhancing his drawing and painting skills by copying pictures in art collections around the city. His artwork drew the attention of his employer; miniature portraits of wealthy people painted on ivory chips could be encased in fancy silver frames and sold, thought Andrews. And the idea proved fruitful as a steady stream of clients entered the store to sit for the young artist. By 1785 Robert was able to capitalize on his talents, entrepreneurial as well as artistic, and paint a sign over his own shop: "Robert Fulton, Miniature Painter."

His artistic prowess reached another Philadelphia resident, Benjamin Franklin, who commissioned a full-sized portrait. So pleased was Franklin with Fulton's work that he advised further study with his friend Benjamin West in London and offered to write a letter of introduction. It was a dream come true. As he explained to Franklin, his parents had known West – even possessed small portraits of them painted by him – and his ambition had always been to emulate the renowned artist. A lung inflammation that may have marked the beginnings of tuberculosis delayed his departure but, finally, armed with Franklin's letter, a 21-year old Fulton sailed for England and five years of study as a student of West.

At the time of Fulton's arrival, England was enjoying an unprecedented prosperity brought on by the industrial revolution, the temporary cessation of foreign wars, and the laissez faire economic policies of William Pitt the Younger. The affluent environment generated progress in all walks of life, but three events in particular would coalesce to bring about Fulton's development of the steamboat. In 1769, engineer James Brindley (1716-1772) built the first English canal of major economic (profitable) importance. Because existing roads and vehicles could handle neither the gentle movement of fragile pottery and glass goods nor the weights of coal, iron and heavy manufactured items demanded by the industrial revolution's newly arising factories, the canal was quickly recognized as the opening venture in an efficient transportation network that would soon span the country. A "canal-mania" investment mentality soon developed and led to the construction of nearly 4500 miles of waterways by 1840. A similar course of development would occur in America fifty years later financed in large part by English money.

Through West, Fulton came into contact with many of the men engaged in the canal business, and his restless mind could only be attracted by the engineering opportunities offered. He was barely scraping out a living with minor portrait commissions during his London years and had come to the conclusion that there was little money to be made as only a good painter. And it was West's opinion that he would never be a great one. As a result, he immersed himself in canal projects and proposed many improvements in construction and excavation equipment, none of which came to fruition. Nevertheless, he learned a great deal about ship design and navigation in narrow and shallow waters, knowledge that would soon serve him in good stead.

Less than one year after Fulton's arrival in England, Robert Barker, an Irish artist living in Edinburgh, patented what came to be known as a "panorama." It was a large-scale circular landscape painting displayed on the illuminated inner walls of a cylindrical building. Seen in the darkness and with no visual distractions, the frameless painting presented to a spectator the illusion of being completely surrounded by an actual landscape. The panorama won almost immediate popularity when it opened in 1794 on London's Leicester Square with a *View of London from the Albion Mills*, and the business thrived for almost seventy years. Early panoramas enjoyed a considerable vogue even in the artistic community. The august painter Sir Joshua Reynolds was quoted as saying that they represented nature "in a manner far superior to the limited scale of pictures in general." And West thought them nothing less than "the greatest improvement to the art of painting that has yet been discovered." So it was only natural for the entrepreneurial side of Fulton to grasp what appeared a great opportunity to combine his art, business and engineering talents and make some money. In 1799, after securing the patent rights to exhibit panoramas in France, he erected a rotunda on the Boulevard Montmartre in Paris and displayed a view of the city painted by landscapist Pierre Prevost. Success was immediate. A few months later, a panorama of Toulon under siege by the British fleet was shown in an identical building next door. With the venture thus firmly established, he sold his French exhibition rights to fellow American James Thayer but retained a percentage of the profits. A *Panoramic View of the Palace and Gardens of Versailles* painted by Fulton's friend, John Vanderlyn, is installed in the American Wing of the Metropolitan Museum of Art in New York City.

Now buttressed by a secure income, Fulton turned his attention to building canals, submarines and steamboats, but no support could he obtain for his proposals from either government or private sources. By happenstance, however, the rotunda provided the venue for Fulton's introduction to the brother of the newly arrived American minister to France and through him, to Robert R. Livingston himself, soon to take part in the Louisiana Purchase Treaty negotiations. Never has there been a more fortuitous meeting of minds.

Livingston (1746-1813) was descended from a politically and socially prominent family of statesmen, diplomats and jurists. He had been a member of the Continental Congress' committee charged with drafting the Declaration of Independence, was an ardent supporter of the Constitution, and, as the first chancellor of New York State, had administered the presidential oath of office to George Washington in 1789. He was also a founder and president of the New York Society for the Promotion of Arts, Agriculture and Manufactures, and steamboating was his passion. Through his thorough knowledge of the law and his far-reaching political influence, he had been able to persuade the New York State legislature to grant him the exclusive privilege of "navigating all boats that might be propelled by steam, on all waters within the territory or jurisdiction of the State, for the term of thirty years." Jokingly labeled the "hot water bill," it also mandated the construction of a boat capable of traveling the 150-mile distance between New York and Albany at an average speed of four miles an hour, little more than a day's trip. In contrast, coach travel at the time required an arduous four or five days. Livingston had previously backed inventor-engineers Nicholas J. Roosevelt and John Stevens in unsuccessful attempts at building a steamboat capable of meeting the specifications.

In the energetic and multi-faceted Fulton, Livingston recognized at once his man for the job. They entered into a partnership agreement, and Fulton proceeded with the design and building of a test boat. A first version failed when the steam engine crashed through the hull in a gale, but a second tested successfully on the River Seine after reconstruction provided a stronger deck. At a length of 66 feet and a beam of 8 feet, it was far too small for commercial operations. A much bigger boat with a more powerful and compact engine was essential if steam transportation were ever to be profitable and Fulton undertook its design. By now, he was able to calculate better than anybody heretofore the requisite size and proportions of such a boat. American John Fitch in 1790 and Scotsman William Symington in 1803 had come close to profitable steamboat operations, but in both cases the problem was an engine too large for a boat too small. And now we come to the third element in Fulton's success story.

In 1769, Scotsman James Watt (1736-1819) patented the most powerful instrument by which the "great sources of power in Nature are converted, adapted, and applied for the use and convenience of men." It was the prototype of the modern steam engine and the great accelerator of the industrial revolution. In partnership with capitalist and inventor Matthew Boulton, he formed the Boulton and Watt Company to develop and exploit the invention. But not until John Wilkinson (1738-1808) invented the boring machine in 1776 (one of the very first machine tools anywhere) could they bore cylinders to the necessary precision for incorporation into a practicable steam engine. By 1790, their steam engines, all for stationary applications, were in great demand. Fulton had visited the Company during his stay in England and learned of its capabilities, and in 1803 he ordered an engine suitable for his needs. It was finally delivered three years later to Charles Brown's shipyard on the East River in New York where his steamboat was built.

The final design for "Fulton's Folly," as it was dubbed, featured a flat-bottomed hull 140 feet long, a beam of 15 feet, a draft of 3 feet and a displacement of 100 tons (the numbers are approximate because of variations in different historical accounts). The 24-horsepower steam engine and boiler were placed amidships between giant paddle-wheels. There were three cabins and sleeping berths for 45 people, adequate deck space, a saloon and a ladies' lounge. It cost $20,000 dollars to build. On 17 August 1807, the newly christened *North River Steamboat of Clermont* was launched on its maiden run with considerable fanfare. As Fulton cranked the engine up to full speed ahead, showers of sparks from the smokestack flew copiously into the air filling the passengers, mostly members of the Livingston family, with trepidation. But suspense and incredulity turned to approval and merriment as the boat proceeded without incident to Clermont, the Livingston estate on the Hudson River, and then to Albany. At Clermont, Robert Livingston announced the betrothal of Fulton to his niece, Harriet Livingston. In a prepared speech, he predicted that the Fulton name "would descend to posterity as a benefactor of the world" and that the century would see vessels crossing the Atlantic with no motive power other than steam. The 150-mile distance up river from New York to Albany was traversed in 32 hours at an average speed of four knots, the down river return in 30 hours. After some modifications, the boat was placed in commercial service on 4 September with a $7 one-way fare and performed profitably until laid up for the winter in mid-November.

In the years to come, steamboat building sprouted. Soon after the birth of the *Clermont*, John Stevens and Nicholas Roosevelt built the *Phoenix*, the first to make an ocean voyage by steam when sent to the Delaware River for commercial service between Philadelphia and Trenton. The "New Orleans," designed by Fulton and built by Roosevelt, was the first to travel down the Ohio and Mississippi Rivers to New Orleans in 1811. In 1819, the *City of Savannah* used an auxiliary steam engine and sails in combination to cross the Atlantic. In 1838, two ships, the *Sirius* and the *Great Western*, crossed solely under steam power. By that time steamships carrying freight and passengers were plying the coastal waters of the eastern seaboard, the navigable streams of the Mississippi River system, and the Great Lakes. And not long after, they were steaming around Cape Horn to the Pacific Ocean and California. Robert Fulton, artist, inventor, engineer and entrepreneur, had liberated sailors from chaotic winds and turned steamboat transportation into a reality. Equally important, he had demonstrated the feasibility of adapting steam engines to moving platforms.

In 1808, Fulton married Harriet and four children resulted. He was developing steamship plans for many of the world's rivers when a recurrence of the lung inflammation of his youth brought on an early death at age 50. On the occasion, Congress wore mourning and businesses in New York closed for a day. He was buried in the Livingston family vault in Trinity Church in New York City.

CHAPTER XVIII

THE BUTTERFLY AGE

It is a fabulous country, the only fabulous country; it is the only place where miracles not only happen, but where they happen all the time.

Thomas Wolfe

The Slater, Whitney and Fulton "butterflys" marked only the beginning. Silver Age chaons, sparked by the random motion of a fully operable "invisible hand," began to "happen all the time." A tidal wave of goods and services from businesses both born and reborn shoved the bell-shaped curve of income distribution sharply to the right and jumped the standard of living to new heights, and nowhere more so than for the middle class. The necessities of life – food, shelter, clothing, transport and communication – became for Mr. and Mrs. Average American more accessible than ever. The annual output of iron and leather goods alone soon equaled in value all the cotton grown in southern fields. An unbelievably rapid development of roads, canals, steamships, and ultimately the railroads distributed a proliferation of industrial and agricultural products nationwide. Telegraph lines spanned the country coast to coast and would have bound the states permanently together were it not for "the folly of human laws." Rotary presses driven by steam engines enabled publishers to print more copies of a book or newspaper in an hour than could be printed on a hand press in a week. A mighty blueprint for an America yet to come was in the making, built on the decentralized plans of millions of private citizens each free to act in his or her own behalf.

Another day, another miracle, or so it seemed. So many contributed, so few succeeded. Farm boy, apprentice, aristocrat, artist, actor, bigamist, jailbird, machinist, businessman – how randomly they popped up, how mightily they tried, those miracle-workers of yesteryear! I should feel remiss if I did not mention, at least briefly, some of their more outstanding accomplishments. Indeed, our god Chaos, father of chaons, demands it, for these are the important people, the ones who made America rich beyond compare. They are the ones who created the industries, the jobs, the products and the services that brought to America the life style we so enjoy today. Their enormous contributions, all but forgotten now, bear eloquent if mute testimony to the vigor of free markets. Only in such markets can all the bits and pieces of unforeseeable reality fall into place. How unfortunate it is that their significance in American history lies buried in the millions of words lavished by historians on those "small men by whom we are governed," politicians and conquerors who almost always do more harm than good.

When in 1834 Cyrus Hall McCormick (1809-1884) patented a horse-drawn reaper for harvesting grains, he became the Fulton of modern agriculture. A son of Robert McCormick, the owner of a prosperous 532-acre Virginia "Walnut Grove" farm, Cyrus displayed all his father's mechanical propensities. When only 15 years of age, he invented a lightweight cradle, which when attached to a scythe, laid out harvested grain in bunches for easier bundling. He observed and aided his father in the farm's blacksmith shop as the latter worked intermittently for more than 15 years trying to replace the scythe with a mechanical reaping device. When Robert finally abandoned the project at the beginning of the 1831 harvest, Cyrus picked up where his father left off, added several key features of his own, and was able to demonstrate a practicable reaper by the end of the same harvest. He spent the next ten years improving the machine and publicizing its great advantages. But during all that time, not a single reaper could he market to dubious and skeptical farmers.

A hard sell though it was at first, the radical and expensive reaper brought McCormick's innate salesmanship talents to the fore. Many of today's marketing techniques, among them low interest loans, written performance guarantees, parts availability, installment selling, advertising promotions, traveling salesmen and consumer education, were pioneered by him. "You must advertise to sell," he insisted. Slowly at first, the "Virginia Reaper" began to sell, and then almost overnight at a pace that outstripped production capacity at the Walnut Grove workshop. Sensing that the agricultural future of America lay on the Great Plains west of the Mississippi, McCormick betook his two brothers in as partners and moved the business to Chicago. Here the enterprise grew by leaps and bounds, until the great Chicago fire of 1871 wiped out both the city and the business. But the company rose phoenix-like under McCormick's management, eventually evolving into the multi-national International Harvester Company.

In 1851, the McCormick reaper found its way across the Atlantic to England. When first placed on exhibition in London's Crystal Palace, a reporter of the *London Times* disparaged it as a "contraption seemingly a cross between a wheelbarrow, a chariot, and a flying machine." Later, after the reaper had demonstrated its prowess in the field, a retraction appeared and the paper's editor expressed his belief that the American reaper was destined alone to be worth more to British farmers than the cost of the entire London Exposition. It gained first place awards at the London Exposition and those in Hamburg, Vienna and Paris. McCormick was elected an officer of the French Legion of Honor and a member of the French Academy of Science, which proclaimed him "as having done more for agriculture than any other living man."

When finally accepted, the reaper opened the agricultural community to a flood of innovative machinery that made American food and fiber production the most efficient in the world. Soaring productivity soon unchained Americans from the land as fewer and fewer farmers were able to produce more in commodities than ever before. In ever increasing numbers, rural Americans found employment, at higher pay and less demanding work, in the newly created industries emerging in cities everywhere. Whereas 90% of the thirteen million people counted by the 1830 census were involved in farming, less than 2% are so engaged today. E. Lee Trinkle, a former governor of Virginia, eulogized McCormick in the following terms: "I have seemed to realize that the glory of service in peace is not always less than the glory of valor in battle; that the hum of the reaper is sweeter than the roar of artillery; that he who feeds the nations is greater than he who rules an empire; that he who conquers famine is greater than he who taketh a city.

"I have looked upon battle flags and thought of that agony and death men call war. And I have lifted up my eyes in prayer that God may yet see fit to fulfill the prophecy of Isaiah, in which we are told: 'They shall beat their swords into ploughshares, and their spears in pruning-hooks; nation shall not lift up sword against nation, neither shall they learn war any more.'"

Two new growth industries, both devoted to food preservation, fostered migration to the cities. Ice harvesting began about the turn of the century and became by 1850 a major component of the gross domestic product. More than sixty kinds of sophisticated new tools for drilling, cleaning, scouring, scraping, planing, cutting, moving, storing and shipping 300-pound blocks of ice spurred its development. Specially designed wagons, ships and railroad cars using saw dust and straw for insulation transported ice to commercial ice houses where it was stacked in winter and stored through the summer. The iceman delivering to domestic iceboxes became as prominent as the milkman. In the 1830s Boston businessman Frederic Tudor was shipping thousands of tons of ice from New England lakes and rivers to New Orleans, Charleston, Havana, the West Indies, and, as a publicity stunt, as far away as Calcutta, India, a voyage lasting 180 days. The industry, which sourced many New England fortunes, peaked in the 1880s, about the time mechanically produced ice technology developed in the southern states. Its end came with the introduction of relatively inexpensive electrically powered refrigerators in the 1920s and 1930s.

In France, Nicolas Appert (1749-1814), a sometime chef, confectioner, baker and brewer, was grappling with another method of food preservation. Why, he wondered, shouldn't meat and vegetables be preserved by packing them in airtight bottles as was done for wine? In 1798, after fifteen years of experimentation, he found an answer. Spoilage could be prevented by storing food in airtight glass jars that had been corked, sealed with pitch, and then heated for varying lengths of time in boiling water. Napoleon himself awarded Appert a 12000-franc prize that had been offered by the French government for a way of preserving military food supplies. Although held as a government secret, the idea soon leaked across the Channel to England where in 1810 Peter Durand patented the use of tin-coated iron containers with a soldered cover for preserving food. By 1814, at the Battle of Waterloo, both sides had canned rations. Fifty more years of progress in the biological sciences were to elapse before Louis Pasteur (1822-1895) could explain that the heat used in the sealing process destroyed the bacteria causing food spoilage.

In 1812 Appert's book, *L'Art de conserver les substances animals et végétales*, was translated and published in New York. Shortly thereafter, Thomas Kensett (sometimes called the father of

American canning) set up a small plant on the New York waterfront and preserved foods using at first glass jars and then tin-coated iron cans. But it was William Underwood (1787-1864) who established the first large-scale operation on Boston's Russia Wharf. Coming to America in 1820 with his mother's recipe for deviled ham in his pocket, he canned a product so successful that it remains popular to this day. Oysters, lobsters, fruits and vegetables, jams and jellies, and mustard were quickly added to his product list. In 1835 he imported tomato seeds from England, grew his first crop and preserved it. Pioneers on their westward treks stocked their covered wagons with his canned goods as did the Union army during the Civil War. The business was taken over by B & G in the 1880s, then by the Pillsbury Company and finally by a British concern, Metropolitan Foods. In other notable developments, Henry Evans received in 1849 a patent for a can-making machine that increased production from five hand-made cans per hour to sixty cans per minute. In 1856, Gail Borden patented canned condensed milk. And in 1858, a patent for the first can opener was issued to Ezra Warner. The century's preservation industry culminated in Clarence Birdseye's invention of the frozen food process sometime in the 1880s.

Francis Cabot Lowell (1775-1817), Harvard graduate and socially prominent Boston merchant, took the textile industry on a great leap forward by performing a Samuel Slater-type feat. Touring England in 1810, he was escorted through a Manchester cotton mill where he witnessed in operation the newly improved steam-powered looms originally invented in 1785 by Edmund Cartwright (1743-1823). By integrating the spinning and weaving operations, these machines converted raw cotton directly into cloth, greatly advancing manufacturing productivity. Although barred from taking any drawings back to America, Lowell, in collaboration with expert machinist Paul Moody, managed to reconstruct from memory the Cartwright looms along with many improvements. With $400,000 raised from private investors, he set up the Boston Manufacturing Company on the Charles River in Waltham, MA. So profitable did the new textile plant prove to be that in 1823, the Company relocated to a massive complex in a town eponymously named in his honor. The work force consisted mostly of rural women (and later immigrants) attracted by the comparatively high wages offered. To meet the needs of its female workers, the Company built dormitories, shops and churches, closely supervised the women's cleanliness and appearance and carefully regulated their behavior. Charles Dickens, who visited the city in 1842, recorded his favorable impressions of the "Lowell System" in his *American Notes*. Another Englishman, one James Montgomery, inspected the operation in 1840 and wrote of the "greater quantity of yarn and cloth from each spindle and loom (in a given time) than was produced by any other factories without exception in the world." In light of the industry's profitability and miraculous growth right from the start, how unfortunate and how unnecessary it was for Congress, under Lowell's urging, to impose a duty of 6¼ cents per yard on imported textiles in the Tariff Act of 1816. This small, "butterfly" duty, to be raised in 1824, again in 1828, and again in 1860, would bring on, as we shall learn, disastrous consequences.

After Lowell, cloth could be machine-produced in quantity. But not so clothing. In all towns and many villages, tailors and seamstresses fulfilled the needs of the local populace as best they could by hand-sewing clothes to order. Not until two men arrived on the world scene, one a sedate apprentice and the other a flamboyant would-be actor who would sire twenty-two children with five different women, did the large-scale production of ready-to-wear clothing become a possibility.

In 1838 Elias Howe (1819-1867) patented a practical sewing machine. A farm boy from Spencer, MA, Howe had apprenticed at a local textile mill at age 16. The Panic of 1837 left him unemployed and led him to Boston where he married and secured work with one Ari Davis, a maker and repairer of precision instruments. Through Davis he learned of earlier attempts to invent a functional sewing machine, none of which were successful, and the supposed fortune that awaited the inventor of such a machine. Beset by frail health, Howe was forced to quit his job and depend on his wife's take-in sewing to support a growing family. While observing her intricate handwork on a day-to-day basis, he thought about the sewing problem. He quickly came to the realization that no machine could duplicate the many motions of the human arm and hand. And almost simultaneously, inspiration struck in the form of a machine-made lockstitch. As opposed to the one thread used in hand-stitching, his machine would use two, one threaded through an eye at the point of a needle and driven through the fabric to form a far-side loop, the other to be shuttled through the loop to complete a tight stitch. He managed to design and build a hand-driven machine that out-sewed five expert seamstresses in an 1845 demonstration. But the cost of the machine, at $300, was far beyond the means of middle class households and not a single one did he sell. He unfortunately possessed none of the marketing flair of a Fulton or a McCormick.

Hoping for better luck abroad, Howe obtained a British patent and sailed for England. But his poor business practices persisted and he managed to lose any advantage his machine may have brought him there. Upon returning to America, he was astonished to find the sewing machine business flourishing. During his absence many other inventors had usurped his discovery and sewing machines of various designs were on the market. The most successful of them belonged to Isaac Merritt Singer (1811-1875).

Singer was born into a German immigrant family in Pittstown, NY, a town not far from Troy. His parents divorced when he was 10 and, not getting along well with his stepmother, he left home to live with an older brother in Oswego. There he grew to his full height of six feet four inches and learned the machinist's trade in his brother's shop. Unhappy with his prospects, he quit his job for a career in show business working as a stage hand, advance man and actor. At age 20, he married 15-year old Catharine Haley and went to live with her family in New York. For the next few years, he worked both as a machinist and as a part-time actor with various groups around the city. In 1836, he took an abrupt leave of his wife and child in New York and joined an acting troupe in Baltimore where he fell in love with actress Mary Ann Sponseler. One year later, he returned to New York and there he fathered another child with Catharine and a son with Mary Ann. That effectively finished the marriage although Catharine did not divorce him until 1860. After two fruitless years as actor and handyman, he left New York with Mary Ann for a job as an unskilled laborer digging an Illinois waterway. At this point, his mechanical talents reasserted themselves and he was able to patent a rock-drilling machine, the rights to which he sold for $2,000. Back into acting he went, using the money to form his own theater troupe, the Merritt Players. When after five years of touring this too failed, he and Mary Ann settled in Fredericksburg, OH, where he found a job in a printing shop.

Singer's next invention, a wood-block cutting machine, brought him to the attention of Orson C. Phelps, the owner of a machine shop in Boston, and there he found the ideal milieu for his talents. When the cutting machine proved unsuccessful, Phelps suggested that Singer improve two current model Lerow & Blodgett sewing machines that needed repair. In 1850, the machines were so badly designed that the majority did not work, and the handful that did required persistent servicing. Singer reacted negatively to Phelps' suggestion: "You want to do away with the only thing that keeps women quiet – their sewing," he pouted. But work on them he did and quickly introduced all the basic features found on today's machines. Patented in 1851, his was the first machine to allow continuous and curved stitching through the use of an overhanging arm for vertical rather than horizontal motion of the needle. It was also the first to use a horizontal table that allowed sewing on any part of the work, the first to use a treadle for motive power, and the first strong enough to sew leather. But it utilized the same lockstitch process that had been patented by Howe and that was to create problems.

With financing from one George B. Zieber, Singer and Phelps founded the "Jenny Lind Sewing Machine Company", named after the "Swedish Nightingale" who had just completed a highly successful concert tour of America. Soon renamed I. M. Singer & Co., the venture was to prove an enormous financial success. But, priced at over $100, the machine found no market at first, neither in the home nor in the garment industry. Undeterred, Singer, as had McCormick, came up with a number of innovative merchandising practices – saleswomen to demonstrate the machines, installment buying, advertising campaigns, sales with service included – and the machines began to sell.

It was at this point that Howe returned from Europe and, funded by a mortgage on his father's farm, began years of legal battles to defend his patent. It was finally upheld in 1854, but the judgment left Singer undeterred. Aided and abetted by a new and secret partner, New York attorney Edward Clark, he rid himself of Phelps and Zieber, paid Howe off with a royalty agreement, and embarked on the greatest gamble of his career.

Soon after Eli Whitney's introduction of interchangeable parts, expert craftsmen could tool them to an accuracy of 1/16 inch. However, firearms manufacturers led by Samuel Colt (1814-1862), demanded better and began developing machine tools, gauges, and milling cutters capable of producing parts to one mil (1/1000 of an inch) and then to 1/10 mil. By 1855, Colt was using the new technology to obtain high quality products at the lowest possible cost. In a Hartford plant constructed along the Connecticut River, he clearly demonstrated the superiority of machine- based fabrication in enhancing both technical excellence and artisanship. His efficient operation enabled him to increase the percentage of unit cost devoted to superior finishes and ornamentations. A talented group of skilled artisans applied the arts of metal plating, engraving and inlaying – as well as carving and incising rare woods, ivory and pearl - into transforming the utilitarian firearm into a lavishly finished *objet d'art, a* "functional sculpture." Consummate salesman that he was, Colt promoted his firearms with specially cased and embellished presentation pieces that heightened the appeal and prestige of his product. His famous revolver, legendary throughout the world because of its high quality and reliability, became a celebrity symbol.

Isaac Singer was quick to see the true potential of Colt's manufacturing techniques and he risked everything to buy the machinery needed for the production of sewing machines. In late 1857, he opened in New York the world's first mass production facility for producing something other than firearms. Unit production costs for his sewing machines amounted to little more than $10. Even when interest, amortization, depreciation and property tax costs were added, the machines generated a handsome profit at their selling price of $50. And, of course, their existed at the time no income tax costs to be passed through to consumers in the form of higher prices. Following the opening of three more New York-based plants in 1858, unit sales topped 3,000 per year. In 1863, Singer and partner Clark incorporated the Singer Manufacturing Company, the owner of 22 patents and $550,000 in capital assets. With the opening of their first foreign factory near Glasgow in 1867 and others in Paris and Rio de Janeiro, the company became one of the first multi-nationals and Singer achieved world-wide renown.

In 1860, Singer's divorce from Catharine Haley was finalized. But, aside from conducting a demanding business life at the time, he was orchestrating a complex, multi-family personal existence as well. With his growing wealth, he had purchased a mansion on New York City's Fifth Avenue and lived there with his "wife" Mary Ann Sponseler and their ten children. But appearances were deceptive, for he had a third family with Mary Eastwood Walters who bore him a daughter and a fourth family with an employee at his factory, Mary McGonigal, who had already borne him five children.

His paradisiacal existence came to an end one day when Sponseler saw him driving openly in a carriage with McGonigal and had him jailed for bigamy. Released on bail, he and McGonigal sailed for Europe in 1862, and there he would remain for the rest of his life.

The couple lived in London at first. But while in Paris on business, Singer met and married Isobelle Eugenie Boyce Summerville in 1865, and this marriage endured. Isaac and Isobelle settled in Devon, England, near Torquay, in an area known as the English Riviera, where they built a 115-room house known as Oldway Mansion. Their son Paris would later redesign Oldway in Versailles-like splendor and, with modern dancer Isadora Duncan (1877-1927), father a son who expired in a car crash at an early age. Isaac died in 1875 leaving his estate to be fought over by his children, many of whom had come to live at Oldway.

Elias Howe finally accumulated a $2 million fortune from royalties but long after his loyal wife had passed on. He died in 1867 at age 48, the year his patent expired. In 1851 Howe had also obtained a patent on what would fifty years later become known as the zipper, but was too consumed in legal battles to follow it up.

It was Secretary of State Daniel Webster (1782-1852) orating at his most eloquent and moving best. Pausing a moment during the course of his two-day plea, he pointed to his client, a man sallow and emaciated from long years of privations and bitter disappointments, in appearance much older than his fifty-two years. "And now," he asked, "is Charles Goodyear the discoverer of this invention of vulcanized rubber? Is Charles Goodyear the first man upon whose mind the idea ever flashed, or to whose intelligence the fact ever was disclosed, that by carrying heat to a certain height it would cease to render plastic the India Rubber and begin to harden and metallize it? Is there a man in the world who found out that fact before Charles Goodyear?"

The year was 1852, the place Trenton NJ, and Webster was taking time off from his "busy" official duties to represent the plaintiff in a patent infringement case *Goodyear vs. Day* before the United States Circuit Court of Appeals. "If Charles Goodyear did not make this discovery," Webster continued, "who did make it? Why, if our learned opponent had said he should endeavor to prove that someone other than Mr. Charles Goodyear had made this discovery, that would have been very fair. On the contrary, they do not meet Charles Goodyear's claim by setting up a distinct claim of anybody else. They attempt to prove that he was not the inventor by little shreds and patches of testimony. Here a little bit of sulphur, and there a little parcel of lead, here a little degree of heat, a little hotter than would warm a man's hands, and in which a man could live for ten minutes or a quarter of an hour, and yet they never seem to come to the point. I think it is because their materials did not allow them to come to the manly assertion that somebody else did make this invention, giving that somebody a local habitation and a name. We want to know the name, and the habitation, and the location of the man upon the face of this globe, who invented vulcanized rubber, if it be not he, who now sits before us.

"Is the discovery so plain that it might have come about by accident? It is likely to work important changes in the arts everywhere. It introduces quite a new material into the manufacture of the arts, that material being nothing less than elastic metal. It is hard like metal and as elastic as pure original gum elastic. Somebody has made this invention. That is certain. Who is he? Mr. Hancock has been referred to. But he expressly acknowledges Goodyear to be the first inventor. I say that there is not in the world a human being that can stand up and say that it is his invention, except the man who is sitting at that table."

One of 32 cases involving infringement of patent #3,633 *Improvements in India-Rubber Fabrics* issued to Charles Goodyear in 1844, it was dubbed "The Great India Rubber Suit". The Court found for the plaintiff, establishing Goodyear as the sole inventor of vulcanized rubber, the first modern "plastic". The birth of polymer chemistry and the great industries producing the wondrous materials so basic to our high standard of living follow from Goodyear's invention.

Goodyear (1800-60) was born in New Haven CT, the son of Amasa Goodyear. A pioneer manufacturer of hardware, Amasa had produced the first pearl buttons sold in America and during the War of 1812 supplied metal buttons to the armed forces. Of a deeply religious nature, Charles' first intent was to enter the ministry, a profession that seemed to offer the most useful career of service. But a change of mind brought him to Philadelphia where he became a partner in his father's hardware firm. Although the business prospered for a time, an injudicious extension of credit led to insolvency. In New York on business during the summer of 1834, Charles happened to buy a rubber life-preserver in a retail store of the Roxbury India Rubber Company of Roxbury MA, America's first rubber manufacturer. Returning a few weeks later, he asked if the Company might be interested in his newly devised valve for improving life-preservers. Sadly, the store manager shook his head. The Company was not in the market for valves now, he informed Goodyear; in fact, it would be lucky to stay in business at all. Formed to manufacture rubber goods made of the miraculous new substance from Brazil, the Company's high expectations had foundered on natural rubber's unfortunate properties under hot and cold conditions. The manager pointed to rack upon rack of rubber goods that had melted into a malodorous goo in the torrid summer heat. At the Company's factory, he confided, the directors had met in the dead of night to bury thousands of melted rubber articles returned by outraged customers. But, he noted, fame and fortune awaited the inventor of a process that would keep rubber dry and firm in summer and flexible in winter.

To Goodyear, his experience with India rubber annunciated a call from God. "There is probably no other inert substance which so excites the mind," he wrote at a later date. "He who directs the operations of the mind can turn it to the development of the properties of Nature in his own way, and at the time when they are especially needed. The creature imagines he is executing some plan of his own, while he is simply an instrument in the hands of his Maker for executing the divine purposes of beneficence to the race." And so it was in the spirit of a crusader consecrated to the task of doing good that Goodyear took a first critical look at this mysterious "gum elastic", a substance with properties so desirable at moderate temperatures yet so gooey and smelly in hot weather and so brittle in cold.

Returning to Philadelphia, Goodyear was immediately clapped into debtor's prison, the usual practice under the laws of the day for bankrupt persons. It was not his first sojourn there and it would not be his last. But his crusade carried on. With a batch of raw rubber procured by a friend and his wife's rolling pin, he conducted his first experiments in jail, kneading and working the gum hour after hour upon a bench and marble slab allowed him by prison officials. He got the idea of mixing a dry powder into the naturally adhesive rubber so as to absorb its stickiness. Out of jail, he tried the talc-like magnesia sold in drugstores and the results looked promising. Working in their small kitchen with his wife and two small daughters, he made up several hundred pairs of magnesia-dried rubber overshoes for sale. But summer came before he could market them and he could only watch as his footwear sagged into a shapeless paste. Because the smell brought nasty complaints from neighbors, he moved his experiments to New York where a friend gave him a fourth floor tenement bedroom to serve as a "laboratory".

By adding another drying agent, quicklime, and then boiling the mixture, he got the best rubber yet. An exhibition of some rubber sheets and other articles at a New York trade show so impressed the judges that they awarded him a medal. But his hopes were dashed when apple juice, vinegar and other weak acids attacked his new rubber. Then in 1836, while trying to remove decorating paint from some samples, he discovered that the application of nitric acid to the rubber surface not only rendered it as smooth and dry as cloth but made it impervious to external influences. Thinking that the secret had been found, he found a partner with capital and leased an abandoned rubber factory on Staten Island. But his partner's fortune evaporated in the Panic of 1837, leaving Goodyear and his family camped in the factory and living on food donations and fish caught in the harbor. Interest had been aroused, however, and he found another partner in Boston who obtained a large government order for mailbags. He set up shop in the deserted Roxbury Company plant in Boston. But by the time the bags were ready for delivery, they had rotted from their handles. Only the surface of the rubber had been "cured". Underneath its dry-as-cloth surface lay the same old sticky gum.

After five futile years, Goodyear was near the end of his tether. Farmers around Woburn MA where he now lived gave milk to his children and let them dig half-grown potatoes for food. The nitric acid process had not solved the problem, Goodyear realized, but it was a major step forward. Fortune finally turned in his direction. In the winter of 1839 came the "butterfly", the accident that led to curing not only the surface but the whole mass of rubber. Stories of the discovery are apocryphal and Goodyear never revealed its circumstances. But it had all the earmarks of Newton's apple, he liked to explain. The accident held meaning only for the man "whose mind was prepared to draw an inference," for the man who had "applied himself most perseveringly to the subject." "The harder you work, the luckier you are," an apropos remark from champion golfer Gary Player, would appear to describe most "butterflys." One of the more persistent stories has Goodyear boiling rubber and sulfur on his wife's kitchen stove when, somehow, a lump of the mixture fell on the red hot iron top. Instead of melting like molasses, it charred like leather, and around the charred area was a dry and springy brown rim so remarkably altered that it was virtually a new substance. The first weatherproof rubber had been made.

The winter after the discovery was the blackest of his life. Dyspeptic and gout-racked, his health broken, he hobbled about on crutches tending to his experiments. He knew now that heat and sulfur miraculously changed natural rubber. But many details remained to be ironed out before the process was perfected – an accurate formula for the mixture, the exact degree of heat and the length of cooking time required. With endless patience, he roasted bits of rubber in hot sand, toasted them like marshmallows, steamed them over the teakettle, pressed them between hot irons. When his long-suffering wife finished baking bread in the oven, he thrust in chunks of evil-smelling gum. At night he lay awake, afraid that he would die and the secret with him. He pawned his watch and household furniture. When even the dinnerware was gone, he made rubber dishes to eat from. Then the food too was gone. He went to Boston looking for backing, found none and was jailed for non-payment of a $5 hotel bill. He came home to find his infant son dead. Unable to pay funeral costs, he hauled the little coffin to the graveyard in a borrowed wagon. Of the 12 Goodyear children, six died in infancy.

At last he found that steam under pressure, applied for 4 to 6 hours at about 270 degrees Fahrenheit, gave him the most uniform results. He wrote his wealthy textile manufacturer brother-in-law – who long before had lectured him on his family obligations and advised him to quit his quest – and informed him that interwoven rubber threads would produce the fashionable puckered effect then much favored in men's shirts. Two "shirred goods" factories were rushed into production and on the ruffled shirtfronts of socialite dandies rubber rode to worldwide acclaim.

As soon as he could, Goodyear disposed of his manufacturing interests that could have made him a fortune and went back to his experiments. He perceived rubber as a "vegetable leather" that defied the elements, an "elastic metal" and wood substitute that could be shaped in molds. Everything was to be made of it – banknotes, musical instruments, flags, jewelry, ship sails and even ships themselves. He had his portrait painted on rubber, his calling cards engraved on it, his autobiography printed on and bound in it. He wore rubber hats, vests and ties, suggested its use in food packaging, paint, wagon springs, ferryboat bumpers, wheelbarrow and carriage tires, inflatable life rafts and "frogmen" suits. But his business dealings were notoriously bad. Royalty rights brought in only a fraction of what they were worth. Shirred goods netted him 3 cents a yard; the licensees made $3 a yard. Patent piracy was so rampant that he finally engaged Daniel Webster to prosecute "The Great India Rubber Suit". At $15,000, the fee was the highest ever paid to a lawyer up to then.

He was slow in filing foreign patent applications. Samples of his heat-and-sulfur treated gum, which he had sent to British rubber companies without revealing any details, were seen by famed rubber pioneer Thomas Hancock. Hancock, who had been trying for twenty years to make weatherproof rubber, noticed a yellowish sulfur "bloom" on one sample's surface and with that clue reinvented the curing process. By the time Goodyear applied for an English patent, he found that Hancock had filed a few weeks earlier. Offered half a share of the Hancock patent, he declined – and lost his English rights. A friend of Hancock christened the contested process "vulcanization" after the Roman god of fire.

At the London and Paris world fairs of the 1850s, Goodyear installed great pavilions built entirely of rubber, floor to roof. When his French patent was canceled on a technicality and French royalties stopped before he could pay his bills, he was seized by gendarmes and hustled off to a 16-day stay at his familiar "hotel" as he called it – debtor's prison. There he received the Cross of the Legion of Honor bestowed by Napoleon III.

When he died, he was $200,000 in debt. Accumulated royalties, however, eventually made his family comfortable. His son Charles Jr. inherited his father's inventive talent and built a small fortune around shoe making machinery.

Today there is a cultivated rubber tree for every two human beings on earth. Three million tree "milkers" harvest the crop. The United States alone imports half of it, and synthesizes as much or more from petroleum. Nearly 300,000 Americans earn their livelihood working in rubber-derived industries that manufacture tens of thousands of polymer products worth many billions of dollars. The whole production apparatus owes its existence to that indomitable fanatic to whom money meant little. "Life," he wrote, "should not be estimated exclusively by the standard of dollars and cents. I am not disposed to complain that I have planted and others have gathered the fruits. A man has cause for regret only when he sows and no one reaps." In 1898, Frank Seiberling memorialized the Goodyear name when he founded the Goodyear Tire and Rubber Company in Akron OH. Its first product line consisted of bicycle and carriage tires, horseshoe pads and, as befitting the gamble that was being taken, poker chips. Charles Goodyear lies buried in New Haven's Grove Street Cemetery, not far from the grave of one of America's and the world's greatest scientists, Josiah Willard Gibbs (1839-1903). Gibbs' enormous contributions to thermodynamics and statistical mechanics laid the theoretical basis for the development of the polymer industries.

"What hath God wrought?" The "lightnings" transmission over wire of these Biblical words (*Numbers 23:23*) in 1844 climaxed a vast communications revolution that unified America during the Silver Age. In 1774 only the post road along the shore from Portsmouth NH to Savannah GA linked the thirteen original colonies. Other than a route between New York City and Albany, no regular communication paths with the interior existed. By 1861, a large network of roads connected the Atlantic with the Mississippi and the Great Lakes with the Gulf of Mexico. There were regular stagecoach runs westward from the seaboard and three lines ran beyond the Mississippi to forts on the far frontier. State and private money funded most of the roads, the one exception being the Cumberland Road, also called the Great National Pike or National Road, which was financed by federal land sales authorized under the Ordinance of 1787. In 1806 Jefferson had signed a bill providing start-up money of $30,000 for an initial survey basing his authority on Article I, Section 8, Clause 7 of the Constitution: The *Congress shall have the power ... To establish post offices and post roads*, a post road at the time being defined as any link between two towns or cities. Construction began in 1811 and was finally completed in 1838 at a cost of $7 million. Beginning at Cumberland MD, the Road cut through the Appalachian Mountains to Wheeling WV on the Ohio River and eventually carried to Vandalia IL on the Mississippi River opposite St. Louis, a distance of almost 600 miles. Although hardly more than a trail in many places, it was for many years the sole link to the western territories, and it pointed the way to the Mississippi and beyond for a great westward migration of settlers. Today's Interstate 70 follows much of the original route.

As in England, however, the road system proved totally inadequate for the movement of heavy loads. It took four horses a whole day to pull a one ton load a distance of 12 miles over level land. Coal from as far away as Newcastle could be shipped across the Atlantic to Philadelphia more cheaply than that mined two hundred miles away. But a canal barge could move 12 tons 24 miles in a day and Americans, as had Europeans, quickly turned to canal building for a more reliable and inexpensive transport of passengers and freight. George Washington had expressed an interest as early as 1770, and in 1785 he, Jefferson and Madison founded the Potomac Company, their objective being the construction of a canal linking the Ohio and Potomac Rivers. Numerous similar projects were undertaken at the same time. But, unfortunately, James Brindley was not around to supervise inexperienced engineers and workmen learning how to take a level, dig channels, remove tree stumps and underbrush, dispose of tons of earth, mix underwater cement, create locks and tend to the hundreds of other problems that arose. As a result, canal building at the time was in a state of abortive achievement. Nobody quite knew how to go about constructing a commercially successful canal and investors both American and foreign lost a great deal of money in the ventures. The Potomac canal, finally completed in 1802, was of limited usefulness because of seasonal low water conditions, chaotic current patterns and winter freezing. For almost a quarter of a century, the Cumberland Road remained the one tenuous link between the emerging west and the established east.

But with the flame of freedom flaring over this typically chaotic scene, many tried their hand at canal building. And, finally, and under the most unlikely of circumstances, a messiah arose. Western settlers, seeking a short route to markets on the east coast and beyond for bulky agricultural products, had long dreamed of a canal connecting Lake Erie with the Hudson River. Gouverneur Morris, one of the most prominent of the Founding Fathers and the owner of land in western New York State, had suggested the building of one in 1790, and his proposal was included in a "Report on Public Roads and Canals" by Secretary of the Treasury Albert Gallatin in 1808. In a 1797 letter from London, Robert Fulton informed President Washington of the great canal improvements he had witnessed in England and gave favorable mention to an Erie-Hudson canal. But nay-sayers cited the enormity of problems – a lack of funds, untrained engineers, an unforgiving terrain of forests, swamps and underbrush, the great length of the proposed canal (at 363 miles the longest ever attempted up till then), the steep ascent and descent from 566 feet at Lake Erie to 675 feet at its peak to sea level at the Hudson River – and deemed the project undoable. Thomas Jefferson, when petitioned for federal funds to undertake an initial survey, refused support. "It is a splendid project," he responded, "and may be executed a century hence."

Into this far from encouraging scene charged DeWitt Clinton (1769-1828), mayor of New York City for ten annual terms between 1803 and 1815, U.S. Senator 1802-3 and governor-elect of the state in 1816. That rare specimen of politician combining entrepreneurial talent with courage and vision, he foresaw the canal as the means of transforming New York into "the granary of the world, the emporium of commerce, the seat of manufactures, the focus of great Bank of the United States by casting the tie-breaking vote in the Senate against its rechartering. A believer in state sovereignty, he had opposed ratification of the Constitution in seven letters to the *New York Journal*, each of which was answered by Alexander Hamilton in the *Daily Advertiser*. And as did most knowledgeable persons of that era, he regarded canal building as essential to American economic growth. His death in 1812 left DeWitt to carry on alone. moneyed operations." His widespread political experience and influence, acquired while serving as secretary to his uncle, Governor George Clinton (1739-1812), was now thrown behind the Erie-Hudson canal project. George Clinton had been one of Washington's brigadier generals during the Revolution and the first and many time governor of New York State. He later became Vice-President of the United States (1804-1812) in which office he killed the 1st

As the pro-canal gubernatorial candidate in 1816, DeWitt embarked on a widespread public relations campaign of letter writing, speech making and petition circulation to win approval for the project. It was not easy. The press lambasted "Clinton's big ditch" mercilessly and most politicians looked aghast at the estimated cost of $7 million. Undeterred, Clinton drafted a "Memorial of the Citizens of New York, in Favor of a Canal Navigation between the Great Western Lakes and the Tidewaters of the Hudson". Submitted to the legislature with more than one hundred thousand signatures attached, it so swayed the lawmakers that they authorized the required funding and the commencement of work. Public opinion appeared overwhelmingly behind Clinton. A state bond issue got matters moving, raising $200,000. Figuring prominently in the initial financing of the canal were the small savings of New York City laborers, many of them recently arrived immigrants. Consolidation of their deposits at the Bank for Savings gave the Bank's trustees the wherewithal to purchase nearly 30% of the new securities by 1821. Almost all the rest was also supplied by small investors. The large northeastern banks, including the 2nd Bank of the United States, never did invest their deposits in this risky venture. Nevertheless, canal securities traded actively on the forerunner of the New York Stock Exchange along with Treasury issues and bank stocks.

Because no experienced European canal engineers would dare touch the project even when offered enormous salaries, Clinton hired a team of American "engineers" with country lawyer Benjamin Wright (1770-1842), a man with no engineering or canal experience whatsoever, as chief. Many would later call him the father of American civil engineering. James Geddes (1763-1838), who had earlier done some preliminary survey work, was appointed assistant chief engineer. Another appointee, Canvass White (1790-1839), traveled to England to learn what he could of English canal construction and came back to invent a waterproof hydraulic cement that could harden under water and still maintain full strength. It replaced the wood and bricks previously used in lock construction and proved essential in sealing the many leaks that developed along the canal length. Other appointees were John Bloomfield Jervis (1795-1885) who would later design and build New York City's Croton water supply system and Nathan Roberts (1790-1852) who designed the canal's unique "double combined locks" at Lockport for the 60-foot drop to Lake Erie. His locks enabled traffic to move simultaneously in opposite directions. All learned on the job in what became a school of engineering in itself and all figured prominently in future canal and railroad building.

Digging commenced on 4 July 1817 on the middle 96-mile segment of the canal from Utica to Rome. That was the easiest part – light soil and no lock requirements – and it was successfully completed in 1819. Clinton had wisely chosen this beginning to get quick results and arouse investor interest. Wealthy Americans, who played no part in the early financing, now bought in led by fur trader John Jacob Astor who invested $213,000, sugar refiner Frederick Havemeyer and tobacco merchant George Lorillard. DeWitt managed funds prudently, resisted pork-barrel add-ons to canal appropriations by the legislature and kept focused on his primary objective. Canal borrowings were completed in 1824. The "engineers" for their part performed miracles. Not even the loss of the more than 1000 workers to "swamp fever" on the Montezuma marshlands west of Syracuse could stop them from expeditiously completing the canal in 1825 on time and under budget. When finished, the canal was 40 feet wide, 4 feet deep and handled barges up to a maximum displacement of 75 tons. It utilized 77 locks, numerous bridges, and aqueducts to carry traffic over rivers and streams including one 600 feet in length over the Genesee River near Rochester. An alongside 10-foot wide towpath provided the means for teams of mules to draw the barges. For years to come, this "wedding of the waters" was the fastest route between western lakes and rivers and the Atlantic seaboard. It cut freight rates from the $100 per ton charged by shippers using mule- and horse-drawn carts between Buffalo and Albany to $10 per ton. And it made Ohio, Michigan, Indiana and Illinois accessible to the thousands of European immigrants who came flooding through the port of New York. Toll revenues soon exceeded $1 million a year, and in 1835 the canal redeemed its entire debt. By 1850 nearly half of all foreign trade was passing through New York piers and the city had leapfrogged over Boston, Baltimore, New Orleans and Philadelphia to become the busiest port in America, moving tonnages greater than the others combined. Perhaps more than any other single factor, the Erie contributed to New York's emergence as one of the world's great cities. And it literally made New York the "Empire State." The engineers "have built the longest canal in the world in the least time, with the least experience, for the least money, and the greatest public benefit" was how canal historian Noble E. Whitford phrased the miracle.

So astonishingly successful was the Erie that politicians in other states rushed into a frenzy of canal building. Most ventures, however, became mired in pork-barrel spending, fraudulent political practices, corruption, and over exuberant planning by inexperienced politicians posing as businessmen. Almost all were either abandoned or turned over to private development. No DeWitt Clinton was to be found among the politicians of any other state. With governments out of the way, the private economy brought into existence more than 4000 miles of canals by 1850, and they had become the superhighways of America. A new era was about to dawn, however, and building stopped abruptly. Following Fulton's steamboat by about twenty years, a steam engine affixed not to a boat but to a moving platform mounted on wheels made its appearance. The railroads had arrived.

In an unforeseeable development seemingly far removed from canal building, the Erie spawned America's first political machine. Conceived and brilliantly operated by then state senator and future President Martin Van Buren (1782-1862), the "Albany Regency", as it was known, would prove instrumental in creating the national Democratic Party. And, as we shall see, it changed American politics forevermore.

A superb portrait of DeWitt Clinton by Samuel Finley Breese Morse (1791-1872) hangs in the Metropolitan Museum of Art. Its bust-length likeness depicts Clinton as the indomitable, headstrong and farsighted person he was. A backdrop of wallpaper, heroically decorated with an overall pattern of monogrammed C's encircled by stars and wreaths, sets off Clinton's aged, jowled face and the black-robed mass of his body. The work potently reflects Morse's ardent belief in art as a means of communication and education. And in its connection to a project linking east and west, especially one of such grandeur as the recently completed Erie Canal, it conferred on him the "noblest delight." This portrait and those of the Marquis de Lafayette, Eli Whitney, Noah Webster, William Cullen Bryant and Presidents John Adams and James Monroe stamped Morse as one of early America's foremost artists.

Morse was born in Charlestown MA, the son of Jedidiah and Elizabeth Ann Finley Breese Morse. Jedidiah, a Congregational minister, had distinguished himself with the 1784 publication of a textbook *Geography Made Easy* that was as well known as family friend Noah Webster's dictionary. At age 14, Samuel matriculated at Yale and there supported himself by painting small portraits of friends, classmates and teachers – one dollar for profiles and five dollars for ivory miniatures. His passion, however, was to paint historical canvases after the style of Benjamin West, and he proceeded to enhance his skills after graduation with four years of study at the Royal Academy in London. An exhibit at the Academy of his six-by-eight-foot The *Dying Hercules* brought critical acclaim but few sales of his paintings. Upon returning to Boston in 1815 and opening an art studio, he found portraiture the only marketable genre.

He married Lucretia Pickering Walker in 1818 and the first of their three children arrived the next year. In 1824 he moved his family to New York hoping to tap into the City's more vibrant art market. There he landed the most coveted commission in town, a full-length portrait of Lafayette (now hanging in New York's City Hall) who was then on a triumphal tour of America. His studio hosted a sketching club of artists that evolved into the prestigious National Academy of Design, the most important art school in America. As the Academy's first president, he played an influential role in the education and training of young artists. His income from painting, however, remained meager. In 1829 he left his children with relatives – Lucretia had died suddenly in 1825 – and sailed once again to Europe for three years of further study and a disappointing response to his paintings. Frustrated by his lack of financial success, he accepted a position as a professor in the newly established art department at the University of the City of New York (soon to become New York University) and returned to America in 1832. And it was on this voyage that the "butterfly" fluttered its wings.

On the boat back home, Morse met one Dr. Charles T. Jackson of Boston who apprised him of what was going on in European electromagnetic research. Their conversations recalled for Morse his student days at Yale when he had been fascinated by professorial lectures on the little understood science of electricity. The production of electric charge by the frictional rubbing of one material on another; the invention of the Leyden jar in 1745 which could store charge for later discharge in the form of a spark; Benjamin Franklin's spectacular kite experiment in which he had stored the lightning's charge in a Leyden jar and identified lightning to be not the weapon of the gods but nothing more than a giant spark; Alessandro Volta's invention in 1800 of the first battery, his "voltaic pile," a column of alternating copper and zinc discs separated by brine-moistened cloth that produced a steady electric current – knowledge of all these phenomena had been tucked away in the far recesses of his brain for more than twenty years and it now came to the fore. He listened intently as Jackson told him about recent developments – Danish physicist Hans Christian Oersted's discovery in 1819 that an electric current produced a magnetism that could deflect the needle of a compass; English engineer William Sturgeon's 1825 invention of the electromagnet, a varnished iron rod bent into a horseshoe shape that became magnetized when current flowed in encircling turns of bare wire; and Michael Faraday's all-important law of electromagnetic induction, discovered just two years earlier, which described how a changing magnetic field created by one circuit induces an electric current in a nearby isolated circuit. Faraday's law was to become the electrical foundation of modern civilization, it being the basis of electric motors, generators, transformers and numerous circuit elements employed in today's manufactures. It seems incredible that layman Morse not only digested all the information imparted to him by Jackson but quickly came to the realization that pulses of electric current could be used to convey information over wires. More amazing still is how he applied his newly acquired knowledge to design in his shipboard sketchbook the prototype of a single-wire electromagnetic recording telegraph.

Back in America, Morse pursued his new passion in a room adjoining his studio. Unable to afford the equipment he needed, he made his own. An old canvas-stretcher to mount the equipment, a home-made battery to provide electricity, bits of insulated wire soldered together to carry current, an old clockwork mechanism to move a paper ribbon on which messages were recorded – all were pressed into service. By 1836 he was able to demonstrate a working telegraph. And in that same year, he painted his last major work, an allegory of the creative process depicted in a complex portrait of his beautiful daughter, Susan Walker Morse.

The first electrical telegraph had been proposed in 1753 and built in 1774. It transported charge from Leyden jars along 26 moistened threads to 26 detecting electroscopes, one for each letter of the alphabet. It was, needless to say, a highly impractical device. An important advance was made in 1825 by American physicist Joseph Henry (1797-1878). He followed up on Sturgeon's invention by constructing a much more sensitive electromagnet that could operate effectively on small currents. It utilized multiple layers of closely wound *insulated* wire, the insulation, it was rumored, coming from his wife's petticoats. In a demonstration of the magnet's potential for electrical signaling over wires, he rang a bell one mile away using his electromagnet to attract a pivoted iron striker. Also, independently of Faraday, Henry co-discovered the law of induction, in recognition of which the electrical unit of inductance now bears his name. Finally, in 1837 Englishmen William Cooke and Charles Wheatstone patented a 6-wire 5-needle telegraph. It proved useful to some railroads but was too costly for widespread commercial use.

Morse's telegraph represented a vast improvement over prior multi-wire systems. A single wire, grounded at both ends to complete the circuit, transmitted pulses of electrical current from a manually controlled switch at one end to a receiving electromagnet at the other. Long and short current pulses became the dots and dashes of the famous Morse code alphabet. Of crucial importance to long-distance telegraphy was Morse's introduction of the "relay," an inductive device whereby one electrical circuit opens and closes a switch in another circuit spatially isolated from the first. By building a telegraph line in segments each containing its own battery and relays, signals of undiminished strength could be carried over great distances. Fortuitously, Morse had the help and advice of Leonard Gale, professor of science at the University, and it was on ten miles of reeled iron wire in the latter's lecture room that the relay was first tested. Copper of sufficient purity and strength would not be available for electrical wiring until the turn of the century. Gale was taken in as a partner in the enterprise as was Alfred Vail (1807-1859) who contributed his mechanical skills and the resources of his family's New Jersey iron works to the construction of better telegraph models.

The telegraph was ready for commercial exploitation but Morse could find no backers willing to finance the construction of a line. Not one of the era's great financiers or politicians could see a future in sparks. What he did find was the first of numerous patent battles when Jackson now claimed priority of invention. Morse's patent, granted in 1840, was not to be upheld by the Supreme Court until 1854. As he later complained to his friend, novelist James Fenimore Cooper, the telegraph had brought him not riches but "litigation, litigation, litigation." In 1838 he surreptitiously took in as a partner Congressman Francis O. J. "Fog" Smith of Maine, chairman of the House Committee on Commerce, in the belief that Smith's influence could be of help in securing federal money. Smith arranged a demonstration in Washington that was attended by President Martin Van Buren and introduced a bill appropriating the necessary funds. But Congress failed to act on it and Morse sailed once again to Europe hoping in vain for success.

In Paris, Morse met Louis Daguerre, creator of the "daguerreotype," and became intrigued by the connection between science and art in the medium that would soon become photography. He brought the daguerreotype back to America, opened a portrait studio in New York and taught the process to others, including future Civil War photographer Mathew Brady (1823-1896).

In 1843 Congress, after years of procrastination, unexpectedly granted Morse $30,000 for the construction of a 41-mile experimental line of iron wire from Baltimore to Washington. By this time Smith, having failed in his 1838 reelection bid, had returned to Maine and become editor of the *Maine Farmer*. There can be little doubt that his highly illicit behavior had served to bring the telegraph to the attention of the political establishment. And it served as well to make him a fortune.

The funds granted, Morse contracted with Smith for the construction of an underground line for the telegraph. At this point in time, Ezra Cornell (1807-1874), one-time carpenter, mechanic and businessman, visited Smith. Having just bought the rights to market a side-hill plow in Maine and Georgia, he needed Smith's help in publicizing it. Smith needed help in laying the line and hired Cornell to build a machine that could plow trenches and lay lead pipe for enclosing the cable. A demonstration of the machine brought Morse to Maine, and he hired Cornell on the spot to supervise construction of the main line. The machine proved effective but the underground cable did not. Twenty thousand dollars was spent before Cornell realized that moisture in the lead pipe leaked through the insulation encasing the iron cable and caused short-circuiting. When Cornell turned to stringing the line overhead on poles using glass insulators of his own design, the project moved expeditiously to completion in early 1844. On 24 May, Morse sat before his telegraph key in the Supreme Court room of the Capitol and sent his famous "What hath God wrought" message to Vail at the Baltimore railroad depot.

Morse, Vail, Gale and Smith now set up the Magnetic Telegraph Company to extend the line from Baltimore to Philadelphia and New York. And other entrepreneurs, their eyes now opened to the potential of the new communications medium, founded a myriad of private competing companies using Morse's patent. Within ten years of the demonstration, 23,000 miles of wire crisscrossed the country. The Associated Press, a pool of six New York daily newspapers organized to share the expense of telegraphing news, began operations in 1848. Mergers on a grand scale commenced in 1851 with the combination of thirteen local companies into the New York and Mississippi Valley Printing Telegraph Company, its name changed five years later to Western Union. The Company completed the first transcontinental telegraph line in 1861. Cornell, one of its founders and directors and for a time its largest stockholder, used his profits to establish on his farmland in Ithaca the great university that now bears his name. Peter Cooper (1791-1883) and Cyrus Field (1819-1892) teamed up to establish the North American Telegraph Company which soon controlled more than half the lines in the country. In 1857 Field began his attempt to lay the first Atlantic cable. The first message, from President James Buchanan to Queen Victoria, was sent in 1858 but the cable stopped working one month later. It began operating successfully in 1866.

Morse became an American hero. His obituary, printed in The *New York Times* of 3 April 1872, reads in part as follows: "Professor Morse died last evening at 8 o'clock, his condition having become very low soon after sunrise. Though expected, the death of this distinguished man will be received with regret by thousands to whom he was only known by fame.

"Few persons have ever lived to whom all depth of industry owe a greater debt than the man whose death we are now called on to record. There has been no national or sectional prejudice in the honor that has been accorded to him, from the fact that the benefit he was the means of bestowing upon mankind has been universal, and on this account the sorrow occasioned by his death will be equally worldwide."

Morse lies buried in Brooklyn's beautiful Greenwood Cemetery, not far from the monument and grave of DeWitt Clinton.

These then were some of the truly greats, those whose unrelenting drive and determination to make a success of their ideas set America apart from the rest of the world. There were thousands more who contributed in ways both major and minor. Only their random selection by the "invisible hand" operating in a free market environment could possibly have singled them out, the relative few who happened to be in the right place at the right time. So powerful was the momentum generated by their unpredictable achievements that the politicians could do little to derail the meteoric economic growth that followed. Not that these experts on everything didn't try. But because they did not have recourse to income taxes and a central bank to confiscate and squander the people's money, government outlays rarely rose above 1% of gross domestic product throughout most of the nineteenth century. Except for the Civil War period, the disasters wrought by nobly-intentioned political expenditures were held to a minimum.

CHAPTER XIX

THE WAR OF 1812

All those who seek to destroy the liberties of a democratic nation ought to know that war is the surest and the shortest means to accomplish it.

Alex de Tocqueville

It was truly a wanton act of folly. On 18 June 1812, at President James Madison's behest, Congress declared war on the world's most powerful nation. The War of 1812, also known in New England as "Mr. Madison's War," is usually treated as a minor event in most history books, but it was hardly that. Its political and financial repercussions reached to the Civil War and beyond and, for a time, threatened to deconstruct a young nation woefully unprepared for battle. George Washington's "providential agency" surely worked overtime to ensure America's survival with the antebellum status quo intact.

The conflict brought into clear view an ugly sectional split between North and South that was to widen steadily thereafter. New England businessmen, their interests tied to shipping and commerce, stood steadfastly opposed to the War. Their opposition led to calls for a separate peace arrangement with England and to the Hartford Convention (December 15, 1814 to January 4, 1815) at which secession was discussed. Moderation prevailed, however, and only amendments to redress the "unfair" political advantage given the South by the Constitution were offered. Up to that time, the "3/5" clause of the Constitution and their greater number had enabled the agrarian southern states to dominate Congress. Support for the War centered there and was led by the "war hawks," political opportunists noteworthy for the war fervor they whipped up. Their vigorous rhetoric may be sampled in 1811 speeches by their most articulate leaders in which they orate their antipathies toward England. Listen to the bombast of Congressman Henry Clay (1777-1852) of Kentucky: "Not content with seizing upon all our property which falls within her rapacious grasp, the personal rights of our countrymen – rights which must forever be sacred – are trampled on and violated by the impressments of our seamen. What are we to gain by war? What are we not to lose by peace? Commerce, character, a nation's best treasure, honor!" And to Congressman John C. Calhoun (1782-1850) of South Carolina who preferred war to the "putrescent pool of ignominious peace."

The strained relations between America and England were rooted in the ongoing Old World slaughters that had started up once again in 1803. After having brought peace through conquest to Europe, Napoleon was intent on bringing Great Britain and her untold riches into the fold. But while France was supreme on land, England controlled the seas and the conflict was a standoff. As the one remaining obstacle to Napoleon's ambitions, the Royal Navy could ill afford any threat to her supremacy. And herein lay the problem. Ever since the Revolution, British sailors had been deserting in droves for the better pay and conditions in the American merchant marine, not to mention escaping from the risk of death and injury in battle. British naval captains, as a result, had long been ordered to board American ships in search of deserters, and in the process "man-stealing" some Americans as well. It remained a constant source of friction between the two countries.

Matters took a turn for the worse when in 1806 Napoleon declared the British Isles under a state of blockade. England retaliated with the 1807 Orders in Council which subjected all neutral shipping to search, seizure and impressments of seamen. Jefferson, however, insisted on freedom of the seas. To instill in the combatants a respect for the rights of neutrals, he resorted to embargo, non-importation and non-intercourse laws, but these proved ineffective. Nothing could deter American business interests from taking advantage of the hostilities to expand both their manufacturing and commercial operations, and a substantial smuggling trade with Britain continued even during the War of 1812. By 1811, according to retiring Secretary of the Treasury Albert Gallatin in a letter to the *New York Evening Post*, 26 January 1812, American exports had grown to over $45 million, $38.5 million of which went to England and her allies. Small wonder that the northern states rejected war with England. Clearly, they did not feel threatened by the occasional loss of a cargo or ship. As an anti-war editorial in the same edition of the *Evening Post* put it: "The anxiety of members of Congress to effect this object ["to compel England to pay more respect to American commerce"] is always the greater in proportion to the distance any honorable member lives from the seaboard."

England too was suffering from the trade disruptions with her former colonies, so much so that Jefferson was able to institute negotiations aimed at resolving the two nations' maritime differences. By 1812, Napoleon had undergone major reverses in Europe and no longer posed the danger he once did. Feeling more securely ensconced on her island fortress, England revoked the Orders in Council on June 16, just two days before America's declaration of war but too late for now President Madison to be notified. The War, however, was not called off when the news broke weeks later.

Aggravating relations between the two countries were uprisings in the Northwest Territories where, it was thought, the British hoped to contain American expansion by establishing a buffer state under the Indian chief Tecumseh. But General and future President William Henry Harrison had effectively neutralized that threat at Tippecanoe in 1811 and Tecumseh was subsequently killed at the battle of the Thames. More insidious were the apparent intentions of the war hawks to expand into Canada, Florida and Texas, the latter two controlled by Spain, England's newly gained ally against France. The British, being preoccupied with Napoleon, were not expected to offer much resistance to such aggression.

Militarily, the War went badly right from the start. An invasion of Canada failed miserably and a British blockade tightened steadily as more and more frigates from Europe were reassigned to patrol duty in the New World. Despite some dramatic victories in single encounters, an American fleet consisting of but sixteen ships of war was a puny match for the Royal Navy. With Napoleon's defeat and exile to Elba in April, 1814, England could entertain plans for the re-annexation of part or all of her former colonies. A three-pronged assault began in August with an expedition to Chesapeake Bay. Seasoned veterans newly transferred from European battlegrounds marched on Washington and burned many public buildings, including the Capitol and the President's house. With Philadelphia and New York there for the taking, England appeared odds-on to restore to America her former colonial status. But, as Robbie Burns had warned, The *best-laid schemes o' mice a' men/ Gang aft agley* ... . Baltimore's Fort McHenry unexpectedly withstood a fierce naval bombardment (inspiring Francis Scott Key to compose the *Star-Spangled Banner*) and the British, enervated by war weariness and a depleted treasury, decided to terminate the campaign. An army of 11,000 from Canada, the second prong of the assault, advanced along General Burgoyne's Revolutionary War route, the plan being to join up with the Chesapeake forces in New York. Once again, however, the British were stymied. An out gunned American flotilla commanded by Commodore Thomas MacDonough won a brilliant naval victory on Lake Champlain, and again the British withdrew. The third prong, consisting of a huge fifty ship armada carrying 7,500 troops, attacked New Orleans and met with disaster. A vastly outnumbered American army won a decisive victory on January 8, 1815, suffering only 8 killed and 15 wounded compared to 2000 casualties for the British. Although the battle took place two weeks after the signing of the Treaty of Ghent that ended the War, it proved highly significant in bringing fame and the future Presidency to General Andrew Jackson (1767-1845).

Peace negotiations, ably conducted by American commissioners Albert Gallatin, John Quincy Adams and Henry Clay, had been under way at Ghent, Belgium, since the previous July. At first recalcitrant in their demands for territorial concessions, the British relented when the stand at Fort McHenry and MacDonough's victory became known. The Ghent Treaty as finally drafted left relations between the two countries much as they were before the War. American casualties amounted to 4200 wounded and 1700 killed. Unfortunately untouched were the politicians who put those poor lads into the war in the first place.

Financing the unpopular War proved difficult. The people's money was no longer easily available because Congress had rejected the rechartering of the 1st Bank of the United States in 1811. On 17 February 1812, the House Ways and Means Committee drew up plans for a 3-year prosecution of a possible war. For the fiscal year 1812-13, a total budget of $26,500,000 was projected including $11 million for the military. To raise the $11 million, the Treasury sold war bonds bearing an interest rate of 6% and redeemable in 12 years. These were sold directly to private banks and individuals with some of the larger banks acting as principals. The ordinary expenses of government (including interest on the remaining $45 million national debt) were to be met by revenues from a doubled tariff schedule, increased "tonnage" fees, and direct taxes on houses, land, slaves, carriages, refined sugar, and spirituous liquors once again. It was not nearly enough. When Congress finally declared war in June, bond subscriptions amounted to little more than $6,000,000 leaving almost $5 million more to be raised. New England banks refused to participate in the bond offerings. Americans of the time, obviously, were hardly enamored at the prospect of war. The island of Nantucket even declared its neutrality in 1814. And, as usually happens when higher taxes are imposed, tax evasion zoomed and revenues fell. Customs receipts in 1813 dropped by 50% even though the British blockade at the time was spotty. All hardly surprising in a war of confused objectives and divided loyalties.

To make up the shortfall, Madison authorized an issue of $15 million in Treasury notes bearing an interest rate of 5.4% and redeemable in specie one year hence. Another issue on the same terms followed in February of the next year. Again, it was not enough, for in 1813 the Treasury ran out of money. All government security holders, contractors and employees, including army and navy personnel, faced a payless and provisionless future. A crisis was averted only when a group of businessmen, headed by shipping magnate Stephen Girard (1750-1831), subscribed to a $10 million loan that enabled the nation to carry on the conflict. Girard, a naturalized French immigrant who had built a global trading business based in Philadelphia, risked almost his entire personal fortune in acquiring more than $8 million of the debt, with fur trader John Jacob Astor and others taking up the rest. Their gamble on a very shaky national government undoubtedly preserved America's independence.

The politicians' insatiable demands for money to finance the War encouraged the formation of "wildcat banks." These undercapitalized banks would take on the government's war debt, add it to their deposits, and issue notes far in excess of specie. It was the same indirect method of printing money that today's governments employ through their central banks, one that avoids the necessity of dangerous and possibly unenforceable tax hikes. Coupled with wartime shortages of civilian goods and services, this new supply of money jumped prices more than 40% over the three war years. War bonds fell to 60¢ on the dollar when in 1814 the government found itself unable to redeem Treasury notes in specie. Suspension of specie payments by private banks followed as a frightened public rushed to convert bank paper into gold. On 26 December 1814, a fourth issue of notes totaling $10.5 million was for the first time not fully subscribed. A fifth issue of almost $5 million on February 24, 1815 dispensed with all the Constitutional formalities. Coming in small denominations of $3, $5, 10, $20, and $50 and bearing no interest or specie backing whatsoever, these notes circulated as the American republic's very first debt-free, interest-free paper currency. The monetary printing press has always been a time-honored method of financing spendthrift governments. The Revolutionary War itself was financed in this way with the printing of "Continentals." And, fifty years later, Abraham Lincoln would drive the printing press to unprecedented limits to finance the Civil War.

Although short-lived, the War of 1812 was to unleash fearsome consequences on unborn future generations. It poses a most interesting question: Would America have been far better off governed under the Articles of Confederation (with limitations on the powers of the states) than under a Constitution of "implied powers"? Under such governance, the three-quarter vote necessary to declare war and appropriate money might well have prevented not only the War of 1812, but also the devastations wrought by future conflicts and economic downturns.

CHAPTER XX

1812: THE AFTERMATH

There are three things that are real in this world — God, human folly, and humor. Since the first two are wholly incomprehensible, we must see what we can do with the third.

The Ramayana

The State is the great fiction by which everybody tries to live at the expense of everybody else.

Frédéric Bastiat, French economist

The scenario should by now be all too familiar to us: *Under the guise of doing good, government taxes, government squanders and government kills.* Whereas the principle of enumerated powers effectively restrains politicians and "binds them down from mischief with the chains of the Constitution," "implied powers" paves "the road to hell" with public service "benignities." Just give those vainglorious politicians – the "correct" ones, of course – all the money they need to realize their noble intentions and they will establish a paradise here on earth – that's the basic assumption of all elitists from Plato to Marx to present-day liberals. But, in light of chaotic unpredictability and its unintended consequences, the whole concept of "implied powers" demands reexamination. The government-sponsored chaos and killing that too often results from professed noble intentions is unconscionable.

War's aftermath usually leads to calls for bigger government, and the War of 1812 proved no exception. Standard operating policy calls for government folly to be corrected by ever greater government folly, and therein lay the future. As we might now expect, the "presence of government" in the post-War years did nothing so much as to introduce anarchy into the nation's drive to "Power, Consequence, and Grandeur." How America's free market economy was able to deliver explosive growth in the face of incessant attacks by chaotic government is a marvel to behold!

His thinking warped by wartime travails, Madison, like Hamilton before him, moves toward "implied powers." In the process, the Republican Party absorbs the Federalist platform to such an extent that only one party remains. It is, supposedly, an Era of Good Feelings, and it temporarily assuages the festering sectional sores soon to break out. In 1816, Madison pierces the protective shield against chaos afforded by "strict construction" and signs two bills.

The first charters the 2nd Bank of the United States for twenty years, the reasons given being much the same as those put forth by Hamilton in 1791. It is naught but a clone of the 1st Bank but three and a half times larger. The great difficulty in financing the unpopular War of 1812 has convinced him of the need for a Bank of England-type institution to accommodate the politicians' insatiable demand for the people's money without resorting to dangerous tax hikes. The other introduces a protective tariff to America. Little did anyone imagine the killing this "butterfly" would lead to 45 years hence.

The 2nd Bank began operations at the end of a strong deflationary period. Money was extremely tight and interest rates high because the War of 1812 had frightened people into converting all the government and bank paper they could into gold and silver. As confidence returned, specie once more found its way back into bank deposits and became available for loans. Tight money gave way to easy money and rampant speculation in western lands, sales of which had been zooming upward ever since passage of the Continental Congress' Ordinance of 1787. Under the Ordinance's terms, the 13 original states relinquished their territorial claims in favor of the national government and federal policy had ever since fostered the privatization of western lands. Before the Revolution, migration westward amounted to only a trickle and stopped at the Appalachian Mountains. Afterwards, however, the movement intensified to flood proportions and extended to the Mississippi River. In 1800, Kentucky and Tennessee were the only states west of the Appalachians, but by 1820, six more were added – Ohio, Indiana, Illinois, Louisiana, Mississippi and Alabama – and the western population had exploded from 386,000 in 1800 to 2,216,000. By 1819, U. S. Government land sales amounted to 3.5 million acres yearly. To make room for the settlers, the native Indian populations were either annihilated or brutally displaced west of the Mississippi. Andrew Jackson's Seminole campaign of 1818 and the Cherokee nation's forced march on a "Trail of Tears" from Georgia to the Oklahoma Territory in the winter of 1838 form genocidal horror stories all their own. Americans were not about to squander an opportunity to own and cultivate land that the Indians had never used productively, especially when huge domestic and foreign markets for western cotton and grains became accessible from the newly acquired port of New Orleans.

As noted by John Kenneth Galbraith in his book, *Money*, the 2nd Bank "joyously participated" in the booming real estate market by facilitating land sales with low interest loans. Its first president, former Congressman William Jones, went along with the easy money policy then in vogue throughout the country. The 2nd Bank's stated mission of reining in a supposed glut of paper money emanating from state banks seemed of little concern to him. Although contrary to the opinion of elitist historians and the Bank's stockholders for whom higher interest rates meant higher profits and dividends, Jones undoubtedly followed the right policy for the time. Under free banking and with the big new Bank in a non-interfering mode, natural checks on the war-induced inflation activated as people sensibly gravitated to the safest banks, those with conservative note issues and fractional reserves of 10% or more. A balance (chaon?) had been struck wherein the nation's inflation was coming under control while at the same time the country found all the money necessary to support a massive expansion of industry, turnpike, canal and farm improvement ventures. But the 2nd Bank's initial capitalization of $35 million (as compared to $10 million for the 1st Bank) had pulled specie out of state banks and concentrated it in the new government-sponsored entity. Coupled with the $3 million in gold needed for the coming redemption of maturing Louisiana Purchase bonds, regional bank reserves diminished and money became somewhat tighter. More than likely, the tightening mildly inhibited booming business activity and land sales. However, there can be little doubt that any slowdown would have self-corrected in short order had the economy remained free of "benign" influences. Rapidly growing foreign investments in America and a strong export trade were more than adequate to replenish the money supply and reestablish strong economic growth. But an "elephant in a china shop" had been created and it was about to make its presence felt.

In 1819 Jones was replaced by Langdon Cleves who immediately instituted a blunderbuss policy of tight money. The resulting loan repayments and land foreclosures forced specie redemption of bank notes and drained reserves from the regional banks. The 2nd Bank's own specie holdings increased to upwards of 50% of deposits. It was exactly the wrong move at the wrong time. The money supply quickly imploded into a vicious depression known as the Panic of 1819. There followed three long years of closed textile factories and iron works in the North, plummeting commodity and land prices in the West, soaring unemployment, failed banks and vanishing savings. Madison and Jefferson themselves almost went bankrupt as money self-destructed. "The Bank was saved, and the people were ruined," was how one contemporary characterized the Bank's reversal of policy. An "immense revolution of fortunes in every part of the Union; enormous numbers of persons utterly ruined; multitudes in deep distress; and a general mass of disaffection to the government" was how John Calhoun depicted the situation. Twelve years later, Senator Thomas Hart Benton would liken the Bank to "the jaws of a monster … One gulp, one swallow, and all is gone!" And, as had been foreseen by William Paterson, the disaffection did not lead to any beheadings or tax revolts. As is still the case today, the public's ignorance of financial affairs ensures an uninterrupted flow of money to the nation's capital. "Who is to regulate the regulators?" Galbraith asks. It is a question that remains to be answered.

As unfortunate and unnecessary as was the Panic in the short run, the unforeseen longer-term consequences proved far worse. To help their businesses weather the economic storm, northern industrial leaders voiced more stridently than ever outcries for protectionism and the end of free trade, what they had been striving for since ratification of the Constitution. Despite his earlier argument against it, Madison signed a protective tariff bill in 1816 that placed duties of 25% on woolen, cotton and iron manufactures and 15% to 30% on all other imports. It was to expire in three years but was extended to 1824. Although aimed at paying the interest on and amortizing over $100 million of accumulated war debt, it established a mercantilist precedent in shielding northern industries from foreign competition. Reaction to the new tariff schedule, however, was at first muted despite the higher prices it entailed. Times were prosperous and redeeming the national debt was everybody's concern. But southern planters soon realized that they were shouldering a disproportionate share of the burden. Although consumers nationwide footed the bill, the South, as the major export arm of the country, found itself in a double bind. The principal revenue source for the federal government was the tariff on imports. And 90% of the tariff revenues came from the South because cotton and tobacco exports were paid in the main by a bartering exchange of imported and, therefore, dutiable manufactures. The higher prices imposed on these by the tariff became a de facto tax on southern planters forcing them to restrict the import of vital textiles and iron goods. That in turn squeezed England and other European nations into buying less raw cotton, which translated into falling cotton prices and rising production costs at a time when all other prices were going up. The South saw the tariff as a government subsidy paid into the pockets of northern manufacturers by all American consumers, and southern farmers most of all. It thrust the South into the same posture relative to the North as that of the American colonies vis-à-vis England before the Revolution. To make matters worse, most of the tariff revenues were spent for government operations in the more populous North and for servicing the federal debt, held in the main by wealthy northerners. The gold specie demanded for the payment of import duties therefore channeled northward for debt redemption, depleting reserves and raising interest rates in the South. Still, the Tariff of 1816 was limited in scope and the problems associated with it provided only a foretaste of what was to come. Aside from the obvious violation of tax uniformity in the Constitution, protectionism raised questions that are still to be answered today: Do the benefits to producers and workers in protected industries outweigh the costs to consumers nationwide? Do protective tariffs allow inefficient industries to persist?

During the first years after the Constitution, a time when manufacturing was in its infancy and farming was by far the country's most important industry, import duties fell more or less evenly among the states and no problem with uniformity in taxation arose. But to serve a population that nearly doubled from 4 million in 1790 to over 7 million by 1810, manufacturing output began to expand rapidly. The Napoleonic Wars in Europe provided further stimulus as both England and France and the neutrals who had previously bought from them now sought American manufactures. By 1816, 100,000 northern factory workers (two-thirds women and children) were producing more than $40 million worth of manufactured goods a year made possible by private capital investments totaling a huge for the time $100 million. Although small compared to agricultural investment, the gap was steadily narrowing. When peace returned, however, European nations resumed normal production and again competed strongly in the prosperous American market. To the dismay of industrial leaders, the easy profits of the war years vanished and that led to more strident calls for tariff protection. Responding to pressures, northern lawmakers introduced protectionist measures at each session of Congress following the 1816 tariff, and with increasing urgency after the Panic of 1819. But manufacturing interests did not yet carry the clout they would soon have and southern Congressmen, in league with those representing New England shipping and mercantile interests, were able to ward off passage of higher tariffs. An 1820 bill to increase duties by a mere 5% died in Congress. Then in 1824 an expanded tariff raising the minimum duty on textile imports to 33% and to an average of 37% on all other goods was signed into law by President James Monroe. Dutiable items included agricultural products such as hemp, wheat and liquor to protect western farmers, textiles to protect northeastern manufacturers, and iron goods to protect the mining and forging industries of Pennsylvania. Now textiles and other manufactures cost a third more because of the tariff and the squeeze was on. Cotton prices by 1827 dropped from 21¢ a pound to 8.8¢. And there was little the South could do about it. Immigration from Europe, as reflected in the 1820 census, was rapidly altering the country's demographics and turning the South into a regional minority. Although the Constitution had been designed to protect just such a minority from oppressive taxation by a "tyranny of the majority," it proved ineffective in practice. What Jefferson and Madison had foreseen in their Kentucky and Virginia Resolutions now came to pass: None of the three branches of government, neither the Supreme Court nor the Congress nor the President seemed interested in fulfilling their sworn oaths to uphold the Constitution. Other than to subsidize northern industrial and agricultural interests fully capable of dealing with foreign competition on their own, there appeared to be no justification for the Tariff of 1824. By favoring one section of the country over another, it clearly violated the general welfare and uniformity requirements of Article I, Section 8, Clause 1 of the Constitution. Moreover, the revenues were not needed since strong economic growth had by then led to a balanced federal budget and a disappearing debt.

Why, it may well be asked, was industrialization not pursued as strongly in the South as in the North? After all, both parts of the country started out as agricultural in nature. And Whitney's cotton gin, by revolutionizing the cultivation of long-staple cotton in the upcountry regions of the South, had transformed subsistence farmers into a class of wealthy landholders. But these planters, along with the rice barons in the down-country coastal regions, believed slavery to be the foundation of their economy and they were not about to give it up. It proved a very unfortunate choice. As Adam Smith had pointed out, a slave economy is terribly inefficient and cannot generate nearly the profits needed for the financing of manufacturing start-ups. Middle and lower class whites, as a consequence, were forced to put up with a standard of living well below that of their northern compatriots. In any event, by the late 1820s, cotton was barely profitable and the South found itself in difficult financial straits. When President John Quincy Adams signed into law the much harsher, Clay-authored Tariff of 1828, the so-called *Tariff of Abominations* or *Black Tariff*, import duties were increased toward 50% on a greatly expanded list of imports and threatened the South with impoverishment. His action placed nullification and secession on the table and precipitated a Constitutional crisis the ramifications of which would lead to the Civil War.

Meanwhile, back at the 2nd Bank, the war between federalists and anti-federalists continued on other fronts. People everywhere outside of Washington, Philadelphia and New York seemed well aware that something had to be done about the Bank and its dictatorial position in the economy. Not only did its unpredictable and tight monetary policies retard economic growth, but its cost-of-money advantage over state banks in negotiating private business loans siphoned capital from rural areas to the "moneyed aristocracy" of the east coast financial centers. Immediately upon its chartering, Indiana and Illinois amended their state constitutions to prohibit Bank branches within their jurisdictions and North Carolina and Georgia laid heavy taxes on the Bank's in-state branches. It was in Maryland, however, where the main action unfolded. The state levied a 2% stamp tax on the notes of the Bank's Baltimore branch with $15,000 to be paid annually in advance. When Bank cashier James McCulloch refused payment, he was convicted in state courts of tax law violation. One of the reasons behind his refusal may have been that he and another officer had negotiated unsecured loans from the Bank in order to speculate in western land deals and the Bank simply did not have the money. In any event, McCulloch petitioned the United States Supreme Court for redress in what became known as the landmark case *McCulloch vs. Maryland* (1819).

Three crucial issues begged for resolution: 1) Does Congress have the power to charter a bank? 2) Does a state have the power to tax an instrument of the federal government? 3) Is the Supreme Court the final arbiter in such matters? In their arguments before the Court, Daniel Webster, the highly paid counsel for the Bank, and Charles Pinckney, government lawyer and twice unsuccessful Federalist candidate for President against Thomas Jefferson and James Madison, spoke for "implied powers" echoing Alexander Hamilton's arguments in 1791. In a 7-0 unanimous vote, the Court concurred. Chief Justice John Marshall (1755-1835) in his brief found the law establishing the Bank well within the purview of the Constitution. The decision occasioned little surprise. As Jefferson well understood, a tenured judiciary salaried with taxpayer money naturally promotes federalism by favoring implied powers. And that issue and that issue alone would become the basis of the coming storms. A lame-duck appointee of President John Adams in 1801, Marshall spent his long tenure on the bench promoting the "benign-dictator" view of government and the Court as supreme arbiter in all matters involving constitutional interpretation. His federalist views were continually challenged by Jefferson, Madison and Jackson, all of whom believed that no government should, through its appointed judges, determine the limits of its own powers. To these popularly elected Presidents, that was tantamount to tyranny. Neither Marshall nor Webster nor Pinckney possessed that instinctive grasp of Adam Smith's "invisible hand" that had guided the Founding Fathers to "enumerated powers." *McCulloch vs. Maryland* was to create a precedent for government intervention into the private economy whenever politicians deemed it necessary.

To his opinion sanctifying "implied powers," Marshall added a limitation on the taxing powers of the states. "The power to tax is the power to destroy," he thundered. A state that can destroy through taxation "an instrument employed by the government of the Union to carry its powers into execution" possesses in effect a veto power over Congress. Because federal law is supreme, Marshall concluded, the Maryland state law was unconstitutional and therefore null and void. As he had for national laws in *Marbury vs. Madison* (1803) and for state laws in *Fletcher vs. Peck* (1810), he once again promulgated his contention that the Court is supreme in deciding the constitutionality of legislation.

The question of the Court's supremacy remained open. Despite *McCulloch vs. Maryland*, many states continued their harassment of the Bank (James J. Kilpatrick, The *Sovereign States: Notes of a Citizen of Virginia* (1957)). In 1819 Ohio enacted an annual tax on a branch Bank of the United States of $50,000. When the Bank refused payment, the state tax collector leapt over the counter, strode into the vaults and helped himself to $100,000 in paper and specie. Today that would be the equivalent of Ohio's governor ordering state troopers to enter the Cleveland Federal Reserve Bank and stripping it of millions in Federal Reserve notes. Relying on the Supreme Court's decision, the Bank sued to get its money back. The Ohio legislature considered the lawsuit a threat to all Americans. It declared itself aware of the "theory" of the Supreme Court's supremacy as final interpreter of the Constitution, but to this doctrine it could never give assent. It quoted Jefferson's Kentucky Resolution of 1798: "…as in all other cases of compact between parties having no common judge," each party "has an equal right to interpret the Constitution for themselves, where their sovereign rights are involved …"

In 1825 Kentucky and Connecticut adopted Ohio's states rights stand toward the Bank and South Carolina in 1829 followed by imposing a tax on Bank stockholders residing in the state. The New York and New Hampshire legislatures enacted resolutions urging that the Bank not be re-chartered while the Virginia legislature prepared a Constitutional amendment establishing a "super-supreme court" to decide questions involving federal vs. states rights. *Obviously, the Supreme Court as a Greek revival oligarchy was not acceptable to most early Americans.* States rights as a check on the tyrannical proclivities of a central government remained the important consideration for them. In the face of such hostility, the Bank's days were clearly numbered.

CHAPTER XXI

ENUMERATED POWERS VS. IMPLIED POWERS, ONCE AGAIN

The World Is Too Much Governed

Slogan adorning the masthead of the Washington *Globe*, circa 1830

James Madison declined a third-term run in 1816 leaving the last of the prominent Founding Fathers, James Monroe, to win in a landslide. In 1821, Monroe secured the nation's southeastern border by purchasing the Florida territory from Spain for $5 million and finalized the northwestern boundary with Canada. In 1823, and with the encouragement of England, he proclaimed what became known as the Monroe Doctrine, which foreclosed the New World as a colonial hunting ground for foreign nations and left Latin America to the mercies of local dictators. He vetoed, as had Madison, what he considered to be unconstitutional internal improvement bills, preferring to leave such tasks to the states and avoid the likelihood of federal "pork." But then he violated the principle of tax uniformity by signing the protectionist Tariff of 1824, and that was to let loose a Pandora's box of troubles.

Monroe also approved a little noticed measure, The General Survey Act of 1824, which authorized the "President of the United States … to cause the necessary surveys, plans, and estimates to be made of such Roads and Canals as he may deem of national importance in a commercial or military point of view." We shall see later that this Act, based on the general welfare and defense provisions in the Constitution, figured prominently in railroad development. And in a reverse twist on the Fulton painter-to-engineer interrelationship, it begat one of the world's greatest artists.

Monroe, too, declined a third-term run in 1824 leaving the field to four principal candidates. This election was the first to be hotly contested. All the previous ones had involved Founding Fathers and little doubt was attached to the outcome. The one major issue had been "enumerated" versus "implied" powers, and that supposedly had been put to rest with the Jefferson presidency in 1801. John Quincy Adams (1767-1848), son of our 2nd President, was the nominee of the Massachusetts legislature (political conventions were still in the future). As Secretary of State under Monroe, he had crafted the Monroe Doctrine and resolved America's boundary disputes with England over the Canada-Maine border. A representative of northern manufacturing interests, he strongly favored implied powers and a more powerful central government. Henry Clay of KY, speaker of the House of Representatives, embraced Adams' statism stand. In a series of speeches before the Senate in 1824, he advocated a program that soon became known as the "American System" – federally funded internal improvements (mainly western roads and canals the costs of which were to be paid by the central government in Washington), tariff protection for American industry, a "sound" banking system headed by the 2nd Bank of the United States to control the financial affairs of the American people, and high prices for western lands to pay for the increased costs of government. For prodding the country into the War of 1812, Clay should have been dispensed with long before, but here he was campaigning for President and threatening America's explosive economic growth with "left-wandering" policies. The staying power of this "corrupt statist," as he has been called, unquestionably rested on his ability to bring "pork" money into his home state. William H. Crawford from Georgia, Monroe's Secretary of the Treasury, was the nominee of a Congressional caucus. He expressed a belief in limited government but a paralytic stroke all but eliminated him from the race. And finally there was Andrew Jackson, United States Senator from TN, iron-willed "Old Hickory" as the renowned hero of the Battle of New Orleans and the Florida Seminole Wars was known. Of his stand on political issues little was known, but there seemed to be no doubt among his supporters that "The World Is Too Much Governed" motto caught the tenor of his thinking. John C. Calhoun of South Carolina, Monroe's Secretary of War and a fifth possible candidate, withdrew to run unopposed for Vice-President.

Jackson won the popular vote handily, garnering 153,000 votes (41%) to Adams' 116,000 (31%) and to Crawford's and Clay's 47,000 each. He also won the electoral vote but failed to get a majority, the tally being 97, 84, 41 and 37, respectively. Pursuant to the 12th Amendment, the election was now thrown into the House of Representatives where each state would cast one vote for any one of the top three electoral vote gatherers. Jackson looked the easy winner, but Clay, although excluded from consideration because of his fourth place finish, wheeled and wheedled, cajoled and threatened, and finally bribed his colleagues into throwing the election to Adams. The final House vote: 13 states for Adams, 7 for Jackson, 3 for Crawford. Adams' first act as President was to choose Clay as his Secretary of State, the office that had with one exception led to the Presidency in prior elections. Rumors of a "corrupt bargain" surfaced incurring the wrath of Jackson and his supporters. Whatever the other consequences of this election, it brought into the open Jackson's anti-Adams, anti-Clay political views: no "American System", no 2nd Bank, no "implied powers," no elitism in government, no strengthening of central authority, and no new taxes.

The stage was clearly set for public decision in the election of 1828. But with the passing of the Founding Fathers, the political scenery had changed. Washington, Adams, Jefferson, Madison and Monroe were household names familiar to all Americans, and none of them even thought of campaigning for public office. After Jefferson's election in 1800, the anti-Federalists – known variously as Republicans, Democratic-Republicans or Democrats – had initiated the beginnings of what today we know as a political party. For their lesser candidates, they organized political campaigns, distributed party literature and used the press to stimulate interest and voter support at the polls. The Federalists, however, had taxed and spent themselves into oblivion and were never a serious factor after 1800 except in the northeast. A one-party system held sway after 1816 (the so-called Era of Good Feelings) and what party organization remained simply withered away for lack of anything to do. But in1824 the old enumerated vs. implied powers controversy, which had been smoldering ever since the end of the War of 1812, broke into the open and split the Jeffersonians into two major groups, National Republicans and Democrats.

As a shrewd observer of the political scene, state senator Martin Van Buren (1782-1862) of New York sensed the change as early as1817. He foresaw that winning elections without the charismatic names of the Founding Fathers heading the ticket would require a much more concerted effort than in the past. Future political campaigns, if they were to be successful, were going to need money, big money. And that is where inspiration struck in the form of the Erie Canal. Originally opposed to the project, Van Buren about-faced when he recognized the enormous patronage potential offered by the Canal. In what soon became known as the "Albany Regency," he gathered about him a talented cadre of legislators, public office holders and newspapermen, all disciples of Thomas Jefferson and ardent believers in the "enumerated powers" interpretation of the Constitution. By handing out patronage jobs on the state-sponsored Erie project, by procuring contracts for businessmen to build short Canal segments, by buying rights-of-way from local land owners and rewarding them with Canal work, by granting printing contracts for state documents to supportive local newspapers, by publicizing the prosperity that would accrue to the communities along the Canal – always with a judicious eye on procuring votes and contributions – the Regency organized a huge constituency of loyal supporters. Regency lieutenants appeared in every county, captains in every town, and confidential agents statewide to keep the leaders apprised of local developments. The *Albany Argus*, along with a network of local newspapers, dispensed the party line throughout the state. Looking to the future, it encouraged promising young lawyers and newspapermen to accept Regency leadership and seek public office under its sponsorship. So successful were its operations that New York politics remained under its control for years to come. A new breed of professional politician had arisen, of a kind familiar today.

In 1821 Van Buren brought his vast organizational skills to the United States Senate. As Senator from New York, he fought legislation that promoted federal programs at the expense of states rights. Public works, he felt, should be undertaken by the states just as New York had done in sponsoring the Erie Canal. As chairman of the Senate Judiciary Committee, he was an outspoken critic of the Supreme Court, especially in its practice of judicial review. As the leader of an anti-Adams coalition in the Senate, he managed the Congressional caucus that nominated Crawford for President in 1824 and suffered a temporary blow when the latter lost out. Whatever else it did, the election revealed to Van Buren the enormity of Jackson's popularity and he resolved to attach himself to what he recognized as the General's very long coattails. But small thinking limited solely to the gratification of his own electoral ambitions was not for a man of Van Buren's caliber. He saw Jackson as the vehicle through which an Albany Regency-type organization could be expanded throughout the country. A national party representing East, South and West, a party that would own and operate the government for the benefit of party workers and be financed with the people's gold – that was his lofty goal. That is not to say he did not have noble intentions as far as the rest of America was concerned. Of course he did. The new party would promote the "greatest happiness of the greatest number" by promulgating Jeffersonian principles throughout the country and electing sympathetic candidates to office. But well-financed campaigns were the first priority, and with their heralded arrival, politics became a business, a very big business.

And so it was in the winter of 1826-1827 that Van Buren set about piecing together the ill-assorted remnants of Jefferson's Democratic-Republican Party with the election of "Old Hickory" as its targeted goal. He initiated conversations with powerful and like-thinking politicians from the South and West, inculcating in them his view of things to come. Vice-President John C. Calhoun (1782-1850) was the first to be so engaged. Born into a family of up-country South Carolina planters made wealthy when Whitney's gin turned long-staple cotton into a hugely profitable cash crop, Calhoun attained public renown as Monroe's nationalistic Secretary of War. His father Patrick had fought in the French and Indian and Revolutionary Wars and opposed the Constitution because it allowed "people other than those of South Carolina to tax the people of South Carolina," thus violating the very revolutionary principle for which he had fought. Young John, after graduation from Yale College, received his legal education in Litchfield CT where Tapping Reeve had founded the first American law school in 1784. Over its 60-year history, the school would graduate 2 Vice-Presidents, over a hundred Congressmen, 28 Senators, 14 governors, 3 Supreme Court justices and numerous state politicians. Upon admission to the South Carolina bar, Calhoun proceeded to make a name for himself denouncing British aggressions against American maritime rights. When elected to the 12th Congress in 1811, he joined up with Henry Clay as one of the original "war hawks" and supported the latter's "American System." The tariff of 1816, however, shook Calhoun's intense nationalism and started him on a path back to his father's beliefs in enumerated powers and states rights. By 1830 he would be regarded as the charismatic champion of Southern interests advocating state nullification of "unconstitutional" federal laws as proposed by Jefferson and Madison in the Kentucky and Virginia Resolutions.

Van Buren reviewed the changing times with Calhoun. A Jackson victory, as he posed it to Calhoun, "as the result of his military services without reference to party … would be one thing. His election as the result of a combined and concerted effort of a political party, holding, in the main, to certain tenets and opposed to certain prevailing principles, might be another and far different thing." A reinvigorated party, he pointed out, could be counted on to protect the special interests of the South by upholding the Constitutional restrictions on the "tyranny of the majority" and, by allying the "plain people" of the North with the planters of the South, diminish sectional criticisms of "African slavery" from northern extremists. In the matter of elections, Van Buren informed him, the old system of nomination by legislative caucus was on its way out – the year 1824 had already seen mass demonstrations against it – and would be replaced by national conventions attended by popularly chosen delegates. Party reorganization and discipline, in the South as elsewhere, were going to be paramount for raising the vast sums of money required. Calhoun was enthralled. He grasped at once all the nuances being enunciated by the "Little Magician," especially the implication that he would continue on as Jackson's Vice-President and possible successor in office.

Note Van Buren's mention of "African slavery." Aside from a small, vocal sect of abolitionists, many of them strongly anti-Catholic and anti-Semitic, most Americans of the time were much too busy enriching the nation's standard of living to worry about the so-called "black problem." Everyone knew that Negroes in America not only enjoyed a far better life than their brethren back in Africa but that they lived twice as long. Northerners and southerners alike thought, if they thought about it at all, that slavery must eventually phase out and that emancipation at best would be a slow, difficult and costly task. Nobody wanted millions of suddenly emancipated slaves thrown on the economy and not even abolitionist extremists wanted them to move north and live alongside them. Indeed, almost all communities had discriminatory and exclusivity laws that prevented such from happening. The states of Illinois and Indiana, in particular, barred slaves from settling there. The "underground railway" for transporting escaped slaves to freedom, we should note, ended not in the northern states but in Canada. Most likely, if they had not proved useful to southern planters, slaves would either have been manumitted or, like the Indians, genocidally removed. Few families, then or now, were about to send their sons off to war on a save-the-slave crusade.

An American Colonization Society, founded in 1816 by one Robert S. Finley, proposed the establishment of an African colony to receive the black population. The Society was supported by, among others, Henry Clay, James Madison, James Monroe, Andrew Jackson, Francis Scott Key, Daniel Webster, William Crawford, Abraham Lincoln and Harriet Beecher Stowe, the author of *Uncle Tom's Cabin*. In a speech that would be delivered on 26 June 1857, Lincoln likened its goal to the Exodus of Hebrews from Egypt: "Let us be brought to believe that it is morally right … to transfer the African to his native clime, and we shall find a way to do it, however great the task may be. The children of Israel … went out of Egyptian bondage in a body." In 1824, Monroe pressured Congress to appropriate $100,000 for the purchase of some West African land from a reluctant "King Peter," and there was born the nation of Liberia, its capital Monrovia named in the President's honor. However, few blacks showed any inclination to leave America. They were not about to give up a standard of living relatively high compared to the rest of the world for the horrors of a life in Africa among the same people who had sold them into slavery in the first place. Emigration remained at a trickle. By 1860 Liberia had a population of less than ten thousand.

Van Buren next turned westward, to Senator Thomas Hart Benton of Missouri, a man of tremendous influence among Western Congressmen and a vigorous Senate leader. He had been Jackson's aide-de-camp during the Creek Indian wars of 1814 in Georgia and Florida, but a duel between his brother and Jackson had ruptured their relations. His life in danger, Benton had resigned his army commission at the end of the War of 1812 and headed west to Missouri. There he became one of the state's first two senators upon its admission into the union as a slave state under the Missouri Compromise of 1820. Ten years after the quarrel, Jackson and

Benton met as Senators in Washington and put their differences aside, Jackson as a man seeking the Presidency well recognizing Benton's potential usefulness.

Benton quickly fell in with Van Buren's plan; he hated Adams and what he stood for and he was more than happy to support Jackson in the coming election. Now soldered into a national party, the Democrats attracted into the fold a large contingent of journalistic and political talent from all over the country. Prominent among them were Thomas Ritchie, editor of the Richmond *Enquirer* and the head of the Richmond Junto, Virginia's equivalent of the Albany Regency; Isaac Hill from New Hampshire who edited the *Patriot* and organized the party in his state; Nathaniel Greene, editor of the Boston *Statesman*; Mordecai Noah of the New York City *National Advocate*; Dabney Carr of the Baltimore *Republican*; and perhaps the most powerful of all, Amos Kendall, editor of the *Argus of Western America* and future business associate of Samuel Morse, who was able to unite all the party factions in Kentucky and steal Clay's home state from under his nose in the next election. There were dozens more, all first-rate politicians. They restructured the party from top to bottom, from local "Hickory Clubs" to central corresponding committees. All of them looked upon newspapers as the greatest unifying force in shaping the public's mind and founded them by the hundreds. There was no other outlet at the time for widespread news coverage. Politically allied newspaper editors were frequently designated as official printers to the House of Representatives, the Senate, the President, the Supreme Court and state legislatures, and their publications received substantial subsidies for the printing of bills, laws, documents, reports, journals and speeches. From 1839 to 1841, the executive office alone spent almost $175,000 on printing contracts. Loyal editors would also receive lucrative patronage appointments; the job of postmaster, which controlled the distribution of mail and most importantly that of newspapers, was most sought after. With a newspaper, said Van Buren, "we can endure a thousand revolutions. Without it, we might as well hang our harps on the willows." Thus began the symbiotic relationship between news people and politicians that characterizes modern times. So rapid was the journalistic expansion that by 1828 there were 600 newspapers published in the country, fifty dailies, 150 semiweeklies and 400 weeklies. Most functioned mainly as political organs, mouthpieces of the party line. The Presidential election of 1828 would see the country literally deluged with a sea of paper telling the American people what they must do and how they must vote to save the Republic.

And how the money rolled in! From carefully staged parades, barbecues, tree plantings, dinners and rallies; from solicitations from those who could afford it and from those whose interests depended on Democratic goodwill; from campaign buttons and clothes; from hickory sticks, hickory canes, hickory brooms, hickory tree plantings and hickory poles "in every village, as well as upon many city streets"; and from popular entertainments – songs, jokes, cartoons, funny stories, poems and puns, most of which poked fun at President Adams and his Secretary of State Henry Clay. All the electioneering gimmicks so familiar today contributed to the raucous enthusiasm that ensued. And it worked, as a huge segment of the population previously suspicious of or at best mildly interested in politics flocked to the Democratic fold. In opposition to Van Buren, two desperately-seeking Presidential aspirants, Henry Clay and

Daniel Webster, spearheaded the formation of the National Republican party. In promoting Alexander Hamilton's federalism and Clay's "American System," its platform relied on a strong central government's guiding hand rather than Adam Smith's invisible hand to spur the nation's economic growth. Webster (1782-1852) was a newcomer to implied powers. As a young lawyer, he identified with New England shipping interests and became an ardent supporter of states' rights and enumerated powers, even to attending the Hartford Convention. When industrialization began to eclipse shipping as the dominant profit-maker in the northeast, he followed the money and switched to "implied powers," exactly opposite to the course pursued by Calhoun. His great oratorical powers quickly led him to the top of his profession, to the House of Representatives in 1813 and to the Senate in 1826. Having excellent contacts with the country's "moneyed aristocracy," he raised considerable funds for the new Party, but neither he nor Clay could match Van Buren's organizational skills, especially in the South and West where Clay's "American System" did not sit well with the people. Americans of the time seemed very much aware that a socialist economy, just as a slave economy, cannot compete with a free economy. In 1836 the Whig Party supplanted the National Republicans and nominated Webster for President, but he was soundly beaten by Van Buren. Abraham Lincoln and John F. Kennedy would later eulogize big government politicians such as Clay and Webster, but never were these statists entrusted with high office in national elections.

CHAPTER XXII

TARIFFS AND SECESSION

I regard free trade as involving considerations far higher than mere commercial advantages, as great as they are. It is, in my opinion, emphatically the cause of civilization and peace.

John C. Calhoun

The election of 1828 was a foregone conclusion. Clay and Webster tried their mighty best speech-making and soliciting funds to elect Adams. But to no avail. The platform of the National Republicans left them with almost no representation in the South and West, and only in the Northeast did they retain a following. The Jackson-Calhoun ticket won 56% of the popular vote and 178 electoral votes as against only 83 for Adams. The effectiveness of Van Buren's efforts shows clearly in the voter turnout. Whereas in 1824 only 3.2% of the total population voted, in 1828 that figure had risen to 9.5%.

Jackson's inauguration as our seventh President brought to Washington a horde of party workers seeking "spoils," their just reward for party service. Jackson and Van Buren were hounded with patronage demands for government jobs – postmasters, auditors, clerkships, bookkeepers, customs collectors, land agents, officer appointments to the armed forces - more than 500 applicants for every position available.

Upwards of 10% of the 10,000 government workers held over from the previous administration faced the dreaded S-word – successor – as they were replaced by newcomers. "The distribution of the patronage of the government is by far the most disagreeable duty of the President," James Buchanan, our fifteenth President, would note later. Amos Kendall controlled and managed the patronage distribution from his post as Postmaster-General, newly elevated to cabinet status, clearing out many friends of Adams and Clay and replacing them with certified Democrats. To some extent, Jackson could claim he was merely following precedent. Washington had given appointments almost exclusively to like-thinking Federalists and Jefferson had replaced them with Democratic-Republicans.

But now, there were many more people to reward and a huge number of new government offices to be created to satisfy them. From the mid-1820s to the end of Jackson's two terms in office, the federal budget nearly doubled from $11.5 million to $22 million. Yet, unlike what happened in Rome, an explosively growing private economy warded off most of the evils heaped on it by the huge increase in federal spending. By 1835, even the federal debt was paid off in full as Albert Gallatin's debt reduction program, initiated in 1801, finally came to fruition. The federal government would operate at a surplus until 1838. Not that this was a panacea of any sort.

Drawing money out of the private economy and into government coffers only decreases efficient private spending overall.

A precedent had been set, however. As the population multiplied and more and more party workers were needed, government bureaucracies would grow irrespective of the country's needs. Throughout most of the 19th century, fortunately, expenditures did not grow nearly as fast as the private economy, and federal outlays remained fixed at about 1% of gross domestic product. Then, too, there were effective term limits in place; civil service jobs usually terminated with the next administration. The tenured bureaucrat did not arrive on the scene until civil service "reform" fifty years hence. With the arrival of the 20th century, however, everything was to change. American politicians were finally to learn "how to drain money from the pockets of the people."

"Spoils" was to be a problem for every subsequent President, but the practice paled into insignificance in the face of two Constitutional crises faced by Jackson. The 1928 Tariff of Abominations signed by John Quincy Adams had brought forth calls for nullification and secession by southern states that were temporarily stilled by Jackson's election. But, unfortunately for the South, Jackson took a different view of the tariff question once in office. Where would the government get the money to pay the mushrooming patronage costs resulting from the Party's reorganization? That was the problem. Especially since the tariff was by far the dominant source of federal income. Sounding much like George III at the Jefferson birthday dinner of 1830, he toasted: "Our Federal Union; it must be preserved." Only to be quickly challenged by Calhoun in a way that the Founding Fathers might have answered: "The Union, after our freedom, most dear." Not until three years later was a new tariff schedule adopted, but when the Tariff of 1832 failed to lower rates on the cloth and iron goods needed in the South, the stage was set for crisis. Calhoun resigned as Vice-President and had himself appointed Senator from South Carolina so as to lead the fight against the Tariff in Congress. Citing Jefferson's Kentucky Resolutions and Madison's Virginia Resolutions of 1798, the South Carolina legislature nullified as unconstitutional both the 1828 and 1832 tariffs and moved toward secession. Jackson responded strongly by threatening military action and treason charges against any person resisting tariff collections. Charleston SC, after all, was the principal port on the Atlantic seacoast for the export of cotton and the reciprocal import of European textiles and iron goods to pay for it. The secession of South Carolina, more than any other state, would have deprived the federal government of much of its needed revenues.

Could anything in the Constitution be construed as preventing a state of the Union from seceding? Hadn't it been generally assumed up to that time that such a course was open to any state that so decided. Did not the Declaration of Independence declare "that all men are created equal; that they are endowed by their Creator with certain inalienable rights; that among these, are life, liberty, and the pursuit of happiness? That, to secure these rights, governments are instituted among men, deriving their just powers from the consent of the governed; that, whenever any form of government becomes destructive of these ends, it is the right of the people to alter or to abolish it, and to institute a new government, laying its foundation on such principles, and organizing its powers in such form, as them shall seem most likely to effect their safety and happiness"? Who is to decide when a new government is to be instituted? Was Jackson not reading into the Constitution a huge extension of Presidential powers, the right to force a state against its will to remain in the Union and collect federal taxes?

Was not the phrase "perpetual union," although conspicuously present in the "Articles of Confederation and Perpetual Union," conspicuously absent from the Constitution. A confrontation was avoided only when Jackson supported a compromise solution, the Tariff of 1833 or "Compromise Tariff," which instituted automatic rate reductions over a ten year period back to the 1816 rates. By this time, Jackson had come to realize that the booming economy was providing sufficient funds not only to pay down the national debt but to support his "spoils system" as well. The new low tariff policy embraced by the Democrats managed to allay sectional frictions until 1861, when newly elected President Abraham Lincoln escalated protectionism to levels never before seen.

It should be noted that acts of defiance against the national government were by no means uncommon. Prior to the Civil War, a number of northern states unilaterally nullified federal laws, most often the fugitive slave laws of 1793 and 1850, and even enacted harsh criminal fines and prison terms for anyone enforcing those laws. In 1838, the state of Georgia ignored a Supreme Court decision establishing the autonomy of the Cherokee nation (Cherokee Nation vs. the State of Georgia, 1831) and forcibly moved the Indians west of the Mississippi.

And, as already mentioned, the New England states had considered secession at the Hartford Convention and may very well have done so had the War of 1812 continued. In 1861, however, hard cash was again on the line. South Carolina refused to allow tariff collections and, as had happened time and time again in both monarchies and republics, the failure to meet tax payments was to be met with savage punishments.

CHAPTER XXIII

ST. ANDREW TAKES ON THE MONSTER

There but for the grace of God goes God.

Winston Churchill's characterization of Sir Stafford Cripps

We are about to enter a period of government-induced chaos that culminates in the Panics of 1837 and 1839-1843, financial collapses that in some respects rivaled the Great Depression one hundred years later. Both were unnecessary tragedies of the first order brought on in the main by the "folly of human laws." And both lend powerful support to my contention that "anarchy is the presence of government." Economists and historians continually visit and revisit these turbulent years, scrutinizing them as case studies of the "business cycle." Few if any of them recognize they are dealing with chaos and that all the explanations and theories advanced vary from "Not even wrong!" to woefully inadequate. Who, after all, can weight the numerous factors involved and discern what "butterfly effects" may have been overlooked? Lacking statistically valid evidence, these searchers after "truth" unearth it in random patterns of historical events, or in "noise" as the statistician would say. And the "truths" they find, obviously, are nothing more than their preconceived philosophic notions of how reality works. Little attention do most of them pay any more to that vast collection of data amassed by Milton Friedman and Anna Schwartz in "A Monetary History of the United States 1867-1960," in which two points are conclusively demonstrated: (1) that the amount of money circulating, the money supply, plays a consistently important role in all economic upturns and downturns, and (2) that no correlation exists between strong economic growth and inflation as long as politicians do not spend too much of the people's money. Point #2 is of especial significance today because most economists seem to believe that strong economic growth goes hand in hand with inflation and that central banks exist to stop it. This belief falls into the "not even wrong" category.

On the basis of Friedman-Schwartz analyses, some writers have found similarities between the earlier Panics and the Great Depression of the 1930s in that one-third of the country's money supply vanished and a huge number of banks (a quarter to a third) closed their doors. Also, in both, wages and prices declined dramatically. But there the similarity ends.

We chaosticians know that no two "business cycles" are ever alike and such is the case here. The years from 1837 to 1843 proved very unique in that gross domestic product, except for the first year when output declined about 5%, continued to grow strongly throughout, by some accounts from 6% to 16% per year. Although wages fell sharply, prices declined even more, by 42%, fast and far enough to restore market equilibrium in short order. Of great significance was the fact that America had no interfering Bank of the United States at the time and Jackson's successors, Presidents Van Buren and Tyler, refused to indulge in socialistic solutions. Their "paralytic helplessness" freed America from political bumbling and enabled her to give birth to a free-banking chaon that spurred non-inflationary economic growth to unprecedented levels.

Unacquainted as they are with modern chaos theory, most writers have failed utterly in recognizing "how sublime order emerges out of chaos." In the two decades following 1840, the new order deregulated banking and gave to bankers the freedom to risk their depositors' money and their own livelihoods on loans to clients as each saw fit. And, as in the pari-mutuel and stock markets, reach a consensus of individual "truths" that gave the best determinant of the amount of money needed for financing a nation's growth.

During the late 1920s and 1930s, in contrast, America had a central bank to contend with. The Federal Reserve, for fear of inflation, clamped an unrelenting monetary squeeze on the economy that played the major role in bringing on and prolonging the Great Depression. Unemployment peaked at 25% of the working force in 1932 and remained at a huge 12% when the nation entered World War II in 1941. The production of goods and services plummeted by 30%. Led by Presidents Herbert Hoover and Franklin D. Roosevelt, politicians ran amuck with government intervention. They not only failed to rid the nation of the woefully inept Federal Reserve System, but saddled America with inefficient government programs, new taxes, subsidies and price supports via production cutbacks that lengthened the Great Depression into the 1940s. Were it not for the printing of astronomical amounts of money to finance World War II – in amounts that no central banker would have undertaken to create in peaceful times – America may well have become a socialist nation with a standard of living to match. The 1930s became an exasperating example of how much harm politicians and economists can do in trying to fix a chaotic situation.

In 1823 Nicholas Biddle (1786-1844) became president of the 2nd Bank of the United States replacing Langdon Cleves who had gotten into difficulties with the stockholders over the dividend rate and with the Board of Governors over expansionist policy. Litterateur, diplomat, politician, statesman and financier, Biddle appeared the perfect reincarnation of Plato's philosopher-king. Enrolled in the University of Pennsylvania class of 1799 at 9 years of age, he was at 13 deemed too young to graduate and was sent to Princeton where he received his degree as class valedictorian in 1801. Jefferson commissioned him to write the history of the Lewis and Clark expedition's survey of the Louisiana Purchase acquisition, but he relinquished the project when elected to the Pennsylvania legislature in 1810. In 1812, he became editor of *Port-Folio*, a leading literary magazine. After serving in the British and French legations and traveling extensively in Europe, he became secretary to President James Monroe. In 1819 Monroe appointed him as one of the 5 government directors of the 2nd Bank of the United States and its president in 1823.

Biddle continued Cleves' tight money policy thereby prolonging the effects of the Panic of 1819 and stunting the country's economic growth throughout the 1820s. The Bank did not participate nearly to the extent it should have in facilitating the transfer of the people's savings to productive enterprises. Its conservative officers and stockholders were not about to involve *their* money in those risky startup ventures that drive a nation to "Power, Consequence and Grandeur." As a result, thousands of businesses could neither expand nor modernize, and thousands of inventions in manufactures, mining, transportation, communication and farming had to mark time awaiting the capital needed for their effective utilization. Not one cent, for example, was invested by the Bank in canals and railroads. What Biddle did do was to establish more Bank branches nationwide to the delight of the stockholders if not to the country at large. By 1830 the 2nd Bank circulated almost 40% of the nation's bank notes and accounted for 15 to 20% of bank loans. Its holdings of specie reserves amounted to one-third of the total for all banks. Cautious reserve ratios upwards of 50% compared to a norm of 10 to 25% for state banks. These figures reveal plainly the Bank's drag on economic growth. If its specie had been spread around to the smaller banks where it could have generated loans at more favorable interest rates, the country's total note circulation would have been much larger and its economic growth rate far greater. Furthermore, the Bank's erratic treatment of regional bank liabilities, at times accepting their notes in payment and at other times demanding specie, generated wide gyrations in the value of local bank notes, the principal currency of the nation.

The Bank's politically correct policy of dispensing liberal emoluments to powerful persons supportive of the Bank augmented under Biddle. Senator Henry Clay, a stout backer of the Bank, facilitated branch openings in KY managed by his political cronies. Almost single-handedly, he established Kentucky as the empire state of "pork" handouts, a "distinction" held by Alaska and West Virginia today. He left Congress in 1822 (after running up almost fifty thousand dollars in debt due to high living) to become the Bank's general counsel recompensed with salary, per case fees, and large land holdings in Ohio and Kentucky. To further his Presidential ambitions, he resigned in 1825 "pleased with his compensation" to become Secretary of State under President John Quincy Adams. Daniel Webster, Congressman from MA (1823-27) and Senator (1827-41) and another of the many recipients of the Bank's largesse, wrote in a letter to Biddle: "I believe my retainer has not been renewed or refreshed as usual.

If it be wished that my relation to the Bank should be continued, it may be well to send me the usual retainer." Other supportive Congressmen were regularly advanced their salaries whenever delays on appropriation bills held up their pay. The Bank also got involved in political matters. Biddle donated thousands of dollars of the Bank's money to the campaigns of John Quincy Adams in 1824 and 1828, promised Bank money to friendly politicians for their internal improvement schemes, paid for the printing of Clay's speeches in support of the Bank, and financed newspaper ads promoting himself and the Bank throughout the country, all of which incurred the wrath of Andrew Jackson and helped bring about the Bank's eventual demise.

Ignoring all the hostile evidence against them, Biddle, Clay and Webster remained convinced both of the Bank's necessity and popularity and pressed for renewal of its charter four years before its 1836 expiration. They would let the 1832 Presidential election serve as a proxy on the Bank's future. And for once, they had a fine idea, one we should consider today.

Why not move the country toward a pure democracy and remove Congressional middlemen from the decision-making process? By letting the people vote on all bills that come up for decision, we could amend the structure of government and get rid of all those dysfunctional and spendthrift Congresses that seldom enjoy much public esteem. We certainly have the technology to do so. Let us never forget Alexander Hamilton's warning of the harm done by too many laws. Any bill failing of voter approval would be relegated to the scrap heap and the powers "left in other hands." Politicians would then be constrained by the silence of the public.

And so the issue was joined. In January 1832, the National Republicans introduced into Congress a bill rechartering the 2nd Bank of the United States. Henry Clay, who had been chosen as the Party's Presidential candidate in the nation's first ever national convention, and Daniel Webster guided the bill to a 28 to 20 passage in the Senate. A month later, on July 3, it rode to victory on a 107 to 85 margin in the House of Representatives. Biddle of course was on the scene contributing "his" money and influence to the Bank's cause. He reminded powerful politicians of past favors, bought advertising space in newspapers to propagandize the Bank's benefits and ordered petitions sent to Congress from every state of the Union. "Now for the President," he chortled on hearing of Congressional approval.

Jackson retaliated with a veto, a power applied only nine times by all former Presidents. In a classic message sent to Congress on 10 July 1832, he rejected the government's right to grant monopolistic privileges to the Bank or any other institution or individual. Such artificial distinctions, he claimed, were a grave distortion of the "necessary and proper" clause of the Constitution and created inequities in a land where equality before the law is mandated for all. He pointed out that only a few hundred investors held stock in the Bank, and yet they divided among themselves the profits collected from all the people. Worse still, 25% of the stock was owned by foreigners (some $8 million worth) who also participated in the profits. He further opined that Article I, Section 8 of the Constitution had given Congress the power "to coin money, regulate the value thereof, and of foreign coin," but that none of the "enumerated powers" permitted it to hand that power over to a quasi-government institution.

Jackson also took up the issue of judicial review: "It is maintained by the advocates of the Bank [the 2nd Bank of the United States], that its constitutionality, in all its features, ought to be considered as settled by precedent, and by the decision of the Supreme Court. To this conclusion, I cannot assent. Mere precedent is a dangerous source of authority, and should not be regarded as deciding questions of constitutional power, except where the acquiescence of the people and the States can be considered as well settled. So far from this being the case on this subject, an argument against the Bank might be based on precedent. One Congress, in 1791, decided in favor of a bank; another, in 1811, decided against it. One Congress, in 1815, decided against a bank; another, in 1816, decided in its favor.

Prior to the present Congress, therefore, the precedents drawn from that source were equal. If we resort to the States, the expressions of legislative, judicial, and executive opinions against the Bank have been probably to those in its favor as four to one. There is nothing in precedent, therefore, which, if its authority were admitted, ought to weigh in favor of the act before me. "If the opinion of the Supreme Court covered the whole ground of this act, it ought not to control the coordinate authorities of this Government. The Congress, the Executive, and the Court, must each for itself be guided by its own opinion of the Constitution. Each public officer, who takes an oath to support the Constitution, swears that he will support it as he understands it, and not as it is understood by others. It is as much the duty of the House of Representatives, of the Senate, and of the President to decide upon the constitutionality of any bill or resolution which may be presented to them for passage or approval as it is of the supreme judges when it may be brought before them for judicial decision." His opinion implied strongly that the Supreme Court, if it did anything, should confine itself to examining "uniformity in the interpretation of the national laws" (Hamilton in The *Federalist* No. 80), to ensure that equality before the law exists for each and every one of us.

Jackson continued by vetting the Bank's profits from private business dealings. "It cannot be necessary to the character of the Bank as a fiscal agent of the Government that its private business should be exempted from that taxation to which all the State banks are liable; nor can I conceive it proper that the substantive and most essential powers reserved by the States shall be thus attacked and annihilated as a means of executing the powers delegated to the general government. It may be safely assumed that none of those sages who had an agency in forming or adopting our Constitution ever imagined that any portion of the taxing power of the States, not prohibited to them nor delegated to Congress, was to be swept away and annihilated as a means of executing certain powers delegated to Congress." And he beautifully summed up his veto message by declaring that the evils of government "exist only in its abuses." "If it would confine itself to equal protection, and, as Heaven does its rains, shower its favors alike on the high and the low, it would be an unqualified blessing. In the act before me there seems to be a wide and unnecessary departure from these just principles." Economic freedom from government for all and no special favors to anyone – it was Jackson's classic statement of laissez faire.

The battle now moved back to Congress where Clay and Webster undertook the difficult next step of convincing Congress to override the veto. In oratorical torrents, they blasted Jackson for exceeding his authority in his "perversion of the veto power." It would almost seem that these two stalwarts had not bothered to read Article I, Section 7 of the Constitution that bestowed the veto power on the President. Of course, not a word was heard of the pecuniary rewards they received from the Bank. Biddle, for his part, mailed out 30,000 copies of Jackson's veto message which he regarded as a gross misuse of Presidential power. In any event, Congress failed to override. The fate of the Bank would now be left to the American people in the election of 1832.

CHAPTER XXIV

END OF THE BANK

I care not what puppet is placed upon the throne of England to rule the Empire on which the sun never sets. The man who controls Britain's money supply controls the British Empire, and I control the British money supply.

Nathan Mayer Rothschild, 1815

Jackson, running with Van Buren as his Vice- Presidential candidate in 1832, again won easily, garnering 55% of the popular vote and 219 electoral votes to 37% and 49 respectively for Clay. Although he took his reelection as a mandate to kill the Bank, Jackson did not mention it in his inaugural address of 1833. But his hostility toward it soon became clear. In his first annual message to Congress, he noted that the Bank had "failed in the great end of establishing a uniform and sound currency" and that he doubted both its constitutionality and its expedience. Thus far, however, there was only a call for changes in the Bank's operations and charter.

Open war against the Bank undoubtedly began in 1829 when Isaac Hill, organizer of a strong and effective Democratic Party organization in New Hampshire and editor of the influential "New Hampshire Patriot," alluded publicly to the Bank's discriminatory loan practices. According to Hill, the president of the Bank's Portsmouth branch had approved a loan to his brother-in-law in Boston while ignoring the needs of New Hampshire merchants who needed only two or three thousand dollars for their businesses. The issue escalated into an election crusade in the efficient Democratic press sloganized by "Democracy Against the Aristocracy," the "Aristocracy" of course being the National Republicans. "Down with bribery – down with corruption – down with the Bank," stormed the Washington Globe. So great did the outcry become that Biddle made a forced journey to Portsmouth to investigate the situation and found nothing of major concern. But Hill had Jackson's ear as a member of his "kitchen cabinet," an unofficial group of close friends and advisers comprising the policy-making arm of the administration, and kept him continually informed of developments. Jackson was livid. "The Monster must perish," he raged.

In 1831, Jackson appointed Roger B. Taney (1777-1864) as Attorney-General and charged him with developing a strategy for killing the Bank. Taney, a Jeffersonian and long a strong supporter of Jackson, was also a proponent of "opening to the most free competition" the profits of banking. By 1833, he was ready to move. He proposed that all future monies collected by the government in taxes, land sales and tariff revenues be placed in a number of selected state-chartered banks, those so designated soon to be called "pet banks" by critics. For its operating expenses, the government would then draw down its deposits at the 2nd Bank until they were exhausted. In this way the removal would be gradual so as to avoid undue shocks to the monetary system. And, thought Taney, without the advantage of interest-free government money to loan out, the Bank's influence on the private economy would quickly wane.

There was a bit of a problem here. In the 2nd Bank's charter, Congress had authorized the Secretary of the Treasury – not the President – to remove government deposits from the Bank if he thought it necessary. Jackson's current Secretary refused to do so, whereupon Jackson fired him and appointed another man who also refused and was fired. His actions outraged Senators who thought the President contravened the Constitution in getting rid of an insubordinate cabinet member without Senate consent. Jackson simply ignored them and gave Taney a recess appointment as Secretary of the Treasury. The latter now launched the official war against the Bank.

Biddle reacted by calling for a general curtailment of loans throughout the 2nd Bank's entire system. Those persons seeking loans were denied, those in debt to the Bank were called on for what they owed, and state banks were directed to redeem their notes in hard money. His order so imploded the money supply that the nation's commercial and manufacturing centers stagnated for lack of working capital. The country was pitched into an economic panic, precisely the effect Biddle wanted. If sufficient pressure were brought to bear on the financial markets, he reasoned, public outcry would force Jackson to restore the government's deposits. During the winter and spring of 1833-4, Jackson received repeated pleas to give in to Biddle and end the squeeze. But he refused to yield.

"Insolvent, you say?" Jackson snorted when approached by business leaders. "What do you come to me for, then? Go to Nicholas Biddle. We have no money here, gentlemen. Biddle has all the money. He has millions of specie in his vaults, at this moment, lying idle, and yet you come to me to save you from breaking. I tell you, it's all politics." In the spring of 1834, Jackson further tightened the noose around the Bank. He ordered the Bank to hand over the government's funds, books, and accounts relating to veteran pensions from the Revolutionary War, the payments of which had been handled by the Bank. They were now to be managed by the Secretary of War. Biddle refused. He told Jackson that the money and the accounts were his to handle as he saw fit, implying that he was above the government's direction, certainly that of the President. Now even Webster, previously a staunch advocate of the Bank, saw the danger, as did many others in Congress. Biddle's arbitrary and disruptive action seemed to prove every accusation leveled at the Bank by Jackson and the Democrats. Here was raw naked power, exercised by one man, that could virtually bring down the nation's financial community. Not until America got a Federal Reserve System in 1913 would such a financial dictatorship be seen again, and it was accompanied by rampant inflation and a long series of depressions and recessions. Quoting Patrick Henry once more: "When men give power, they know not what they give."

Although the panic evaporated in July of 1834 when Biddle relented and stopped the curtailment of loans, the die had been cast. Future President James Knox Polk of TN (1795-1849), chairman of the House Ways and Means Committee and one of Jackson's protégés, now introduced a series of four resolutions: the Bank should not be rechartered; the government's deposits should not be restored to the Bank; the government's money should remain in the "pet banks"; and, finally, a committee should be selected to investigate the Bank's affairs. All passed. Jacksonian America saw central banking for what it is, a bald grab for the people's money by rapacious politicians in league with a "moneyed aristocracy." "I have obtained a glorious triumph," enthused Jackson. "The House vote has put to death that mammoth of corruption and power, the Bank of the United States." Jackson himself was almost put to death in 1835 when Richard Lawrence fired two pistols at point-blank range in an attempted assassination.

Miraculously, both guns misfired. Found innocent by "reason of insanity," Lawrence later boasted that powerful European bankers promised him protection.

Without government deposits, the Bank withered. In 1836, it became just another state bank chartered in Pennsylvania, and its branch banks became independent institutions in other states. On a level playing field, Biddle could no longer compete with regional banks and his bank expired in 1841. Biddle himself was pauperized.

CHAPTER XXV

A FREE-BANKING CHAON

A democracy cannot exist as a permanent form of government. It can only exist until the voters discover that they can vote themselves largesse from the public treasury. From that moment on, the majority always votes for the candidates promising the most from the public treasury, with the result that a democracy always collapses over loose fiscal policy.

Scottish historian Alexander Tyler, circa 1787, The *Fall of the Athenian Republic*

Beset by physical ailments from old dueling wounds, Jackson chose not to serve a third term in 1836. But once again, the "freest country of the universe" found the right man in the right place at the right time to steer her through the turbulent times to come. That staunch Jeffersonian adherent of "enumerated powers," Vice-President Martin Van Buren, handily defeated Whig candidate Daniel Webster and became the nation's 8th President. The year 1834 had seen a realignment of political parties, mainly through the replacement of the National Republicans by the Whigs, that being the classic name designating opposition to concentrated political power in the hands of a chief executive. Van Buren would soon face the worst financial crisis in the young nation's history.

In his inaugural address, Van Buren called for "strict adherence to the letter and spirit of the Constitution" and for "friendship of all nations as the condition most compatible with our welfare and the principles of our government." As Secretary of State during Jackson's first term, he had achieved a long-standing goal of American foreign policy in opening direct trade with the British West Indies, a region closed to shippers since the Revolutionary War. As Vice-President, he had persuaded Jackson to veto all appropriations for internal improvement ventures, including Henry Clay's Maysville "road-to-nowhere" in Kentucky. Opposition to such pork-barrel handouts would soon become part of Democratic canon. As an advocate of free trade, he put the Democratic Party squarely behind tariff reductions. And his abhorrence of war led him, as President, to avoid conflict with England over a Maine-Canada border dispute, to refuse support of a Canadian revolt against England in 1837, and to oppose the annexation of Texas over the threat of war with Mexico The diversion of government funds to "pet banks" and the end of Biddle's squeeze in 1835 had brought on a sudden expansion of the banking system's loan portfolios and a surge in the money supply. Increases in vault specie from newly discovered silver mines in Mexico and decreased opium imports from China (payable in silver) may also have contributed. Before the economy could adapt by producing a compensating surge in the production of goods and services, a two year 15% per annum inflation ensued. Easy credit skyrocketed government land sales from $2.6 million in 1832 to almost $15 million in 1836, most transactions in the form of banknotes. Jackson, from boyhood distrustful of banks and frightened by the amount of paper now in government hands, reacted with an executive order, the Specie Circular of July 1836, which required payment in gold or silver for all government lands. Prospective land purchasers reacted by converting banknotes into specie, and that of course forced banks to curtail loan activity so as to maintain reserve ratios at acceptable levels. Looking back, one would not have expected the relatively small dollar amounts involved to have caused any disruption in the financial markets, especially since federal spending at the time seemed insignificant at 1% of gross domestic product. But public concern mounted day by day. If the government wanted to hold gold and silver in preference to banknotes, so did private depositors, one might think. Other factors – the uncertainty caused by the expiration of the 2nd United States Bank and Henry Clay's push for another, an increase in interest rates by the Bank of England which cut into foreign investment in America, a temporary adverse balance of payments, heavy borrowing by many states for pork-barrel spending on internal improvement ventures, and who knows what other overlooked "butterflys" – may have shaken the public's confidence in the banking system. In any event, redemptions escalated from a trickle to a torrent. Just two months after Van Buren's inauguration, a major financial panic engulfed the country's eight hundred banks forcing all but six to suspend specie payments for banknotes. On 10 May 1837, bank runs reached New York City where many regional banks kept their deposits. More than $700,000 in specie was drawn down from the City's banks causing them to suspend the following day. The Panic of 1837 had begun.

"Still-around" Henry Clay shouted for instatement of his "American System" – another Bank of the United States, high tariffs and government subsidized internal improvements. Van Buren responded by doing almost nothing. In September he explained his inaction to a special session of Congress in the following terms: "All communities are apt to look to government for too much. Even in our own country where its duties and powers are so strictly limited, we are prone to do so, especially at periods of sudden embarrassment and distress." Cautioning against yielding to this temptation, he pointed out that "all former attempts on the part of Government" to "assume the management of domestic or foreign exchange" had in his opinion proven "injurious." What was needed was a "system founded on private interest, enterprise, and competition, without the aid of legislative grants or regulations by law," one that embodied the Jeffersonian maxim "that the less government interferes with private pursuits the better for the general prosperity." "Government measures," he maintained "would not promote the real and permanent welfare of those they might be designed to aid." And as far as another Bank of the United States was concerned, he noted that "a national bank [the Bank of England] possessing powers far greater than are asked for by the warmest advocates of such an institution here has also proved unable to prevent an undue expansion of credit and the events that flow from it." To people like Van Buren and Jackson, the evils of a central bank were patently clear. Thanks to them, America remained free of the "Monster" until 1913.

Let me note again that the *price level for goods and services in 1789 was higher than that in 1913*. No overall inflation existed during that long period of explosive growth, little government and free banking.

What Van Buren did do was *slash* government spending. He halted the distribution of surplus federal funds to state governments – begun under Jackson after the federal debt had vanished – and cut back on "internal improvements," especially for rivers and harbors. At the suggestion of Postmaster General Amos Kendall, he eliminated a heavy postal subsidy for newspapers, instituted by Alexander Hamilton in 1792, which resulted in newspapers providing no more than 15% of postal revenues even though accounting for more than 95% of deliveries by weight. After spiking to $37.2 million in 1837 from $30.9 million in 1836, federal expenditures declined to $24.3 million in 1840. And the Panic of 1837, despite its severity, was over almost before it began. After dropping by 20% and wiping out the inflationary binge of the previous two years, prices stabilized. Banks resumed specie payments in 1838 and the economy apparently returned to normal. But the threat of political intervention in the economy was hardly over, although much of it now sprang forth from state politicians.

The success of the Erie Canal had inspired those aspiring entrepreneurs to issue more than $100 million in state bonds of very dubious quality to finance lavish and wasteful "infernal" improvement ventures. But people did not buy in the amounts expected and, as a result, state-chartered banks were legally pressured – that is, threatened with cancellation of their charters - into taking on much of the debt. Evidently, the public judged their elected representatives for the spendthrifts and grafters they were and instead of buying bonds were redeeming banknotes for specie. Because of the ensuing financial stringency, many states defaulted on their bonds, $60 million worth out of a total of $170 million by 1844. Arkansas, Michigan, Mississippi and the Florida Territory repudiated their debts outright. Reserve ratios collapsed once again forcing banks to close their doors, half of them this time around. One third of the nation's money apparently vanished during the deflation of 1839-1843 but prices declined even more. Van Buren's slashes in inefficient government spending coupled with his refusal to bail out state governments and support prices left relatively greater buying power in private hands and, considering the economic growth rate during the period, mitigated deflationary effects considerably.

The centerpiece of Van Buren's special message was a call for the complete separation of the government's fiscal operations from banks. Through an Independent Treasury, he maintained, government could easily and safely conduct its own affairs without relying on any kind of bank paper. There would be no unbridled government spending financed by a government-sponsored bank. Banknote payments to and from the Treasury would be gradually phased out and replaced with hard money, the details to be handled in sub-Treasury buildings in many major cities. A Greek-revival structure that once housed sub-Treasury operations still exists on New York City's Wall Street. Considerable opposition, however, developed from the Whigs who championed another Bank of the United States.

The threat of renewed regulation of the banking system would hang over the financial markets for several more years and undoubtedly contributed to the next round of bank suspensions in 1839. But losses of federal deposits as a result of that collapse drove Congress into passing an Independent Treasury bill that Van Buren signed into law on 4 July 1840.

It is of interest to note a proposal by Senator from Pennsylvania and future President James Buchanan advocating the payment of government obligations through the issue of unbacked paper money by the Treasury. Its great advantage, as Presidents Lincoln and Kennedy would come to understand, was an interest- and debt-free currency and no costly apparatus to handle the government's fiscal operations. Buchanan's idea derived from the successful financing of the Revolutionary War and in part the War of 1812 through the issue of such paper money. In addition, the English Bank Restriction, which suspended specie redemption of the pound from 1797 to 1821 and helped pay for the Napoleonic Wars, furnished another reassuring precedent for the safe issue of unbacked currency.

Of course, war financed in this way must be paid through inflation, but that appears by far the cheapest means of doing so. If done in peacetime, inflation need not result, providing government spending were efficient. If not, the blame is easily established and automatic controls forcing government to downsize can be instituted. But, horrors! Neither the banks nor Hamilton's "moneyed aristocracy" would have access to taxpayer-supported, relatively risk-free government bonds and the interest payments thereon. And without Paterson's perpetual government debt, government spending would be clearly in the open and effectively constrained. "Money created out of nothing" would not be stealthily available to politicians.

With government spending at less than $25 million a year, the Independent Treasury probably caused few if any ripples in the nation's finances. But the Panic knocked Van Buren out of the Presidency, narrowly defeated by military hero William Henry "Tippecanoe and Tyler Too" Harrison. Clay got Congress to rescind the Independent Treasury in 1841 and again tried to translate his American System into law, including the re-establishment of another government-sponsored bank.

But Harrison died within a month of taking office and was succeeded by Vice-President John Tyler of Virginia (1790-1862), a former Democrat whose Jeffersonian views surprisingly reasserted themselves. To the great good fortune of the young nation, Tyler twice vetoed Clay's efforts to reestablish another Bank of the United States. It might be noted that Tyler received hundreds of letters threatening his assassination during his term of office.

As one of his last acts as President in early 1845, Tyler arranged the formal entry of Texas into the Union as the 25th state. Andrew Jackson, in retirement at his Hermitage home in Tennessee and long a proponent of annexation, exulted. He lived to see his friend and admirer James Polk elected President in 1846, defeating Clay who was running for the third and last time. Polk ran on a platform of geographical expansion known as "Manifest Destiny." Over Van Buren's protests, he went to war with Mexico in 1846 acquiring California, New Mexico, Arizona and Utah in the Peace Treaty of 1848. But he avoided war with England (as demanded by the "fifty-four forty or fight" extremists) by compromising on the Oregon Territory boundary dispute, setting it at the 49th parallel. And in still another beneficial example of tax reduction, his Secretary of the Treasury Robert J. Walker (1801-1869) sponsored the Walker Tariff Act of 1846 which lowered the tariff to one of its lowest points in American history. As a result, the economy boomed to such an extent that no tax increases were necessary to pay for the Mexican War. Finally, Polk reinstated the Independent Treasury in 1845, and from then until the Federal Reserve System was established in 1913, the government was its own banker.

Once free of government intervention, the huge monetary demands of an exploding economy were met with remarkably little turmoil. The nation's currency derived for the most part from the checks and notes of incorporated commercial banks redeemable into specie on demand. Private competition among banks, not the ministrations of a benign central banker, regulated the creation and circulation of paper money and brought about uniformity in bank reserve ratios.

Any bank indulging in an excess issue of notes quickly saw its deposits wither as depositors shifted to safer banks. Innovations such as deposit protection and central clearing houses for banknotes made their appearance. In the seventy years 1790 to 1860 deposits soared from a negligible amount to over $220 million. In a bank's home territory, most banknotes circulated at par; in distant places they might trade at a discount that did not exceed costs of shipment. Private banks, legally excluded from banknote issue, offered other financial services. There were over 1100 by 1860 compared to 1600 state-chartered banks.

In 1829, banks chartered in New York came under the state's Safety Fund law, which required an annual payment of ½% of their capital for a period of six years. The obligations of failed banks were paid out of the fund. So successful was the scheme that the fund had a surplus of $10,000 upon its termination in 1866, an indication that no depositor lost money due to a bank failure. This pioneering idea quickly spread to many other states.

In New England, bank notes circulated at par because of regulation by the Suffolk system, the first successful private clearing house in the United States. From the 1820s until the Civil War, it handled daily note redemptions averaging $400 thousand by 1834 and $750 thousand by 1850. In 1853, the New York Clearing House Association opened for the daily settlement of net balances arising among the City's fifty-two banks.

Traveling in the United States in the 1830s, the French economist Michel Chevalier observed that banks had "served the Americans as a lever to transfer to their soil … the agriculture and manufactures of Europe and to cover their country with roads, canals, factories … with everything that goes to make up civilization." "Is there any instance in any of the United States, where any town or city has increased to any considerable extent without the aid of banking institutions?" asked Albert Gallatin in 1836, then serving as president of the National Bank in the City of New York. He wished for slower economic progress, but recognized that "this does not accord with the extraordinary and irresistible energy of this nation." In that same year, Congressman from New York Nathaniel P.

Talmadge defended state banks against centralized control and accused "political economists" of being "frightened at this prosperity and blind to the cause which makes us, above all others, a happy, great and prosperous people." And what could that cause be, he asks? "Sir, it is contained in two words: it is our credit system." In 1837 Joseph Vance, governor of Ohio, reminded the legislature that bank "credit has given us one of the most enterprising and active set of businessmen that have lived in any age or any country … Credit has bought our land, made our canals, improved our rivers, opened our roads, built our cities, cleared our fields, founded our churches, erected our colleges and schools." Future economic adviser to Abraham Lincoln, Henry C. Carey, praised American banks for having "brought the owner of capital into direct communication with the active, the industrious, and the enterprising who desired to use it." Banking guru and author Carter H. Golembe credits the state banks for "the rapidity and character of western growth" from 1830 to 1844. And in 1843 Calvin Colton, author, journalist and minister, noted that "it is to this system of a sound credit currency, that, as a nation, we owe our unrivalled march to prosperity and wealth." New York's Free Banking Act of 1838 had invited investors with a minimum capital of $100,000 to associate themselves for banking purposes. Called "a second Declaration of Independence," the Act was adopted in most states by 1861.

There were almost five banks for every 100,000 citizens in 1860 compared to three in 1820. Bank capital doubled between 1834 and 1860. In New York City alone there were more than 8000 bank stockholders as compared to London and Paris where only a small number of very wealthy capitalists were bank owners. "Yet not everything could have been wrong," writes John Kenneth Galbreath, admonishing the critics of free banking in his book *Money*, "for those who spoke most despairingly of the monetary aberrations of the United States in the last [19th] century spoke always admiringly, and sometimes ecstatically, of the nation's economic development. Nothing like it had ever been seen before. One of two things must be true. The monetary arrangements must have had some redeeming aspect. Or else they were exceptionally unimportant." Galbreath, indeed, had spotted a free-banking chaon.

Business welfare masquerading under the guise of "internal improvements" was conspicuously absent even at the state and local levels of government by 1860. Such had been the corruption, mismanagement and graft accompanying these projects that every state except Massachusetts had amended its constitution to prohibit them. "I cannot find any authority in the Constitution for public charity. [To approve such spending] would be contrary to the letter and the spirit of the Constitution and subversive to the whole theory upon which the Union of these States is founded," announced President Franklin Pierce (1804-1869) as he vetoed another in a long line of Whig sponsored "internal improvement" bills in 1853. His successor, James Buchanan, signed into law the Tariff of 1857 which revised duties downward to a historically low average of 17% ad valorem. Buchanan also called attention to the huge expansion of the American merchant marine in his request for "a reasonable increase of the Navy which is at present inadequate to the protection of our vast tonnage afloat, *now greater than that of any other nation,* as well as to the defense of our seacoast" [italics mine]. Like the tropical ocean surface in the absence of storms, economic calm prevailed amidst almost unimaginable economic growth. But unpredictable and unavoidable hurricane-like instabilities must be expected every once in a while, and one of short duration erupted in the Panic of 1857.

For six months the money supply shrunk and prices plummeted. But Buchanan took Van Buren's approach and did nothing; government spending remained constant and businesses and banks were allowed to fail. The result? The economy found itself in full recovery by the next spring. In 1860 the expectation of war frightened businessmen into cutting back on bank loans, and the consequent effect on the money supply caused what is now termed a "growth recession." By 1860, Adam Smith's invisible hand had bestowed on an independent America seventy-seven years of unprecedented growth and prosperity. With the successful manufacture and sale of steam engines in large numbers, the amount and reliability of available power soared to undreamed heights.

Newly invented machines and interchangeable parts enabled most Americans, both skilled and unskilled, to find work on farms and in factories. The capital invested in industry almost doubled during the 1850s, from $530 million to over $1 billion.

Industrial and urban property advanced rapidly in value finally topping that of all farms and plantations from the Atlantic to the Pacific. Iron products and leather goods, including boots and shoes, alone equaled in value of annual output all the cotton grown in southern fields. Telegraph wires brought the day's news quickly to all the principal regions of the country "from sea to shining sea." A burgeoning railroad system distributed the growing bounty of manufacturing and agricultural wealth to all the major towns and cities between the east coast and the Mississippi River. The 8th census, taken in 1860, reported a population of 31 million people – two million more than Great Britain – and 1,385,000 employed in manufacturing establishments and enterprises. The leading commodities were, in dollar order, flour and meal, cotton goods, lumber, boots and shoes, leather, clothing, woolen goods, machinery, books, newspapers, sugar, liquors, furniture, bar and rolled iron, agricultural implements, paper, soap and candles. The census could declare that America had ceased being a mere supplier of raw materials for foreign manufacturers: "It is safe to assume … that one third of the whole population is supported, directly or indirectly, by manufacturing industry … The nation seemed speedily approaching a period of complete independence in respect to the products of skilled labor." Clearly, on the eve of the Civil War, there seemed every reason to believe that the nation could proceed uninterruptedly along the path to becoming "the greatest and most formidable that ever was in the world." But, alas, it was not to be. Beyond all notice, the requisite bits and pieces for the hurricane to come had been falling into place for decades and awaited only some "butterfly's flap" to set it off. It came with the Panic of 1857, and it revived blatant cries in the North and Northwest for a new wave of protectionism.

CHAPTER XXVI

THE AMERICAN RAILROAD CHAON

Sooner or later in life, we all sit down to a banquet of consequences.

Robert Louis Stevenson

It was the race of the 19th century. The contestants: Dobbin, a stagecoach horse endowed with exceptional speed and stamina, and the *Tom Thumb*, a diminutive steam engine with a vertical boiler designed and built at Baltimore's Canton Iron Works by inventor, engineer, industrialist and philanthropist Peter Cooper. The course: a nine-mile stretch of the Baltimore and Ohio Railroad from Riley's Tavern to the Mount Clare depot in Baltimore. The date: 18 September 1830.

The race condition: each contestant to draw a wagon load of 24 people the entire distance. Three years earlier, a group of Baltimoreans had incorporated the B&O in the state of Maryland with the objective of running the line eventually to the Ohio River at Wheeling in what is now West Virginia.

Baltimore, at the time the second largest city in the country, sorely needed a route westward because its seaport was beginning to feel the effects of competition with New York and its Erie Canal. Construction on the first 13 miles to Ellicott's Mills had been completed in 1829 and operations begun with horse- and mule-drawn wagons. Even wind-driven sail wagons were tried. But at a passenger cost of 75 cents for a ride taking 90 minutes (an average speed of 9 miles per hour), operations were unprofitable. Stagecoach interests continually denigrated the significance of the new railroad and insisted that the fastest and most reliable means of transportation could be provided only by horses on post roads. That was the challenge taken up by Cooper.

At the start, Dobbin took off quickly and was a quarter mile ahead before the *Tom Thumb* could drum up a full head of steam. But the iron horse gradually caught up and the two went neck and neck for a short while as Dobbin felt the whip. After that, the race appeared to be no contest until, a few miles before the finish, the locomotive's blower belt slipped and brought it to a halt. Cooper, who acted as both engineer and fireman, burnt and lacerated his hands trying to replace it, but by the time he did, Dobbin was too far ahead and won the race. The B&O board members, however, remained unconvinced by the victory and courageously opted to risk their own and their stockholders' money on steam propulsion, primitive though the state of the art was.

They had little to go on, but railroading was in the air. Hundreds of short-line horse- and mule-drawn railways financed almost exclusively by small investors were in existence. The common people were convinced that a new and more efficient transportation system was vital for a country the size of America and that it would soon be forthcoming. And how right they were! Despite its many faults, the railroad quickly proved itself far more preferable to canal and river navigation as a means of transportation. The lessons learned in building and operating these pioneering roads led to such rapid improvements in technology, procedures and capabilities that the industry spearheaded 19th century economic growth and industrialization. We today are indeed fortunate that Hamilton's "moneyed aristocracy" was not able to direct the flow of the considerable investment capital required away from these new ventures. Neither the well capitalized northeastern banks nor the 2nd Bank of the United States, for example, ever evinced any interest in railroad investment. The New York Stock Exchange listed only a small number of railroad stocks before 1860 and the leading companies, the Baltimore & Ohio and the Pennsylvania, did not even appear. Some state governments, it is true, did guarantee newly issued stocks and bonds, but this could never have been done without popular approval.

In 1825 John Stevens (1750-1828), the engineer first associated with Robert Livingston in trying to build a commercially successful steamboat, was exhibiting a steam locomotive of his own design that traversed a small circular track on his Hoboken NJ estate at speeds up to 13 miles per hour. Stevens had been arguing in favor of railroad rather than canal building since 1810, but Livingston, curiously enough, opposed the idea. The latter's opposition had much to do with Stevens' failure to obtain the necessary financing for his proposals. In England, the Stockton and Darlington Railway opened in 1825 for public traffic using the *Locomotion*, a steam locomotive built by George Stephenson (1781-1848) and regarded as the first to be placed in commercial service. On its test run, it pulled six loaded coal cars and 450 passengers in 21 wagons at a speed of 9 miles per hour on level ground. But Stephenson did not think the locomotive would be of use on steep grades because of traction problems. In 1828 Horatio Allen (1802-1899), an engineer employed by the Delaware and Hudson Canal Company, was sent to England to assess Stephenson's locomotives and quickly foresaw the potential of railroad transportation. "There is no reason to believe that the breed of horses will be materially improved," he wrote, "but the present breed of locomotives will furnish a power of which no one knows the limit." He bought four engines and shipped them back to the West Point Foundry in New York City where their design and engineering details were carefully noted. Especially of note was the boiler's horizontal placement which allowed for much larger capacity and power. It was the Delaware and Hudson Company's intention to transport anthracite coal from its mines in northeast Pennsylvania to New York City by rail and canal. One of the locomotives, the *Stourbridge Lion*, went to Honesdale PA where it was given a much ballyhooed trial on 8 August 1829. With Allen at the controls, it successfully navigated a two-mile test run and return. The seven ton engine, however, proved far too heavy to be sustained by wooden rails and it was placed in stationary service. At about the same time, the *Tom Thumb* demonstrated the feasibility of steam traction by successfully negotiating the sharp curves and steep grades on the B &O's newly laid track. But weighing in at less than a ton and generating only one horsepower, it was severely underpowered and could not draw sufficiently heavy loads for profitable operations.

Concurrently with Baltimore at the time, Charleston SC was experiencing a similar problem. With vigorous cultivation exhausting the soil in the coastal regions, farmers were forced to move further and further westward into the up-country regions close to the Savannah River on the Georgia border. It soon became cheaper and more convenient to ship cotton and other cash crops by river to Savannah GA rather than to Charleston. Threatened with the loss of its export business, Charleston's businessmen, as did those in Baltimore, looked to the new railroad as their means of survival. They persuaded the state legislature to charter the South Carolina Canal and Railroad Company (or the SOLA as it was known) with the objective of building a 136-mile line from Charleston to the small Savannah River town of Hamburg, just across from the river port of Augusta GA. Horatio Allen was hired to manage the spectacularly ambitious project. Upon its completion in 1833, it would cost almost $1 million and become by far the longest railroad in the world.

To provide engine power for the line, Allen ordered a locomotive of his own design from the West Point Foundry. Dubbed the *Best Friend of Charleston*, it was delivered by packet boat early in 1830 and became the first in America to be placed in commercial service. Another, the *West Point*, made its debut a few months later. A third, the *DeWitt Clinton*, went to the Mohawk and Hudson Railroad in New York.

The SOLA employed wooden rails capped with flat one half inch thick iron straps. Although the 3-ton *Best Friend* could travel at 25 miles per hour on short, straight stretches, the high probability of derailment resulting from the inadequate track structure limited its speed to 10 miles per hour. But railroad technology was advancing with miraculous speed. John Stevens' son Robert invented the iron T-rail along with a hook headed spike for fastening it to cross ties, an arrangement that is standard today. The new rail made for much greater speeds and efficiency and by 1836 was quickly taken up by all carriers. And as Horatio Allen had foreseen, more powerful locomotives were appearing almost daily.

Within two years of the Tom Thumb-Dobbin race, the Baltimore and Ohio had replaced its horses with steam-driven locomotives. And by 1852 it had completed its line westward and begun service to Wheeling on the Ohio River. But long distance travel on most other railroads involved frequent transfers of people and freight from one short line to another, and it made for inefficient and unprofitable operations. The roads did not even fit together because the standard gauge of 4 feet, 8½ inches would not be adopted nationwide until 1886.

Although limited merger and acquisition activity had occurred earlier, it swung into high gear after 1850. I note, as but one example of small investor ownership and trackage, the Albany to Buffalo route which gave birth to one of America's great transportation systems and ensured New York City's continued dominance in commercial and financial affairs. The route was served by nine different roads connected end to end for the most part:

the Mohawk and Hudson (opened in 1831 using the *DeWitt Clinton* locomotive with 18.2 miles of track and 277 stockholders); the Mohawk Valley (opened in1836 under the name Utica and Schenectady with 78 miles of track and 687 stockholders); the Schenectady and Troy (opened in 1842 with 21 miles of track and one stockholder); the Rochester and Syracuse (formed by the merger in 1853 of the Auburn and Syracuse, the Auburn and Rochester, and the Syracuse and Rochester Direct Railroads with 80 miles of track and 947 stockholders); the Buffalo and Rochester (opened in 1850 with 262 stockholders, formed from a merger of the Tonawanda Railroad opened in 1837 with 44 miles of track, the Attica and Buffalo Railroad opened in 1843 with 31 miles of track, and the Buffalo and Rochester Railroad opened in 1850 with 27 miles of track); the Rochester, Lockport and Niagara Falls (opened in 1838 with 262 stockholders and 77 miles of track); the Rockport and Lake Ontario (opened in 1852 with 6 miles of track); the Buffalo and Niagara Falls (opened in 1845 with 22 miles of track); and the Buffalo and Lockport (opened in 1853 with 36 stockholders and 12.3 miles of track).

By 1851 it had become clear to the directors and officers of all these publicly owned roads that mergers and cost-cutting were essential for establishing profitable operations. Raising prices was not an option given the competition provided by the Erie Canal. Free market rates had settled in at about $1.10 per ton-mile via the Erie Canal, and $3.50 per ton-mile via railroad for the Albany to Buffalo run. In 1853, less than two years later, in what appeared to be an insuperable accomplishment, the railroad managements had hammered out all the numerous financial and technical details attending the multiple mergers and the great New York Central Railroad System was born. In Pennsylvania, the merger of over a hundred roads created the Pennsylvania Railroad and gave Philadelphia a route west to Pittsburgh and the Ohio River. With the completion of an engineering marvel of the time, the horseshoe curve piercing the 2300-foot Allegheny Mountains near Altoona, travel time on the Philadelphia-to-Pittsburgh run was cut from three and a half days to thirteen hours or less.

Once again we see a free market "mobocracy" exhibiting a wisdom that exceeds that of any one of us! With people pursuing what they perceived as their own best interests free of government interference, Adam Smith's invisible hand produced a self-organized and unbelievably efficient transportation system. The railroad offered by far the most viable means available for the movement of raw materials and capital equipment to factories and farms and for the distribution of manufactured and agricultural products over the length and breadth of the land. As such, its importance was widely recognized and it became the stellar growth industry of the 19th century, attracting huge amounts of both domestic and foreign investment capital and the most talented of young entrepreneurs. Trackage grew from 23 miles in 1830 to 2818 miles in 1840, a figure far greater than the 1800 miles in all of government-saturated Europe, including Great Britain. In the next decade, trackage more than tripled to 9021 miles and tripled again to 30626 miles by 1860. No other statistic attests more dramatically to America's phenomenal growth at the time, and only in a market economy largely free of government-issued chaos could it have happened.

The General Survey Act of 1824, signed into law by James Monroe as a post-road and defense necessity, boosted early railroad development. Under its terms, both Presidents John

Quincy Adams and Andrew Jackson assigned United States Army engineers to survey routes and aid in the construction of roadbeds, bridges and tunnels. Thomas Jefferson had in 1802 approved a bill establishing an engineering school and military academy at West Point NY.

Although initially opposed to a standing army, Jefferson undoubtedly had a change of heart when Napoleon appeared on America's western boundary. The miserable performance of the military during the War of 1812 had prompted Madison and the army brass into sending Colonel Sylvanus Thayer (1785-1872) and Major General Winfield Scott (1786-1866) to Paris after the fall of Napoleon. There the two immersed themselves in the curriculum of the *École Polytechnique* and, after two years study, returned with a library of more than 1000 books on engineering, mathematics and the military arts. Appointed superintendent of the United States Military Academy in 1817, Thayer introduced the modern *École* regime that combined officer training with a highly technical undergraduate education. West Point became the nation's chief source of civil engineers and its graduates, as teachers, writers and practitioners, fostered science and engineering at Cornell, Harvard, Princeton, Rensselaer and other colleges.

Simultaneously, Scott totally revamped army accounting and administrative procedures to ensure professional rigor and accountability.

Among the West Point engineers assigned by President Adams to the Baltimore and Ohio Railroad were Major William Gibbs McNeill and Lieutenant George Washington Whistler, the latter an assistant professor of drawing at the Academy and a master of projective geometry. Beginning with their first report to the Board of Directors in 1828, they adhered to the precedent-setting standards developed by Scott and Thayer for army engineers. Written up in railroad periodicals, their procedures were closely studied and taken up by most other lines. In 1831, Whistler married McNeill's sister, Anna, and their union sired one of America's and the world's foremost artists, James Abbott McNeill Whistler (1834-1903). Anna is the famous figure in Whistler's painting, *Arrangement in Grey and Black: Portrait of the Painter's Mother*. American engineers being in demand abroad, George Whistler betook his family to Russia in 1842 to supervise construction of the Moscow to St. Petersburg railway. He died of cholera in 1849, two years before its completion.

CHAPTER XXVII

THE FIRST TRANS-CONTINENTAL RAILROAD

To the United States belongs the honor of this work. From its inception to its consummation, it is purely American — American genius conceived the plan, American science pronounced it practicable, American capital furnished the sinews, and American energy prosecuted the gigantic enterprise to its completion in spite of the most formidable difficulties.

Editorial in the *Aspinwall Courier*, circa 1855

Closer to home, America's railroad chaon continued its spontaneous, self-organized evolution when American entrepreneurs undertook the building of the world's first transcontinental railway. The brainchild of William Henry Aspinwall (1807-1875), a remarkably prescient and astute young shipper and financier, the railroad would become a conduit through which flowed the wealth of many nations.

Continuing a long line of visionaries who followed Vasco Nuñez de Balboa's (1475-1517) discovery of the Pacific Ocean in 1513, Aspinwall recognized the strategic position of the Isthmus of Panama for the development of inter-oceanic trade.

The first, Charles V (1500-1558) of Spain, dreamed of a canal connecting the Atlantic and Pacific Oceans. A shorter, safer and less expensive route than that around Cape Horn at the southern tip of South America was sorely needed to repair back to Spain the gold and silver plundered from Mexico's west coast and Peru. He ordered surveys undertaken for a trans-Isthmus canal, but settled for El Camino Real, a 55-mile long, seven-foot wide stone "highway" connecting Panama City on the Pacific side of the Isthmus with Portobelo on the Atlantic side. Charles' son, Phillip II (1523-1598), finally decided the cost of a canal to be much too great and rejected the idea. That left him money enough to squander on the Spanish Armada for an attack on England, for the continued subjugation of the Netherlands, and for expelling the Jews and Moors from Spain. In later centuries, England, France and Portugal also entertained notions of a canal but nothing came of them.

In 1695 William Paterson of Bank of England fame persuaded the Scottish Parliament to create the "Company of Scotland Trading to Africa and the Indies." His objective, known as the "Darién Scheme," was to establish on the Isthmus of Darién (as he called Panama) an entrepôt around which Scots could settle and "thus hold the key of the commerce of the world." The colony would foster free trade, offer shelter to the ships of all nations and sponsor tolerance of race and religion, ideas far ahead of their time during this era of mercantilism. For its services, the Company would exact a tribute of ¼% on the value of all goods passing through its facilities. With one supreme stroke, he argued, Scotland could tap into the world trade that was so rapidly enriching England and be raised from the poorest to the richest of nations. At the time, England and Scotland shared a common monarch, William of Orange, but otherwise were politically and commercially independent.

Paterson's trail-blazing proposal had originally caught on in London where those English and Dutch investors locked out from purchasing shares in the East India Company quickly snapped up £500,000 of Company stock. At this point, however, the government intervened and forced the Company to cancel all subscriptions and return the shareholders' money.

England at the time was at war with France and William, his hands full trying to fend off the French in Holland, did not wish to offend Spain which claimed Darién as part of New Grenada (the future Colombia). Paterson then repaired to Edinburgh where again he found no shortage of investors. He sold over £400,000 of stock and the Company was in business. Five ships were acquired to carry colonists to their new home. From the thousands who volunteered, Paterson selected 1200 to accompany him to Panama.

Sailing in July of 1698, the expedition endured a very rough crossing during which many passengers died, including Paterson's wife. The ship arrived on the Isthmus three months later at a point 200 miles west of Cartagena and 150 miles east of Portobelo, and there the colonists established the town of New Edinburgh. It being the dry season, building and planting were able to proceed reasonably well. But then began the six month rainy season, and for this the colony was totally unprepared. Famine, disease, and hostile attacks by Spaniards decimated the population. After seven months and four hundred deaths, the decision was made, over Paterson's violent objections, to abandon the colony and return to Scotland. A very ill Paterson had to be carried aboard ship.

A second and larger expedition of six ships and 1600 people left Scotland before the fate of the first became known.

They took up the deserted settlement, but hundreds of the new arrivals quickly succumbed to the same tropical afflictions as the first. Three months after the landing, a fleet from Cartagena arrived to press the Spanish claim to the land. So appalled was the Spanish commander at the condition of the colonists that he offered to let them leave unscathed. Only one ship, however, with fewer than 300 survivors managed the return to Scotland.

Not for another 150 years would a serious attempt be made to take advantage of Panama's strategic importance. Paterson recovered from his illness and spent his last years writing and trying to convince King William to revive the Darién Scheme, but without result.

The 1848 Treaty of Guadalupe Hidalgo ending the war with Mexico ceded a vast amount of western land to the United States. Together with the Oregon Territory claimed under the Louisiana Purchase Treaty, these almost inaccessible possessions posed immense problems of communication with America's east coast. Three routes connecting the Atlantic with the Pacific Ocean were available at the time, the first a perilous 2000-mile four-to-six month crossing of the American west by foot and covered wagon. The mortality rate from accidents, disease and Indians was high and only a trickle of people attempted this. A second option was the four-to-six month 13,000-mile voyage around Cape Horn braving the world's roughest seas in the Drake Passage. The third, as advertised for those with destination California in mind, was for travelers to make the "pleasant voyage to Panama, stroll across the fifty miles of Isthmus to the Pacific and, after another easy sea voyage, find themselves in San Francisco," 6,000 miles and a time duration of only three to four weeks. A young army officer trudging across the Isthmus in 1852 offered a contrary opinion, that "The horrors of the road in the rainy season are beyond description." Lieutenant Ulysses S. Grant was at the time en route to garrison duty in California with a large detachment of 400 men from the U. S. Army's Fourth Infantry Division together with their families. Yellow fever, cholera, dysentery, heatstroke and drowning claimed the lives of 150 people under his command – men, women and children. Even the mules found the going almost impassible so obliterated had the paths become from washouts and sinkholes. Grant never forgot that ghastly hike through swamp and jungle and in his old age talked more of Panama's horrors than those of the Civil War.

During his Presidency, he authorized seven expeditions to Panama and Nicaragua seeking the best route for the construction of a canal. An alternate 175-mile route through Nicaragua to the north had been discussed by many including naturalist, writer, explorer and statesman Alexander Humboldt, DeWitt Clinton and Horatio Allen, none of whom had traveled there.

In 1832, at age 25, William Aspinwall began his career in the family business of Howland & Aspinwall, a New York merchant firm specializing in the Caribbean trade. Upon gaining control in 1835, he expanded the company's routes to South America, Asia and Europe. Realizing that faster ships generated higher profits, he commissioned the noted naval architect John William Griffiths (1809-1882) to build the *Rainbow* and *Sea Witch*, two of the first China clipper ships. By cutting the travel time to Asia to three months, these sleek vessels proved highly profitable to the New England shipping community as their cargoes of tea, silk, spices, coffee, china ware and opium were quickly snapped up in American markets. But Aspinwall was not one to stand on his business laurels and his mind quickly turned to a grander scheme of things.

At the conclusion of the Mexican war in 1848, President Polk negotiated treaties with both Nicaragua and New Grenada securing the right of passage across the Isthmus for United States citizens. Soon after, the U. S. Post Office Department proffered ocean mail contracts for servicing an Atlantic route from New York City to Chagres, Panama, and a Pacific route from Panama City to California and Oregon. Despite its lack of a deep water harbor, Chagres, about twenty miles southwest of Portobelo, had become the main jumping-off point for the Isthmus crossing because of its location at the mouth of the Chagres River and the near obliteration of El Camino Real due to neglect. Travelers would take *cayucas* or dugout canoes upriver as far as it was navigable and then follow jungle paths for some twenty miles to the town of Las Cruces near present-day Gamboa, about 38 miles from Chagres. The remaining 12 miles to Panama

City could then be trekked on the Las Cruces Trail, a very narrow cobblestone path that had been built in 1530.

Estimated time of crossing, four to five days. Fifty years later, the Chagres River would be dammed to form Gatun Lake, eighty-five feet above sea level and a major section of the Panama Canal

Several months were to elapse before responsible bidders on the mail contracts appeared. The Atlantic run seemed profitable mainly for having Charleston, Savannah, New Orleans and Havana as ports of call. But the Pacific service was universally considered a losing proposition because of the west coast's lack of industry, coal supplies, repair yards and port facilities. George Law (1816-81), steamboat operator and building contractor for canals, railroads, ship terminals and bridges, won the Atlantic contract in the name of the United States Mail Steam Line Company. William Aspinwall, along with his associates, diplomat, lawyer, explorer, amateur archaeologist and author of popular travelogues John Stephens (1805-1852) and banker Henry Chauncey, incorporated the Pacific Mail Steamship Company in New York and took on the Pacific contract along with the responsibility for transporting mail across the Isthmus. The assumption was looked on as foolish in the extreme by all their fellow steamship operators.

But Aspinwall, familiar as he was with the profits generated by the Asian trade, had something much grander in mind. An interoceanic railroad across the Isthmus, he knew, would shave some 6,000 miles off travel distances to Asia and California, thus greatly lowering insurance costs and payrolls for shipboard personnel, and reducing the wear and tear on passenger and merchant vessels. Aspinwall ordered three new wooden-hulled, paddlewheel steamers to inaugurate the California-Oregon service.

The *California*, launched in May of 1848, departed New York in October and became the first steamship to navigate the Straits of Magellan. It was quickly followed by its sister ships, the *Oregon* and the *Panama*. These steamers would soon become the backbone of Aspinwall's trading empire on the Pacific coast. Law, having no ship ready at the time, chartered the *Falcon*, a small steamer displacing 890 tons, and inaugurated service to Chagres. It sailed from New York on 1 December 1848 with all but 29 of its 129 berths empty, just four days before President Polk announced the discovery of gold in California. By the time the ship arrived in New Orleans, the news had spread far and wide, and nearly two hundred heavily armed gold prospectors stormed aboard and refused to get off. The captain finally agreed to sail after cramming bunks and bedding into every nook and cranny he could find and taking on extra supplies. At Chagres, the Falcon was unable to anchor near the town because of un-navigable reefs and sand bars and had to proceed to the safety of Limón Bay about 10 miles to the northeast. There the passengers paid dearly for native boatmen to ferry them to Chagres where there were far too few *cayucas* available for the river transport to Las Cruces.

Normally used for banana shipments, they could carry at most 4 to 6 passengers. Confusion and rowdiness mounted with the arrival of more and more ships from both America and Europe.

In the meantime, the *California*, after its trip around the Horn, reached Panama City on January 17, 1849 to find more than a thousand "forty-niners" waiting to board for the trip to San Francisco. Riots broke out when it was learned there were berths for only 250, and sailing was delayed until January 31.

In San Francisco, 365 passengers disembarked along with the ship's entire crew. Three months would elapse before the captain could hire replacements for the return to Panama.

The gold rush catapulted Aspinwall's folly into a source of gold all its own. No one was laughing anymore. And to compound Aspinwall's huge success, Commodore Matthew Perry (1794-1858) opened Japan to foreign merchants in 1853 bringing still more trade through Panama. Aspinwall had taken the first steps toward enacting his grand plan in 1847 when he and his associates acquired an exclusive concession from New Granada allowing the construction of an Isthmus crossing by some combination of road, rail, river or canal. Thereupon, he dispatched Stephens, Chauncey, Company engineer James L.

Baldwin, and Colonel George W. Hughes commanding a group of engineers on loan from the army's U. S. Topographical Corps to survey the land and lay out a line for a possible railroad. The most worrisome problem in their eyes was the continental divide the altitude of which would determine whether a steam engine could traverse the steep track grades required for the short 11-mile distance to the Pacific coast. To their great fortune, they discovered a summit gap only 287 feet above sea level, what is now known as the Gaillard (formerly the Culebra) Cut of the Panama Canal, which allowed lesser grades and shortened the line. All agreed that the project should go ahead. Their estimated cost of construction, $1 million; their estimated building time, six months. They were to be severely disillusioned.

In 1850, the Panama Railroad Company was incorporated in the state of New York with a capitalization of $1 million and the stock, offered at $100 a share, quickly sold out. Stephens in Bogota signed a contract with the government of New Grenada granting the Company the exclusive privilege of establishing "an iron railroad between the two oceans across the Isthmus of Panama." It would run from Portobelo to Panama City and follow closely the route of the old El Camino Real. But they reckoned without George Law who had bought or taken options on all the ground sites around Portobelo that could possibly be used for a shipping terminal. These he offered to the Railroad Company at a price it could not afford.

After poring over old maps of the area, Aspinwall and his associates decided that Manzanilla Island in Limón Bay, twenty miles southwest of Portobelo, offered the only suitable deep-anchorage harbor and there they decided to locate the railroad terminus. A low, swampy plot of land 600 acres in area and infested with mosquitos, snakes and alligators, it was separated from the mainland by a narrow arm of the Bay. Two engineering contractors who had had much experience working on canals and railroads in America and New Granada, "Colonel" George M. Totten and John C. Trautwine, signed on for the building of the railroad. Upon arrival in Panama, however, they saw immediately that the construction estimates for the railroad were far off the mark and asked to be released from their contract lest they go bankrupt. To this the Company assented and hired them back as engineers. John Stephens, president of the Company, and James Baldwin now assumed the responsibility for getting the railroad built.

Beginning with an acute labor shortage caused by the California gold-rush, Stephens and Baldwin faced almost intractable problems in getting started. Stephens sent agents scurrying to Europe, Asia and the West Indies to hire workers, an initiative that proved highly successful given the conditions of unemployment, starvation and oppression that existed in much of the world. Soon, boatloads carrying thousands of workers began arriving regularly. With no place to live, they were initially quartered on old ships anchored in Limón Bay.

Baldwin undertook the difficult and costly task of procuring and importing food, clothing, materials and equipment from New York two thousand miles away. May 1, 1850 saw the first sod turned on Manzanilla Island, and it was not long before a causeway to the mainland was built and a rudimentary bedroom town set up. First called Aspinwall, it would later stand at the entrance to the Panama Canal and be renamed Colón.

On the mainland, an environmental chamber of tropical horrors awaited the builders. A stifling heat prevailed the year round, and a six-month rainy season forced workers to toil waist-deep in mud and water. Insects, snakes and alligators were a constant menace. Bottomless mangrove swamps swallowed thousands of tons of rocks and dirt and still no solid ground on which to lay railway tracks emerged. The lead engineer, convinced that the project was futile, wished to resign but Totten persuaded him to stay on and complete the job, which he finally did. Sickness so decimated the work gangs that they were replaced every week with fresh ones. There was a death for every crosstie laid, some claimed. Of a thousand Chinese coolies who arrived on the *Rainbow* and *Sea Witch*, only 250 survived, many committing suicide when the Company cut off their opium supply. Simply disposing of dead bodies became a problem. A ghoulish business of pickling cadavers in brine and selling them to medical schools and hospitals around the world sprang up. By March 1851, rails stretched out only two miles to Monkey Hill, a piece of solid ground on which lived thousands of chattering monkeys. There Baldwin faced three more miles of swamp and quicksand over which he had to lay a roadbed.

Making progress even more difficult for Stephens and Baldwin was fierce competition from ferry operator, shipper and future railroad magnate, Cornelius Vanderbilt (1794-1877).

There will be more to say about this great entrepreneur later, but a few words now are of relevance. A blue-eyed, flaxen haired, boisterous youngster, he worked his father's Staten Island farm until his 16th birthday at which time he received a $100 "butterfly" present from his mother. From that moment on, money became his passion. "I have been insane on the subject of moneymaking all my life," he recounted later. Using the $100 to buy a small flat-bottomed, two-masted sailing vessel, he established a ferry service between Manhattan and Staten Island. No weather too stormy to sail, no competitive price too low to undercut, no job too difficult to undertake – those were the attributes of his business style, and they acquired for him a reputation for reliability, fearlessness, competitiveness and frugality that he never lost. The War of 1812 saw him supplying six army bases around New York Bay and conveying agricultural produce from the farms along the Hudson River to New York City. With his savings he bought interests in other boats, including some plying the coastal waters between Chesapeake Bay and New York.

In 1817, his ferry operation having lost its competitive edge to steamboats, Vanderbilt sold all his sailing vessels and went to work as a captain for one Thomas Gibbons ferrying passengers between New Jersey and New York. He immediately reconditioned Gibbons' two small steamboats, selected new hard-bitten crews and within a year turned a losing venture into a profitable one. He charged a below-cost $1 for passage compared to $4 for his competitors and made up the losses by raising prices for food and drink in the steamboat's bar. There remained one big problem. As an unlicensed steamboat operator, Gibbons was in violation of the "hot water bill" passed years before in 1798 and renewed for a term not exceeding thirty years by the New York State legislature in 1808. The bill granted Robert Fulton and Robert Livingston the exclusive privilege of steamboat navigation on all New York waters and permitted the seizure of unlicensed steamboats and the collection of penalties for every trip made.

The Fulton-Livingston monopoly had had it vigorously enforced ever since the appearance of a competing steamboat on the Hudson River in 1810. Violators were denounced as rogues, rascals, law-breakers and ingrates. It would not be the last time that Vanderbilt competed against a state-sponsored monopoly.

Although harried incessantly by New York City police, Vanderbilt managed to avoid arrest and seizure. In 1820, the New Jersey legislature, seeking to aid its citizens, passed an act providing that if anyone be "enjoined or restrained by any writ or injunction by the Court of Chancery of the State of New York … from navigating any boat or vessel moved by steam or fire … on the waters between the ancient shores of the State of New Jersey and New York, the plaintiff or plaintiffs in such writ or order shall be liable to the person or persons aggrieved for all damages, expenses and charges occasioned thereby, to be recovered by triple costs … ." A situation had developed wherein two sovereign states had passed laws in direct conflict and it became the cause célèbre of the day. There was even talk of an interstate war.

Also in 1820, Aaron Ogden, a licensed steamboat operator suffering under Vanderbilt's competition, brought suit against Gibbons for violating New York law. New York courts upheld Ogden and the case reached the Supreme Court of the United States in 1824. Dubbed *Gibbons vs. Ogden*, it would soon become a Constitutional landmark. The unfamiliar names attached to the case obscure both its importance and the great personalities who took part. Except among Hamilton's "moneyed aristocracy," the Supreme Court at the time commanded very little respect around the country, especially in the hinterlands where its 1820 2nd Bank decision aroused great antipathy. But this case was entirely different, based as it was squarely on "enumerated powers," the "commerce clause" of the Constitution [Article I, Section 8, Clause 3]: "The Congress shall have the power … To regulate commerce with foreign nations, and among the several States, and with the Indian tribes." How precise and concise the wording is! By simply granting to the federal government the sole power to regulate interstate commerce, the clause excises a maze of local rules and regulations and, most importantly, curtails governmental powers overall.

Gibbons and Vanderbilt retained Daniel Webster to represent them. Then at the height of his oratorical powers, Webster launched into an exhaustive analysis of interstate commerce and navigation, concluding finally that the "hot water bill" violated the "commerce clause" of the Constitution.

The Supreme Court, Chief Justice John Marshall presiding, concurred and Marshall wrote the majority opinion. The decision nipped in the bud the state-legislated chaos that was about to flower from a myriad of restrictions on interstate commerce. Connecticut and Louisiana already had laws on the books limiting navigation in their waters and other states were considering them. Had the Court's opinion been ignored, our great free trade union might well have followed the course of the 2nd Bank and vanished. It did not, however, for the Court this time around had attuned itself to popular sentiment, and the private economy took quick advantage of it. From only eight in 1819, the number of steamboats on the Hudson sprouted to more than a hundred in 1840. (See once again on page 138 the excerpts from Hamilton's *Federalist* articles No.11 and No. 22 that laid the basis for the commerce clause). Of especial significance, I should note here, is what Webster and Marshall did *not* say in their arguments. Nowhere did they imply that the federal government had any right to interfere in private business affairs, as the clause would so be reinterpreted sixtythree years later.

The end of the Fulton-Livingston monopoly brought fierce competition and lower fare and freight charges to the Hudson River. Operators and shipbuilders vied to get a share of the tremendous volume of passengers and freight moving through Albany, the eastern terminus of the Erie Canal. Bigger and faster steamboats appeared every year, the goal being a daylight journey of less than ten hours on the New York- Albany run. In 1826, the time was reduced to fifteen hours, in 1836 to ten hours, and finally in 1864 to seven hours by the *Chauncey Vibbard.* So great did the rivalry for record runs become that a race was arranged between two of the fastest boats, the *Oregon* owned by George Law and the very luxurious *Cornelius Vanderbilt* owned by Vanderbilt, with a side bet of $1000 between the owners. The race course was from the Battery at the foot of Manhattan Island to Ossining thirty-five miles up the Hudson and back. The *Oregon* won by 1500 feet and Vanderbilt took the result badly. Almost certainly it figured in his decision to compete with Law on the New York-Panama run and establish a route to California through Nicaragua.

In 1850, Vanderbilt paid the Nicaraguan government $10,000 for the exclusive right of transit across Nicaragua. His plan was to establish an Atlantic shipping line servicing Panama and Nicaragua in competition with Law, then to navigate the San Juan River to Lake Nicaragua using small steam-powered boats, cross the 50 mile width of the Lake using steamships, and finally journey by stagecoach to the Pacific coast on a 12-mile macadam road he intended to build along with port facilities. To the distress of Stephens and Baldwin, he sent agents to bribe railroad workers to come work for him in Nicaragua, thereby forcing constructional delays over and above those caused by the environment. By 1852, his operation was in full swing attracting

28,000 "forty-niners" a year, as many as the Panama route. His route was 600 miles and two days shorter and his fare $200 lower than Aspinwall's $600. So profitable was the operation – he was netting over $1 million a year – that Vanderbilt at age 59 decided to take his first vacation. For that purpose, he commissioned a steam yacht, the *North Star*, and embarked on a triumphal tour of Europe. That voyage aroused an interest in trans-Atlantic shipping, and he entered into competition with the Cunard and Collins lines. In 1847, Congress had granted Edward K. Collins a subsidy of $3 million plus $385,000 per year to compete with European shippers. Lobbyist Collins spent lavishly to retain his government largesse, entertaining Congressmen and influential politicians like President Millard Fillmore and his entire cabinet. But by 1858, the Collins Line had become so inefficient that Congress ended the subsidy. Vanderbilt's venture, however, proved unprofitable and he turned his attention to railroading. And there we shall meet him again later in this history.

Back at the railroad, Baldwin finally overcame the quicksand problem with an ingenious solution, one that is used today for erecting buildings in sandy areas. He hooked together lines of flatcars loaded with dirt, rocks and debris, sank them to their buoyant depth and used them as platforms on which to float a roadbed. Still, time was fleeting and the expectation of quick profits had vanished. By November of 1851, the rails extended to Gatun on the edge of the Chagres River valley, only 7 miles from Aspinwall, and the Panama Railroad was facing a bleak financial future. The $1 million capital raised from the original stock issue had been spent and now there were soaring construction costs, material shortages, the competition from Vanderbilt, and a plummeting stock price to be dealt with. Trautwine resigned and returned to the United States. Aspinwall reacted quickly. He dipped into his private fortune to keep the Railroad solvent, resolved his differences with Law and placed faster and more luxurious ships on the Atlantic run to counter Vanderbilt's shorter Nicaragua route.

Law for his part bought a large block of stock in the Railroad and undertook the building of docks and warehouses on the shores of Limón Bay.

At this point, a most fortuitous tropical hurricane probably saved the Railroad from extinction. Two of Law's steamers carrying 1100 gold-rushers arrived at Chagres simultaneously with the storm. Unable to discharge passengers, the ship captains sought refuge in Limón Bay until they could safely return to Chagres. While waiting for the weather to subside, the travelers heard what sounded like the toot of a train whistle. They clambered up to the deck and saw what they believed to be a miracle, a freight train chugging its way across the causeway from the mainland. They rushed to the railroad office and demanded of Colonel Totten that they be permitted to ride the train to its end near Gatun rather than return to Chagres. Totten refused, not wishing to delay railroad construction. But when they persisted, he charged an outlandish fare of $25 for the train ride and $10 for a walk along the tracks. It seemed a bargain to the eager forty-niners and by the end of the day, Totten had collected almost $7000. Suddenly, the Railroad was in the passenger business and making money.

When the news reached New York, the stock price zoomed. A new issue quickly raised $4 million and there was little doubt now that the Railroad would be completed, even though 1852 turned out the worst year yet: Railroad president John Stephens died of yellow fever, a 300-foot wooden bridge across the Chagres at Barbacoas collapsed in a flood to be replaced by a 600-foot iron structure, and Baldwin's entire engineering staff of 50 men died of cholera. But in that same year, men and materials were shipped around Cape Horn to Panama City and construction started on the Pacific portion of the Railroad.

January of 1854 saw a months-long excavation begin at Culebra on the continental divide and, finally, on 12 January 1855, the work gangs from the Atlantic met those from the Pacific. Totten, who along with Stephens supplied the driving force for the project, drove in the final spike during a torrential rainstorm. And on the next day, the first train ever steamed from one ocean to another taking only four hours instead of the four to six days for the former crossings.

It had taken five years and $7.5 million to build and had cost six to twelve thousand lives (no one could be sure of the exact number). But the Panama Railroad revolutionized world trade routes. It brought the Orient thousands of miles closer to the American east coast and hastened the development of the west coasts of North and South America. Hundreds of thousands migrated to California via the Railroad and the Panama Canal itself may never have been built except for its presence

George Totten stayed on as chief engineer of the Panama Railroad until 1875. He designed a lock canal for crossing the Isthmus as opposed to a sea level one and that brought him to the attention of Ferdinand de Lesseps, the builder of the Suez Canal. De Lesseps appointed him chief engineer of the French company attempting to build an Isthmus canal, but that project never came to fruition. For his contributions, Napoleon III awarded Totten a gold ring studded with diamonds in the form of an imperial crown. He is commemorated only by his etched profile on a small plaque in the Panama City railroad station.

He died in 1884. A brief obituary in The *New York Times* stated only that he was a retired engineer, nothing about his being the man directly responsible for building the world's first transcontinental railroad.

William Aspinwall retired in 1856 and began years of extensive world traveling. Howland & Aspinwall became, and was to remain so for many years, the foremost mercantile firm in New York. After settling down in New York, Aspinwall helped found the Metropolitan Museum of Art and the American Society for the Prevention of Cruelty to Animals. He also became a grand-uncle of future president Franklin Delano Roosevelt. Only a nondescript red granite monument in Colón commemorates the great achievement of Aspinwall, Stephens and Chauncey, whose railroad raised the standard of living of millions worldwide.

CHAPTER XXVIII

THE SECOND TRANS-CONTINENTAL RAILROAD AND BEYOND

The place is fast becoming civilized, several men having been *killed there already.*

Salt Lake City *Deseret News* 18 March 1869

Looking for an honest politician is like looking for an ethical burglar.

H. L. Mencken

To the Editor:

I wish to protest the appalling physical condition of the Long Island Railroad. The crumbling stations, the dirty and crowded old cars, and the deteriorating roadbed and track make the system dangerous to life and limb, not to mention the extreme discomfort and inconvenience associated with commuting. Why, come to think of it, there was better transportation two thousand years ago.

Sincerely yours
Outraged Commuter

To the Editor:

May I say to Outraged Commuter that I am aware of problems in the areas to which he refers and that every effort is being made to correct them. However, I do not understand how he can justifiably write that there was better transportation two thousand years ago.

Sincerely yours,
President, Long Island Railroad

To the Editor:

In my Bible, it states that Jesus rode into Jerusalem on his ass, and that's more than I have been able to do in ten years of commuting on the Long Island Railroad.

Sincerely yours,
Outraged Commuter

Adapted from the "Letters to the Editor" column in the *New York World-Telegram*, circa 1937

"Anna, I am going to California to be the pioneering railroad engineer of the Pacific Coast," announced Theodore Dehone Judah (1826-1863) to his wife in 1854 just after returning from a meeting in New York with San Francisco businessman Charles Lincoln Wilson. Wilson had hired him to design and build a railroad connecting Sacramento CA with the gold fields in the Sierra Nevada foothills twenty-two miles to the east. The job offer would become the "butterfly" marking the birth of the world's second trans-continental railroad.

Judah attended the Rensselaer technical school in Troy NY as a youngster and, upon graduation, worked on a railroad connecting Troy and Schenectady. Engineers being very much in demand during this boom period of railroad building, he immersed himself in a long series of construction jobs in Vermont, Massachusetts and Connecticut. His work on the Niagara Gorge Railroad capped his reputation as a top flight engineer and led to the meeting with Wilson.

The Judahs quickly removed to Sacramento, taking the Nicaragua route offered by Vanderbilt. Once there, Judah set about bringing into existence the Sacramento Valley Railroad, the first in California. Financed solely by San Francisco businessmen, it was completed in 1856. Its eastern terminus was Folsom, a newly created town that became a hub of mining activities and the western terminus of the Pony Express. But Judah had something much grander in mind than the building of another mundane short line railroad.

The gold rush of 1849 had exploded California's population from a few tens of thousands in the1840s to almost 100,000 by 1850. It would be 400,000 by 1860, most of the migration being carried by the just finished Panama Railroad.

Talk of an American transcontinental line uniting the state with the east coast was bruited about constantly, and not just in California. Bills granting land and subsidies of as much as $90 million toward the construction of a Pacific railroad had been introduced into the United States Congress ever since California attained statehood in 1850. In 1852, Jefferson Davis, Secretary of War under President Franklin Pierce and future president of the Confederate States of Americas, directed the U.

S. Army Topographical Corps to conduct surveys for finding the most suitable routes. These, as published in the Pacific Railroad Surveys of 1855, identified five possibilities. Few, however, took the idea seriously. Building a railroad over 8000- foot passes in the Sierra Nevada

Mountains only 100 miles east of the Pacific Ocean, scaling steep precipices and bridging deep gorges, all this coupled to snowfall averaging more than 30 feet per year, made any such project sound as visionary as a man-to the- moon mission. Adding to the difficulties was a fierce competition between political leaders of the North and South as to whether the projected railroad would follow a northern or southern route. And, of course, there were enormous financial problems to be dealt with.

Judah's grand mission from the beginning was to build that trans-continental railroad, and none of the difficulties associated with it deterred him one iota. He drew up a detailed 13,000-word proposal – "A Practical Plan for Building the Pacific Railroad" – and distributed it widely at his own expense to Congressmen, legislators, department heads and influential people in California and Washington DC. In it, he pointed out that the project had been "in agitation" for more than 15 years, and that although the U. S. government had spent much money and time seeking routes, no proper survey of any one of them yet existed. "The project is a popular one," he maintained. "If investors felt confident in the practicability of the project, money can be raised through stock and bond issues. Can the United States Government do it? Have they done it? Have they tried? No, and they will not, and what is more, the people do not care to have them, for they have little confidence in their ability to carry it out economically, or to protect themselves and the treasury from the rapacious clutches of the hungry speculators who would swarm around them like vultures round a dead carcass. ... The road should be built by the spontaneous free will of those of the people who favor and are willing to pay for it, and who desire to protect the public purse from plunder, believing themselves better able to manage it than their political representatives." Judah also gave cost estimates. Considering that 25,000 miles of railroad had been built in the past twenty years for about $1 billion, he thought the new road could be built for at most $150 million.

At one of his public presentations, he met Leland Stanford (1824-1893), a Sacramento grocer who had become wealthy selling supplies to gold prospectors. As Stanford recalled the meeting: "In 1860 there was a gentleman by the name of T. D. Judah ... who had made surveys over the mountains with reference to building of a line of railroad connecting the Atlantic and the Pacific ... We discussed the question thoroughly in all its bearings, and the more we talked of it the better we liked it. Mr. Crocker then came in, together with some other citizens, and between Crocker, Huntington, Hopkins, Judah, Bailey and myself we raised some money towards making explorations which we thought necessary before forming a company. We awaited the result of those explorations and the reports made by Mr. Judah before we concluded to form a company, which we did in 1861." Collis Huntington (1821-1900) and Mark Hopkins (1813-1878) partnered in a dry goods store in Sacramento specializing in mining supplies, as did Charles Crocker (1822-1888); James Bailey was a jeweler. Related Crocker: "We didn't know one thing about railroads, but we supported the idea." Stanford, Huntington, Hopkins and Crocker would soon become famous as the "Big Four."

Each of the five men put up $1500, and Judah set out to chart the Sierra Nevada Mountains. He had the good fortune to meet Daniel Strong, a local miner who had surveyed a route for a wagon road leading up to the Donner Pass (named for the Donner party tragedy in the winter of 1846-7). Strong thought that the route might be suitable for a railroad in that it offered a manageable, continuous grade up to its highest point at 7200 feet. Most of the rest of the Sierra Nevadas were double-ridged, making for two difficult ascents to the peaks. After verifyng Strong's assessment firsthand, Judah convinced the others to incorporate the Central Pacific Railroad in California and form a Board of Directors composed of them and a few other interested parties. The initial capitalization was for $8.5 million, and the Board members shared equally in a modest $159,000 worth of stock of par value $100. Judah became the Railroad's chief engineer and lobbyist in Washington for government aid. His lobbying efforts played an essential role in drafting the Pacific Railroad Act of 1862, formulated to furnish government support for the private construction of a transcontinental railroad. But, as of the moment, the public was not buying in and no building was possible.

During these same years, a young railroad engineer, Grenville Mullen Dodge (1831-1916), was surveying the Platte River Valley west of Omaha NB, through which would later run the talked-about trans-continental railroad. In 1856 or 1857, as he recalled, he had a chance meeting with a prominent railroad lawyer named Abraham Lincoln at the Pacific House hotel in Council Bluffs, Iowa, across the Missouri River from Omaha. Lincoln, in town to give a speech and look after some real estate holdings, had had Dodge pointed out to him as a man who knew more about railroads than any "two men in the country." Sitting on the hotel stoop after dinner one night, Lincoln learned from Dodge the results of his western surveys.

The conversation fixed in Lincoln's mind the feasibility of a northern route for a transcontinental line, as supported by most northern politicians. Like Lincoln, many of them, including Democratic Senator Stephen A. Douglas from Illinois, happened to own land in the area. They could hardly have been averse to such an undertaking.

Like Judah, Dodge had dreamed of such a railroad, ever since at age 14 he began working and surveying for the Illinois Central, a line running from Chicago to New Orleans. He was soon hired to build a proposed Mississippi and Missouri Railroad by Thomas Durant (1820-1885) who would later become vice-president and the driving force of the Union Pacific, the eastern half of the proposed transcontinental railroad. When the Civil War broke out, Dodge enlisted in General Ulysses S. Grant's army of the western sector and quickly rose to the rank of major general for his prowess in reconstructing destroyed railroads and bridges. At War's end, he resigned his commission, ran for Congress as a representative from Iowa and won the 1866 election without bothering to campaign. He was out west surveying, having been hired by Durant to draft a route for the Union Pacific.

The year 1862 had seen the Republicans live up to their platform promise of a transcontinental railroad by passing the Pacific Railroad Act. The intent, as stated in the preamble, was "To aid in the construction of a railroad and telegraph line from the Missouri River to the Pacific Ocean and to secure to the government the use of the same for postal, military and other purposes." The Act chartered the Union Pacific Railroad to lay trackage from Omaha NB to some as yet undetermined point west of the Rocky Mountains, and it also authorized the Company to issue 100,000 shares of stock of par value $1,000.

Not since the expiration of the 2nd Bank of the United States had the federal government chartered a private business. The sale of that $100 million worth of stock, it was assumed, would be sufficient to cover the costs of building. The Central Pacific Railroad (already in existence) was authorized to build from Sacramento to a point 150 miles east of the Sierra Nevada Mountains (a distance later extended).

The word "aid" in the preamble of the Pacific Railroad Act has been subject to all degrees of confusion and misinterpretation by later writers who seemed to be under the simplistic impression that the federal government subsidized the railroad. That was definitely not the case, because, as we shall learn, the government had no money or gold to hand out in 1862. What could be raised from taxes, bonds and the issue of a limited amount of unbacked paper money called "greenbacks" all went into financing the Civil War, and there was no central bank to supply whatever more the politicians needed for their spending proclivities. The "aid" granted by the Act consisted of 6% government bonds redeemable in thirty years, to be doled out to the two railroads based on the mileage of track laid and the terrain encountered (flat, desert or mountainous). Bonds are not money, however, and since neither one of the railroads had the funds to start construction, this provision did little to help at this point. Furthermore, it seemed unlikely that the railroads could raise money by selling the bonds once obtained because Treasury itself could not sell more than it already had. In 1862 a Union victory was far from assured, and the public was gathering up all the gold it could.

The Act further stipulated that all interest paid on the bonds and their redemption at maturity were liabilities of the railroads, not the government, and would come out of future earnings if any. To ensure payment of those liabilities, the government would hold a first mortgage on the railroad's assets and, if earnings failed to materialize, could sell them to protect its investment.

In addition to the bonds, free public land was meted out to the railroads, ten sections (a section equals one square mile) for each mile of track in an alternating checkerboard pattern.

But neither was land the equivalent of gold or banknotes, and it had little value without a railroad running nearby. It had been expected that the Act would help the railroads raise money by enhancing the attractiveness of their stock issues in the marketplace. It didn't. The public was not buying and the railroads were not "a-building." In the spring of 1863, a concerned Lincoln summoned Dodge to Washington for consultation. As Dodge wrote later: "In the discussion of the means of building the road, I thought and urged that no private combination should be relied on, but that it must be done by the government. The President frankly said that the government had its hands full. Private enterprise must do the work and all the government could do was to aid.

What he wished to know of me was what was required from the government to ensure its commencement and completion. He said it was a military necessity that the road should be built." Dodge obviously disagreed with Judah about the role government should play.

In 1864, Lincoln signed an amended version of the Railroad Act enhancing the "giveaways." It doubled the land grant to twenty sections per mile and included mineral as well as timber rights. Additionally, the companies were authorized to issue their own 6% 30-year bonds, and these would constitute a first mortgage lien on railroad property. Subsequent issues of government bonds would be relegated to second mortgage status. The Act also reduced the par value of the stock to $100 and increased the allowed number of shares to one million.

On 23 October 1863, Central Pacific workers began laying down spike and rail, "the first certain step taken in building the great Pacific Railroad," as reported by the *Sacramento Union*. By then, Stanford had become governor of California and inveigled the legislature into granting some support ($10,000 for each mile of track laid in California) to the Railroad. In addition, San Francisco voters approved a bond issue providing $600,000 in cash for railroad construction, and to this the Big Four added their own money, borrowing on their personal security. Theodore Judah, however, did not witness the eventful start. Irreconcilable differences over financing and the government land grants had sprung up between him and the other Board members, and he was in New York hoping to raise the funds needed to buy them out. Rumor had it that Cornelius Vanderbilt was interested. But en route east crossing the Isthmus of Panama, Judah contracted yellow fever and died exactly one week after the first rail was laid. His place was taken by his capable assistant chief engineer Samuel Montague who would see the project through to its completion.

By the spring of 1864, Central Pacific tracks reached to only 18 miles east of Sacramento. The Union Pacific was also experiencing extreme difficulty raising money. Vice-president Durant had managed to sell only $2 million worth of stock with which to begin construction, and not until July 1865 was track being laid outside the city limits of Omaha. Both railroads remained in a precarious financial condition until, with the end of the Civil War and the passage of the amended Railroad Act, interest perked up in the stock of both companies. With the government no longer soaking up money for war expenses and the repeal of wartime taxes in sight, capital soon became available for the economy to resume its "overexuberant" pre- War growth rate.

The pace of building improved slowly. By July of 1864, the Central Pacific rails had reached to Newcastle, 31 miles from Sacramento, and Charles Crocker and Company, the building contractor for the Railroad, was trying to hire five thousand laborers for the next 23-mile stretch to Colfax. "Labor is dear and scarce in this state," Stanford explained in a letter to President Andrew Johnson in December of 1865. "A large majority of the white laboring class on the Pacific Coast find more profitable and congenial employment in mining and agricultural pursuits than in railroad work." Crocker solved the problem by hiring Chinese workers, explaining that any race that could build the Great Wall of China could build a railroad. Ten thousand Chinese would soon constitute more than 90% of the work force.

In September 1867, the foothills of the Sierra Nevadas were reached at Cisco, 93 miles from Sacramento, and the town became the staging area for the final assault on the summit at Donner Pass. Although construction costs had mounted to $100,000 per mile (payable in gold), Collis Huntington was able to sell sufficient stock and bonds to keep abreast of expenses.

1866 had seen work started on thirteen tunnels needed to breach the Sierra Nevada fortress. The total length of all tunnels stretched to 6,213 feet, the Summit at 1,695 feet being the longest. Pick and shovel, black blasting powder and one-horse dump carts to move equipment on the Donner Pass wagon road were the only means available for getting the work done. Much of the Summit tunneling was in hard granite rock, and work progressed initially at the excruciatingly low rate of about 14 inches per day using powder. It seemed that the tunnel would never be finished. But with the arrival of Scottish chemist James Howden, hired by Crocker for the on-the-spot manufacture of recently invented nitroglycerin, the penetration rate advanced to 22 inches, more than a 50% increase. It marked the first use of the explosive in the United States. Even with the nitro, digging the Summit tunnel took 13 months.

And then the snows came – and overwhelmed the whole work force. Related Superintendent of Buildings and Bridges Arthur Brown: "Although every known appliance was used to keep the road clear from snow that winter [1866-67], including the largest and best snow-plows then known, it was found impossible to keep it open over half the time and that mostly by means of men and shovels, which required an army of men on hand all the time at great expense." But how was snow to be kept off the tracks? Continued Brown: "It was decided that the only positive means of protecting the road was by snowsheds and galleries. Although the expense of building a shed nearly forty miles in length was almost appalling and unprecedented in railroad construction, yet there seemed to be no alternative … We therefore had to gather men from all quarters and pay high wages – carpenters $4 per day, and suitable laborers about $2.50 to $3. We employed about 2,300 men, with six trains distributing material. … Some of these galleries extend back up the slope of the mountain several hundred feet from the center line of the road. [They] were built along the side of the mountains where the slope of the roof conforms with that of the mountain, so the snow can pass over easily. In other places massive masonry walls were built … to prevent the snow from striking the sheds at right angles. It was necessary to build sheds and galleries of enormous strength by bracing them against the mountain side, framing them and interlacing them with beams and cross-beams." Snow sheds and galleries were constructed for almost the entire forty-mile distance between Alta on the western and Truckee on the eastern slope of the Mountains, 115 miles from Sacramento. It cost over $2 million.

"It took three years to build the road across the Sierras," wrote Superintendent of Construction J. H. Strobridge. "If the country had been level, the road could have been built to Omaha in less time, and for less money, while if built with ordinary exertion the cost would have been 70% less."

The orders were to rush construction as fast as men and money would do it. Graders were sent far ahead of the track layers as the heavy snows in winter stopped all work except in the tunnels. The men who had been digging on the roadbed were sent across the mountains and into Nevada Territory where there was not sufficient snow to interfere.

Three locomotives were loaded on big sleds at Cisco in the winter of 1867, [and] hauled over the summit to Truckee. Twenty flat cars and forty miles of iron were taken over in the same way."

Work on the Union Pacific proceeded very slowly. By the end of 1865, the railroad had spent $500,000 and laid only 40 miles of track – "two streaks of rust across the Nebraska prairie." But building accelerated in 1866 when Durant hired Dodge as chief engineer and former Union brigadier general Jack Casement and his brother Dan as contractors. Mountains presented none of the formidable grading problems that beset the Central Pacific. The Sherman or Evans Pass through the Black Hills of Wyoming (now called the Laramie Mountains) offered a gradual grade to the highest point attained by the Union Pacific at 8,248 feet. A dispute as to whether Dodge (who named the Pass for Civil War General William Tecumseh Sherman) or James Evans discovered it has been resolved in favor of the latter. South Pass through the Rocky Mountains, part of the Oregon or Mormon Trail, offered another easy grade. The highest summits attained by the two railroads were commemorated in the following exchange of communications:

Sherman's Summit, April 16, 1868, via Cheyenne, April 17

To Leland Stanford, President Central Pacific Railroad

We send you greeting from the highest summit our line crosses between the Atlantic and Pacific Oceans, 8200 feet above tidewater. Have commenced laying iron on the down grade westward.

T. C. Durant

Vice- President, Union Pacific Railroad Office Central Pacific Railroad Company Sacramento, April 17, 1868

We receive your greetings with pleasure. Though you may approach the union of the two roads faster than ourselves you cannot exceed us in earnestness of desire for that great event. We cheerfully yield you the palm of superior elevation; 7042 feet has been quite sufficient to satisfy our highest ambition. May your descent be easy and rapid.

Leland Stanford

President, Central Pacific Railroad Company

The "great event" took place on 10 May 1869 just north of the Great Salt Lake at Promontory Point, Utah – 1,861 miles from Omaha and 690 miles from Sacramento. Stanford drove in a golden spike, and America was joined "from sea to shining sea."

Anna Judah survived her husband by almost 32 years. She was not present at the "golden spike" ceremony. "It seemed as though the spirit of my dead husband descended on me and together we were there unseen and unheard of by man," she reminisced.

II

Union Pacific vice-president Thomas Durant was a graduate of the Albany Medical School. His interests, however, shifted quickly from medicine to the burgeoning fields of railroad construction and finance. He did well speculating in the stock of budding railroads, but great wealth came only during the Civil War. Acting on confidential information supplied by Grenville Dodge, now a high-ranking military officer, he marketed contraband cotton to northern mills at inflated prices.

A vigorous trade between North and South, as we shall see, obtained throughout the War. When the Pacific Railroad Act of 1862 chartered the Union Pacific, he bought enough stock (at par) to put himself in a dominant position on the Board of Directors, install himself as vice-president and William B.

Ogden, formerly the first mayor of Chicago, as president. As was the usual practice in those days, he then set up a separate company to carry out the actual construction work. For this purpose, he bought a company chartered in Pennsylvania, the Pennsylvania Fiscal Agency, and in 1863 changed its name to Crédit Mobilier Company of America. Capitalized at $2.5 million, its only stockholders were Durant and a select few to whom he sold shares. At this point, however, the stock appeared valueless as no earnings were in prospect; the Railroad simply did not have funds enough to start construction.

By 1867, however, Durant was able to sell Union Pacific stock and thereby provide the capital for building. Crédit Mobilier then secured a lucrative contract from the Union Pacific calling for the construction of 667 miles of track at prices ranging from $42,000 to $96,000 per mile, a total amount of $47 million. This was far above the cost of building and netted Crédit Mobilier a profit estimated at $23 million. It provided the wherewithal for the declaration of a huge first year dividend of approximately $248 in cash, Union Pacific stock and 1st mortgage bonds, this on stock purchased at $100 par. These lucrative dealings, I must point out, were made possible by the Pacific Railroad Act, in which Congress greatly overcapitalized the Union Pacific at $100 million – that being the amount of stock that could be sold to the public at par.

Consequently, the public's stock holdings were "watered"; they did not represent as much value as they should have. But we must understand that these calculations excluded the value of the Union Pacific's extensive and now much more valuable land holdings. In any event, the nation got a transcontinental railroad. And neither the public nor the government lost money as all bonds were redeemed and all interest on them paid out from the Railroad's future earnings. Furthermore, the presence of the Railroad greatly enhanced the value of the government's remaining acreage. It is likely that similar type manipulations went on with the Central Pacific, but a convenient fire destroyed all records.

In 1867 Oliver Ames became president of the Union Pacific. His brother Oakes Ames, a Congressman from Massachusetts and a member of the House committee that had drawn up the 1864 Pacific Railroad Act, sat on the Crédit Mobilier Board. Among the select few invited by Durant, the brothers had committed much of their family's fortune to buying stock in Crédit Mobilier. They owned a shovelworks business started by their father and had become wealthy selling shovels to gold miners. Through Collis Huntington, Oakes was also an early investor in the Central Pacific. When news of Crédit Mobilier's highly profitable contract with the Union Pacific leaked out, Oakes was besieged by other politicians demanding a piece of the action. "There were so many who talked to me about getting an interest in it," he later confessed, "that I cannot remember all the names." To defer any Congressional investigation, he sold stock at par – in blocks of ten or twenty – to two Senators and nine Congressmen, including Vice-President Schuyler Colfax and future President James A. Garfield, recording all transactions in a little black ledger. All recipients were Republicans except for one lone Democrat, James Brooks of New York, who bought stock in his son's name. As a government director on the Board of the Union Pacific, Brooks was prohibited from owning stock in Crédit Mobilier. Although no public market for the stock existed, it was undoubtedly worth at least two or three times the $100 par value.

In 1872, a law suit by a disgruntled stockholder precipitated a Congressional investigation. Oakes Ames produced his ledger, but his revelations brought forth few repercussions. Ames and Brooks were merely censured; nobody else was implicated. Eight years after Oakes Ames' death in 1873, the Union Pacific commissioned a 60-foot memorial monument to the Ames brothers from architect Henry Hobson Richardson, whose notable designs include Boston's Trinity Church and Chicago's Marshall Field store. The "Ames Pyramid" is built of solid granite and stands in Sherman Pass at the high point of the line. Sculptured likenesses of the two Ames brothers by famed Augustus Saint-Gaudens adorn the structure. The Union Pacific tracks have long since moved, and the monument now stands alone in a barren landscape.

Congress responded to the Crédit Mobilier scandal by unleashing a flood of regulations that ultimately micromanaged the Union Pacific into bankruptcy in 1893. Almost all decisions involving prices, wages, track extensions and borrowings required bureaucratic approval. The line was finally restored to profitability by Edward Harriman (1848-1909). In 1893, James J. Hill (1838-1916) completed the building of an extraordinarily successful Pacific railroad, the Great Northern, with no government subsidies, no land grants and no scandal attached.

Running from the Great Lakes to the Puget Sound in Washington across appallingly difficult terrain, it is generally considered the greatest feat of railroad building in American history. Hill controlled over ten thousand miles of railroads, settled his vast domain with homesteaders, introduced scientific farming, supported schools and churches, and generally directed the development of the entire Northwest. We shall meet Harriman and Hill again in Volume II.

After the hiatus during the Civil War, railroad expansion continued unabated, reaching a peak of almost 167,000 miles (three-quarters of the distance to the moon) by 1890. Passenger and freight revenues climbed over the $1 billion mark, more than twice the federal government's income in 1890. Railroad debt of $5.1 billion was almost five times the national debt, again singling out the comparative insignificance of government spending during this time of vigorous economic expansion.

Such was the pace of the expansion that inequities, dislocations, sharp competitive practices and fraudulent watered stock deals inevitably arose. Stinging indictments of rebates, drawbacks, pools and traffic agreements, and the long and short-haul evil were bruited about by disadvantaged farmers suffering under the Republican high tariff policies, muck-raking journalists and power-hungry politicians. But, clearly, the public in general was extremely well served.

Witness again the extraordinarily high and strongly rising American standard of living, made possible in large part by the most efficient, innovative, and far-flung railroad system the world had ever seen. By the time Congress got around to reinterpreting the "commerce clause" of the Constitution and passing in 1887 the Interstate Commerce Act to eliminate the "excesses of competition," the railroads had ironed out most of the so-called abuses. The marketplace, as always, ran far ahead of the law. And, as usual in a chaotically changing world, the politicians knew not the consequences of their actions.

Beginning with the new Act, a flood of regulations would engulf the entire railroad industry and micromanage it into the deplorable state of affairs described so amusingly in the exchange of letters heading this chapter. No efficient chaonic companies combining air, rail and road transportation could now be born. No innovative technological developments, such as 400-mile-an-hour trains magnetically levitated above the rails, would now develop. Ahead lay only chaos for the industry.

CHAPTER XXIX

THE AMERICAN HOLOCAUST BEGINS

Lincoln has become one of the national deities, and a realistic examination of him is thus no longer possible.

H. L. Mencken (1931)

Because no great strength would be required to hold back the rock that starts a landslide, it does not follow that the landslide will not be of major proportions.

Milton Friedman and Anna Schwartz, A *Monetary History of the United States 1867-1960*

The North had adopted a system of revenue and the disbursements in which an undue proportion of the burden of taxation has been imposed on the South, and an undue proportion of its proceeds appropriated to the North ... the South, as the great exporting portion of the Union, has in reality paid vastly more than her due proportion of the revenue.

John C. Calhoun

Slavery? Ah, humbug!

Charles Dickens

As sure as there is a God in Heaven, we will have fearful times in our country should the North elect Lincoln. His election will not only be an insult to the South, but will be regarded as a declaration of war.

John Hodgson, publisher of the *Jeffersonian*, West Chester, PA

Though I approve the war as much as any man, I don't quite understand what we are fighting for.

Nathaniel Hawthorne

"What on earth is the North fighting for?" asked a special correspondent sent to America in 1862 to cover the Civil War for *Macmillan's* magazine, a British monthly. What, indeed, we must now ask? Just how do we justify the slaughter of 620,000 young men and 50,000 civilians in a nation of but 31 million people? If applied proportionately to today's population of 300 million, these numbers would equate to 6,000,000 and 500,000, adding up to *six and a half million deaths* overall. And if these figures are not sufficiently barbaric, add to them a half million wounded and disabled and untold numbers diseased by a wave of syphilis that engulfed the country. So monstrous becomes the butchery and carnage laid bare in our Civil War that it is small wonder that historians tend to cloak its origins in obfuscation and, as they do all too often, spin monstrous deeds into noble endeavors by deified individuals. The greater the killing, the greater the veneration, it would almost seem. What did the North have to gain by preserving the Union? What did the South have to lose? These are the questions that demand answers.

That slavery was the "one cause" of the Civil War has become the politically correct stance, today's common knowledge, and other views to the contrary have virtually disappeared. But, as I have implied all along and as the more hard-nosed of my readers will understand, it is money that matters. And even though often camouflaged from view in a background of initial conditions, it usually matters in a big way.

Except, as Charles Adams writes in his book *Those Dirty Rotten Taxes*, "among Ivy League Civil War historians who … live in an economic cloistered world, which minimizes the role money plays in the affairs of men." Even among economists, the "money-does-not-matter" school oscillates in and out of favor as they try to cope with chaotic "business cycles" one after the other. "One can read through the annual *Proceedings* of the American Economic Association or of the Academy of Political Science and find only an occasional sign that the academic world even knew about the unprecedented banking collapse in process [during the Great Depression of the 1930s], let alone that it understood the cause and the remedy," write Milton Friedman and Anna Schwartz in their *A Monetary History of the United States*. Predicting a chaotic future is tortuous, but discerning the distant past is equally so, especially when monetary affairs are downplayed. As summed up by Professor Avery Craven of the University of Chicago in 1951, there are always "remote or background causes, and immediate causes, and causes resting on other causes." We, however, shall follow the money. Where does it come from? Where does it go? The answers will serve to clarify our vision enormously. Blood flows freely only when money matters.

Abraham Lincoln, the surprise nominee of the Republican convention, won the 1860 Presidential election garnering less than 40% of the popular vote. He received no electoral votes in fifteen states and not a single popular vote in ten. A North-South split in the Democratic Party virtually guaranteed his election. Within the next three months, seven "cotton" states led by South Carolina seceded from the Union.

The others were Alabama, Florida, Georgia, Louisiana, Mississippi and Texas. Citing the Declaration of Independence and the Kentucky and Virginia Resolutions of Jefferson and Madison, the legislative bodies of these states maintained that they had every right to do so. Indeed, as I have already noted, Henry Cabot Lodge asserts in his *Life of Webster* that this was the prevailing view of the Founding Fathers. In corroboration, Thomas Jefferson had specifically sanctioned the right of voluntary disunion when there was talk after the Louisiana Purchase of dividing the nation into an Atlantic federation and a Mississippi federation: "Let them part by all means if it is for their happiness to do so. It is but the elder and the younger son differing. God bless them both, and keep them in Union if it be for their good, but separate them if better." Secession talk had arisen in three earlier crises – the Whiskey Rebellion of the 1790s, the Hartford Convention of 1814, and South Carolina's nullification of federal tariffs in 1832. In every one of these instances of "civil disobedience," money was the common denominator. There was not even the remotest mention of slavery. And now it was South Carolina once again leading the way. Why, South Carolina? If slavery were the sole cause of the new secession problems, why not one of the other six "cotton" states? And once again, money is the most probable answer. South Carolina stood to suffer most under the trade barriers that formed the cornerstone of the Republican Party platform. A new protectionist tariff introduced into the 36th Congress by Republican Representative Justin Morrill had already passed the House of Representatives by the lopsided vote of 105 to 64 in May of 1860, and it awaited almost certain passage in early 1861 by the Northern dominated Senate. Unlike the historically low ad valorem Tariff of 1857, this one contained specific duties – 50% on iron products and 25% on textiles – that were much higher even than those of the Tariff of Abominations. Moreover, it imposed duties on a greatly expanded list of agricultural, mining and fishing products in addition to manufactures. Under it, the average tariff doubled to 36.2%. All the compromises that had been worked out since the nullification crisis of 1832 were about to be thrown out the window. In a historical repeat, South Carolina's cotton planters, along with the shippers and merchants of Charleston, once again stood to lose heavily from the viciously high tariff schedules on the vital iron and textile manufactures that paid for the South's cotton exports. Upon completion of the SOLA Railroad in 1832, South Carolina had ascended to first rank both as a producer and exporter of cotton, and her citizens could hardly be expected to exchange their prosperous livelihoods for almost certain impoverishment.

Under the circumstances, the state simply could not afford to remain in the Union. And as Northern businessmen and politicians well knew, the new and larger government being planned in Washington could ill afford the loss of tariff revenues from South Carolina.

In February of 1861, delegates from the cotton states convened in Montgomery AL to draw up a constitution for the Confederate States of America. Their litany of grievances, the "requisite bits and pieces for the hurricane to come," is well documented in a speech delivered earlier by Senator Robert Toombs of Georgia in November of 1860: "The instant the Government was organized, at the very first Congress, the Northern States evinced a general desire and purpose to use it for their own benefit, and to pervert its powers for sectional advantage, and they have steadily pursued that policy to this day. They demanded a monopoly of the business of shipbuilding, and got a prohibition against the sale of foreign ships to citizens of the United States, which exists to this day.

"They demanded a monopoly of the coasting trade, in order to get higher freights than they could get in open competition with the carriers of the world. Congress gave it to them, and they yet hold this monopoly. And now, today, if a foreign vessel in Savannah offers to take your rice, cotton, grain or lumber to New York, or any other American port, for nothing, your laws prohibit it, in order that Northern shipowners may get enhanced prices for doing your carrying. This same shipping interest, with cormorant rapacity, have steadily burrowed their way through your legislative halls, until they have saddled the agricultural classes with a large portion of the legitimate expenses of their own business. We pay a million of dollars per annum for the lights which guide them into and out of your ports. We built and kept up, at the cost of at least another million a year, hospitals for their sick and disabled seamen, when they wear them out and cast them ashore. We pay half a million per annum to support and bring home those they cast away in foreign lands. They demand, and have received, millions of the public money to increase the safety of harbors, and lessen the danger of navigating our rivers. All of which expenses legitimately fall upon their business, and should come out of their own pockets, instead of a common treasury.

"Even the fishermen of Massachusetts and New England demand and receive from the public treasury about half a million of dollars per annum as a pure bounty on their business of catching cod fish. The North, at the very first Congress, demanded and received bounties under the name of protection, for every trade, craft, and calling which they pursue, and there is not an artisan in brass, or iron, or wood, or weaver, or spinner in wool or cotton, or a calico maker, or iron-master, or a coal owner, in all the Northern or Middle States, who has not received what he calls the protection of his government on his industry to the extent of from fifteen to two hundred per cent from the year 1791 to this day. ... No wonder they cry aloud for the glorious Union. ... By it they got their wealth; by it they levy tribute on honest labor. It is true ... that the present tariff [the Tariff of 1857] was sustained by an almost unanimous vote of the South; but it was a reduction – a reduction necessary from the plethora of the revenue; but the policy of the North soon made it inadequate to meet the public expenditure, by an enormous and profligate increase of the public expenditure; and at the last session of Congress they brought in and passed through the House the most atrocious tariff bill that ever was enacted, raising the present duties from twenty to two hundred and fifty per cent above the existing rates of duty. That [Morrill tariff] bill now lies on the table of the Senate. ... "Thus stands the account between the North and the South. Under its ordinary and most favorable action, bounties and protection to every interest and every pursuit in the North, to the extent of at least fifty millions per annum, besides the expenditure of at least sixty millions out of every seventy of the public expenditure among them, thus making the treasury a perpetual fertilizing stream to them and their industry, and a suction-pump to drain away our substance and parch up our lands."

What Toombs came down hard on was the unconstitutional non-uniformity of so many of the laws adopted since ratification of the Constitution. The Constitutional guarantees against minority oppression by a "tyranny of the majority" were simply not working and, as a sectional minority, the South could hope for no redress in Congress. Nor was there any hope in the judiciary because no Supreme Court ever has paid any heed to Hamilton's admonition in The Federalist (No.

80)   to limit judicial review to the "mere necessity of uniformity in the interpretation of national laws." In December of 1860, South Carolina addressed the other slave holding states in these terms: "… And so with the Southern States, towards the Northern States, in the vital matter of taxation. They are in a minority in Congress. Their representation in Congress is useless to protect them against unjust taxation, and they are taxed by the people of the North for their benefit, exactly as the people of Great Britain taxed our ancestors in the British Parliament for their benefit." Nowhere in his speech did Senator Toombs mention slavery. He didn't have to. Why? Because there was no concession on slavery that the North would not have granted to preserve the Union. Listen to Lincoln's plea in his inaugural address 4 March 1861 for the cotton states to return to the Union: "Apprehension seems to exist among the people of the Southern states that by the accession of a Republican Administration, their property and their peace and personal security are to be endangered. There has never been any reasonable cause for such apprehension. Indeed, the most ample evidence to the contrary has all the while existed and been open to their inspection. It is found in nearly all the published speeches of him who now addresses you. I do but quote from one of those speeches when I declare that 'I have no purpose, directly or indirectly, to interfere with the institution of slavery in the states where it exists. I believe I have no lawful right to do so, and I have no inclination to do so.' Those who nominated and elected me did so with full knowledge that had made this, and many similar declarations, and had never recanted them. And, more than this, they placed in the platform for my acceptance, and as a law to themselves, and to me, the clear and emphatic resolution which I now read: *Resolved*, That the maintenance inviolate of the rights of the states, and especially the right of each state to order and control its own domestic institutions according to its own judgment exclusively, is essential to that balance of power on which the perfection and endurance of our political fabric depend; and we denounce the lawless invasion by armed forces of the soil of any state or territory, no matter under what pretext, as among the gravest of crimes." Indeed, a proposed 13th Amendment to the Constitution had already been approved by both the House and Senate, to wit: "No amendment shall be made to the Constitution which will authorize or give to Congress the power to abolish or interfere, within any State, with the domestic institutions thereof, including that of persons held to labor or service by the laws of such State."

If any further light need be shed on Lincoln's attitude toward slavery, it is expressed in a letter to Horace Greeley, publisher of the *New York Tribune*, 22 August 1862: "My paramount object in this struggle is to save the Union, and is not either to save or to destroy slavery. If I could save the Union without freeing any slave, I would do it; and if I could save it by freeing all the slaves, I would do it; and if I could save it by freeing some and leaving others alone, I would do it." Obviously, Lincoln did not regard slavery as a "blood flows freely" issue. To "Preserve the Union," he was prepared to make any sacrifice whatsoever – except for giving up the new Morrill Tariff. That he alluded to further on in his inaugural: "The power confided to me will be used to hold, occupy, and possess the property and places belonging to the Government and to collect the duties and imposts; but beyond what may be necessary for these objects, there will be no invasion, no using of force against or among the people anywhere." And there it was, Lincoln's ultimatum to the South: "Collect the duties and imposts" or invasion! Was it to be monetary aggression or military aggression? But southerners knew all about Lincoln's stance long before. In a speech delivered at Galena IL 23 July 1856, he had answered a charge by former President Millard Fillmore that the election of a Republican president in that year's election would dissolve the Union. "Who are the disunionists, you or we?" Lincoln asked in rebuttal. "We, the majority, would not strive to dissolve the Union; and if any attempt is made it must be by you, who so loudly stigmatize us as disunionists. But the Union, in any event, won't be dissolved. We don't want to dissolve it, and if you attempt it, *we won't let you*. With the purse and sword, the army and navy and treasury in our hands, and at our command, you *couldn't do it*. This Government would be very weak indeed, if a majority, with a disciplined army and navy, and a well-filled treasury, could not preserve itself, when attacked by an unarmed, undisciplined, unorganized minority. All this talk about the dissolution of the Union is humbug – nothing but folly. We *won't* dissolve the Union, and *you shan't*." Is it any wonder that the South saw in Lincoln a reincarnation of King George III, another stubborn, uncompromising politician embarked on a crusade to do good and damn the consequences? Unfortunately for the hundreds of thousands soon to die, Lincoln had learned nothing from the British invasion of the American colonies eighty years earlier.

He seemed oblivious to "the agony and death men call war." A sampling of newspaper editorials at the time reveals them to be in complete agreement with Toombs. On 10 October 1860, one month before Lincoln's election, the editor of the influential *Charleston Mercury* charged that a Republican administration would "plunder the South for the benefit of the North by a new protective tariff." And two days before the November election, he followed that up with: "The real causes of dissatisfaction in the South with the North are in the unjust taxation and expenditures of the taxes by the Government of the United States, and in the revolution the North has effected in the government, from a confederated republic to a national sectional despotism." The *New Orleans Daily Crescent*, on 21 January 1861, observed that "They [the South] know that it is their import trade that draws from the people's pockets sixty or seventy millions of dollars per annum, in the shape of duties, to be expended mainly in the North, and in the protection and encouragement of Northern interests. ...These are the reasons why these people do not want the South to secede from the Union. They [the North] are enraged at the prospect of being despoiled of the rich feast on which they have so long fed and fattened, and which they were just getting ready to enjoy with still greater *gout* and gusto. They are as mad as hornets because the prize slips by them just as they are ready to grab it." The Northern newspapers were a bit slow to catch on.

Originally for a moderate and conciliatory policy toward the South, they switched to an all-out call for military action when on 11 March 1861 the cotton states adopted the Confederate Constitution and chose Jefferson Davis (1808-89) as provisional president. In competition with a high-tax, protectionist North, there would now arise a free-trade zone comprised of a southern confederation of states. "Preserving the Union" meant protecting northern jobs and livelihoods from a newly arrived "freest nation in the world." "Blockade Southern Ports," demanded the *Philadelphia Press* on 18 March. "At once shut up every Southern port, destroy its commerce, and bring utter ruin on the Confederate states," editorialized the *New York Times*. But the *Boston Transcript* of 18 March summed up most incisively the panicky thoughts developing in the North: "It does not require extraordinary sagacity to perceive that trade is perhaps the controlling motive operating to prevent the return of the seceding states to the Union which they have abandoned. Alleged grievances in regard to slavery were originally the causes for the separation of the cotton states; but the mask has been thrown off and it is apparent that the people of the principal seceding states are now for commercial independence. They *dream* that the centres of traffic can be changed from Northern to Southern ports. The merchants of New Orleans, Charleston and Savannah are possessed with the idea that New York, Boston, and Philadelphia may be shorn, in the future, of their mercantile greatness, by a revenue system verging on free trade. If the Southern Confederation is allowed to carry out a policy by which only a nominal duty is laid upon imports, no doubt the business of the chief Northern cities will be seriously injured thereby.

"The difference is so great between the tariff of the Union and that of the Confederate States that the entire Northwest must find it to their advantage to purchase their imported goods at New Orleans rather than New York. In addition to this, the manufacturing interests of the country will suffer from the increased importation resulting from low duties … The [government in Washington] would be false to its obligation if this state of things were not provided against." During the weeks following his inauguration on 4 March, Lincoln carefully weighed the alternative futures open to him. Seven states had seceded, but eight border states – Arkansas, Delaware, Kentucky, Maryland, Missouri, North Carolina, Tennessee, and Virginia had not. In each of these states, strong backers of the Union maintained control awaiting developments. In Virginia, the legislature convened a special convention in Richmond to discuss an Ordinance of Secession.

On 3 April, Lincoln requested a meeting with an emissary from that meeting apparently to find out what was going on. One Colonel John B. Baldwin hurried to Washington the next day and was immediately ushered into Lincoln's presence in the White House. Testifying years later on 10 February 1866 before the Reconstruction Committee of Congress, he gave the following account of the interview which I summarize in part: Lincoln began by saying the Virginia convention was an embarrassment to him and that he wanted it adjourned *sine die* [without fixing a date for future action]. Baldwin told him that Union supporters were in control of the convention and that they could not do that without weakening their case. But something positive from Lincoln was needed to keep matters in hand. He urged Lincoln to withdraw the troops stationed at Fort Sumter in Charleston SC, the site of custom house tariff collections, and Fort Pickens in Pensacola FL, and declare he was doing so for the sake of peace. "If you take that position, there is national feeling enough in the seceding States themselves and all over the country to rally to your support, and you would gather more friends than any man in the country ever has." To which Lincoln responded: "What about the revenue? What would I do about the collection of duties?" Baldwin: "Sir, how much do you expect to collect in a year?" Lincoln: "Fifty or sixty millions." Baldwin: "Why, sir, four times sixty is two hundred forty. Say 250 million dollars would be the revenue of your term of the Presidency; what is that but a drop in the bucket compared with the cost of such a war as we are threatened with? ... If you do not take this course [withdrawal of the troops], if there is a gun fired at Sumter – I do not care on which side it is fired – the thing is gone." Replied Lincoln: "Oh, sir, that is impossible." Repeated Baldwin: "Sir, if there is a gun fired at Sumter, ... Virginia herself, strong as the Union majority is now, will be out in 48 hours."

At that point, Lincoln brought the interview to a quick close. He did not inform Baldwin – had not even informed his cabinet – that preparations were already under way to reinforce the troops at both Sumter and Pickens. The Virginia convention, unaware of Lincoln's intentions, voted 60 to 53 against secession. All changed when General P. G. T.

Beauregard, in command at Charleston, received word of the reinforcements being sent by Lincoln. He commenced bombardment of the Fort, and on 12 April Sumter surrendered with no loss of life. The action provided Lincoln with an excuse for proceeding with military operations, and he betook it upon himself on 15 April to issue a first call for troops, a power granted in the Constitution only to Congress: "... Now, therefore, I, Abraham Lincoln, President of the United States, in virtue of the power in me vested by the Constitution [?] and the laws, have thought fit to call forth, and hereby do call forth, the militia of the several States of the Union, to the aggregate number of seventy-five thousand, in order to suppress said combinations [the cotton states already seceded], and to cause the laws to be duly executed." Lincoln also ordered a blockade of southern ports. And as Baldwin had counseled, Virginia, North Carolina, Tennessee and Arkansas immediately seceded, more than doubling the strength of the Confederacy. The people of those states wanted no truck with a President who could trample on the Constitution with impunity. And they were certainly not about to send their boys and pay taxes to kill their southern brethren. On 18 April Virginian militia men captured the Union fort and arsenal at Harpers Ferry and two days later occupied the navy yard at Norfolk – after all, it was the South's money that had in the main paid for these installations. There was no backing away now; war had begun. But as far as Lincoln was concerned, blood could now flow freely. Two hundred fifty million dollars of the North's money was in jeopardy!

And now the question becomes: Why in the world was the tariff money of such importance that Lincoln would risk war over it? Led by a multitude of great men like Lowell, McCormick, Goodyear, Howe, Singer and Morse, America had experienced two decades of unimaginable advances in her standard of living, and it had occurred with the historically low Walker tariff as the main source of government revenue. The federal debt, which vanished for the first and only time in the nation's history when Treasury redeemed the last government bond during the Jackson Administration, reappeared after the Panic of 1837. At $46 million, it proved easily manageable, financed as it was by an issue of Treasury notes sold through state banks without any central bank help. By 1846 when Polk took office, it had decreased to $16 million. Expenditures associated with the Mexican War and the Whig administration of Zachary

Taylor and Millard Fillmore (1849-1853) jumped it up to $68 million. But Jeffersonian Democrat Franklin Pierce (1804-1869), elected in 1852, reduced it by more than half to $28 million. Never again would it be that low.

Clearly, government revenues were not a problem during the 1840s and 1850s. But the Whigs had done poorly in the 1852 Presidential election. Even with Mexican War hero General Winfield Scott as their nominee, the Party carried only four states. Wrote Horace Greeley, "We consider the Whig Party a thing of the past." The country obviously persisted in its distaste for Henry Clay's "American System" of high tariffs, centralized banking and federally funded internal improvements, the cornerstones of Whig policy. But not so Lincoln. For him Clay was both idol and mentor. In 1832, when he first entered politics, he announced to the voters: "My politics are short and sweet, like the old woman's dance. I am in favor of a national bank ... in favor of the internal improvements system and a high protective tariff." As a young member of the Illinois legislature, he wholeheartedly favored government-sponsored canal and railroad projects that, because of graft, corruption and mismanagement, drowned the state in bankruptcy – it defaulted on interest payments due on a huge $12 million borrowed in the American and European capital markets. This experience with government chaos left Lincoln unguided, however, for he never deviated from the Whig line.

In the 1840, 1844 and 1848 elections, he barnstormed around Illinois ardently and eloquently defending Clay's statist beliefs.

He became the Party's mouthpiece, speech making and fund raising around the country. Whig interests supported him throughout his career and he owed his Presidential nomination in 1860 to the protectionist delegations of Pennsylvania and New Jersey. In a letter dated 11 October 1859, he stated that he was "an old Henry Clay tariff Whig" and that "I have made more speeches on that subject [in favor of a high protectionist tariff] than any other. I have since not changed my views." Nor did he ever change. "The tariff is to government what a meal is to a family," he spouted forth in a speech on 2 February 1861.

In 1854 a new political alliance with changed colors and unchanged spots formed. It consisted of old Whigs, abolitionists, some anti-slavery Democrats and two splinter parties – the Free-Soilers who were mainly concerned with obtaining free land for western settlers, and the Know-Nothings who considered Catholic immigration and office-holding the greatest threat to the country. At conventions in Michigan and Wisconsin, the name "Republican" was adopted for the new party and quickly spread eastward. Like the title of Plato's *Republic*, however, the name was a misnomer because the new party advocated big government policies directly opposed to those of Thomas Jefferson. John C. Fremont, the renowned "Pathfinder" of western exploration, became the Party's first Presidential candidate in 1856, but he was handily beaten by Democrat James C. Buchanan of Pennsylvania in a three-way race that included former Whig President Millard Fillmore running on the Know-Nothing ticket. At the1860 Republican convention, free land for western settlers ("Vote yourself a farm") and a proposed trans-continental railroad were wedded to the "American System" in the Party platform. And Resolution 12 still called for the protectionism that had brought on the 1832 secession crisis: "That while providing revenue for the support of the General Government by duties upon imports, sound policy requires such an adjustment of these imposts as to encourage the development of the industrial interests of the whole country …" And right here in the financing of a greatly expanded centralized government – coined Lincoln's "New Deal" by historian Daniel Elazar – is what Lincoln needed the money for. There were internal improvements ("corporate welfare," as it was termed by the Democrats) to be funded, promises of subsidies to the Party's manufacturing and mercantile connections redeemed, and infrastructure provided for the "free" land meted out to western settlers. There were also thousands of new government jobs to be created for the hordes of party workers who would soon comprise by far the greatest patronage administration up to that time. As Lincoln himself wrote of his campaign managers who secured the nomination for him, "They have gambled me all around, bought and sold me a hundred times." Revenues from the old 1857 Tariff accounted for 95% of tax receipts, but these barely covered the current $80 million a year in current federal spending. Much more would be needed to fund the Lincoln "New Deal." The time's apostle of big government and protectionism, influential economist and lobbyist for the Pennsylvania iron industry Henry C. Carey, although recognizing the accomplishments of free banking, thought that government could do a better job than Adam Smith's invisible hand. He wrote books arguing that laissez faire was not applicable to America and blamed the Panic of 1857 on the "heresy" of free trade. The success of the new administration, he assured Lincoln, depended on the money to be brought in by the Morrill Tariff. The only alternative was a direct tax on property, but that was out of the question; the Constitutional requirement of apportionment would have the more populous North paying most of the bill. Lincoln, as an old time mercantilist Whig, needed no convincing. But, like George III, he would soon find out that raising taxes not only raised government deficits, but led to horrendous consequences as well.

There were numerous dissenters to Republican policy in the North. The Chicago *Democrat* noted that many editors "with Whig proclivities" were taking advantage of the crisis to foist the "antiquated doctrine" of protectionism on the public.

Horace Greeley chimed in with "Let the erring sisters depart in peace." He would later change his mind and support the War unreservedly in return for administration favors. It remained for abolitionist Wendell Phillips in Boston, echoing Adam Smith's admonition in The *Wealth of Nations* to let the American colonies secede from England, to offer the most sensible resolution of the crisis: "Let the South march off, with flags and trumpets, and we will speed the parting guest … All hail, disunion! … Let the border states go. Then we part friends. The Union thus ended, the South no longer hates the North … The laws of trade will bind us together, as they do all other lands." Taking our cue from Wendell Phillips and Horace Greeley, let us take a peek at the Confederate Constitution to see what a free Southern republic might have been like. A Constitutional Convention convened on 4 February 1861 in Montgomery, Alabama, and completed its work less than one month later, on 1 March. Among its forty-nine delegates were Alexander Stephens who would become Vice-President of the new nation, Senator Robert Toombs whom we have already met, Robert Barnwell Rhett, a former

Congressman and Senator from South Carolina known as the "Father of Secession," and Georgia attorney Howell Cobb, Secretary of the Treasury in Buchanan's administration and former speaker of the United States House of Representatives, all brilliant men who in their deliberations displayed an understanding of world chaos and the limitations of reason that approached those of the Founding Fathers. Having lived for decades under the U.S. Constitution, they were well aware of its strengths, which they tried to copy, and what they perceived as its flaws, which they tried to eliminate. In but few word changes they reestablished in their new document the Jeffersonian ideal of limited government through an "enumerated powers" interpretation of the original.

The new Constitution's preamble reads as follows: "We, the people of the Confederate States, each State acting in its sovereign and independent character, in order to form a permanent federal government, establish justice, insure domestic tranquility, and secure the blessings of liberty to ourselves and our posterity – invoking the favor and guidance of Almighty God – do ordain and establish this Constitution of the Confederate States of America." The great change here is the omission of the "promote the general welfare" phrase contained in the preamble of the 1789 Constitution. The Confederate Fathers considered any reference to "general welfare" an open door to government intervention in private affairs whenever, as is always the case, the intentions are presumed "noble." And, of course, that was to happen with increasing frequency in post Civil War periods.

The vitally important Article I, Section 8, Clause 1 of the original, was also rewritten to give to the Confederate Congress the power "To lay and collect Taxes, Duties, Imposts and Excises, for revenue necessary to pay the Debts, provide for the common Defence, and carry on the government of the Confederate States; but *no bounties shall be granted from the treasury, nor shall any duties, or taxes, or importation from foreign nations be laid to promote or foster any branch of industry,* and all Duties, Imposts and Excises shall be uniform throughout the Confederate States" [italics mine]. Again, "general welfare" is omitted and, in addition, the italicized phrase renders both protectionism and government subsidies to well-connected special interests unconstitutional. This provision is further reinforced later in Section 8: "The Congress shall have the Power ... To regulate Commerce with foreign Nations, and among the several States, and with the Indian Tribes; but neither this nor any other clause contained in this Constitution, shall ever be construed to delegate the power to Congress *to appropriate money for any internal improvement intended to facilitate commerce; except for the purpose of furnishing lights, beacons, and buoys, and other aids to navigation upon the coasts, and the improvements of the harbors, and the removing of obstructions in river navigation; in all such cases such duties shall be laid on the navigation facilitated thereby, as may be necessary to pay the costs and expenses thereof*" [italics mine].

Of the greatest significance was a move to protect minority interests from a "tyranny of the majority" on monetary matters, the uniformity issue that the 1789 Convention wrestled with. The Confederate solution is contained in Article I, Section 9: "Congress shall appropriate no money from the Treasury except by a vote of two-thirds of both Houses ..." unless requested otherwise by the President. Without a Presidential request, therefore, a simple majority could no longer suffice for spending bills. If Sections 8 and 9 had been written into the U.

S. Constitution, the regional interests of the South would have been amply protected; revenues from overbearing legislation like the Morrill Tariff could not have been appropriated without Southern acquiescence. The Civil War itself may well have been averted.

Pork-barrel spending came in for special consideration, first of all through granting the line-item veto power to the President in Article I, Section 7: "The President may approve any appropriation and disapprove any other appropriation in the same bill." In addition, no "Christmas-tree" appropriations, spending add-ons unrelated to the main subject, or hidden expenditures (the "earmarks" mentioned earlier) were permitted. All appropriations had to "relate to but one subject ... expressed in the title." The changes, as small as they were relative to the whole, were expected to keep the Confederate government small and unintrusive. Under such governance, there can be little doubt that a republic to the South would have been a fierce competitor of the North. Indeed, in one of its first actions, the new government enacted into law a copy of the free-trade Tariff of 1857. But it was nothing the North could not have handled.

After all, that was the economic reality in place during the prosperous decades preceding the current crisis. In all probability, the competition provided by the Confederacy would have forestalled the greatly enlarged government envisioned by the Republicans. But Lincoln removed the rock holding back the landslide to ever more government intervention into business and financial affairs, and that landslide today has reached socialist proportions. By 1900, federal spending would more than quintuple to over $500 million from the $80 million in 1860. Fortunately, it hardly mattered. Led by a new generation of swashbucklers – men like Alexander Graham Bell, Andrew Carnegie, Thomas A. Edison, Henry Ford, James J. Hill, Edward Harriman, John D.

Rockefeller and Cornelius Vanderbilt – productivity gains in the private economy kept government outlays at about 1% of a rapidly expanding GDP. And this despite government-issued chaos that brought on scandals and panics, one after the other.

As for the South, its standard of living would lag far behind the North for more than a hundred years.

Insofar as slavery is concerned, there was little difference between the United States and Confederate Constitutions. Whereas the former ended the importation of slaves after 1808 (by which time New England shippers had made fortunes in the slave trade), the latter simply forbade it.

Neither Constitution prohibits slave ownership and, I might add, neither do the Old and New Testaments. And that brings up one final question: How in the world did slavery ever become ingrained in our nation's history as the "one cause" of the Civil War? And for the source of that fabrication, I must point to that I-square beyond compare, Karl Marx, and the long line of his disciples who inhabit the "Groves of Academe." Marx at the time of the Civil War was scratching out a living in a London Soho garret as a foreign correspondent for Horace Greeley's *New York Tribune* and a Vienna newspaper, *Die Presse*. Both he and Friedrich Engels were refugees in England, having been declared *persona non grata* in most other European countries for their part in the general uprisings of 1848 and the publication of the *Communist Manifesto*.

Managing editor of the *Tribune* Charles Dana had hired him in 1851, paying him five dollars per article.

In October 1861 Marx published an extensive analysis of the American Civil War in both papers. After dismissing the arguments in the London news media – The *Times*, *The Economist*, *The Examiner* and The *Saturday Review* – that the Morrill Tariff brought on the War, he states categorically that "The whole movement was and is based ... on the slave question." And his "reasoning" follows: "Naturally, in America everyone knew that from 1846 to 1861 a free trade system prevailed, and that Representative Morrill carried his protectionist tariff through Congress only in 1861, only after the rebellion had already broken out. Secession, therefore, did not take place because the Morrill Tariff had gone through Congress, but at most, the Morrill Tariff went through Congress because secession had taken place." In other words, Marx rules out the Morrill Tariff as a possible cause of the War simply because of its time of passage into law, after secession had taken place. One learns much about a person from what he or she says or writes, and sometimes even more from what is not said. Marx, like so many social scientists, here displays no consideration at all for the role played by expectations in human affairs. Expectations, as we have seen, imply many possible future outcomes and their accompanying probabilities, not certainty, and that line of thought is anathema in deterministic thinking. That the expected passage of the Morrill Tariff could have led to secession seems beyond his comprehension. How such a smart-smart-smart-stupid man could have influenced so many millions of intellects is truly mind-boggling. The same line of "reasoning" was to be employed by future historians in accounting for the Great Depression of the 1930s, to wit, President Calvin Coolidge was in office beforehand and therefore responsible for that debacle.

But let me backtrack a bit. As I have noted, the Morrill Tariff bill passed the House of Representatives by the lopsided margin of 105 to 64 in May of 1860, six months before that year's Presidential election. By employing some intricate parliamentary maneuvers, Southerners delayed passage in the Senate until the next session of Congress in 1861, after the next election. In so doing, they expected that a Democrat sympathetic to the South's interests, either Senator from Illinois Stephen A. Douglas or Vice-President John Breckinridge of Kentucky, would become President and veto the new tariff bill.

Incumbent President James Buchanan, a northerner from Pennsylvania, was expected to sign it if passed by the Senate, having switched gears since his approval of the 1857 Tariff. As far as the South was concerned, everything depended on that fall's election.

For most of the nation's prior history, slavery was a tempest only in the Washington teapot. A Lincoln speech in Charleston IL on 18 September 1858 undoubtedly reflected the public's attitude: "I will say then, that I am not nor ever have been, in favor of bringing about in any way the social and political equality of the white and black races: that I am not, nor ever have been, in favor of making voters or jurors of Negroes, nor of qualifying them to hold office, nor to intermarry with white people; and I will say in addition to this that there is a physical difference between the white and black races which I believe will for ever forbid the two races living together on terms of social and political equality. And inasmuch as they cannot so live, while they do remain together there must be the position of superior and inferior, and I as much as any other man am in favor of having the superior position assigned to the white race." Every northern state had passed laws legalizing most of Lincoln's opinions. His home state of Illinois had even amended its constitution to make it illegal for blacks to move in. The exclusion of slavery from the territories coupled with its protection in those states where it already existed, as advocated in the Republican platform, probably had the same purpose: keep the blacks out.

The slavery issue first surfaced in 1820 when Missouri applied for statehood. At the time, the Union was equally divided between eleven "slave" and eleven "free" states so that the South, having just as many Senators as the North, could exercise some control over any discriminatory or non-uniform tax and spending legislation introduced by Northern Congressmen. Missouri statehood threatened to upset the balance. But all was amicably settled by the Missouri Compromise which admitted Missouri into the Union as a slave state and Maine as a free state. In the future, slavery would be banned in territories north of latitude 36°30′ (the southern boundary of Missouri) and permitted south of that line. During all the wrangling, no move toward secession or freeing the slaves appeared.

Slavery resurfaced as an issue in 1850 when California sought entry into the Union as a free state. That threatened once again to upset the balance of power in the Senate because there would then be sixteen free states versus fifteen slave states. For the first time, the North would have a majority in both Houses of Congress. Again, a compromise alleviated most concerns.

Proposed by Henry Clay, it was drafted into five separate bills and steered through Congress by Senator Stephen A. Douglas (1813-1861), chairman of the Committee on Territories. The most important items in this Compromise of 1850 were those relating to the territories and to the recapture of fugitive slaves: California was admitted as a free state and the lands acquired from Mexico in the Treaty of Guadeloupe Hidalgo were organized into the territories of New Mexico and Utah. It was implicitly understood that the final decision on their slave status should be left to their inhabitants when they achieved statehood. "Popular sovereignty" was the name given to the idea by its supporters and "squatter sovereignty" by its detractors. The Missouri Compromise, it was presumed, would remain in force. In return for this agreement on the territories, the South got a new and much more stringent fugitive slave law.

Many Southerners, led by Robert Rhett, termed the Compromise a bad deal. Not only was the South now a minority in Congress, but on geographic and demographic considerations the North's preponderance was certain to increase. Whereas a vast region of the country was available for settlement north of 36°30′, the only land remaining to the south of that line consisted of what is now modern Oklahoma, and that was reserved for the Indian tribes removed from Georgia and Alabama during the 1830s. Nine southern states sent delegates to a convention in Nashville to discuss the Compromise. But Rhett's call for immediate secession was rejected when the Convention endorsed the 1850 Compromise.

Moderation reigned. In the words of presiding officer Judge William L. Sharkey, the Convention had not been called "to prevent but to perpetuate the Union." At this point, it was quite apparent that the South remained guardedly committed to the concept of national unity and open to compromise. With the Walker Tariff in place, non-uniform tax and spending policies posed few problems.

For three and a half years, national harmony prevailed, and Jeffersonian Democrat Franklin Pierce from New Hampshire carried all but four states in the Presidential election of 1852. Anti-slavery feeling, as indicated by the surprisingly poor showing of the abolitionist Free-Soil candidate, John P.

Hale, declined sharply. But the conflicting interests of North and South resurfaced again in 1854 when Senator Douglas introduced his Kansas-Nebraska bill in the Senate. It called for dividing the land west of Missouri and Iowa and north of latitude 36°30′, what today comprises the states of Kansas and Nebraska, into two territories. Considered an Indian homeland, the region was sparsely settled. But population pressures were mounting. Reports of an especially fertile soil and its suitability for the planting of wheat, corn, oats and rye had brought forth a steadily rising migration westward. Then, too, through here lay the northern route of the proposed trans-continental railroad.

Douglas' bill threatened even more the balance of power in the Senate. Three months of bitter debate followed, and once again Douglas led the forces of compromise. The final bill included the repeal of the Missouri Compromise, which had forbidden slavery north of 36°30′, and the adoption of "squatter sovereignty" for the new territories. In this form, it received southern approval and President Pierce signed it into law. There was little doubt that Nebraska would eventually become a "free" state, but Kansas was questionable as pro- and antislavery forces vied for control. Some bloodshed arose, probably more from battles over land ownership than slavery.

Exaggerated slogans like "Bleeding Kansas" far overstated the reality. Few slaves were introduced into the state because it was evident to all that slave labor was much too costly for profitable operations. Even Karl Marx understood that: "The cultivation of the southern export articles, cotton, tobacco, sugar, etc., carried on by slaves, is only remunerative as long as it is conducted with large gangs of slaves, on a mass scale and on wide expanses of a naturally fertile soil, which requires only simple labour. Intensive cultivation, which depends less on the fertility of the soil than on the investment of capital, intelligence and energy of labour, is contrary to the nature of slavery. Hence the rapid transformation of states like Maryland and Virginia, which formerly employed slaves on the production of export articles, into states which raise slaves to export them into the deep South. Even in South Carolina, where the slaves form four-sevenths of the population, the cultivation of cotton has been almost completely stationary for years due to the exhaustion of the soil. Indeed, by force of circumstances South Carolina has already been transformed in part into a slave-raising state, since it already sells slaves to the states of the extreme South." Not surprisingly, Marx could not relate slavery to the forced labor prescribed for the populace in the *Communist Manifesto*. Both communism and slavery suffer from the same fatal flaw, the one instilled in our barnyard hen. It is the incentive to do as little as possible.

Obviously, slavery in America was a dying institution and would have disappeared, as it did throughout most of the civilized world, without war. Great Britain had ended slavery peacefully throughout the Empire with the Emancipation Law of 1833, which allocated £20 million to buy the slaves' freedom from their owners. No serious reprisals against former owners occurred upon emancipation, not even in Jamaica where a population of 30,000 whites owned 250,000 slaves. Most Americans believed that emancipation on similar terms would happen eventually throughout their young nation. Clearly, the South's main interest in Kansas as a "slave" state lay in protecting her interests in the Senate, not the introduction of slaves. It should also be clear that in view of the prevailing free-trade policy at the time and the vanishing of the Whigs as an effective political party, "Kansas-Nebraska" was not an issue of secession proportions. Note also that were the South to secede, all chance to introduce slavery into the territories would be lost. That aspect of the problem simply did not matter.

But, unfortunately for the South, the Democratic Convention of 1860 split wide open on the issue of "squatter sovereignty." The passage of the Morrill Tariff by the House of Representatives and the expectation that it would soon become the law of the land once again put the South's interests at risk from Northern monetary aggressions. Southern representation in the Senate relative to that of the North had to be maintained at all cost, and for help in achieving that goal, southern Democrats demanded federal protection for slave property brought into the territories. They could no longer afford to support squatter sovereignty because it had in practice brought about the exclusion of slavery wherever applied. When Douglas and the northern Democrats refused to give it up, secessionists led by William L. Yancey, a former Congressman from Alabama, prodded the southern delegations into convening their own convention. Yancey saw "a house divided against itself" as a much more viable political arrangement than a Union, even though the North was offering slavery more vigorous protection than it had ever before enjoyed. With the southerners gone, Douglas was able to gain the nomination for President at the northern Democrat convention, while Breckinridge became the nominee of the southern Democrats. A third convention nominated Tennessean John Bell to run on the Constitutional Union ticket; its platform, the shortest ever, merely advocated adherence to the Constitution and national unity. With three Democratic candidates in the running, the election of Lincoln appeared much more likely. But, as Yancey had probably foreseen, there would be no backtracking now. The Panic of 1857 and the political attempt to "fix" it with the Morrill Tariff had set the stage for secession.

It remained for Charles Dickens (1812-1870) to pronounce his now forgotten summary of the controversy in the British weekly, *All the Year Round*, 21 December 1861.

"Slavery? Ah, humbug!" he wrote. "Union means so many millions a year lost to the South; secession means the loss of the same millions to the North. The love of money is the root of this, as with many many other evils. ... the quarrel between the North and the South, as it stands, is solely a fiscal quarrel." Earlier that year, Greeley had tired of Marx's obiter dicta and dispensed with his services. That left Marx free to finish his magnum opus, the deterministic, "not-even-wrong" *Das Kapital*, and organize the first Communist International. How unfortunate it is that his version of Civil War "truth" has persisted!

CHAPTER XXX

BLOOD AND MONEY I

The big heart of the people is still in the Union. Less than a hundred politicians are endeavoring to destroy the liberties and usurp the rights of more than thirty millions of people. If the people permit it, they deserve the horrors of the civil war which will ensue.

Editorial in the Raleigh NC *Banner* 1861

Speech should only be free when it is loyal ... Whenever the press becomes dangerous to the existence of the government, it must be checked by law.

New-York Times editorial 20 August 1861

The "enforcement of the laws" is getting on famously. Newspaper offices are gutted ... with great success, by "loyal multitudes." Congressmen are burnt in effigy, in the most creditable and satisfactory way. In Massachusetts, where they always do such things best ..., they add tarring and feathering, and riding on a rail, to the list of their efforts on the behalf of the Constitution. Nothing can surpass the noble and generous patriotism with which the citizens of Haverhill possessed themselves of the person of the editor of a "secession sheet" (meaning an unhappy man, who dared to oppose abolitionism and war) – they covered him with a "coat of tar and feather," rode him on a rail through the town and then compelled him to make recantation of his opinions, on his knees, in the midst of brutal and horrible indignities. "I am sorry," the wretched victim was made to say, "that I have published what I have and promise that I will never again write or publish articles against the Union. What a triumph of reason and free institutions!

Francis Key Howard, editor of the Baltimore *Daily Exchange*, 24 August 1861

Money is the heart of war.

Peter the Great of Russia

By the end of 1861, war costs for the North alone were escalating toward one million dollars a day. The year had seen the first trickle of blood, a trickle only in light of what was to come. Under pressure from northern newspapers to bring the "rebellion" to a quick end, Lincoln had backed a plan drawn up by General Irvin McDowell for a direct attack on Richmond, the recently established capital of the Confederacy. For the march south, McDowell gathered together a Union army of 34,000, mostly raw recruits drawn from Lincoln's 75,000 volunteers. Time was pressing because their three-month term of enlistment ended in August, one month hence. Blocking the Richmond road was General Beauregard and an army of 25,000 deployed along Bull Run, a narrow creek of water near the important railroad junction of Manassas, twenty-five miles southwest of Washington. Here it was on 21 July that the first major battle of the war took place. Gathered in the hills overlooking the site were hundreds of spectators, including newspapermen, Senators and Congressmen. They had come from Washington in stylish carriages, in buggies, in wagons, on horseback and on foot to picnic and enjoy the killing. But their expectations for a quick and easy Union victory were quickly dashed. A day of confused fighting saw the invading army routed and both Union troops and onlookers engaged in a panic-stricken flight back to Washington. Northern losses totaled 460 killed, 1124 wounded and 1312 missing or captured compared to 387 killed, 1087 wounded and 13 missing for the South. Outstanding battlefield tactics were displayed by Brigadier General Thomas J. "Stonewall" Jackson (1824-63), whose brigade held like a "stone wall" throughout the fighting.

"Give me 5,000 fresh men and I will be in Washington City tomorrow," Jackson told President Jefferson Davis, who visited the battlefield that evening. In all likelihood, Jackson could have shot the "less than hundred politicians" responsible for the War and saved the lives of hundreds of thousands.

Unfortunately for the South, Davis had second thoughts after first consenting. His early strategy called for a purely defensive war, one that did not foreclose on the ongoing possibility of compromise. He had yet to recognize the "blood and money"- thirsty monster he was dealing with. Even George III had given up on the Revolutionary War with the "mere" loss of Cornwallis' 5000-man army at Yorktown.

The Union rout at Bull Run confronted Lincoln with the likelihood of a long, bloody and expensive war. No thought of compromise entered into his thoughts, however. What he saw were two great enemies – a much stronger than expected Southern army in front of him and a recalcitrant Northern populace to his rear, one that might just rebel against financing a conflagration such as this. Killing politicians was a frequent occurrence in those days and the new administration could hardly afford to let the practice get started in America. The beheadings of the French Revolution, just sixty-five years earlier, and the general uprisings of 1848 that nearly begot repeat performances across Europe must have proved especially worrisome to a minority President engaged in an unpopular war. Bull Run acquainted Lincoln and his cohorts with the sudden realization that the heads of government, not merely those of soldiers and sailors, were also on the block this time around. His fears would soon protrude into an amateurish meddling in military strategy that greatly prolonged the War.

The immediate problem centered on Maryland, a border state thoroughly southern in mentality. Because the District of Columbia lay sandwiched between her southern boundary and Virginia, it was a state Lincoln could not afford to lose. Thus far, Maryland had not joined her sister states in secession, but there was little doubt as to where the people's sympathies lay.

In the 1860 election, Lincoln had garnered only 2300 votes and Douglas less than 6000 out of a total of nearly 92,000, most voters going for anti-Republicans Breckinridge and Bell. For his inauguration, both Lincoln and his luggage had to be smuggled through Maryland to prevent incident. Outright resistance occurred just three days after Lincoln's call for volunteers, when an angry crowd of southern sympathizers in Baltimore blockaded a troop train carrying a regiment of Massachusetts recruits to Washington. The first seven cars managed to get through the sand and cobblestone dumped on the tracks only after the rear cars were unhitched, and that left two hundred soldiers to rejoin their comrades by marching through the city. Shooting incidents occurred, leaving several soldiers and civilians dead and wounded.

Flouting all Constitutional restraints, Lincoln took no chances on losing the state. He directed General-in-Chief Winfield Scott to anticipate a vote on secession by the Maryland legislature and, if such should appear likely, "to adopt the most prompt and efficient means to counteract, even, if necessary, to the bombardment of their cities." Although no action on secession was taken, Lincoln on 27 April suspended habeas corpus everywhere between Philadelphia and Washington. It was a power granted by the Constitution only to Congress, not to the President. Shortly thereafter, Baltimore came under military rule. To avoid further incidents, federal marshals and soldiers seized several police commissioners and incarcerated them in Fort McHenry. There they were held incommunicado despite protests from families and friends.

Stated Major General John Adams Dix, one of the men overseeing the turmoil: "The loss of Baltimore would have been the loss of Maryland; the loss of Maryland would have been the loss of the nation's capital, and perhaps, if not probably, the loss of the Union cause." On 6 August, Lincoln signed the Confiscation Act of 1861, a throwback to the Alien and Sedition Acts of 1798. The legislation signaled an all-out assault on the First Amendment's guarantees of freedom of speech and press. Any person suspected of southern sympathies could now be arrested and his/her property (including slaves) forfeited solely at the discretion of federal officers. "Be it enacted by the Senate and House of Representatives of the United States of America in Congress assembled, That if, during the present or any future insurrection against the Government of the United States, after the President of the United States, by proclamation, that the laws of the United States are opposed, and the execution thereof obstructed, by combinations too powerful to be suppressed by the ordinary course of judicial proceedings, or by the power vested in the marshals by law, any person or persons, his, her, or their agent, attorney, or employee, shall purchase or acquire, sell or give, any property of whatsoever kind or description, with intent to use or employ the same, or suffer the same to be used or employed, in aiding, abetting, or promoting such insurrection or resistance to the laws, or any person or persons engaged therein; or if any person or persons, being the owner or owners of such property, shall knowingly use or employ, or consent to the use of employment, of the same as aforesaid, all such property is hereby declared to be lawful subject of prize and capture wherever found; and it shall be the duty of the President of the United States to cause the same to be seized, confiscated, and condemned." Lincoln well understood that in his precarious position he could not tolerate dissension in the news media. The prospect of a war so costly in lives and money demanded a redeeming cause, if only for the self-preservation of government officials rather than vague principle. "Preserving the Union" – that was the brainwashing to be administered throughout the North. For the average American, it meant preserving jobs and livelihoods from the economic attacks of what promised to be a formidable free-market competitor to the south. For the "moneyed aristocracy," it meant higher profits to be accrued through Republican mercantilist policies. Contrary opinions were not to be tolerated. Publishers and editors in opposition felt particularly threatened, and their fears were soon justified. Those newspapers and journals voicing anti-Lincoln or anti-War opinions were held to be in violation of the Confiscation Act. More than 300 were denied use of the mails or physically shut down. Seven thousand others, out of fear of reprisals, shifted their allegiance to the President and his policies. Seven – the West Chester PA *Jeffersonian*, the Easton PA *Sentinel*, the Bridgeport CT *Farmer*, the Canton OH *Democrat*, the Concord NH *Standard*, the Bangor ME *Democrat*, and the Clinton KS *Journal* – saw their establishments demolished. Faceless hoodlums, violent mobs and even federal troops burned vital subscription lists, scattered printing type, and broke as best they could huge and costly printing presses. When John Hodgson, publisher and editor of the *Jeffersonian*, decided to continue publishing his anti- Lincoln and anti-War views by utilizing the machinery of a friendly Democratic newspaper in Philadelphia, he was closed down once again, this time by federal deputy marshals. They handed him a document that in part called for them to "take, hold, and keep possession of the building, as well as all property of every kind whatsoever, used in and about the publication of said newspaper." Upon what authority was suppression of the newspaper being taken? Hodgson asked.

"… Upon the authority of the President of the United States," the document read.

Although the military occupation of Baltimore in April had temporarily calmed the secession crisis in Maryland, the state remained a hotbed of resistance, especially after the butchery at Bull Run. A reconvening of the Maryland legislature scheduled for September again raised the strong possibility of a favorable secession vote. "The passage of any act of secession by the legislature of Maryland must be prevented," wrote Secretary of War Simon Cameron to the commander of the Baltimore jurisdiction, General Nathaniel Banks, soon to retire in favor of General Dix. "If necessary, all or any part of the members [of the legislature] must be arrested.

Exercise your own judgment as to the time and manner, but do the work efficiently." During the early morning hours of 13 September, the arrests began. Supervised by secret agent Allan Pinkerton, who would later found the detective agency bearing his name, a score of suspected southern sympathizers were routed out of bed and hustled to Fort McHenry. Among those arrested were state legislators thought to favor secession, Congressman from Maryland Henry May, and Francis Key Howard, editor of the Baltimore *Daily Exchange*. It was on that very day forty-seven years earlier that Howard's grandfather, Francis Scott Key, had witnessed the bombardment of Fort McHenry and penned "The Star-Spangled Banner." On the day before his arrest, Howard's paper had been denied use of the mails in accordance with a directive to local postmasters from Postmaster-General Montgomery Blair in Washington: "I believe the *Exchange*, *Republican*, and *South* should be suppressed. They are open disunionists." Those arrested were quickly shuttled out of Maryland to Fort Monroe in Virginia and then to Fort Lafayette in New York where they joined hundreds of other political prisoners.

Known at the time as the "American Bastille," after the Paris prison used during the French Revolution for the same purpose, Fort Lafayette occupied a small rocky island in New York harbor near where now stands the Brooklyn tower of the Verazzano Narrows Bridge. Today it is referred to as the "American gulag." Upon his release fourteen months later, Howard would write of the day of his treatment: "The flag which he [Francis Scott Key] had then so proudly hailed, I saw waving, at the same place, over the victims of as vulgar and brutal a despotism as modern times have witnessed." Similar tactics employed in Missouri and Kentucky prevented those border states from seceding.

As many as 40,000 citizens throughout the North may have been incarcerated as political prisoners for opposing administration policies. The trials and tribulations of Clement

L. Vallandigham, a former Congressman from Ohio and voluble opponent of the War, inspired Edward Everett Hale's book, The *Man Without a Country*. On 13 April 1863, Vallandigham had been dragged from his home at 2 o'clock in the morning and arrested by a company of troops. The charge: making derogatory references to Lincoln and stigmatizing the war effort during a speech to a large audience in Columbus OH.

He had apparently violated General Order No. 38 issued by Major General Ambrose E. Burnside, Commander of the Department of the Ohio, which forbade expressions of sympathy for the enemy. Taken to Burnside's Cincinnati headquarters, he was denied a writ of habeas corpus, tried by a military court and convicted of expressing "treasonable sentiments." An embarrassed Lincoln commuted his two year prison sentence to banishment from the Union, and Vallandigham was handed over to Confederate soldiers at Murfreesboro TN. From there, he made his way to Wilmington NC, shipped out to Bermuda and then to Canada. Outraged at his treatment, Ohio Democrats nominated him for governor and he ran in absentia. Although defeated by a 288,000 to 187,000 vote, his showing revealed the large anti-War sentiment existing in the North. In 1864, the Supreme Court decided, in *ex parte Vallandigham*, that no writ of habeas corpus could be issued in a "military" case even though Ohio was not in a military zone.

Bull Run exposed the enormity of financial problems facing both North and South. As Colonel Baldwin had tried to counsel Lincoln, the revenues collected by the federal government hitherto were "but a drop in the bucket compared with the cost of such a war as we are threatened with." Lincoln had remained unconvinced. After all, federal budgets during the 1850s never amounted to more than $60 million, and most of it was covered by tariff receipts. And if the South could be subjugated quickly, war spending would remain negligible.

Now, however, Baldwin's assessment of reality intervened. Of a sudden, everyone realized that this war was not going to be the brief police action originally envisioned, a point driven home to Congress on 1 August. At a strategy meeting with the Senate Finance and House Ways and Means Committees, newly appointed Secretary of the Treasury Salmon P. Chase (1808-73) estimated government expenditures for the coming fiscal year 1861-2 at the unheard of total of

$318 million, six times higher than in the previous year. He notified the Committees that the Treasury had at the start of hostilities only $3 million in specie to pay for $65 million in authorized expenditures, and that he had managed to borrow only $16 million to meet immediate needs. He proposed raising $240 million through further debt issues and $50 million in new taxes and higher tariff rates. It was a tall order, to say the least. Former Treasury issues in the Buchanan administration had failed to sell as much as $10 million in single offerings.

Throwing hundreds of millions of debt securities onto the credit market would certainly depress government bond prices drastically. It was a scary scenario but one that could be avoided, Chase assured the legislators, by involving the large European investment houses in the underwritings. He would dispatch August Belmont, an ardent supporter of the War and the Rothschild Bank agent in America, to Europe for that purpose. For his present needs, he requested the authority to borrow $100 million with three-year notes bearing 7.3% interest, plus an additional $50 million if necessary. Congress acceded to Chase's proposals without serious debate.

On 11 August, Chase traveled to New York for a meeting with the City's leading bankers. Accompanying him was Jay Cooke, a young financier whom we shall presently meet. Chase presented a plan to raise a flabbergasting $150 million in gold specie to defray the rapidly rising military expenditures. In return for the gold, the banks would receive $150 million in United States government bonds, the gold to be held in Independent Treasury depositories and not in bank vaults. Chase feared that borrowings of the magnitude contemplated, coming on top of commercial loans, could sink reserve ratios to frighteningly low levels and spark bank runs by the public. Such a happening could force the banks to suspend and possibly dry up the government's source of funds; commercial bank notes unbacked by gold might become unacceptable as payments for war expenses. To the bankers, however, Chase argued that such a contingency was unlikely.

Deposits of military payments and the resale of the bonds to the public plus the interest on those bonds, which had to be paid in gold, would quickly replenish bank reserves. To pacify the bankers even further, he assured them that Congress would dedicate the revenues from new income and property taxes for the specific purpose of defraying the payment of bond interest.

Because the New York banks had on hand only $63 million in gold, a compromise was finally negotiated wherein the bonds would be issued in three installments of $50 million each.

In July, Lincoln had signed into law the Revenue Act of 1861, which contained the nation's first income tax. It provided that "there shall be levied, collected, and paid, upon annual income of every person residing in the United States whether derived from any kind of property, or from any profession, trade, employment, or vocation carried on the United States or elsewhere, or from any source whatever," a tax of 3% on incomes above $800 (about $10,000 in today's dollars) and 5% on individuals living outside the country. Being a direct and unapportioned tax, it was another desecration of the Constitution. But such a tax seemed a safe bet because its introduction in England in 1799 to help pay for the Napoleonic wars had not induced any large scale revolt. However, the tax raised no revenue because a second income tax passed the next June took effect first. A property tax provision in the Act raised $20 million, but it was repealed in early 1862 because of western opposition; farmers with large land holdings found themselves paying an inordinate share of the tax compared to city folk. It was the same non-uniformity in law faced by the South with the passage of the Morrill Tariff. Holding to the agreement reached by Chase with the bankers, Congress also included in the Act an authorization for $150 million in 7.3% Treasury notes redeemable in three years, these to be issued in $50 million installments and sold through the state banks. The year's fund raising concluded on 17 November when Congress, acting on its own behalf as a commercial bank, further authorized an issue of $33 million in demand notes (convertible into gold) in denominations of $5, $10 and $20.

But events were unfolding much faster than any of the politicians had expected. Costs associated with another call for volunteers by Lincoln, this time for an astounding 600,000 men, drained the Treasury of reserves. Another battle, this time at Balls Bluff near Leesburg VA in October, cost the Union force more than half its 1720 men in killed, wounded, captured and missing, and it threw further doubt on the North's ability to prosecute the war successfully. Compounding the developing chaos was the November "Trent Affair," which almost brought England into the War on the side of the Confederacy. Captain Charles Wilkes, a noted Antarctic explorer and now in command of the American warship *San Jacinto*, stopped the British mail steamer *Trent* and forcibly removed two Confederate commissioners en route to England. Confrontation was averted only when the two prisoners were released in January after protracted negotiation.

In the light of these events, Chase's fears came to the fore. A gold rush on New York banks shrunk their reserves by a third and forced them to suspend convertibility of their bank notes. Banks in other cities soon followed, as did Treasury on its demand notes. A frightened public was obviously converting paper money into gold at a rapid clip. In early 1862, the nation's money supply consisted solely of inconvertible bank and Treasury notes plus a small supply of gold and silver coins that were rapidly disappearing from circulation. Soon, only pennies remained. To facilitate transactions, the banks issued fractional bank notes, but these wore out so rapidly that the government made their issuance in denominations less than $1 a federal offense. Ordinary postage stamps began serving as a coin proxy, and then, during the period from August 1862 until 1875, Treasury issued more than $368 million in a fractional currency ranging in denominations from 3 cents to 50 cents.

The notes were nicknamed "shinplasters" by soldiers who used them to line their worn-out boots. Finally, to cap the financial chaos, Belmont reported that the English and French governments and the great European banking houses had emphatically refused to lend any money to the Washington government.

On 3 February 1862, Chase informed a stunned Congress that "The Treasury is nearly empty." And, he might have added, we have no central bank to create for us all the money we need. A panicky debate on what to do followed. At this point, New York Congressman Elbridge G. Spaulding, undoubtedly under the urging of Lincoln, introduced legislation authorizing the issuance of a paper money. Unbacked by precious metal, it would nevertheless be legal tender for all transactions including the purchase of government bonds, but not for the interest on those bonds and not for import duties.

Objections based on the Constitutional clause empowering Congress only "to coin money" were countered by Spaulding with "The bill before us is a war measure." As would happen countless times in the future whenever the politicians so decided, the "overriding" needs of government took precedence over the Constitution. Had the Constitution been adhered to, the coming slaughter could have been stopped in its tracks.

On 25 February Lincoln signed the Legal Tender Act of 1862 and, for the second time in her short history, America got a debt-free, interest-free currency to pay for war. The first instance, as we remember, occurred just after the War of 1812, in February of 1815, when the Madison government issued five million dollars in unbacked paper notes. "Greenbacks," as the new money was called, consisted of bills printed on one side in green ink; the other side, in black and white, displayed a portrait of Secretary of the Treasury Chase. The Act authorized an issue of $150 million, but subsequent Acts in March and June of 1863 put $300 million more into circulation.

Altogether, greenbacks defrayed about 15% of the $3.5 billion cost of the War to the North. The remainder was covered by bond issues (65%), tariffs and a host of new taxes (20%). Both greenbacks and state bank notes served as currency during this "greenback era," and soon a third type – national bank notes – would be added. In the South, unbacked Confederate notes paid almost 95% of War costs.

The suggestion for paper money issuance first came from one Colonel Edward Dick Taylor, a friend of Lincoln. They had first met as opposing members in the Illinois legislature, Lincoln just beginning a political career and Taylor a businessman well connected in banking circles. A letter from Lincoln to Taylor two years after the Act (quoted in Emil Ludwig's *Lincoln* biography) recounted the turn of events as follows:

My dear Colonel Dick: I have long determined to make public the origin of the greenback and tell the world that it was Dick Taylor's creation.

You have always been friendly to me, and when troublous times fell on us … I said in my extremity, 'I will send for Colonel Taylor – he will know what to do.' I think it was in January 1862, on or about the 16th, that I did so. Said you: 'Why, issue treasury notes bearing no interest, printed on the best banking paper. Issue enough to pay off the army expenses and declare it legal tender.' Chase thought it a hazardous thing, but we finally accomplished it, and gave the people of the Republic the greatest blessing they ever had – their own paper to pay their debts. It is due to you, the father of the present greenback, … and I take great pleasure in making it known.

How many times have I laughed at you telling me, plainly, that I was too lazy to be anything but a lawyer.

Yours truly,

A. Lincoln

The letter shows how quickly Lincoln grasped Colonel Taylor's point, the absurdity of a currency based on government debt. Once freed of wartime financial pressures, he gave every indication of adopting greenback issue as permanent policy and the cheapest and safest way of getting the money needed for his projected political establishment. It may have done him in.

The Legal Tender Act also authorized the issuance of $500 million in bonds bearing an interest rate of 6%. Known as the 5/20s, they matured in twenty years and could be redeemed in five. Although they could be bought with greenbacks, interest and redemption were payable in gold. But the public was not buying. At this point, obviously, most people did not regard a Union victory as a good bet, nor did they believe that the government would have the gold to redeem the bonds even if the North won. By the end of 1862, Chase had managed to sell only $23.7 million worth of them. Most of the year's expenditures had to be defrayed with greenbacks, and these in terms of gold were fast depreciating in price. The physical amount of gold, after all, remained about constant. With so much new paper money appearing in the marketplace and the supply of civilian goods and services diminishing in the face of war production, inflation began to ramp up. By the end of 1862, the purchase of a pre-War dollar's worth of gold required $1.30 in greenbacks. At the low point in 1864, the greenback price of gold was more than $2.50. But inefficient spending such as for war must be paid somehow, and in this case, it was through the inflationary prices charged in public markets. From 1860 to the end of the War in 1865, prices rose about 75% while wages in contrast went up by less than half. Inflation is, in its effect, exactly the equivalent of a consumption tax in that it limits the public's power to spend. War in general must force a decline in living standards as production shifts from civilian to military needs.

Aside from playing a major role in financing the War, greenbacks spared future taxpayers some of the immense costs associated with bond underwritings and interest payments, which would have amounted ultimately to more than $4 billion.

The inflation tax, you see, has a great advantage – a zero collection cost. The first greenback issue had gone through without incident and the resulting inflation was quite manageable. There is another great advantage to paper money issue: Should inflation surface during peacetime, over-issue of paper money is easily established as the cause – and it tells politicians to reign in their spending. However, Hamilton's "moneyed aristocracy" objected vehemently. They did not want to see their fixed income investments – bonds, mortgages, contractual obligations and business receivables – repaid in ever cheapening greenbacks. Paying the inflation tax was certainly not for them. "To pay taxes is ignoble," declares Greatauk in Anatole France's *Penguin Island*. "Being noble, I shall not pay. It is for the rabble to pay." The bankers for their part were also upset. They saw an opportunity lost for making the large commissions associated with government bond underwritings, especially during wars.

Even the Rothschild-controlled *Times* of London weighed in: "If that mischievous policy which had its origin in the North American Republic should become indurated down to a fixture, then that government will furnish its own money without cost. It will pay off its debts and be without a debt. It will become prosperous beyond precedent in the history of the civilized governments of the civilized world. The brains and wealth of all countries will go to North America.

That government must be destroyed or it will destroy every monarchy on the globe." The wealth of Rothschild consists of the bankruptcy of nations, it has been said, and that vast financial empire clearly regarded paper money as a threat to its existence. In the face of such opposition at home and abroad, the administration limited its issuance of greenbacks to $450 million. Thus began a vicious and ongoing propaganda campaign against a debt-free, interest free currency that could have given "the people of the Republic the greatest blessing they ever had" and saved American taxpayers trillions of dollars. Quoting from A *Monetary History of the United States*: "… in light of the U. S. experience in two World Wars, especially World War I, the financing of the Civil War involved surprisingly little inflation …. The tendency in the literature … to regard the financing of the Civil War as a disgracefully inflationary episode reflects the implicit application of standards of monetary rectitude that, to the modern student, seem almost utopian in light of the monetary vagaries of the past half century [1917-1967]." For comparison, from the end of 1915 to the spring of 1920, a time during which America fought in World War I and the Federal Reserve System controlled the money supply, prices rose almost two and one-half times from their beginning level, greatly exceeding the 75% increase during the far more devastating Civil War years 1860-1865.

In a quandary over their poor sales, Chase turned to Jay Cooke (1821-1905) for help in marketing the 5/20s. The second of three brothers born in the frontier hamlet of Sandusky OH about one hundred miles west of Cleveland, Cooke by the age of 18 was exhibiting the financial wizardry of a William Paterson. In 1837 he joined the large private banking house of E. W. Clark & Company in Philadelphia and became a partner a short three years later. The firm was one of many that acted as a clearing house for transactions involving inter-bank notes during the free-banking era, and it also handled the safekeeping and transfer of funds, functions formerly assumed by the 1st and 2nd Banks of the United States. Other of its activities included the flotation of federal, state, municipal and railroad bond issues, and the purchase and sale of western lands and land warrants. During the Mexican War of 1845, the house realized considerable profit from underwriting government war debts, and the experience prepared Cooke for his coming role as "financier of the Civil War." However, the Panic of 1857 caught E. W. Clark & Co. in an overextended financial condition. Sharp declines in the values of its land and security holdings deprived the company of the cash needed to meet its current obligations, and the ensuing bankruptcy forced Cooke to find other means of employment. He responded by founding Jay Cooke & Company, capitalized with a modest $150,000.

His "butterfly" came in 1861 when the state of Pennsylvania authorized a $3 million bond sale for financing an adequate defense against a potential Confederate attack. Using the connections established during his long tenure with E. W. Clark, he convinced Pennsylvania officials of his ability to sell a significant portion of the bonds, and the underwriting was divided equally between Cooke and Drexel & Company, a firm ten times larger.

It was in the Pennsylvania bond sale that Cooke originated entirely new underwriting tactics from those used hitherto. After the demise of the two Banks of the United States, both the federal and state governments had handled their borrowing activities through major banks and brokerage houses, firms that either held the securities in their reserves or sold them to their wealthiest customers. Ordinary citizens were given little opportunity to participate. As we have seen, the Bank of England followed this policy. Cooke, on the other hand, by-passed the large institutions and sold directly to the people. He distributed circulars in stores, in public buildings and in railroad cars, bought advertising space in local newspapers and obtained editorial comment favorable to the sale. And despite the state's notoriously bad credit rating, incurred by a reckless spending spree on "internal improvements," the underwriting proved enormously successful. It so enhanced Cooke's reputation that his company was appointed the official depository for state funds. That brought in a large flow of non-bond related money and enabled Cooke to expand his financial activities considerably.

Henry Cooke, the youngest of Jay's three brothers, was closely connected with Ohio politicians. As part owner and editor of an influential daily newspaper, the *Ohio State Journal*, he had strongly supported Chase's political aspirations and also those of John Sherman (1823-1900), brother of General William Tecumseh Sherman. Both Chase and Sherman were instrumental in the organization of the Republican Party in Ohio, and Chase had served both as a United States Senator from Ohio and governor from 1855 to 1860. He became a leading Presidential candidate at the Republican convention in 1860, but his strongly abolitionist stance militated strongly against him. Elected once again to the U. S. Senate in 1860, he served only two days before being appointed Secretary of the Treasury. His seat was taken by Sherman who, as former chairman of the House Ways and Means Committee, had helped steer the Morrill Tariff Act through Congress. In 1890 he would lend his name to the Sherman Anti-Trust Act, which empowered bureaucrats and lawyers rather than the marketplace to determine the most efficient size of private companies. The Cookes had lobbied long and hard in Republican circles to get Chase and Sherman into positions of power in the new administration. They clearly foresaw the coming of war and were determined, as attested to in a remarkable letter from their father, a lawyer and former Congressman himself, "to make money out of government contracts."

On 12 July 1861 Henry transmitted to Chase a message from Jay, "that I hold myself at his [Chase's] service and, pay or no pay, I will do all I can to aid him in Treasury matters. I feel, however, that if he would give me a chance I could show him a way to raise the money." Now in 1862, with the sale of the 5/20s foundering, Chase decided to take Cooke up on his offer and appointed Jay Cooke & Company as the government's sole financial agent for marketing the 5/20s. Past bond sales were not even close to selling on the scale now needed, and Chase recognized Cooke's tactics in Pennsylvania as the best if not the only chance he had of raising a sufficient amount of money. Cooke did not disappoint him. He played the key role in solving the Union's monetary problems, and because of him, Lincoln was able to prosecute the War to its conclusion financially unencumbered and simultaneously institute his "New Deal." For marketing the 5/20s, Cooke partnered with Anthony Drexel of Drexel & Company and went in for mass salesmanship on a scale never before attempted. Again, he bypassed the banks and went directly to the public. In language that was a rarity in those days, he sold patriotism: "The soldier at the front must be supported in the rear; it was every American's war and idle dollars should be lent to the boys in blue and not stuck under mattresses." Nor did he neglect financial gain: "But independent of any motives of patriotism, there are considerations of self-interest which may be considered in reference to this loan. It is a 6% loan free from any taxation." And he could have added that the bonds were redeemable in gold and thereby immune from the inflation tax.

To get his message across, he plastered the nation with flamboyant posters and advertisements in newspapers across the country, not only in the metropolitan dailies with large circulations but in obscure small town weeklies as well. Bonds in denominations as low as $50 rather than the usual par value of $1000 were offered and installment buying was encouraged.

An army of 2500 sub-agents scoured the remotest hamlets and villages, and even mining camps, for customers. His agencies remained open night and day serving coffee and doughnuts free to customers. When he used the new telegraph facilities to confirm the purchase and sale of bonds, his company became the first "wirehouse." At the peak, Cooke was selling more than $2 million worth of bonds per day. Wrote Henry to Jay, 31 October 1863: "…At half past seven I am here at the office after the biggest days work on record – too tired to give you anything but a summary … the office was besieged inside and out. Scores had to wait and wait, although we had four subscription tables at full blast. Local sales to customers amounted to $1,800,000. Our orders from the west etc. were a trifle over $900,000, and the subscriptions from New York and Boston, Baltimore, etc. were a trifle over $10 million making a total of between 13 and 14 millions. We sold bonds until we had not a single bond left on hand." By December of 1863, Cooke had sold $400 million of the 5/20s. Between February and July of 1865, the government was again beset with disappointing sales of a new issue of 7/30 notes by the national banks, and Cooke was called on once again. His sale of $850 million of these debt securities assured the soldiers of their pay and supplies during the final days of the War. Altogether, with commissions of at least ¼%, he realized more than $5 million on the sale of $2 billion worth of debt. His efforts vested America's middle class with a huge financial stake in a Union victory and certainly helped quell anti-War sentiments. A Union defeat could have turned the bonds into worthless paper.

Future war bond drives would be patterned after Cooke's pioneering salesmanship. A portrait of Cooke by the renowned American artist, William Merritt Chase, hangs in the board room of the Citigroup Corporation in New York, one of forty or more primary "merchants of debt" in today's $9 trillion government bond market. It aptly commemorates the first of the country's investment bankers.

CHAPTER XXXI

BLOOD AND MONEY II

But oh! How wondrously they slew/ With what they had to go on.

Phyllis McGinley, The *Conquerors*

"It scared the hell out of me. It conjured up images of Civil War battles, row after row of men going up and replacing those who had fallen. I knew we would get to the top of that mountain, eventually — but how many men was it going to chew up?"

James Bradley quoting Captain Dave Severance on his viewing of a map of Iwo Jima in *Flags of Our Fathers*

One death is a tragedy, a million deaths a statistic.

Joseph Stalin

I see more barbarism and sin in continuing this war than in the sin and barbarism of African slavery.

Clement L. Vallandigham

I saw in States' Rights the only availing check upon the absolutism of the sovereign will, and secession filled me with hope, not as the destruction but as the redemption of Democracy . . . I deemed that you [Lee] were fighting the battles of our liberty, our progress, and our civilization; and I mourn for the stake which was lost at Richmond more deeply than I rejoice over that which was saved at Waterloo.

British historian Lord Acton in a letter to General Robert E. Lee

    With the War's finances more or less assured, the killing soon climbed to hideous heights. Huge armies, in numbers never before seen in the Americas, came into being. In the North, George B. McClellan (1826-1885), welded more than 125,000 raw recruits into an organized and disciplined force known as the Army of the Potomac. McClellan, the son of a Philadelphia surgeon, entered West Point at 15 years of age and graduated second in the class of 1846. He entered military service as a 2nd lieutenant in the Corps of Engineers and served with distinction in the Mexican War. Twenty of his classmates would become general officers in the coming Civil War. He resigned his commission in 1857 to become Chief Engineer of the Illinois Central Railroad and, during this tenure, cooperated occasionally with a railroad lawyer named Abraham Lincoln.

After the July disaster at Bull Run, Lincoln recruited him from his post as president of the Ohio and Mississippi Railroad and appointed him a major general in the regular army, outranked only by General-in-Chief Winfield Scott whom he would soon succeed.

Concurrently, Confederate General Joseph E. Johnston, West Point class of 1826 and also a Mexican War veteran, created the Army of Northern Virginia, 75,000 strong. The two armies would soon clash on the outskirts of Richmond in the first climactic battle of the War. Everyone agreed that taking the Confederate capital, the major arsenal of the South, would in all probability bring the War to a quick conclusion, and Lincoln favored confronting Johnston in a direct move south to Richmond. The Bull Run rout had raised fears of raids on Washington, and he was very insistent on keeping the Army of the Potomac between the capital and the "Rebels." But McClellan demurred. From his military point of view, the supply line to Richmond would stretch too long and be too exposed to attack. And, furthermore, the topography south of Fredericksburg offered too many almost impregnable defensive positions. Against the likes of Johnston, Beauregard and "Stonewall" Jackson, a frontal assault such as Lincoln had in mind could pile up massive casualties without any assurance of success. Instead, McClellan opted for a flanking attack on Richmond via the lightly defended Yorktown peninsula, where Washington had bottled up Cornwallis to end the Revolutionary War. His plan called for a naval landing at Union-held Fort Monroe on the eastern tip of the peninsula, from which point there would be a short seventy-mile march northwestward to Richmond with the navy protecting the army's flanks. 30,000 men under General McDowell in Washington and another 38,000 under General Nathaniel Banks in the Shenandoah Valley fifty miles west would be held in reserve to protect Washington and ready to march south when called. In support of the land operations, naval warships would sail up the James River and lend their guns to the final assault on Richmond. If all went well, the Army of Northern Virginia would find itself clamped between the jaws of a giant pincer movement, vastly outnumbered and subject to annihilation. When almost all Union commanders indicated their support for McClellan, Lincoln approved the plan, albeit reluctantly. On paper, it promised a quick end to the War and a low casualty count. But *Mousie* ... .

On 29 April, after an uneventful voyage to Fort Monroe from Alexandria VA via the Potomac River and Chesapeake Bay, McClellan started his army up the peninsula. There had been a delay occasioned by the surprise appearance on 8 April of a Confederate ironclad vessel in Hampton Roads at the mouth of the James River. Originally the USS Merrimack and now rechristened the CSS Virginia, she was the South's hope for lifting the blockade imposed by Lincoln after the fall of Sumter. On her first day out, she rammed and destroyed two Union warships, and her captain awaited the morrow before taking on the rest of the Northern fleet. The event sent shockwaves through the Navy and forced McClellan to delay his sailing. Another day, however, brought another surprise with the appearance of a just-built Union ironclad, the USS Monitor. Ironclads had made a first appearance in the Crimean War of 1848 and about a hundred had been built by foreign navies, but none by the United States until now. On the 9th and 10th of April, the Monitor and the Merrimack engaged in the first battle between ironclads, but neither could inflict much damage on the other. When McClellan and the navy brass convinced themselves that the Monitor had neutralized the Merrimack, the transport operation proceeded. The delay, however, gave Johnston all the time needed to establish a virtually impregnable ring of fortifications around Richmond. On 9 May, the Merrimack was scuttled when Union troops occupied her home base at Norfolk.

McClellan moved deliberately up the Peninsula, avoiding casualties as much as possible. "Every poor fellow that is killed or wounded almost haunts me!" he wrote in a letter to his wife. Heavy rains and determined opposition from Major General John Magruder commanding a small force of perhaps 13,000 Confederates slowed the advance somewhat. But there seemed to be no rush. Johnston's Army of Northern Virginia, having moved south to block McClellan's advance, was locked in a tightening grip from which there seemed to be little hope of escape. Johnston, of course, was well aware of his predicament, and he reacted with verve and daring. Taking into account Lincoln's inordinate concern about protecting Washington, he dispatched "Stonewall" Jackson to the Shenandoah Valley for the specific purpose of harassing McDowell and Banks and posing a threat to the capital. Jackson's "foot cavalry" performed magnificently. With never more than 17,000 men engaging 50,000 to 60,000 Union troops in the Valley, Jackson waged a dazzling war of movement. By defeating no less than three commands sent to destroy his demiarmy, he frightened Lincoln and Secretary of War Edward Stanton into making the fatal mistake of keeping McDowell and Banks near Washington and preventing them from joining McClellan. The timidity displayed by the "small men by whom we are governed" would prolong the War for three more years and cost hundreds of thousands of lives.

By the end of May, the Army of the Potomac had reached the environs of Richmond, only six miles from the capital. At this point, Johnston launched a vicious counterattack in a battle known as Seven Pines in the South and Fair Oaks in the North. Although the result was a stalemate, it stopped the advance. At Drewry's Bluff on the James River, a Union squadron found the way to Richmond blocked when its naval guns could not be elevated sufficiently to hit the Confederate batteries. Casualties on both sides were unprecedented, on a scale never before seen. Politicians and generals got their first inkling that military tactics had fallen far behind technological advances in killing. A typical battle saw infantry-men marshaled into double-rowed lines advancing on each other in close formation, elbow to elbow and shoulder to shoulder. Firing at distances of only one hundred yards or less, they made easy marks for the .58 caliber rifled muskets that were replacing the smooth-bores of earlier times. With a recently developed paper cartridge holding the powder, a musketeer was expected to load and reload quickly enough to fire three shots a minute. Cannons exacted a fearful toll. Loaded with grape, canister, solid balls, chains, and rusty iron scrap, they served as over sized shotguns firing point-blank into enemy infantry lines. Not until near the War's end did the long lines of infantry and artillery disperse and disappear into the earthworks and natural ground cover that would characterize future wars.

Rather than racking up more casualties than necessary, McClellan decided to wait for the expected arrival of McDowell before launching the final assault. He also awaited a number of big siege guns with which he hoped to level the Richmond fortifications. These were to be transported by rail from the big Union base at West Point on the York River. But, unfortunately for McClellan, delay again opened a time window for the unexpected to happen. Johnston was wounded at Seven Pines, and that brought about a momentous change in Confederate leadership. He was replaced by Robert E. Lee (1807-1870), an even more capable general and a man not afraid to gamble everything when he thought the reward justified the risk. The fifth child of Revolutionary War hero, Henry "Light Horse Harry" Lee, he was graduated second in the West Point class of 1829 and, like McClellan, entered service as a 2nd lieutenant in the Corps of Engineers. After serving as an aide to Winfield Scott in the Mexican War, he became superintendent of the Military Academy at West Point in 1852. Scott wanted him for a command in the Union army when hostilities broke out, but Lee could not find it in his heart to war on his fellow Virginians. Instead, he became Jefferson Davis' military adviser. Once in command, he reorganized the battered Army of Northern Virginia and, with stunning speed and decisiveness, launched an offensive that came close to annihilating McClellan's Army of the Potomac.

On 26 June, a series of battles known as the Seven Days now ensued. Knowing that McDowell would not be coming, Lee spotted his opportunity. Leaving only a token force under Magruder to defend Richmond, he drove his army of 55,000 en masse against McClellan's exposed right wing north of the capital. Unlike Lincoln, he was not afraid to risk the fall of his capital city to gain a conclusive victory. And the gamble paid off when his troops decimated the Union V Corps and forced it back onto the main body. Recognizing the peril in what was now a flank attack in force, McClellan managed to retreat to Harrison's Landing on the James River with Lee in hot pursuit. There, under cover of navy artillery, he was able to ward off annihilation despite wave after wave of Confederate infantry assaults. And there the Army of the Potomac would sit, never bestirring itself. McClellan simply refused to engage in any further offensive action until supplied with substantial reinforcements, and these were not forthcoming. He believed that he faced 200,000 troops in Richmond, and there was too little information available to dispute him. Furthermore, his big siege guns could no longer reach him, the railroad from the York River being now in Confederate hands. On 3 August, he was notified that the Army would be withdrawn from the Peninsula and returned to Washington.

A sickening number of casualties on both sides bloodied the battlefields. The Peninsula Campaign cost The Army of the Potomac almost 16,000 men in dead and wounded. The Army of Northern Virginia lost even more, 20,000. It was precious manpower that the South could ill afford to lose. I cannot read or write about these horrors without my heart going out to all those young men, to those from the North fighting for empty slogans and to those from the South fighting both for their homes and the Jeffersonian principle of limited government. Almost never mentioned in historical accounts of the battles is the stench of dead bodies permeating the battlegrounds. During World War II, I myself served in Manila for a year after its retaking by General Douglas MacArthur. Because the Japanese defenders of the city refused to evacuate, almost all buildings had to be demolished by artillery with the soldiers inside. Only the San Miguel brewery was left intact. One year later, when I left, the odor of corpses was still as strong as ever. It was something nobody ever got used to. I might mention that whiffs of that stench reappeared at my Brooklyn home borne on northwest winds from the World Trade Center after the terrorist attack on 9/11.

The successful defense of Richmond was perceived in the South as a glorious victory, a morale builder sorely needed in lieu of the loss earlier that year of New Orleans and western Virginia. But Lee could hardly afford to rest on his laurels. McClellan was only a days march from Richmond and, even more alarming, a new Union army was being pieced together in northern Virginia by Major General John Pope, an officer who had enjoyed a measure of success in the west. If ever the forces of McClellan and Pope merged, Lee with perhaps 55,000 men would be facing an army of 200,000, and that he knew he could not cope with. The South had in total possibly 500,000 men of military age compared to over 2 million in the North, a four to one advantage. To have any chance at all against such odds, Lee had to conduct a war of movement, hit and run, divide and conquer. Only in this way could he take on and destroy Union armies one at a time and possibly force Lincoln into negotiations. When Lincoln relieved McClellan of his command and ordered the Army of the Potomac back to Washington, Lee had to move fast, and he did. His window of opportunity would not remain open for long. In mid-July, he reorganized his army into two commands, one under "Stonewall" Jackson and the other under James Longstreet. Taking another daring gamble, he turned his back on McClellan and sent Jackson on a long circular movement to the northwest that would bring him to Pope's rear, while he and Longstreet followed as quickly as they could. On 25 August, Jackson captured the huge Union supply depot at Manassas in a surprise attack and then, after sacking and burning the base, retired to the surrounding hills to await Lee and Longstreet. Pope, unaware of Longstreet's coming, massed virtually his entire army for the blow that he thought would crush Jackson once and for all. Not until Longstreet launched a flanking attack on 30 August did Pope realize what he was up against, and only the hurried arrival of reinforcements from Washington prevented the complete annihilation of his army. Again, the casualties – the butcher's bill, as many called it – in the two day battle were horrendous. Pope lost 14,500 men and Lee 9,500.

Lee now had back-to-back victories, but neither was decisive in the way he had hoped for. Both Union armies were still intact. Somehow, he had to draw Pope's army out from behind the strong fortifications around Washington, engage it in battle and destroy it. And he had to do it before the Army of the Potomac returned in force to Washington from Harrison's Landing on the Peninsula. If he could bring it about, Washington would be his for the taking.

And so it was that Lee once again defied the odds, risking everything to win all. A thrust into Maryland, he calculated, was the best way to instigate the decisive battle he desired.

Although destitute of clothing, equipment and food, his army's morale was soaring. And though over matched by a two to- one disadvantage in manpower, it would, he believed, be adequate for the kill.

On September 4, Lee crossed the Potomac and advanced on Frederick MD. And, as figured, the Washington forces, now reorganized as the Army of the Potomac with McClellan again in command (there seemed to be no one else fit for the job) moved westward to intercept him. The two armies, Lee's with less than 40,000 men and McClellan's with 75,000 and more arriving daily, met on 18 September at the town of Sharpsburg on Antietam Creek in the bloodiest one-day battle of the War. Union losses totaled 2,108 killed, 9,549 wounded and 753 missing; Confederate losses were 2,750 killed, 9,024 wounded and 2000 missing. More than one out of every four men in action became a casualty. The result was a stalemate, but so battered were the Confederate forces that Lee had to withdraw back across the Potomac, once again denied a decisive win. The Army of the Potomac fared little better, and McClellan opted for giving his men a respite from the killing rather than pursuing Lee on the latter's home grounds. A sortie the next day across the Potomac was driven back with heavy losses, confirming McClellan in his decision to pause and repair damages. Lincoln, however, found McClellan's failure to pursue Lee inexcusable, and in early November replaced him with one of his subordinates, Major General Ambrose Burnside.

But something more than just firing generals had to be done. "Preserving the Union" was losing its potency as the redeeming cause for the "butcher's bills" that arrived daily from the campaigns in the east and west. Even worse, army enlistments were drying up amid steadily rising anti-War sentiments. Five days after Antietam, on 22 September, Lincoln issued the Emancipation Proclamation. Although a "war measure," as he put it, intended to abort British support for the South and justify all the bloodletting, it marked the first and possibly only time in his career that Lincoln adhered to Adam Smith's "invisible hand" in setting policy. By taking the first step toward providing a maximum of freedom for a long enslaved portion of the population, he prepared the way for the South's reconstruction after the War. Indeed, post-bellum cotton production fueled by wage labor rather than slave labor recovered quickly, and by 1870 was greater than ever. To foreign correspondents, however, the Proclamation was naught but a brilliant propaganda coup. As a cynical editor put it in the London *Spectator* of 11 October 1862, "The principle [of the Proclamation] is not that a human being cannot justly own another, but that he cannot own him unless he is loyal to the United States." In his December 1862 State of the Union message to Congress, Lincoln followed up with three proposed amendments to the Constitution, firstly that slaves not freed by the Proclamation (those owned by Union loyalists) be freed gradually over a 37-year period ending 1 January 1900; secondly, that owners be compensated for the loss of their slave property; and thirdly, that the government deport freed Blacks, at government expense, out of the country and relocate them in Latin America or Africa. For Lincoln, emancipation and deportation were inseparably connected. As Secretary of the Navy Gideon Wells wrote in his diary, Lincoln "thought it essential to provide an asylum for a race which he had emancipated, but which could never be recognized or admitted to be our equals." Congress refused to consider

Lincoln's proposals, and eight months later the 13th Amendment to the Constitution was ratified. It freed four million slaves into poverty everywhere in the United States without gradualism, compensation, or deportation.

American blacks were hardly immune from the ongoing horrors of war. Beginning in 1863, 200,000 of them were admitted into the Union army and 38,000 died, mostly from disease. In 1862, Rufus Saxton, head of the Department of the South, allotted two acres of abandoned lands to black families for their own use, provided a portion of their cotton production went to the government. There were few takers. Thousands followed on the heels of Union armies seeking food and shelter. Many were placed in "contraband camps," where suffering and disease led to mortality rates estimated as high as 25%.

To everyone's astonishment, General Burnside moved, and moved fast. In mid-November he marched the Army of the Potomac, 120,000 strong, to the north bank of the Rappahannock River near Fredericksburg VA, leaving Lee well to the west. The road to Richmond, only fifty miles away, seemed wide open. But again, *Mousie* played his part. The river was near flood stage and impossible to ford. Because of bureaucratic bungling, the promised pontoon bridges had yet to be delivered and would not be until 9 December. That gave Lee the time he needed to whip his men back into shape, speed the army to Fredericksburg, and take up almost impregnable defensive positions on the high grounds just south of the town. General Joseph Johnston knew the area well and, when informed of the coming battle, had few fears of a Union victory despite the preponderance in manpower. "What luck some people have," he wrote. "Nobody will ever come to attack me in such a place." But Burnside, being unfamiliar with the area, knew not what he faced. By 12 December, the Army of the Potomac, although still intact, was in full retreat back across the Rappahannock, having suffered dreadful losses – 12,500 Union dead, wounded and missing against 5000 Confederate casualties.

Neither rising body counts nor declining enlistments deterred Lincoln in his unconscionable drive to do "good" with other people's lives. The next commander appointed for the "march to Richmond" was Major General Joseph "Fighting Joe" Hooker. Under him, the Army of the Potomac confronted Lee in early May of 1863 at Chancellorsville, ten miles west of Fredericksburg. Although the Army of Northern Virginia had been reduced to less than 40,000 men because of Longstreet's departure south for the foraging of provisions, Lee's brilliant tactics once again sent the Union forces reeling back across the Rappahannock in full retreat. "Give us victories," Lincoln had urged Hooker. He got, instead, ignominious defeat, and 24,000 more American casualties, 14,000 Union and 10,000 Confederate. Unfortunately for the South, one of her casualties was "Stonewall" Jackson, shot by his own men. His presence at the coming battle of Gettysburg might have spelled the difference between defeat and victory.

On 3 March 1863, Lincoln signed the Enrollment Act of Conscription that subjected all able-bodied men between 20 and 45 years of age to military service. Wildly unpopular, it provoked nation-wide protests. Most serious were those in New York where Governor Horatio Seymour and other Democratic leaders proclaimed the law unconstitutional. In New York City, four days of large-scale, bloody riots erupted in July just after accounts of the carnage at

Gettysburg were published in the newspapers. Mobs overpowered police and militia, attacked and seized the Second Avenue Armory with its rifles and guns, and set fire to the building. Blacks and abolitionists were especially singled out for assault and many beaten to death. Robbing and looting flourished. Since the act provided for draft exemption on the payment of $300, the Tammany city government voted to pay the money for anyone who might be conscripted. Lincoln rushed the New York 7th regiment back to the city from Gettysburg, and with the help of the police, militia, naval forces and West Point cadets, it managed to restore order. Seymour urged a court test of the law's constitutionality, but it never came to pass. Estimates of property damage amounted to as high as $2 million and casualties to 1000. The original purpose of the law was to spur enlistments, and this it seemed to accomplish. Only 150,000 new recruits, three-quarters of them substitutes, were drafted.

Just days after Chancellorsville, Lee decided for the second time to invade the North. A war of maneuver still afforded his outnumbered army its best and possibly only chance of victory. The Army of the Potomac, now commanded by Major General George Gordon Meade, moved quickly north in pursuit. The two armies met at Gettysburg and there, beginning on 1 July, 160,000 Americans fought to the death in a three-day battle that marked the turning point of the War. Again, the butcher's bill was enormous. Although Union casualties amounted to 20,000 men (25% of the total force), the Confederates suffered even more with a catastrophic loss of 28,000 men (40%). The campaign would mark the last time Lee felt strong enough to take the offensive. After the battle, he led his men on a painful, ten-day retreat back across the Potomac, but his Army of Northern Virginia had survived to fight once again. Although not as badly battered, Meade decided his men needed time for recuperation, and to Lincoln's fury, did not pursue.

Lee's failure to destroy the Union army at Gettysburg was accompanied by an equally calamitous blow to Confederate aspirations when General Ulysses S. Grant occupied Vicksburg MI on the Mississippi River after a 28-day siege. With Memphis and New Orleans already in Union hands, this river port remained as the sole barrier to the shipment of midwestern produce to New Orleans and overseas, and its fall considerably ameliorated western opposition to the War. Vicksburg, furthermore, served as the only conduit for the shipment of military contraband to Confederate armies along the Mississippi River. Foreign vessels would call at the "backdoor" Mexican port of Matamoros just across the Rio Grande River from Brownsville TX and exchange sorely needed munitions and other supplies for cotton, sugar and rice. A railroad from Brownsville to Vicksburg then transported these to points of need. Nassau, Bermuda and Havana also served as booming contraband depots for blockade-runners to Wilmington NC, Charleston SC and Savannah GA. The Rhett Butler character in the novel and movie *Gone With The Wind* operated out of Wilmington. Despite the disruptions of war, Adam Smith's "invisible hand" was very much in operation. North and South depended on each other, the former for cotton, sugar, rice and tobacco and the latter for salt, shoes, clothing and munitions. Market forces were much too extensive for government agents to control, and black market operations continued in full swing throughout the conflict. No war was necessary to

"Preserve the Union," only less government. As abolitionist Wendell Phillips had so accurately intoned, "The laws of trade will bind us together, as they do all other lands."

In the end, a killer President finally got a killer general to carry out the mass murders needed to end the War. Lincoln appointed Grant as General-in-Chief in recognition of his bloody victories at Shiloh and Vicksburg in the western theater, retaining Meade as commander of the Army of the Potomac. Confident that he could defeat Lee's forces by grinding them down in a war of human attrition, Grant crossed the Rapidan River in the spring of 1864, and the nation entered the final and most bitter phase of the War. As had the others before him, Grant quickly discovered that there would be no easy wins against Lee. Wilderness, Spotsylvania, Cold Harbor, Petersburg - the casualties in these final campaigns of the War dwarfed those earlier. Taking losses of as much as two to one, Grant pushed relentlessly on to Richmond. It took another year of fighting before Lee finally realized that the South had no young men left to sacrifice. For all practical purposes, the War ended with his surrender at Appomattox on 9 April 1865, just five days before Lincoln was assassinated.

CHAPTER XXXII

THE FRUITS OF WAR

When the government fears the people, it is liberty. When the people fear the government, it is tyranny.

Thomas Paine

A billion here, a billion there, and soon you're talking about real money.

Everett Dirkson, Senator from Illinois

On 19 November 1863, Abraham Lincoln delivered his terse and oft-quoted Gettysburg Address. Orating on a battlefield that had seen 48,000 casualties in three days of furious fighting, he began his speech employing language found in both the Bible and the Declaration of Independence: "Four score and seven years ago our fathers brought forth upon this continent a new nation, conceived in liberty and dedicated to the proposition that all men are created equal." And he ended it with "that this nation shall have a new birth of freedom; and that this government of the people, by the people, for the people, shall not perish from the earth." Now, as is so often the case, much more can be learned about a person not from what is said but from what is not said. And what Lincoln did not say speaks volumes. By invoking Scripture, he implicated God as the scapegoat for all the killing. He, Lincoln, had been given the power; he, Lincoln, knew the Truth and the Good; and he, Lincoln, was merely carrying out God's will "on earth, as it is in Heaven." Law and order, it had to be upheld; the Union, it had to be preserved. A George III reincarnated, that is how he appeared to many. Not a word did he say about those other lines in the Declaration of Independence, "... that whenever any form of government becomes destructive of these ends [life, liberty, and the pursuit of happiness], it is the right of the people to alter or to abolish it, and to institute a new government ..." In Lincoln's eyes, it would seem, the Declaration of Independence justified rebellion, but not secession. Which leads us to the final line in the speech: "... that this government of the people, by the people, for the people, shall not perish from the earth."

Just what kind of government did Lincoln have in mind? Certainly not Jefferson's idea of limited government based on "enumerated powers." According to his long-time friend and law partner, William Herndon, Lincoln "hated Jefferson as a man and a politician." What Lincoln meant was the old Whig idea of a big, intrusive, mercantilist government based on "implied powers," the kind of governance so emphatically rejected by Americans in previous elections. As put forth by Senator Sherman in phrases befitting Karl Marx, "Nationalize as much as possible, even the currency, so as to make men love their country before their states. All private interests, all local interests, all banking interests, the interests of individuals, everything, should be subordinate now to the interest of the Government." It was the intention of the Republican Party, as it is with both Republicans and Democrats today, to make Americans mere servants of the state, not the other way around. "Ask not what your country can do for you, but what you can do for your country," John Kennedy would spout forth one hundred years later. And, with southern representation gone and Republicans dominating the Congress, changing the nation's course presented little problem. Republicans would steer the ship of state into the future not with Adam Smith's "invisible hand" or Oliver Wendell Holmes' "cautious hand," but with Karl Marx's increasingly heavy hand.

The Revenue Act of 1 July 1862, passed soon after the Legal Tender Act, provided a foretaste of Lincoln's "new birth of freedom." It was the country's first T. O. E. – a tax on everything. It levied monthly taxes on the gross receipts of transportation companies, on bond interest, on the surplus funds accumulated by financial and insurance institutions, and on auction sales of hogs, cattle and sheep. It levied a quarterly tax on the gross receipts from newspaper advertisements. It imposed a labyrinth of annual licenses on bankers, auctioneers, wholesale and retail dealers, pawn brokers, distillers, brewers, jugglers, confectioners, horse dealers, cattle brokers, candle makers, soap makers, coal and oil distillers, peddlers, apothecaries, photographers, lawyers and physicians. It charged hotels, inns and taverns with license fees of $5 to $200 depending on yearly rents, eating establishments $10, theaters $100, circuses $50, bowling and billiard rooms according to the number of alleys and tables. Personal property – carriages ($1 to $6), gold watches ($1 or $2), gold and silver plate (50¢ and 5¢ per troy ounce), yachts and pleasure boats ($5 for a displacement of 10 tons or less and $100 for displacements of more than 10 tons), pianos and other parlor instruments ($2 or $4), billiard tables ($10) and feathers, leather, iron goods, gunpowder and telegrams among a vast number of other items - became taxable on an annual basis. Furthermore, it placed a 2% tax on state bank notes and reintroduced from colonial days the stamp duties on legal and business documents, medicines, playing cards and cosmetics. All this on a nation that had been free of internal taxation since the War of 1812!

In addition to the excises, a new income tax supplanted the one passed in the previous year. It taxed net incomes of $600 to $10,000 at 3% and those above at 5%. As a graduated tax, it violated the uniformity provision of the Constitution, but no challenge arose. Also imposed for the first time were a small inheritance tax and withholding taxes on dividends, interest and federal salaries. The tax raised only $2.7 million in 1862-1863, but that jumped to $20.2 million in the next year. Because the taxmen believed that many large income-earners were eluding them, Congress raised the rate on incomes over $5,000 to 10% and authorized revenue agents to estimate incomes. The fine for non-compliance was increased to 25% of the amount due and that for filing a fraudulent return to 50%. Tax returns were even made available to the newspapers in a move to increase compliance. By 1866, income tax revenues totaled $73 million, 30% of federal revenues, primarily derived from three states, New York, Pennsylvania and Massachusetts. But hostility toward the tax built up steadily, and it petered out in 1872. For the next forty-one years, the federal government would be supported solely by consumption taxes, mainly tariff duties, as it had for most of its existence.

The Revenue Act also created a Bureau of Internal Revenue to supervise tax collection. George Boutwell, the first Commissioner of Internal Revenue, described the Bureau as "the largest government department ever organized." Shades of Diocletian! While Boutwell and his staff of bureaucrats prepared the maze of regulations and forms used in assessing and collecting the taxes, Lincoln issued a series of executive orders dividing all states and territories into collection districts. For each district, he appointed a collector and an assessor. Each district was further divided into divisions headed by an assistant assessor and deputy collectors. All persons, partnerships, firms, associations and corporations were required to submit to the assessor of their district a list showing the amounts of their annual incomes, all articles subject to tax, and the quantity of taxable goods to be sold. And it was still not nearly enough to pay the $3.5 billion cost of the War!

With Jay Cooke & Company fully engaged in selling the 5/20s and the state-chartered banks loathe to buy government bonds except at very high interest rates, the time had come to secure the extra financing needed for both the War and Lincoln's "New Deal." Only with a new monetary system in place could this be done. The very efficient free-banking chaon of the previous decades had to be discarded in favor of something more conducive to government spending, something like William Paterson's "Fund for Perpetual Debt" and Alexander Hamilton's Bank of the United States. To this end, the Cooke brothers got Chase and Sherman to sponsor the National Currency Act of 1863, later to be amended by the National Banking Act of 1864. Its preamble reads as follows: "An Act to provide a National Currency by a pledge of United States Bonds, and to provide for the circulation and redemption thereof." The Act created a system of mini-Banks of England, nationally chartered and empowered to issue a uniform currency supplied by the Comptroller of the Currency, a newly formed office (OCC) in the Treasury Department. It was expected that the new national banks would soon supersede and do away with state-chartered banks, thereby basing the nation's money supply squarely on the size of the government debt. As with the 1st and 2nd Banks of the United States, none of the Constitution's enumerated powers permitted politicians to print money or charter a private institution. Nevertheless, the new banking system would persist unchallenged until replaced by the equally unconstitutional Federal Reserve Act of 1913.

As we chaosticians might expect with the onset of centralization, it caused more monetary instability than ever before. Severe and widespread economic disruptions erupted during the Panics of 1873, 1884, 1890, 1893 and 1907, and to these were added frequent liquidity squeezes, bank runs, stock market collapses and bank failures. It is hard to know what else our confiscatory lawmakers could have expected; a large fraction of the money supply now depended on government spending rather than on the needs of businessmen and farmers.

And, as it had for England, the new policy of a perpetual national debt would have perpetual military ramifications in times to come. Along with the extraordinary spending power handed to politicians and the huge profits derived from servicing the debt would come men of great power, men who knew not the consequences of their actions; but, of course, they thought they did. Again, the question surges to the fore: Do central banks operated by political appointees do a better job of stabilizing markets than the cumulative private decisions of hundreds of bankers each of whose livelihoods hang on the line?

Under the terms of the Currency Act, any association of people could apply to the Comptroller of the Currency for a bank charter, providing they met certain financial requirements and complied with numerous regulations. An initial capital of not less than $100,000 was required for banks located in cities with a population greater than 50,000 and not less than $20,000 for smaller communities. An association could then buy 6% U.S. bonds and, after transferring them to Treasury, receive from the Comptroller of the Currency newly created currency not exceeding 90% of the par value of said bonds. As with the Bank of England, the association would then benefit not only from the 6% interest on its bonds deposited at Treasury, but also from the interest on its loan portfolio. Because of its government bond backing, the new currency, like the Federal Reserve note of today, incurred interest payments ultimately to be borne by the taxpayer. Notes in denominations of $1, $2, $3, $5, $10, $20, $50, $100, $500 and $1000 were authorized. They bore the name of the issuing bank and were legal tender for all payments, including those for taxes and public lands, but not those for import duties and the interest on government bonds, both of which still had to be paid in gold. The Act limited the total issue of currency to $300 million. In the wake of the Panic of 1873, Senator Sherman sponsored a bill eliminating the ceiling.

Jay Cooke received the initial charter under the new Act when he organized The First National Bank of Philadelphia. As fiscal agent for the government, Cooke's house occupied the enviable position of selling bonds to the new national banks in addition to having the other benefits of government debt. But the build-up of the national banking system did not proceed as expected; most state-chartered banks refused to convert and remained outside the system. The member banks of the New York Clearing House (whose notes commanded a premium over greenbacks) refused even to admit the newly organized national banks into membership, considering them dangerous institutions subject to tyrannical regulation. Restrictive reserve ratios of 25% mandated for big city banks and 15% for smaller country banks were particularly oppressive. These compared to the 10%-15% ratios in common practice during the freebanking era. Many state banks could afford neither the capitalization requirements for conversion nor the costs of compliance. By the end of 1863, only 71 national banks were in operation compared to over 1600 state banks. One year later, there were still only 638.

To speed up the formation of national banks, Lincoln signed into law the National Banking Act of 1865. It levied a 10% tax on the notes issued by state banks, to take effect 1 July 1866, and effectively removed the profitability from their issue. Conversions now proceeded in droves. By the end of 1865, there were 1601 national banks, 922 of which were state bank conversions, and less than 300 state banks. The latter, it was thought, were on their way to extinction. Fortunately, it did not happen, for by 1867 the decline had ceased. In the following four years, their number expanded so rapidly that deposits at non-national commercial banks roughly equaled deposits at national banks. The reason? Commercial banks introduced nontaxable checking accounts to replace note issue. From then until now, a dual banking system has prevailed with the two classes of banks about equal in the sizes of their deposits. Competition obviously leveled the playing field for debt financing. We can only imagine what might have happened to America's growth rate in the post-bellum decades if our banking system at the time consisted only of a government-sponsored monopoly of national banks. As it was, Treasury's monetary powers were still great because its ability to deposit and withdraw funds from commercial banks affected reserve ratios. But the heady pace of post-War economic expansion held the proportion of government spending to GDP at the remarkably low figure of 1%. Treasury bank deposits, as a result, remained small relative to either its currency holdings or the public's bank deposits, thus limiting the deleterious effects of constant Treasury meddling in the money markets. Economic progress in the southern states lagged far behind the rest of the country as the South went from the chaos of war to the chaos of reconstruction. Northern farmers too did not fare well. With the introduction of new machinery, they over-produced for the domestic market and were forced to depend more and more on foreign markets to get reasonable prices and profits. But the Republican high tariff policy penalized them in exactly the same way as southern cotton planters, and they too suffered.

Lincoln's "New Deal" removed the rock that held back the landslide toward the bloated, hyper-regulating government we have today. In short order, the nation got, in addition to a new central banking system and taxes on everything, a high tariff and an expanded postal monopoly (1861), a Department of Agriculture, a Homestead Act, the Morrill Land-Grant College Act, and a Bureau of Printing and Engraving (1862), a National Academy of Science and "free" urban mail delivery (1863), an Office of Immigration, a Railway Mail Service and a Money Order System (1864). Despite the escalating costs of the War, Lincoln found the money to staff all the newly established bureaucracies. And as had been foreseen by John Calhoun fifteen years earlier, America saw the beginnings of a major special interest constituency, an "active, vigilant, and well trained corps, which lives on Government, or expects to live on it; which prospers most when the revenues are greatest, the Treasury the fattest, and the expenditures the most profuse," and which will faithfully support "whatever system shall extract most from the pockets of the rest of the community, to be emptied into theirs." An extensive evaluation of that "active, vigilant, and well-trained corps" I reserve for Volume II of this history.

The House of Cooke met chaos in 1870. Overextended through the financing of a second American trans-continental railroad, the Northern Pacific, Jay Cooke & Company declared bankruptcy. That opened the door for new firms to become major players in the ever-growing government debt market, the most influential by far being Drexel, Morgan & Company. Cooke himself was lucky enough to make more than a million dollars in a Nevada silver mine speculation.

CHAPTER XXXIII

OUR FATHER WHO ART IN WASHINGTON: HOW HE TAKETH FROM US OUR DAILY BREAD

Something Wicked This Way Comes

Ray Bradbury title

You furnish the pictures and I'll furnish the war.

Newspaper publisher William Randolph Hearst, cable to artist Frederic Remington in Cuba, 1898

The makers of our Constitution undertook to secure conditions favorable to the pursuit of happiness ... They sought to protect Americans in their beliefs, their thoughts, their emotions and their sensations. They conferred, as against the Government, the right to be let alone — the most comprehensive of rights and the right most valued by civilized men. To protect that right, every unjustifiable intrusion by the Government upon the privacy of the individual, whatever the means employed, must be deemed a violation of the Fourth Amendment.

Supreme Court Justice Louis Brandeis (Olmstead vs. United States, 1928)

Having left home to escape Napoleon's compulsory draft, a teenage, Austrian-born Francis Martin Drexel (1792-1863) wandered Europe supporting himself as an itinerant painter of houses and coaches. Never could it have entered his mind that thirty years later he would follow in Robert Fulton's footsteps and transform himself from artist to entrepreneur and help found a financial dynasty that persists to this day. After floundering about in various jobs and developing his artistic talents, he decided that there existed little opportunity for success in Europe and sailed for America in 1817. Settling in Philadelphia, he married and installed himself in a studio painting portraits. His work was quickly recognized. In 1818 the Philadelphia Academy of Fine Arts hung no fewer than nine of his oils and a number of his crayon drawings, and he contributed regularly to their exhibitions. From 1826 to 1830, he toured Bolivia, Chile, Ecuador and Peru painting portraits of political leaders. Dissatisfied with the profits derived from an artistic career and facing severe competition from the likes of

Thomas Sully and members of the famous Peale family, he made several attempts at entering the business world. Finally, in 1837 at age 46, he put his palette aside for good and opened a currency brokerage office in Louisville KY. The demise of the 2nd Bank of the United States had opened new horizons for brokers. Through an inter-bank clearance network for the notes of state-chartered banks – other than gold and silver the only money available at the time – they provided liquidity to the currency markets and, if successful, could derive a tidy profit for themselves. Drexel & Company was soon able to expand its operations into a private bank and, when the Mexican War broke out, float government bonds to help the politicians pay for it. The Company also entered the emerging field of railroad financing, a business ignored as much too risky and even disreputable by the large northeastern banks.

In 1851, father Francis turned the firm over to his two sons, Anthony Joseph and Frank, and taking advantage of the California gold rush, opened a highly profitable branch in San Francisco. To meet the increasing demands for railroad funds, Drexel & Company expanded to Chicago and New York, and later allied itself with the large London bank of George Peabody, one of whose partners was Junius Spencer Morgan (1813-1890). Morgan, who hailed from a wealthy New England family, took over the Peabody bank in 1864, renaming it J. S. Morgan & Company. In London, he handled most British investments in U. S. government bonds and, in one of the more spectacular transactions of the time, headed a syndicate that loaned the French government $500 million to help finance the Franco-Prussian War. Nothing, he learned, generates debt – and profit – like war. The greater the debt, the higher the profits.

In 1870, Junius Morgan, together with his son John Pierpont (1837-1913) and Jay Cooke's former partner, Anthony Joseph Drexel (1826-1893), organized Drexel, Morgan & Company, the name changed to J.P. Morgan & Company upon Drexel's death. When in 1870 Congress authorized the sale of $1.5 billion of Treasury securities carrying interest rates varying from 4% to 5% in exchange for higher yielding wartime issues, Drexel, Morgan seized the opportunity to break Cooke's monopoly and become the chief source of government financing. In 1871, the new company underwrote the army payroll; in 1872, in conjunction with the London banks of Nathan Mayer Rothschild, Junius Morgan and the Baring Brothers, it underwrote $300 million of government securities at 5% interest; in 1876, there was another $300 million with Seligman Brothers of New York added to the syndicate; and in 1877, the same partners, with Rose & Company added, refinanced another $700 million of 4% government debt. After the Panic of 1893, Wall Street firms headed by J. P. Morgan bought $200 million worth of government bonds for gold, thereby helping to preserve the credit of the United States. The discount on the purchase was rumored to be large, but never divulged. It should be understood that from the Civil War to the 1890s, virtually no manufacturing operation had reached a size necessary to take advantage of the corporate form. Bond underwritings, therefore, were confined largely to railroad, state and U. S. government securities. By 1890, railroad passenger and freight revenues had climbed over the $1 billion mark, more than twice federal tax receipts.

Their appetites whetted, American investment bankers now wanted more in the way of profits and looked to expand operations abroad. Following in the footsteps of the Rothschilds, the Barings and other great European merchants of debt, they too hoped to profit from underwritings in foreign markets. A series of articles on their objectives in the 1894 *Bankers' Magazine* concludes with this provocative statement: If "we could wrest the South American markets from Germany and England and permanently hold them, that would indeed be a conquest worth perhaps a heavy sacrifice." Or, in other words, for economic and financial gain – war! It was not only for the rabble to pay taxes in support of government debt, it was for the rabble to die for it. And, coincidentally, American foreign policy switched abruptly from one of peace and nonintervention to one of imperialist expansion. And the national debt escalated accordingly.

As the world's foremost industrial and agricultural power at the time, it was all but inevitable that America's presence in international affairs should grow. Commercial relations with other countries had to be negotiated, business interests abroad and trade routes protected, and national security provided for. The world had become much smaller since the days of Washington's Farewell Address and the avoidance of foreign entanglements. But the Founding Fathers, cognizant of the rise of the British Empire, had foreseen the eventuality of a nation that would ultimately advance to "Power, Consequence and Grandeur." And they specifically authorized the federal government to conduct foreign affairs and establish a strong national defense. There can be little argument as to the prerogatives of government in this area. No better way of handling such matters has been suggested, even though political mismanagement almost always entails terribly excessive waste and inefficiency. Even so, a country as rich as America at the time should have experienced few financial problems in handling her expanded international commitments. But, as Adam Smith had advised English politicians long before, a policy of imperialism and colony acquisition, as opposed to free trade, generates budget deficits and little in the way of benefits. And that was how it would play out for America.

The Spanish-American War of 1898 became the first important manifestation of what would be called "dollar diplomacy." An explosion aboard the U. S. battleship *Maine* in Havana harbor – undoubtedly caused by spontaneous combustion in her coal storage bins, a not uncommon occurrence of the times – sunk the ship and railroaded us into a seemingly senseless war with Spain over Cuba. The Spanish government wanted no part of war and would have acceded to almost any terms offered to avoid it, including Cuban independence. Also opposed was President William McKinley (1843-1901), a Civil War veteran well acquainted with the horrors of that conflict. But "yellow press" journalism about alleged Spanish atrocities and threats to American sugar interests compelled McKinley to ask for a declaration of war. Congress complied and appropriated $50 million to finance that "splendid little war." It set a precedent. The American taxpayer would now be called on to underwrite the risks attending to imperialist initiatives both public and private.

Fifty-four hundred dead were recorded as a result of the War, four hundred in battle and the rest from yellow fever, dysentery and heat prostration. Although Cuba and the few other islands still held by Spain in the New World offered few attractions, the War put Latin American countries on notice that America intended to intervene in their affairs whenever "necessary." American troops would be sent south no fewer than thirty-two times in the next thirty years – to Nicaragua, Panama, Honduras, Haiti, the Dominican Republic, and Mexico. Cuba came under American "protection" and Puerto Rico was annexed. At the same time, our new imperialist politicians, headed by Assistant Secretary of the Navy Theodore Roosevelt, grasped the opportunity to make America's presence felt in Far Eastern markets by ordering the seizure of the Spanish-held Philippine Islands. A naval squadron commanded by Admiral George Dewey took Manila in May of 1898 aided by Emilio Aguinaldo, a Filipino independence fighter who had long sought secession from Spain. But when America reneged on her promise of independence, Aguinaldo conducted a guerrilla war against an American army of 70,000 that saw the killing of 20,000 Filipino combatants and a huge number of civilian casualties. American casualties were 4374 from all causes, including 1037 killed and 2818 wounded. Thus began the "righteous conquest of foreign markets," as it was later phrased by Woodrow Wilson.

A gigantic public works project became the next item to weigh on the federal budget. As we have already noted, an inter-ocean Isthmus canal had been discussed for centuries, and America's new imperialism revived interest in it. Two fact finding commissions appointed by Congress in the late 1890s favored a canal through Nicaragua as most practicable from both engineering and financial standpoints. It would follow the route pioneered by Cornelius Vanderbilt in 1852. Two earlier attempts at building a canal through Panama by private French companies, the first headed by Suez Canal builder Ferdinand de Lesseps, had failed with the loss of more than 20,000 lives and hundreds of millions of francs. Even though de Lesseps had ridden the Panama Railroad with Colonel Totten to assess the costs, he drastically underestimated them. Labor shortages arising from disease, mainly yellow fever, and inadequate excavation equipment had quickly burned up available cash. Because Europeans had not enthused over the project, de Lesseps had managed to raise only an unnerving 8% of the project's estimated cost of $100 million.

Had he survived the assassination attempt on his life in 1901, President McKinley would probably have signed a bill authorizing funds for a Nicaraguan canal. At this point, stockholders of the French Compagnie Nouvelle du Canal de Panama, the successor to the de Lesseps company, and Philippe Bunau-Varilla, its chief engineer, saw an opportunity to recoup their losses. Although virtually bankrupt and unable to obtain the funds necessary to continue work on the canal, the Compagnie did possess a concession from the Colombian government to build a canal across Panama, at that time a province of Colombia. This they offered to the United States government for $100 million, and Bunau-Varilla hired lobbyist William Nelson Cromwell, a New York lawyer with close ties to the Republican Party and J. P. Morgan, to press their case. The price of the concession was much too high, given a cost estimate of canal construction by American engineers of $400 million, and it made the Panama route financially undoable. Cromwell and Morgan, however, formed a secret syndicate of Wall Street firms that managed to buy most of the stock in the Compagnie from small European stockholders for somewhere between $3.5 and $12 million and then priced the concession to the U. S. government at $40 million. After some intense lobbying and a $60,000 donation to a Republican campaign fund chaired by Senator Mark Hanna of OH, Congress and McKinley's successor in the Presidency, Theodore Roosevelt, approved the Panama route.

In January 1903, Congress approved a payment of $10 million plus $250 thousand annually for the right of America to build and operate a canal. The Colombian Senate, however, rejected the proposed treaty, outraging President Roosevelt. "We may have to give a lesson to these jackrabbits," he stormed. Soon after, in 1904, he added the "Roosevelt corollary" to the Monroe Doctrine: "Any country whose people conduct themselves well can count upon our friendship. Chronic wrongdoing, however, … may force the United States to exercise an international police power." Especially, I might add, to free foreign investments of any risk, the cost of course to be borne by American taxpayers.

Seeing their $40 million going down the drain, the Wall Street syndicate arranged with Bunau-Varilla to instigate a secession movement in Panama. Financed with $250 thousand, he equipped a force of one hundred men to set up a new and independent government. By "happenstance," the U. S. battleship *Nashville* arrived in Colón on 2 November 1903 and prevented the disembarkation of 450 Colombian marines arrived by gunboat to quell the rebellion. On 4 November, the new Panamanian "government" declared its independence and appointed Bunau-Varilla minister to the United States. On 18 November, the United States signed a treaty with Panama giving her a ten-mile wide "Canal Zone" strip across the Isthmus for building the canal. The newly installed government ended up with the original package of $10 million plus the annual fee of $250 thousand originally earmarked for Colombia, and the Wall Street syndicate pocketed $40 million of U. S. taxpayer money.

Carlos Juan Finlay (1813-1915), a Cuban physician, first postulated the mosquito as the carrier of yellow fever in 1881. He conducted years of research to verify his theory, but few in the medical profession took "the mosquito man" seriously. At the time, Louis Pasteur's germ theory of infectious diseases had yet to achieve widespread recognition. Only when Major Walter Reed (1850-1902) arrived in Havana after the Spanish- American War as head of the U. S. Army Yellow Fever Commission was Finlay's work carefully evaluated. Finlay opened all his records to the Commission, furnishing the basis for Reed to conduct an elaborate series of controlled experiments that confirmed the mosquito theory. Using army volunteers as guinea pigs – courageous men indeed considering that mortality rates for the disease hovered about 45% and could approach 85% - he established beyond doubt the mechanism by which the disease was transmitted. The first steps to combat the constantly recurring yellow fever epidemics in Havana came with the arrival in 1898 of Colonel William Crawford Gorgas (1854-1920), Chief Sanitation Officer for the Department of Cuba. Skeptical at first, Gorgas became an ardent believer in the new theory and launched a massive program to eradicate the Aedes mosquito, the carrier of the disease. He segregated stricken patients, quarantined infected communities, and listed and eliminated every possible mosquito breeding ground in the city. It took more than two years, but in the end he freed Havana of the disease. His success prompted his assignment to Panama, where he again succeeded in stamping out yellow fever. His work made possible not only the building of the Panama Canal, but also the virtual elimination of the disease worldwide.

With the yellow fever problem solved, there remained intractable engineering problems to be dealt with. George Washington Goethals (1858-1928), taking over after two chief engineers on the project had resigned, managed to excavate the crumbling sub-strata encountered at the Culebra Cut, level mountains to reduce the altitude of the canal, build concrete locks on a scale never before attempted, exercise a tight vigil over expenses, and finally complete the canal in 1914 under budget. Without the extraordinary efforts of Finlay, Reed, Goethals and Gorgas – and let us not forget William Aspinwall whose Panama Railroad proved essential for the transport of men, equipment, dirt and rock – the Panama project could have been a $400 million fiasco for the American taxpayer. It was a lot of money for the time, considering that the government's yearly tax receipts averaged about $600 million over those years.

Was it worth it? Who knows? As a pure business proposition, no private promoter other than de Lesseps thought so, and he failed. And the "invisible hand" did not pick out another William Aspinwall to undertake the building of an Isthmus canal. Because America's trans-continental railroads had greatly diminished the importance of such a waterway, the main impetus for the project was as a defense measure; a one ocean navy could handle both the Atlantic and Pacific if the need arose. As it was, the project significantly accreted the national debt. That would climb to $2.6 billion in 1910 versus $1.2 billion in 1900.

A busybody *extraordinaire* in the mode of Alexander Hamilton, President Theodore Roosevelt appeared on the political scene after the McKinley assassination in 1901. Ignoring George Washington's sage advice on the avoidance of foreign entanglements, he created two "butterflys" that have had lasting effects on America's future course. His "mediation" in 1905 of the Russo-Japanese War handed Korea over to Japan and helped balloon her imperialist ambitions to the point of attacking Pearl Harbor in 1941. For his efforts, Roosevelt was awarded the Nobel peace prize in 1907. His intervention in the 1908 Algeciras conference to resolve conflicting foreign commercial interests in Morocco favored France, irritated Germany, and exacerbated the frictions that eventually lead to World War I and America's involvement in it. On the domestic front, Republican Roosevelt followed Republican Lincoln and hatched a "square deal" of bureaucratic agencies empowered to do good. Here I only need mention that these initiatives helped mushroom government debt to new heights and led to persistent calls for reinstatement of the income tax, a dead issue since its expiration in 1872. Not that the politicians were ignorant of its vast potential for draining money from the citizenry's pockets. Members of Congress had in fact introduced no fewer than 68 bills hoping to revive it, all of which died for lack of support. When in 1893 one finally made it into law, it was struck down by the Supreme Court as an un-apportioned and therefore unconstitutional direct tax. Nonetheless, the Democratic Party, repudiating its Jeffersonian heritage, supported an income tax amendment in the party platforms of 1896 and 1908. Roosevelt and his successor in office, William Howard Taft (1857-1930), also called for its enactment. In 1909, with both political parties in accord on grabbing the people's money, a proposed amendment passed overwhelmingly in Congress and was sent off to the states for ratification. Not much opposition was expected from western and southern states; very few of their citizens made enough money to be affected. The northeastern states, where all the rich supposedly dwelt, were expected to balk. They didn't. Politicians there well recognized the bounty up for grabs. By constitutionalizing the income tax, they could also provide for themselves through state and local income taxes. Remember, the people were not voting on this issue so affecting their pocketbooks; according to Article V of the Constitution, their elected representatives in the state legislatures were deciding for them.

With Wyoming's ratification of the 16th Amendment in 1913, Americans placed at the disposal of politicians easy access to their money. "All good citizens will willingly and cheerfully support this, the fairest and cheapest of all taxes," proclaimed the tax-writing House Ways and Means Committee. Ah, yes. Humpty-Dumpty again! As with most political pronouncements, this one meant exactly the opposite. What matter to these "robber barons" that they were creating a giant octopus whose tentacles snaked right around the Bill of Rights and into the most private of all concerns, a person's finances. What matter that they were granting to a very expensive government tax-collecting agency Gestapo-like powers. What matter that they were making war much easier to finance. "The legislature [Congress] is in session," Daniel Webster had warned, "and no man's property is safe." The first income tax bill, passed in a special session of Congress in 1913 and signed into law by newly elected President Woodrow Wilson, placed a tax of 1% on incomes above $3000 and a surcharge of between 2% and 7% on incomes above $20,000. But from a wee acorn a great oak tree grows, and Americans would soon pay dearly for giving up their precious "unalienable right" to financial privacy, supposedly guaranteed by the Fourth Amendment to the Constitution: "The right of the people to be secure in their persons, houses, papers, and effects, against unreasonable searches and seizures, shall not be violated … ."

The National Banking Act of 1863 was obviously not working. Another in a long line of panics erupted in 1907, and it brought forth calls for a government-sponsored central bank to solve all our economic problems. If some centralization of the banking system under the National Banking Act did not work, why not give the politicians all the power necessary to make it work properly? And so the great banking minds from all over the world gathered at Jekyll's Island off the coast of Georgia to confront chaos, and what they came up with was the Federal Reserve System – an oxymoronic benign-dictator solution! When President Taft expressed his opposition, former President Roosevelt was brought out of retirement to run as a third party candidate in the 1912 election, ensuring the defeat of Taft and the election of "Democrat" Woodrow Wilson who was known to favor a central bank. The bill establishing the Federal Reserve barely squeaked through Congress, and Wilson signed it into law on 23 December 1913. Gone now were any restraints on government spending. Gone now was the possibility of a free-banking chaon. And gone was all chance for a tax-free nation with a debt-free, interest-free currency. Pandora's box was opened wider, and America would get in the next hundred years an insidious package of war, depression, inflation, monetary instability and a mountainous pileup of national debt. Fortunately, despite all the chaos heaped on it, our largely free market economy was able to deliver a four-fold advance in our standard of living, a rate much reduced from the prior hundred years.

In 1914 World War I broke out in Europe. In that same year, the House of Morgan, through its connection with the House of Rothschild bank in London, became the fiscal agent of the British and French governments, responsible for underwriting their war bonds in America and purchasing goods and munitions for use against Germany. It was a godsend. The near bankruptcy of the New York, New Haven and Hartford Railroad, in which Morgan owned a large position, had shaken the company's financial foundations. The great profits from war activities, however, soon remedied that situation. In 1914 Morgan made its first loan of $12 million to Russia. There followed a $50 million loan to France and, then, through various banking syndicates, loans amounting to more than $1.5 billion to Allied governments. The profits and fortunes of American bankers and exporters became irretrievably tied to an Allied victory – a German win would have probably rendered all the loans un-repayable. And so began a propaganda campaign of stupendous proportions in which an inflammatory "yellow press" corps exploited alleged German atrocities toward civilians and the sinking of British "passenger" ships by German submarines to push America into a ghastly foreign war. Neither a stalemate through exhaustion nor a German victory, the most likely outcomes without American intervention, posed any threat to the nation.

Woodrow Wilson, former president of Princeton University, author, teacher, lecturer, political scientist and intellectual mutton head for all ages, won reelection in 1916 on his record of "keeping us out of the war." But it was not long before he reneged on his promise. Suddenly become a visionary with grandiose ideas, he planned to intervene and make the world safe for democracy, establish a world government to abolish war and resolve all disputes between nations, and just possibly become the first President of the World. To realize these goals, he had to have a say in the peace treaty. And to have a say in the peace treaty, America had to fight. Wilson was very much aware that a major obstacle, financing a war of this magnitude, had been removed by the new income tax and the Federal Reserve System. Getting the people's money was not a problem any more. America entered the War "to end all wars" and broke a stalemate in favor of the Allies.

What was our reward? 124,000 American soldiers killed and 236,000 wounded; a top income tax rate jumped to 77% and millions of previously untouched people filing returns; a national debt standing at $25.9 billion; and the country gripped in an exceptionally severe post-War depression – the new Federal Reserve System notwithstanding. Grim, yes, but what happened on the foreign scene was more catastrophic still. A League of Nations formed and was rejected by the U. S. Senate. Who needed another layer of government on top of the abysmal ones now in power? America seemed to say. The Versailles Peace Treaty negotiations got under way, and while Wilson hallucinated in the nobility of his vision, the victorious Allies drew up the crushing terms that backed Germany into a corner, reduced her to desperation, and paved the way for Adolf Hitler, Josef Stalin and World War II. The war "to end all wars" became the war "to end all peace." The carving up of Palestine, part of the Turkish Ottoman Empire and a German war ally, into Jewish and Arab pieces has consequences of tremendous import for us today almost one hundred years later. Can anyone imagine a more terrifying scenario of post-World War I events that might have followed a German victory?

In Ian Fleming's book *Goldfinger*, the title character speaks of a low probability event as "happenstance" upon one occurrence, "coincidence" upon two occurrences, and "enemy action" upon three occurrences. So, let me conclude Volume I of this history with this pertinent question: What can be made of the following list of "low probability" events, through all of which stalk money and death?

1) In 1811, Vice-President George Clinton breaks a tie in the Senate by voting against the re-chartering of the 1st Bank of the United States. He dies less than a year later.

2) In 1832, President Andrew Jackson vetoes a bill rechartering the 2nd Bank of the United States. "You are a den of vipers and thieves," he rages to the bankers, "and I intend to rout you out, and by the eternal God, I will rout you out." In 1835, as noted earlier, Richard Lawrence fails in attempting to assassinate him.

3) President John Tyler, during his term of office 1841-1845, twice vetoes attempts to reinstate a Bank of the United States. He receives hundreds of letters threatening his assassination.

4) Early in 1865, President Abraham Lincoln gives every indication of financing government with unbacked paper currency issues rather than the debt securities he was forced to accept during wartime exigencies. "The money power preys upon the nation in times of peace and conspires against it in times of adversity," he declares. "It is more despotic than monarchy, more insolent that autocracy, more selfish than bureaucracy. It denounces as 'public enemies' all who question its methods or throw light upon its crimes." He is assassinated shortly thereafter by John Wilkes Booth who, along with Rothschild-related bankers Jacob Schiff, Abraham Kuhn and Solomon Loeb, belongs to a secret organization known as the "Knights of the Golden Circle." Izola Forrester, Booth's granddaughter, writes in her book *This One Mad Act* that Booth had been in close contact with mysterious Europeans and had made at least one trip to Europe prior to the assassination.

5) President James Garfield (1831-1881) declares in a speech shortly after his inauguration: "Whosoever controls the volume of money in any country is absolute master of all industry and commerce ... And when you realize that the entire system is very easily controlled, one way or another, by a few powerful men at the top, you will not have to be told how periods of inflation and depression originate." After but four months in office, he is assassinated by Charles Guiteau.

6) In 1900, President William McKinley, an anti-imperialist and hard money advocate, is assassinated by Leon Czolgosz. Originally an espouser of high tariffs, McKinley is about to deliver a speech announcing a new policy of free trade and reciprocal tariff arrangements with Latin America. "Big Stick" Theodore Roosevelt becomes President.

7)   Warren G. Harding (1865-1923) is elected President in a landslide vote in 1920 succeeding Woodrow Wilson. In a brilliant first State of the Union address, he points to the menacingly high national debt and threatens to end a major tax haven of the "moneyed aristocracy": "I think our tax problems, the tendency of wealth to seek non-taxable investments and the menacing increase of public debt, Federal, State, and municipal, all justify a proposal to change the Constitution so as to end the issue of non-taxable bonds. ... the drift of wealth into nontaxable securities is hindering the flow of large capital to our industries, manufacturing, agricultural, and carrying, until we are discouraging the very activities that make our wealth." Despite a severe depression, a crashing stock market and a 15% unemployment rate left over from Wilson, Harding does nothing except reduce income taxes and government spending, despite much advice to the contrary. "Less government in business and more business in government" had been his campaign slogan. By 1922, the depression is over. Returning from a visit to Alaska in July of 1923, Harding develops a severe case of food poisoning and dies of what appears to be either a stroke or a heart attack in San Francisco on 2 August. There is no autopsy. Successor President Calvin Coolidge completes Harding's "return to normalcy" with a further tax reduction to a 25% maximum, paving the way for the massive economic boom of the "roaring twenties." The money lost in the Teapot Dome scandal, for which historians unanimously condemn Harding, is but a drop in the ocean compared to the scandal of World War I.

8)   Louis T. McFadden (1876-1936), Congressman from Pennsylvania and Chairman of the House Committee on Banking and Currency from 1920 to 1931, undergoes two attacks on his life. While alighting from a taxi in front of a Washington hotel, he is the target of two revolver shots. Both miss and are embedded in the cab body. At a Washington political banquet, he almost expires from food poisoning. His life is saved when a physician in attendance procures a stomach pump and administers emergency treatment. McFadden is a vociferous opponent of the Federal Reserve System.

9)   President Harry S. Truman (1884-1972) cuts government spending by two-thirds after World War II despite predictions by Keynesian economists of dire economic consequences. Business booms. On 1 November 1950, two Puerto Rican assassins fail in an attempt to assassinate the President in his temporary residence at Blair House.

10)   President John F. Kennedy (1917-1963), who had taken the first step toward abolishing the Federal Reserve, is assassinated soon after by Lee Harvey Oswald who in turn is murdered by Jack Ruby who in turn dies while awaiting trial.

11)   Robert F. Kennedy (1925-1968), younger brother of John and a shoo-in Presidential candidate for the 1968 Presidential election, is assassinated by Sirhan Sirhan. There can be little doubt that Robert, as Attorney-General in his brother's administration and his trusted advisor, supported John in his action against the Federal Reserve.

CHAPTER XXXIV

C.O.I.T.U.S.
COALITION OPPOSED TO THE INCOME TAX IN THE UNITED STATES

Anybody can make history; only a great man can write it.

Oscar Wilde

Non-fiction is non-existent.

Burton P. Fabricand

Vox populi, Vox Dei

Poet and novelist Peter Rosegger, the phrase "The voice of the people is the voice of God" being his response to Gustav Mahler's dismay at the huge popular success of Richard Strauss' opera *Salome.*

Government is the problem; government is not the solution.

President Ronald Reagan's first inaugural address

Learning hurts. If it doesn't hurt, you're not learning.

Burton P. Fabricand

On a tour of China in 1985, I had the pleasure of meeting Deng Xiaoping (1904-97), Secretary General of China's Communist Party and a truly extraordinary person in my estimation. That you will never hear from our I-square historians, however, for he is the man who introduced into China the novel idea of letting the people rather than the politicians spend their own money. Deng, a friend of one of our group members, arranged a chartered flight to Xian for us and a banquet in the Great Hall at Beijing when we got back. He also spoke like Ronald Reagan: "If you want to bring the initiative of the peasants into play, you should give them the power to make money." And that is exactly what we saw the peasants doing throughout China, people everywhere selling lovely, home-made red jackets, fans and other trinkets for a dollar or two. Since then, China has grown almost as strongly as 19th-century America, and she has become a formidable competitor for the world's resources. That holds true as well for many other newly-arisen powers – Japan, India, Russia, Brazil and the European Union, the latter having reinvigorated Old World economies through its establishment of a huge free trade zone. Their meteoric growth rates relative to ours threaten to reduce twenty-first century America to a third-world status should present trends continue.

My history takes us into the present, to a time when we Americans are about to "sit down to a banquet of consequences." We have squandered too many trillions of dollars for too long, and our luck is about to run out. No longer can we afford thousands of "bridge-tonowhere" programs, inefficient agencies at the federal, state and local levels, and a fraudulent tort bar. These massive and costly intrusions into the private economy have deprived us of the freedoms that made our country great. More and more of our money gets piped into political pockets leaving less and less in private hands for funding research and development, start-up businesses, the modernization and expansion of productive facilities, and the millions of other beneficial ways in which people spend their own money. High taxes are "hindering the flow of large capital to our industries, manufacturing, agricultural, and carrying, until we are discouraging the very activities that make our wealth," as President Warren Harding put it. We are, in effect, killing the goose that lays our golden eggs. Oh, for politicians in the mode of William Pitt the Younger, the Jeffersonian Democrats and Deng Xiaoping, all of whom understood that the basis of democracy and capitalism is, if I may paraphrase the Biblical Moses, "Let my people spend."

What we do today is exactly the opposite; we let the politicians spend for us. Each failure of government policy is met with more government policy to correct what went on before. It is diametrically opposite to private business practices. Our great minds in Washington DC try to "fix" the chaos caused by their meddling in social and economic problems with ever more government programs. Even spurious environmental problems such as "global warming" come under their purview when it comes to getting our money. One might think that in today's technological society, passing a college physics course should serve as a prerequisite for entering the legal profession and politics. But then, attendance at law schools would probably fall to near zero.

As we have seen when dealing with chaos, fixing it almost always engenders unintended consequences and makes matters worse. Our political experts-on-everything have little understanding of the harm they do, no comprehension of the calamities that their noble intentions may beget. And neither does a public brainwashed by a subservient news media and educational establishment into believing that government is the solution and not the problem. Have we become the unknowing children of Hamelin following the Pied Piper of Washington DC into an economic chamber of horrors?

Until the 21st century, unimaginable technological advances have neutralized government-issued chaos and kept the private economy prosperous. But now all has changed. Further progress becomes more and more unlikely as the number of non-producers approaches and threatens to exceed the number of producers. Chaos is being generated on a scale never before seen. It shows up in the huge inflation of the 20th century, in an ever-growing government debt, and in the hyper-regulation of the private economy. No longer can we hope to live smugly off the savings bequeathed to us by our forefathers. No longer do we enjoy the competitive advantages we once had over the government-saturated nations of the 19th and 20th centuries. As befell Rome, the collapse in our currency's value foreshadows a decline in living standards. In the 1970s, the dollar bought 360 yen; today it buys only 100. In 2002, 87¢ could buy one euro; today, it takes $1.60. If its dilution continues at its present pace, can "dollar zero" be far off?

What can be done to stop this march to national suicide? Before attempting an answer, "let experience be our guide" and allow me to recapitulate the lessons learned in Volume I. First and foremost is the fact that private spending in free markets is remarkably efficient. That "truth" was demonstrated beyond a reasonable doubt in the pari mutuel and stock markets and, more importantly for our purposes, in the American consumer markets from 1789 to 1913. During that long span of years, the dollar actually *increased* in value. No correlation existed between strong economic growth and inflation as most economists seem to believe today, except during times of excessive government expenditures. Only with the creation of a central bank, the Federal Reserve System, and the introduction of the income tax in 1913 did that false notion come into fashion. Those two monstrosities placed at the disposal of politicians all the money desired and, of course, made their urge to spend irresistible. If that spending had proved efficient, any inflation should have proved miniscule; the increased production of goods and services would have offset the new money created. That did not happen. What we got instead was a nation "too much governed," all made possible by a tyrannical income tax and a Federal Reserve monetary printing press.

The voice of the people is heard in their spending in free markets. That is another way of defining Adam Smith's "invisible hand." If we are not to abort our drive toward a higher standard of living both for us and our children, we must listen to it. Only in this way can we defy chaos and learn to handle society's very complex problems. "Reason will lead us astray" when dealing with chaos, as our Founding Fathers understood.

The 21st-century's banquet of consequences now comes clearly into focus. We enjoy a standard of living far too high for a government far too big. Once we recognize that "truth," what must be done becomes obvious. First and foremost, we must rid ourselves of the Federal Reserve and the income tax, both of which permit politicians to grab an inordinate amount of our money. There is no need to issue paper money through a private central bank headed by, of all people, a benign dictator in the form of an unelected economist or banker. Why not just let Treasury do it to pay government's obligations, as Abraham Lincoln did during the Civil War? It would give to the people "the greatest blessing they ever had," a debt free, interest-free currency. It is simply outrageous for we the people to pay, as we now do, a half trillion dollars in interest on our currency and bank deposits in support of government debt, and that is in addition to taxes. Furthermore, if Congress should appropriate too much money for inefficient purposes, it would show up in the inflation rate and be clearly visible. Elective action to correct any abuses could then be taken. Can you hear the screams arising from our merchants of debt and the growing hordes of mercenaries feasting on government handouts should this come about?

While we are at it, why not follow Thomas Jefferson and eliminate all internal taxes at the national level along with the exorbitant cost and tyranny of income tax collections? Taxes are unnecessary if government can pay its bills through paper money issuance. America could then return to its 19th-century status of unbelievably strong advances in the standard of living unhindered by too much government. The "invisible hand" would be in complete charge. There would be far fewer nobly-intentioned government programs that sooner or later almost always turn into compost. There would be far fewer bureaucratic regulations that curtail individual freedoms and prevent the emergence of chaons. Once again, we could take pride in an America aspiring to "Power, Consequence, and Grandeur," an America that would have few worries about her place among the world's leading nations.

CHAPTER XXXV

BOOM ...

Secretary Mellon gained more applause for his tax proposal than John Barrymore in Hamlet. It was a tremendous surprise to the professional politicians.

Time Magazine, 19 November 1923

Round up the usual suspects!

Screenwriters Julius J. and Philip G. Epstein and Howard Koch, the line delivered by actor Claude Rains in the movie *Casablanca*

"Nine-tenths of [visitors to the White House] want something they ought not to have. If you keep dead still, they will run down in three or four minutes."

Calvin Coolidge

He was born soon after the Civil War on 2 November 1865 in the small town of Marion OH.

After college and with the help of his father, he acquired the *Marion Star*, a small local newspaper of which he was the chief-ofeverything officer. He bought the newsprint and ink, set the type, ran the presses, wrote the articles and editorials, and sold the advertising. Under his guidance, the *Star* grew into a powerful voice for Republican views in a Democratic region of the state.

He was elected to the state Senate in 1899, to lieutenant governor in 1904, and to the United States Senate in 1914. Nominated by the Republicans, he won the 1920 Presidential election by a landslide 60% majority.

As President, he inherited the worst depression yet experienced by the nation, an unemployment rate of 15%, a wartime inflation that had jumped prices 2½ times, a dangerously unbalanced budget, a skyrocketing national debt, confiscatory taxes, and a people disillusioned and exasperated by a ghastly and useless war. Taking immediate action, he appointed an Adam Smith disciple in the mold of William Pitt the Younger and Albert Gallatin to carry out his program of "normalcy." And, once again, the elitists were confounded, for business boomed. As Secretary of the Treasury, Andrew William Mellon (1855-1937) sponsored legislation that slashed income tax rates down from the top rate of 77% during the Wilson administration to 25% by 1929, ended scores of nuisance taxes on telegraph, telephone, gifts, transportation services and theater admissions, eliminated "excess" profits taxes, lowered the Wilson capital gains tax to 12.5%, dismantled a huge wartime spending apparatus, and cut back sharply on government expenditures. As a result, government tax receipts from an exploding private economy surged to over $4 billion, ensuring balanced federal budgets and a much smaller national debt. And, with more money left in the hands of the people, there ensued the tremendous standard-of-living advances that characterized the 1920s. His example, wholly or in part and with similarly beneficial results, would be followed by future Presidents Harry S. Truman, John F. Kennedy, Ronald Reagan and George W. Bush.

The man responsible for resurrecting our nation's drive to "Power, Consequence, and Grandeur" is commonly considered to be America's worst President – Warren Gamaliel Harding.

"Hmm," we must now ruminate, "how did the achievements of such an apparently great man get spun into such disrepute?" Judging from the above record, we would indeed be most fortunate were he to occupy the Oval Office today. But to answer the question, I must once again "round up the usual suspects." Which means, of course, that influential cadre of academic "I-square" historians whose interpretation of events so displays the "intelligence that can be invested in ignorance when the need for illusion is great."

Suppose I begin with Arthur Schlesinger Jr. According to this bestselling author, the 1920s mark a terrible decade, a dismal valley between Woodrow Wilson's "New Freedom" and Franklin Roosevelt's "New Deal." As he sees it, that foolish, short-sighted Harding-Coolidge-Hoover trio succeeds an idealistic, heroic Wilson and precedes a reincarnation of Wilson in Rooseveltian form. In his *Cycles of American History* (Houghton Mifflin, 1986), Schlesinger finds "truth" in random patterns of history. He divines a "thirty-year cycle [that] accounts both for the era of public purpose – TR in 1901, FDR in 1933, JFK in 1961 – and the high tides of conservative restoration – the 1920s, the 1950s, the 1980s." Obviously a believer in the socialist idea that the business of America is government, he finds himself easily mesmerized by the noble intentions of Wilson and the two Roosevelts. Indeed, in his book (*The Age of Roosevelt: The Coming of the New Deal.* Houghton Mifflin, 1958), he sees Wilson as playing John the Baptist to the messiah of Franklin Delano Roosevelt. Of course, it goes without saying that he displays no understanding of chaos and little knowledge of the financial misdeeds of the times. Nor does he, like all his ilk inhabiting the sanctuary of academe, recognize the huge advances in living standards enjoyed by middle-class America in that "dismal valley" of 1920s prosperity.

I continue with Allan Nevins and Henry Steele Commager, whose A *Pocket History of the United States* (Pocket Books, 1976) also became a best-seller: In it, we find the following: "The idealism of the Wilson era was in the past; the Rooseveltian passion for humanitarianism was in the future. The decade of the twenties was dull, bourgeois, and ruthless. 'The business of

America is business,' said President Coolidge succinctly, and the observation was apt if not profound. Wearied by idealism and disillusioned about the war and its aftermath, Americans dedicated themselves with unabashed enthusiasm to making and spending money. Never before, not even in the McKinley era, had American society been so materialistic, never before so completely dominated by the ideal of the marketplace or the techniques of machinery." How fortunate, I can only reiterate, that government in the 1920s was not the business of America, as it would become with the appearance of the "New Deal" in the 1930s! How lucky we were once again that activist politicians did not dominate the marketplace, monsters who knew not the consequences of their actions!

In a history of the Ford Motor Company (Allan Nevins and Frank Hill, *Ford: Expansion and Challenge, 1915-1933*, Scribner 1957), Nevins had previously applied his prejudices to the coming of the 20s: "The nation, as Wilson's towering vision crashed into the dust and Harding, Coolidge, and Mellon opened an era of selfish materialism, grew cynical." What that seems to mean is that Americans, to Nevins' chagrin, rejected Wilson's hallucinations in favor of less government and much lower taxes. How I do regret that all these authors had no chance to risk their lives together with all those other young men who were so uselessly killed in World War I! Another historian, William Leuchtenberg, writes of "the bleak intellectual mood of the period" [*The Perils of Prosperity 1914-1932*, University of Chicago Press, 1958]. Others considered the era one of "false prosperity," a "fool's paradise" in which most of the newly created wealth went to the rich. To them, Harding proved the feeblest of Presidents. Although possessed of good intentions and a warm heart, he existed in a mental fog, abysmally lacking in intelligence and force of character; in short, a boob. Even journalist and Professor of Business History Robert Sobel, the author of an otherwise sympathetic biography, *Coolidge: An American Enigma*, could write nonsense such as "the Harding policies had next to nothing to do with the recovery" [from the 1920-21 depression].

What are we to make of all this? Are we to assume these historians know more than the American "mobocracy" did at the time? What were all those "stupid" people thinking who overwhelmingly put Harding into office? Judged by the election results, they obviously considered Woodrow Wilson the boob, not Harding, and WWI a catastrophe. And just what did most Americans of the time think of the 1920s? We can get a good idea of middle-class American thought from a classic 1929 study by Robert and Helen Lynd, two sociologists I had the pleasure of knowing when teaching at Sarah Lawrence College in 1950. In their book, *Middletown: A Study in Modern American Culture*, Harcourt Brace & World, 1956 ed.), they report many interviews such as this with an ordinary housewife in Muncie IN: "I began to work during the war [World War I], when everyone else did; we had to meet payments on our house and everything else was getting so high. The master objected at first, but now he don't mind. I'd rather keep on working so my boys can play foot ball and basketball and have spending money their father can't give them. We've built our own home, a nice brown and white bungalow, by a building and loan like everyone else does. We have it almost paid off and it's worth about $6,000. ... We have an electric washing machine, electric iron, and vacuum sweeper. ... I bought an icebox last year – a big one that holds 125 pounds ... We own a $1,200 Studebaker with a nice California top, semi-enclosed. Last summer we spent our vacation going back to Pennsylvania – taking in Niagara Falls on the way. The two boys want to go to college, and I want them to. I graduated from high school myself, but feel if I can't give my boys a little more all my work would have been useless." How touching becomes this interview from the past when considered from today's exalted standard of living! Just imagine what the life of an ordinary housewife must have been before the 1920s, not to mention that of her mother and grandmother. Or what ours may have been like if Wilson's "towering vision" had prevailed into a socialist future. Let us look at some statistics. In 1923, our automobile industry sold a record 3.6 million cars; in 1924, 3.2 million. New-fangled radios appeared in 2.7 million households, more than twice as many as in 1923. Sales of refrigerators, vacuum cleaners, washing machines and clothing boomed. Never before had Mr. and Mrs. Average American been so well off. Obviously, prosperity was not confined to the few rich as so many "Isquare" writers were to maintain.

In the matter of public finance, the Republican Party platform for the 1924 Presidential election accurately recounts the successes of the Harding administration: "We believe the achievement of the Republican administration in reducing taxation by $1,250,000,000 per annum; reducing of the public debt by $2,432,000,000; installing a budget system; reducing the public expenditures from $5,500,000,000 to approximately $3,400,000,000 per annum, thus reducing the ordinary expenditures of the government to substantially a pre-war basis, and the complete restoration of the public credit; the payment or refunding of $7,500,000,000 of public obligations without disturbance of credit or industry – all during the short period of three years – presents a record unsurpassed in the record of public finance." I must note that government spending was still almost 5% of gross domestic product, a much higher percentage than that throughout most of the 19th century but much lower than today's 25%, a figure that makes no allowance for the regulatory costs imposed on the private sector or state and local taxes.

The national debt stood at $25 billion in 1920 (up from little more than $2 billion in 1910). If we assume an average interest rate of 5%, our government paid out to its debt holders $1.25 billion. That figures to more than 30% of the total of tax receipts, an amount earmarked merely for paying the interest on the national debt! Obviously, Wilson was well on his way to bankrupting the country. By 1930, the debt was down to $16 billion despite the huge tax cuts enacted. As we have witnessed earlier, tax cuts again led to increased tax revenues through booming business profits and to a steadily dropping percentage of gross domestic product contributed by government expenditures. It is small wonder that John Dean, former counsel to President Richard Nixon and author of *Warren G. Harding* (Times Books, 2004), could write that "reputable historians had written absolute crap about Harding." And, I might add, his observation could be easily extended to much of what is written about American history! Clearly, our statist historians have failed utterly in understanding the power of efficient markets and the wisdom of the people.

Warren Harding died unexpectedly in 1923, just two years into his term of office. But once again, "the freest country of the universe" found the right person for the job, the man who would "hinder the horse the least." Calvin Coolidge embraced Harding's program and carried it through to completion. As a result, the 1920s stand out in American history as a time of high prosperity and steady economic growth, a decade during which an enormous construction boom rebuilt America's cities and infrastructure, mass-produced automobiles, radios and appliances reshaped American life, and a revival of optimism about the future sparked a great bull market in stocks. Belying once again the pronouncements of present day economists on the incompatibility of growth and deflation, the 4.7% per year rise in GDP coincided with a general price *decline* of approximately 1% per year. In terms of a constant dollar, GDP growth was well over 5% per year. In his final annual message to Congress in 1928, President Coolidge noted that since 1922 real wages had risen by 12.9% and in some industries by as much as 38%. And because of the decrease in living costs, real wages had increased even more. In retrospect, the 1920s seem like one of the more golden of golden ages. By every reasonable expectation, the economic growth that made America the wonder and mystery of the world should have continued, as it was to do many years later. Unfortunately, what happened was unreasonable in the extreme, and it could all be traced to abysmally incompetent Federal Reserve bureaucrats. As had been feared by the Founding Fathers, too much power in too few hands all too often leads to nationwide debacles.

Let me conclude this chapter with a word about the Teapot Dome scandal. During the early years of the 20th century, the navy converted the fleet from coal to oil propulsion, the explosion aboard the battleship *Maine* having awakened the authorities to the dangers of spontaneous combustion. For fear that available oil supplies in the United States might be insufficient for future needs, the Navy Department in 1912 established oil reserves at Elk Hill CA and three years later at Teapot Dome WY. Harding's Secretary of the Interior Albert Fall, after having managed to shift control of both reserves from the Navy Department to the Interior Department, leased the Teapot Dome reserves to the Mammoth Oil Company in return for a royalty and the construction of a pipeline to Kansas City. Harry Sinclair, an important contributor to the Republican Party, controlled Mammoth Oil. Fall also leased Elk Hill to the Pan- American Petroleum and Transportation Company, headed by an old friend Edward Doheny, in return for a royalty and the construction of storage tanks. Fall explained that the oil was being drained, quite legally, by wells on adjoining lands and that the reserves would be depleted in a few years. By leasing the land, Fall argued, the government received royalties that would otherwise be lost.

It turned out that Fall had received more than $400,000 in bribes and payoffs for his "services." But Doheny later testified that Fall was not the only government official with whom he had dealings. Several Wilson administration figures had also been on his payroll, including four cabinet members. Among them was William Gibbs McAdoo, Wilson's son-in-law and Secretary of the Treasury, and also a front-runner for the Democratic 1920 and 1924 Presidential nominations. Doheny had retained him as his attorney for $25,000 a year and a $900,000 contingency fee. "I hired them for their influence" testified Doheny. "Just what Mr. Doheny hoped to get in return remains to be explained, but it looks as if it might have something not unlike political influence. If this is true, Mr. McAdoo was converting his former public positions … into a source of enormous private profit," (from an article in the *New Republic* magazine 5 March 1924).

Only rarely do we read about the Wilson administration's involvement with Teapot Dome characters. Most historians confine their outrage over official bribery to the Harding and Coolidge administrations. When all the Congressional investigations ended in May of 1924, only Fall, Sinclair and Doheny were indicted. In 1929 Fall was sentenced to one year in jail and a $100,000 fine; Sinclair and Doheny were acquitted. The public had long since grown bored with the whole affair, and accounts of it were to be found only in the back pages of the daily newspapers. We are all aware, are we not, that money accumulating in political capitals brings on a rush of people who "want something they ought not to have."

CHAPTER XXXVI

... AND BUST

Every man, wherever he goes, is encompassed by a cloud of comforting convictions, which move with him like flies on a summer day.

Bertrand Russell

The euphoric Coolidge era ended abruptly with the traumatic stock market crash of 1929 and the Great Depression of succeeding years. A deadly sequence of new lows in stocks alternated with new lows in the economy, generating unprecedented suffering and millions of wasted lives. Wherever the blame lay, capitalism seemed kaput, many thought, and the only way to go was toward more government involvement in economic functions. "We gave them their chance, and look what they did with it," remonstrated a not-too-bright Mayor of New York City Fiorello H. La Guardia, referring to businessmen.

What did happen? Again we have "I-square" historians and economists putting forth "absolute crap" in trying to absolve "infallible" government from taking any blame for the chaos it brought about. Most writers are guided by English philosopher and economist John Stuart Mill who wrote more than one hundred fifty years ago: "There cannot, in short, be intrinsically a more insignificant thing, in the economy of society, than money; except in the character of a contrivance for sparing time and labour. It is a machine for doing quickly and expeditiously what would be done, though less quickly and commodiously, without it: and like many other kinds of machinery, it only exerts a distinct and independent influence of its own when it gets out of order." "Perfectly true," comment Milton Friedman and Anna Schwartz on Mill's observation in their A *Monetary History of the United States.* "Yet also somewhat misleading, unless we recognize there is hardly a contrivance which man possesses which can do more damage to a society when it goes amiss." Ah, yes! But understanding the role of money in our society takes a bit of reflection. And it is so much easier for the simple-minded among us to blame the disaster on the Harding-Coolidge-Hoover trio of Republican Presidents and businessmen in general. Thanks to Friedman and Schwartz, however, a consensus of opinion has crystallized, and it is simply this: Money matters!

Let us backtrack a bit. In 1913, a newly elected President Woodrow Wilson signs the Federal Reserve Act after it had barely squeaked through a poorly attended pre-Christmas session of Congress. It is another desecration of the Constitution's "enumerated powers" because none of these empowers Congress to create an independent agency controlling the country's money. It also desecrates the ideals of Jefferson's Democratic Party in its drive to inflict bigger and better government on the American republic. The new monetary authorities promptly fulfill the politicians' expectation of easily available money by financing America's entry into World War I. But the new agency fails miserably in holding down inflation, one of its prime objectives. Prices jump by 150% in the five-year period from 1915-1920, twice the 75% increase during the Civil War period from 1860-1865, a time during which the government helped pay for a much more devastating conflict by printing its own debt- and interest-free currency.

After the War, the Wilson administration does little to bring down wartime taxes and spending. After all, Wilson's "towering vision" has to be financed. But inefficient government expenditures continue wartime inflation and force the Federal Reserve to "sock it to the private economy." A progression of interest rate increases from 1919 to 1921 brings on the worst depression ever experienced by the nation up till then. We have the usual *modus operandi* of central banks: Slash efficient private spending in favor of inefficient government spending. Did these monetary "experts" have a clue as to what they were doing, not to mention the consequences thereof? If we read through the annual reports of the Federal Reserve and the papers and diaries of the System's governors for those years – writings that cannot be read without sensing the omnipresence of chaos – we find naught but sharp disagreements on credit policy. Even at the nadir of the depression, during the spring of 1921, they could come to no consensus on the need for lowering interest rates. When President Harding tells reporters "that the Federal Reserve Board has to lower rates generally," the only two governors favoring a decrease in rates change their minds, feeling that they had to appear independent of the President. It remains for Harding to take the obvious steps of slashing taxes to keep more money in the hands of the people and down-sizing government to reduce its inefficient spending. That is exactly the recipe our great country needs in our own time if some future "Edward Gibbon" is not to write "The Decline and Fall of the American Republic."

In the *Tenth Annual Report* (1923) of the Federal Reserve Board, we find a ten-page section that seeks to establish an adequate guide to credit policy. There it states that such policy "is and must be a matter of judgment" based on the fullest possible range of evidence about changes in production, trade, employment, prices and inventories. What kind of gobble-de-gook is this? Instead of a scientifically based guide to future prediction, we get from these Fed governors a glittering platitude: Do the right thing at the right time! How have we Americans been so stupid as to put up with such nonsense for so long? Whatever possessed us to grant these sophists such power over our livelihoods and money? Why were we not guided by Andrew Jackson's experience in his slaying of the "monster" – the 2nd Bank of the United States – eighty-five years earlier? Are we to allow our politicians to build on their own failures until another "shot heard round the world" is fired?

Thanks to their tax and spending cuts, Harding and Coolidge detoured Wilson's drive to big government. And whether by happenstance or plain good fortune, the Fed's random walk of interest rate changes during the middle 1920s – a time representing what Friedman and

Schwartz call "the high tide of the Reserve System" – did not derail the ongoing prosperity. Indeed, it is possible that the monetary authorities kept interest rates too low, thereby encouraging the speculation that eventually led to Florida's real estate boom and bust in 1925. The situation has strong parallels with the current sub-prime mortgage boom and bust of 2002-08.

By early 1928, however, the country's luck began to run out. It was then that the Marxist fossils comprising the Federal Reserve Board convinced themselves that they knew more about the stock market than the investing public. In a statement released to the press in February of 1929, they expressed concern about "the excessive amount of the country's credit absorbed in speculative security loans," what today is called "irrational exuberance." And then, just to confuse the issue, they then asserted in their *Annual Report* for 1929 (also released at that time) that the Board "neither assumes the right nor has it any disposition to set itself up as an arbiter of security speculation or values." These contradictory statements notwithstanding, it seems indisputable that curbing the stock market boom was the dominating factor in the disastrous initiatives taken by the Board during 1928 and 1929. Remember, there was no inflation to curb; consumer prices were falling. If the Federal Reserve Board governors had curbed their ignorance rather than the stock market, the country might well have been spared the Great Depression.

The actions taken by the Fed consisted mainly of hikes in the rediscount rate (today shortened to the discount rate). This is the interest rate charged to commercial banks for borrowing money directly from the Fed, money that could then be used for loan originations. It was then the principal tool used for controlling the country's money supply. In 1928 the Fed raised the discount rate three times, from $3\frac{1}{2}$% to 5%, and then in August 1929, just before the crash, to a "last-straw" 6%. It was clearly too much. Loan originations contracted and bank deposits withered. As we remember, banks record loans as deposits (those bookkeeping entries of fractional reserve banking) which can then be transferred from one pocket to another by means of bank checks or notes, and this makes up most of what we call the money supply. The decline in loan activity brought on the self-destruction of money through the multiplying factor now acting in reverse - an implosion rather than an explosion of the money supply. In short, the Fed's curtailment of loan activity in 1928 and 1929 brought the money supply well below that necessary to support existing levels of business activity and stock market prices. Obviously, something had to give, either stock prices or business activity or both.

The hand-to-hand currency in public hands (about $4\frac{1}{2}$ billion at the time) consisted of Federal Reserve notes, the national bank notes issued under the National Banking Act of 1864, silver certificates (paper money backed by silver in the U. S. Treasury first issued in 1878), greenbacks, gold and some gold and silver coinage. That money did not self-destruct. However, the part of the money supply consisting of checking accounts was about eleven times the hand-to-hand currency in 1929, and these accounts were backed only by the banking system's promise to pay. Depositors wishing to withdraw deposits and convert them into currency, or gold if so desired, could not do so if a run on their bank forced it to suspend payments. In the malaise to follow, those people fortunate enough to put their currency and gold under the mattress rather than in banks or stocks made out very well. Their money increased in value as prices fell. In contrast, the, money in many stock investments and bank deposits simply vanished.

The minutes of an executive committee meeting of the New York Federal Reserve Bank 19 May 1930 (as quoted in A *Monetary History of the United States*) confirm the deflationary policy of the time by admitting that "we had encouraged a deflation of credit during the years 1928 and 1929, that the rate of increase in total volume of credit in use had been below normal ..." Friedman and Schwartz furnish additional support: "The money stock [of the nation] ... declined slightly, being lower at the cyclical peak in August 1929 than 16 months earlier in April 1928. From the time our monthly series starts in 1907, the only previous occasions on which the stock of money was below its level 16 months earlier were during the sharp contractions [depressions] of 1907-08 and 1920-21. There is on record no prior or subsequent business expansion during which so long a period passed without a rise."

Was the stock market speculatively overpriced in 1929, as so many unknowing historians maintain? If we take a look at the average price-to-earnings ratio of the blue-chip Dow-Jones stocks, it stood at 16, just what it is today. This ratio spells out the risk in owning the stock, it being the number of years it will take, as judged by the investing public, for the sum of the company's earnings to equal its current stock price. Companies well regarded by investors have high ratios, and more risky companies lower ratios. One of the highest price-to-earnings ratios of the 1920s belonged to the Radio Corporation of America, one of the era's premier growth industries. Considering the projected sales of its recently introduced radios and "talking machines," and with television looming on the horizon, its ratio of 26 seems modest indeed. For a comparison, look at today's Google sporting a ratio of 45. There can be little doubt that the stock market, in its role as the appraiser of the country's future, stood in its accustomed position of being exactly where it should have been. By every reasonable expectation, the nation's exuberant growth should have continued unabated, as it was to do less than twenty years later. Unfortunately, what happened was unreasonable in the extreme.

The Dow-Jones Average peaked at 382 on 5 September 1929, the Standard & Poor's composite price index of 90 common stocks at 254 on 7 September. Obviously anticipating trouble, the market then declined sporadically until 23 October when selling became panicky. On the day of the crash, 29 October, the Dow-Jones fell to 200 and the Standard & Poor's to 162. Nearly 16½ million shares traded, overwhelming stock exchange clerks who had to work far into the night recording transactions. The daily average in September had been 4 million. Both averages bottomed out for the year in mid-November, 195 and 141 respectively, a drop of almost 50% in less than two months. The estimated loss in value of all stocks listed on the New York Stock Exchange in October approached $15½ billion. It was nothing compared to what was coming.

August 1929, the month the discount rate reached its "butterfly" peak at 6%, saw the beginnings of a precipitous decline in business activity. From then to the stock market crash of 29 October, industrial production fell at an annual rate of 20%, wholesale prices at 7½%, and personal income at 5%. After the crash, the decline continued unabated. By October 1930, production had fallen 26%, prices 14%, and personal income 16%. Coinciding with these declines, the country's money supply began to self-destruct, beginning with the liquidation and repayment of brokers' loans, the money borrowed by investors from the banking system to buy stocks. This time around, however, no loan originations replaced many of those lost, and that caused the banking system to lose deposits. From August 1929 to October 1930, the money supply declined 2.6%, a more sizable decline than during the whole of but four of the most severe previous depressions, those of 1873-9, 1893-4, 1907-8 and 1920-1. The on-going annihilation of money pressured personal incomes downward and, coupled with the loss of savings in the market crash, shocked the people's expectations of a dazzlingly bright economic future. Even if the contraction in business activity had come to an end in late 1930 or early 1931, this depression would have ranked as one of the worst on record.

In the November following the crash, the Fed tried to stimulate bank loans by lowering the discount rate in steps from 6% to 2½% the following October 1930. It also engaged in open market buying of government securities to put more money into the private economy. But it was all too little and too late; the damage had been done. The Fed's discount rate reductions marched well behind market rates – no bank could afford to borrow money at the discount window at 2½ % and loan it out at 1%. People were not borrowing, banks were not lending and, as a result, money kept disappearing. The great uncertainties inherent in all business activities were further compounded by the antics of a government authority that obviously had no idea as to what it was doing. And to make matters worse, the Hoover administration joined in by passing the Hoot-Smalley Tariff in 1930. It raised protectionism to the highest level ever and effectively increased the taxes borne by the citizenry.

In October 1930, the monetary character of the depression changed dramatically. The continuing losses of deposits began to affect the banking system, and the dire consequences fell on all banks, albeit unevenly. Because the high tariff policies of Republican administrations had had the farm belt reeling ever since Civil War days, a banking panic first erupted there. Perhaps it began on a day when some farmer sought to withdraw money from his account and found the door to his local bank locked. The bank's officers, faced with too many nonperforming outstanding loans (those on which interest payments had stopped), discovered that they could not satisfy all requests for the conversion of deposits into currency and had suspended withdrawals. It was the straw that broke the camel's back. A contagion of fear swept throughout the country as depositors ran to their banks trying to get their money. Bank suspensions rose rapidly, to 256 banks holding $180 million in deposits in November 1930 and 352 holding $370 million in deposits in December, including the largest commercial bank ever to have failed up to that time, the Bank of the United States with over $200 million in deposits (not to be confused with the government-chartered 1st and 2nd Banks of the United States in earlier history). In the three months from October 1930 to January 1931, the money supply declined by 3%, or more than in the preceding fourteen months.

This first banking crisis leveled off in early 1931 as depositors slackened their demand for additional currency. To many, the first few months of 1931 seemed to have the earmarks of a cyclical bottom and the beginnings of a revival in economic activity. If these tentative stirrings had been reinforced by a vigorous expansion of Federal Reserve open market purchases of government securities to expand the money supply and get more money into the private markets, or if, as had always happened in the past, an outstanding private individual had arisen in this time of need to lead the banking system back to health, or if a Harding- Coolidge type tax cut had been imposed to put money directly back into people's hands, a sustained recovery might have begun. But, alas, it was not to be. Everyone waited for decisive Fed action, and all they got was "paralytic helplessness." None of the money annihilated in the 1929 crash, the amount obviously needed to return the economy to its former prosperous level, was going to be recreated; that was now clear. Their confidence jolted once again by the Federal Reserve's impotency, depositors in March 1931 resumed the conversion of deposits into hand-held currency.

From February to August 1931, commercial bank deposits fell by $2.7 billion or nearly 7% of total deposits, a decline greater than that from August 1929 to February 1931. In the same six months, the money supply fell by nearly 5½%, or at a rate of 11% per year. An influx of foreign gold, at the time an important part of bank reserves, moderated the fall somewhat relative to the decline in deposits. At the time, even the Fed was required to maintain a gold reserve of at least 40% of its note issue and convert its notes into gold on demand. The drafters of the Federal Reserve Act obviously had great misgivings about granting the Fed unlimited power to issue Federal Reserve notes, something it is able to do today.

A second and much more serious banking panic erupted in September 1931 after Britain went off the gold standard (the pound could no longer be converted into gold). Anticipating a similar action by the United States, foreign central bankers and private citizens converted substantial amounts of dollar assets into gold and exported it out of the country. Because of the low level of money-market interest rates in the United States, foreign central banks had been selling shortterm American securities for several months prior to September. The selling now assumed panic proportions, and it forced the Fed to react vigorously to quell the foreign drain before the Treasury's gold stock vanished. On October 9, the Fed raised the discount rate from 1½% to 2½% and then to 3½% on October 16, the sharpest rise in so short a time in the whole history of the Federal Reserve System before or since. Its action increased the rate of return on short-term domestic securities sufficiently to stem the gold outflow. But, at what cost?

As we might expect, unintended consequences followed swiftly. The Fed's move intensified the banking system's already critical financial difficulties and brought on a spectacular increase in bank failures and bank runs. Besides making borrowing at the Fed's discount window unaffordable, the higher interest rates depressed the prices of bonds held in the investment portfolios of many banks, bonds which they had been selling to obtain currency. "Within a period of a few months United States Government bonds have declined 10 per cent; high grade corporation bonds have declined 20 per cent; and lower grade bonds have shown even larger price declines. Declines of such proportions inevitably have increased greatly the difficulties of many banks, and it has now become apparent that the efforts of individual institutions to strengthen their position have seriously weakened the banking position in general" (from a preliminary memorandum for an Open Market Policy Conference, January 1932).

In October 1931, 522 commercial banks holding $471 million in deposits locked their doors, and in the next three months 875 more banks with $564 million followed suit. All told, in the six months August 1931 to January 1932, 1,860 banks with deposits of $1.5 billion suspended operations. Over the same period, those banks that managed to stay afloat lost five times more, or 17% of their initial deposits. And the money supply fell by 12%, or at an annual rate of 31%, by far the biggest decline in American history.

Under heavy Congressional pressure to act, the Fed from April 1932 to August 1 embarked on open-market purchases of securities amounting to a paltry $1 billion. But its action seemed to have some effect. Wholesale prices started to rise in July, as did industrial production in August. Factory employment, railroad ton-miles, and numerous other economic indicators told a similar story. Although personal income continued to fall, it was at a much reduced rate. As in early 1931, many of the earmarks of an economic revival appeared. And at this point, in May of 1932, a massive intervention into the private economy on the political level entered the picture in the form of a gigantic tax hike. It generated government issued chaos on a scale hard to believe.

The sharp decline in personal income and business profits in the year following the 1929 stock market crash lowered government tax receipts to a level far below expenditures, producing a budget deficit of $900 million. By 1932, it had increased to more than $2 billion and led to calls for higher taxes by President Hoover and Andrew Mellon, the latter near the end of a long stint as Treasury Secretary. In a curious about-face from his tax policies during the Harding and Coolidge administrations, Mellon now favored tax increases, not tax cuts, to cure a hemorrhaging federal budget. Hoover, himself Secretary of Commerce under Harding, also failed to be guided by experience. And what the country got was another tax-on-everything. The Revenue Act of 1932, passed into law in May, raised the top income tax rate to 63% from 25% for individuals and from 12.5% to 13.75% for corporations, doubled the estate tax, and accompanied these with a slew of excises on lubricating oil, gasoline, malt syrup, brewer's wort, tires, toilet articles, furs, jewelry, automobiles, trucks, radio and phonograph equipment, refrigerators, sporting goods, cameras, firearms, matches, candy, chewing gum, soft drinks and electricity. Unbelievably, the government and the Fed were now operating at cross purposes with each other. On the one hand, the Fed was trying to put money into people's hands through open-market purchases of securities and, on the other, the politicians were trying to take it away! Talk about anarchy being the *presence of government*!

On 8 July 1932, the Dow hit its low of 41, a drop of almost 90% from its high of 340 on 3 September 1929. It was accompanied by drop in the gross domestic product of 46%. Adjusting for a 30% decline in prices and a population increase of 2½%, everyone on average had become at least 20% poorer over this period. To get an idea of the devastation caused by the Depression, picture the losses as distributed along a bell-shaped curve peaked at a 20% loss and think of the huge number of people who lost from 25% to 100% of their wealth. Another indicator of those calamitous times is the unemployment rate; it jumped from 5% to a nightmarishly high 25%!

A typical rebound in business activity from the abyss, beginning in the summer of 1932, now ensued. All expectations of imminent disaster, it would seem, had been factored into market prices. Again, a rise in industrial production portended the end of the Depression. But, the election of Franklin Delano Roosevelt brought with it rumors – later confirmed by actual events – of a dollar devaluation. People expected that Treasury would soon buy gold for $35 per ounce rather than the current $20.67 per ounce, almost doubling its price. Another rush to convert bank deposits into Federal Reserve notes and other currency, which could then be used to buy gold, developed. And, for the first time, depositors also demanded gold coin and Treasury gold certificates. On this go round, however, the crisis spread further than ever before. In early March of 1933, a heavy gold drain reduced the New York Federal Reserve Bank's reserve ratio below the legal limit and caused the Federal Reserve Board to relax its reserve requirement for thirty days. New York's Governor Herbert Lehman declared a state banking holiday effective March 4, and the governors of Illinois, Massachusetts, New Jersey and Pennsylvania followed suit. Also on March 4, all twelve of the Federal Reserve Banks remained closed, as did all the leading stock and commodity exchanges. "The central banking system, set up primarily to render impossible the restriction of payments by commercial banks, itself joined the commercial banks in a more widespread, complete, and economically disturbing restriction of payments than had ever been experienced in the history of the country" (from A *Monetary History of the United States 1867-1960)*. "I concluded [that the Federal Reserve System] was indeed a weak reed for a nation to lean on in time of trouble," commented President Hoover. But no move did he make toward slaying the "Monster."

On March 6, a newly inaugurated President Roosevelt proclaimed a nationwide banking holiday that closed all banks until March 9, later extended. The announcement was accompanied by a suspension of gold redemptions in the United States and gold shipments abroad. Ever since, we in the United States have been on a fiduciary standard – the dollar has value only in the sense that other people are willing to accept that piece of green paper as legal tender for the payment of goods and services. No specie backs the dollar.

On March 9, Roosevelt signed the Emergency Banking Act of 1933. It continued and confirmed the March 6 proclamation and granted the President emergency powers over gold and currency movements. The next day, on March 10, Roosevelt issued an executive order extending the restrictions on gold and foreign exchange dealings beyond the banking holiday proper and, in effect, prohibiting gold payments by banking and non-banking institutions.

On 5 April 1933, Executive Order #6102 forbade the "hoarding" of gold and required all holders of gold, including member banks of the Federal Reserve System, to deliver their holdings of gold coin, bullion and gold certificates to Federal Reserve Banks on or before May 1, except for rare coins, reasonable amounts for use in industry and the arts, and a maximum of $100 per person in gold coin and gold certificates. The gold coins and certificates were exchanged for other currency or deposits at face value; the bullion brought the legal price of $20.67 per fine ounce.

On June 5, all gold clauses in public and private contracts, past and future, were abrogated. The Supreme Court, paying no attention to the Constitution's sanctity of contracts provision and its prohibition on *ex post facto* laws, upheld the right of Congress to do so in private, state, and city obligations, but not in those of the U. S. government. As heretofore noted, anything goes when politicians feel the need to spend money. The dollar's sole link to gold now resided only in the requirement that the Fed hold a 40% reserve in gold against its note issue. When the Fed's gold holdings approached the 40% restriction in 1945, the required reserve was lowered to 25%. The link was completely severed on 15 August 1971 when President Richard Nixon ended Treasury purchases and sales of gold and released the Fed from its gold reserve requirement. Ever since, the Fed has had the power to "create as many dollars as it pleases, any time it pleases, and for any reason it pleases."

De facto dollar devaluation took effect on 31 January 1934 when President Roosevelt, acting under the authority of the Gold Reserve Act of 1934, specified a fixed buying and selling price of $35 per ounce for gold. Since Treasury had formerly valued its own gold holdings at $20.67 per ounce, it realized a large "paper profit" of nearly $3 billion from the dollar revaluation. Now Treasury could turn over the gold (in the form of gold certificates) to its Federal Reserve account and receive either notes or checks amounting to $3 billion in newly created money. The devaluation of the dollar in effect raised the prices of agricultural imports and, as was intended, helped beleaguered farmers raise domestic prices. Note the huge loss of money suffered by private citizens because of the forced gold tender the previous April.

Now began even more massive intrusions into our free markets. More government! That was the solution. Extract wealth from society's most productive people and businesses and redistribute it to the less productive – *after the* politicians and bureaucrats have taken their cut. And, society's producers, like our barnyard hen who baked no more bread, thereupon marketed less food, less clothing, less shelter and less of all the other necessities and niceties that make up our standard of living. Roosevelt even outdid Hoover on income tax hikes. The top rate went to 79% in 1935, and in 1941, to 90% on incomes above $100,000. It is small wonder that business investment withered in the face of outright confiscation of investor capital. (In 1943, Roosevelt tried once again to kill our capitalistic system by proposing a $25,000 limit on after-tax incomes, but even a Democratic Congress could not go along with that.) A paltry interest rate of 1% or less on short-term, taxpayer-guaranteed federal debt indicated a great demand for this unproductive but relatively safe haven for funds. Nobody, but nobody, suggested Harding's solution of cutting taxes and government spending. Letting the people keep and spend their own money was decidedly out of favor.

From 1932 to 1937, the gross domestic product rose unevenly by a strong 59% in constant prices, aided and abetted by government pump-priming (spending) and a flight of capital from abroad. In the wake of Adolph Hitler's rise to power in Germany, Europeans were shipping their gold to America for safekeeping. Without that inflow, the Depression might have been far worse. The most notable feature of the recovery from the 1932 trough, however, was its incompleteness: Unemployment remained large, 5.9 million out of a labor force of nearly 54 million, or 11%, at the 1937 peak; unutilized manufacturing capacity proliferated; and private construction at the 1937 peak continued sharply lower than that in the 1920s, one-third as much. The recovery in industrial production was disproportionately concentrated in government purchases and non-durable goods and services, which pointed to an unusually low availability of investment capital for building new plant and equipment and for sponsoring research and development Government spending rose to almost 10% of GDP from 3% during the 1920s.

On President Hoover's recommendation, a number of special monetary institutions had been established to spend the people's money for them. In January 1932, the Reconstruction Finance Corporation was given the authority to make loans to banks, to other financial institutions, and to railroads, many of which were in danger of default on their bonded indebtedness. Capitalized at $500 million (to be supplied by the Federal Reserve), it could in addition borrow $1.5 billion for its purposes. In July 1932, its borrowing power was further advanced to $3.3 billion. During the remainder of 1932, its loans to banks totaled almost $1 billion. In May 1932, a bill to provide federal insurance for bank deposits passed the House of Representatives but failed in the Senate. In July 1932, the Federal Home Loan Bank Act passed. It could make advances to savings and loan association, savings banks, and insurance companies on the security of first mortgages they held. In addition, Hoover expanded federal expenditures on public works. Once again, the "great minds" ignored the Constitution's "enumerated powers" and enlarged government to "fix" the chaos their meddling created in the first place. Money that could have been better spent in the private sector would now be spent inefficiently in the public sector.

Roosevelt's new "New Deal" expanded Hoover's initial efforts enormously. With this administration, the Democratic Party outdid even the Republicans in repudiating their Jeffersonian heritage of limited government. We got an alphabet of soup of nobly-intentioned government acts and agencies – AAA, CCC, FDIC, FERA, FFMC, FHA, FSA, FSLIC, HOLC, NIRA, NRA, PWA, RA, REA, SEC, TVA, WPA – turkeys some of which still hang heavy around our necks, growing ever larger, ever hungrier and ever more costly to feed. This comes on top of many other agencies launched by previous administrations – the ICC which wrecked the railroad industry, the FDA which has killed far more people than it has supposedly saved by delaying the introduction of life-saving pharmaceuticals and making them far more expensive to produce, the anti-trust antics of the Department of Justice which grants to ignorant bureaucrats the power to determine the most efficient size of private businesses, the FRB which tries to control the economy. Thanksgiving for many of these birds, it seems, never comes. Many of their harmful consequences continue to modern times, to wit, a subsidized passenger railroad system, a dying pharmaceutical industry, the savings and loan bankruptcies of the 1980s, and the sub-prime mortgage panic of 2007-8.

In 1936, the Fed let fly another of its arrows from its quiver of powers. For fear that the huge gold inflow from Europe would spark inflation, it employed a newly authorized tool to deflate the money supply. It was a power granted just one year earlier on the grounds that the failure of the Federal Reserve System to stem the 1929-1933 economic collapse and prevent the subsequent banking panics could be attributed to its inadequate powers — the usual excuse to enlarge government intrusion into the private sector. What the great minds did was to bludgeon the financial markets with a doubling of the reserve requirement from 13% to 26% for the big banks in central reserve cities, sharply cutting their ability to grant loans. The action tanked the money supply and drove the economy back almost to where it had started up in 1932. Unemployment took a great leap upward to 19%. "It is a natural human tendency," comment Friedman and Schwarz, "to take credit for good outcomes and seek to avoid the blame for bad. One amusing dividend from reading through the annual reports of the Federal Reserve Board seriatim is the sharpness of the cyclical pattern in the potency attributed to the System. In years of prosperity, monetary policy is said to be a potent instrument, the skillful handling of which deserves credit for the favorable course of events; in years of adversity, monetary policy is said to have little leeway but is largely the consequence of other forces, and it was only the skillful handling of the exceedingly limited powers available that prevented conditions from being even worse."

After the debacle of 1937, the Fed reduced the reserve requirement to 22½ % and then locked itself into a passive mode until 1940. As it had during World War I, it concerned itself mainly with papering over the gap between government revenues and expenditures (averaging more than $5 billion per year over the 1935 to 1939 interval), and this was to continue throughout World War II. The gross domestic product recovered to its 1929 and 1937 levels thanks in the main to an increased money supply induced by newly arrived gold from Europe. But distortions in the economy continued, and unemployment remained very high at 12% of the work force. A population increase of more than 7% caused the GDP per capita figure to wallow sharply below the level of 1929. Confessed Secretary of the Treasury Henry Morgenthau: "We are spending more than we have ever spent before and it does not work … We have never made good on our promises … I say after eight years of this Administration we have just as much unemployment as when we started … And an enormous debt to boot!"

CHAPTER XXXVII

WORLD WAR II AND THE RETURN OF PROSPERITY I

It is foolish and wrong to mourn the men who died. Rather we should thank God that such men lived.

George S. Patton

The terrible Ifs accumulate!

Winston Churchill

I

A book of history speaks of many things – of money and politics, of war and revolution, of art and science, of "unalienable rights," and of philosophy. And, of all these, philosophy is perhaps the most important because it conditions the way we look at all the others. It endows experience with structure, meaning and direction as opposed to indiscriminate perception and uninformed judgment. For what is philosophy other than a total vision of how the world works, a comprehensive model of reality housed within the black confines of the human skull. It is a picture pieced together from sense impressions, by electric currents originating in body sensors which, when transmitted to the brain and processed, get displayed as consciousness. The modern digital computer operates in an amazingly similar fashion, with data bits substituting for the sensory stimuli of sight, sound, taste, touch and smell. And just as the computer's display depends on how it is programmed, so too does our view of reality relate to how we are influenced by family, teachers, friends and the news media. Philosophy, then, is the programming of the human computer.

I have endeavored, dear reader, to program you into a philosophy of uncertainty, one based on Adam Smith's invisible hand and an all-knowing free market. It is perhaps the only philosophy in accord with modern chaos theory. Almost all others prefer the "supremacy of reason" as their basis for explaining how the world works. But because such philosophies apply only to a geometrically perfect world, they are of the "not even wrong" variety. We, on the contrary, shall "let experience be our guide." And, as cautioned by Founding Father John

Dickinson, we shall examine the "terrible Ifs" of the 20th – and 21st-centuries knowing that all too often "reason will lead us astray."

It was the 14th day of May in the year of our Lord 1940, and "Oh, What a Beautiful Morning" had dawned. A cloudless sky of azure blue; robins, blue jays, wrens and cardinals chirping happily away as they gathered twigs for their regeneration of species; tulips in full bloom and peonies ready to burst; butterflies flittering among the fresh greens of spring – could my Long Island bit of the universe ever have been lovelier? And, suddenly, how it all blackened! At home for the school lunch break, I snapped on the radio to find out the latest happenings in the "phony war" that had begun in Europe the year before when Germany *and* Russia jointly invaded Poland. It was phony no longer. "French forces are engaging German tanks at Sedan," the loudspeaker blared forth. Sedan! I jumped up, startled. Sedan! Forty miles south of the northern anchor of the Maginot Line bastion, bordered by the supposedly impassable Ardennes Forest where the Germans had routed the French army in the Franco-Prussian War of 1870, even to capturing Emperor Napoleon III. How in the world had German tanks managed to break through? And I knew right then and there that what I had dreaded all through my teenage years would come to pass. Not a week – not even a day – had gone by when I had not hoped that the war everybody knew was coming would start and get over with by the time I was old enough to be in it. That is, everybody knew it but the small men by whom England and France were governed at the time. In 1936 Hitler had tested their resolve by sending German troops storming into the demilitarized Rhineland and found it wanting. Playing on this display of weakness, he then began the subjugation of Europe – Austria, Czechoslovakia, Denmark and Norway. He even consummated a pact in 1939 with arch enemy Josef Stalin to split Poland between Germany and Russia, and that left Communists around the world with a lot of explaining to do. With each conquest, I could feel the dead hands of those smart-smart- smart-stupid drafters of the Versailles Treaty, Premier Pierre Clemenceau of France, Prime Minister David Lloyd George of Great Britain and President Woodrow Wilson of the United States, reaching ever further from the grave to enslave millions of young men in another great war to the death. And I was to be one of them.

"As you was!"

"You three men. Half of you come here."

It was my first day of active duty, 30 June 1943, and a tough, old three-striper had met me and twenty other men as we stepped off the train at Fort Dix NJ. I looked intently at the sergeant. Was he serious? Was I hearing things? He took us to the mess hall for an evening meal consisting of cubes of pork fat and then to our barracks. The next morning the company commander addressed us. He looked the spitting image of Teddy Roosevelt and dressed similarly. "Men," he said, "don't sit in the poison ivy." There could be no doubt. I was in the army now, yanked out of college for what appeared to be years to come. A quick end to the War was nowhere in sight. The French had surrendered soon after Sedan, most of their vaunted army having been entrapped in Belgium, and the German invasion of Russia was proceeding relentlessly. All Europe suffered under Nazi dominance. A Japanese naval squadron commanded by Admiral Isoroku Yamamoto had attacked Pearl Harbor on 7 December 1941, and by the end of 1942 Japanese armies had conquered almost all of southeast Asia and solidified their hold on the island fortresses in the Pacific.

But Hitler was unable to subjugate England after the fall of France. And the attack on Pearl Harbor failed, as Yamamoto well understood, in that it did not destroy the American aircraft carriers based there. Both these non-events would prove decisive in the coming years.

By the end of 1943, there could be little doubt that the tide had turned against the Berlin-Tokyo axis. German armies were in full retreat, having been stopped at El Alamein in Egypt and at Stalingrad, Moscow and Leningrad in Russia. In the Pacific theater, the Japanese navy had been severely mauled in the battles of the Coral Sea and Midway Island. And America's great industrial machine was pouring out tanks, airplanes, ships and munitions in unbelievable quantities. Her "robber baron" businessmen had performed miracles in converting from peace to war production, aided in great part by the substitution of a business-friendly, free-market climate for the 1930s New Deal hostility. Industrialists could now spend contracted money as they saw fit. "If you are going to try to go to war, or to prepare for war, in a capitalist country, you have got to let business make money out of the process or business won't work," proclaimed Republican Secretary of War Henry Stimson. To which Undersecretary of the Army added, "We had to take industrial America as we found it." How fortunate!

After basic infantry training, I was transferred to the Army Signal Corps and thence to a technical support group in Warrenton VA, located on a site near the future CIA headquarters. Our mission: to establish direct communications with the Nationalist Kuomintang government of China headed by Generalissimo Chiang Kai-Shek in Chunking, the provisional capital. It was hoped that aid to Chiang would continue and help him tie up hundreds of thousands of Japanese soldiers on the Asian mainland. During our preparations, however, Chinese Communist forces led by Mao Tse-Tung threatened Chunking and we were diverted to Manila in the Philippine Islands. The Communists had been gaining power ever since 1933, the year in which America's nationalization of silver wreaked economic chaos on China. The Japanese invasion in 1937 had brought about an uneasy truce between Mao and Chiang, but with the end of the war in sight, fighting once again broke out between the two factions.

In January of 1945, our group established General Douglas MacArthur's message center in a partially bombed-out building on the banks of the "blue" Pasig River. As working personnel in top secret surroundings, we were privy to much scuttlebutt emanating from the communications passing through GHQ. It treated us to a privileged view of the war.

Still talked about months after his appearance was *Mousie* and his role in prolonging the European War into 1945. But let me recapitulate. On D-Day, 6 June 1944, American and British forces invaded France and managed to establish a beachhead on the Normandy coast. It stretched from Caen in the east to the Cotentin Peninsula some thirty-five miles to the west. But there the invasion stagnated, confined by fierce German resistance. It appeared to many that the horrors of World War I's trench warfare would re-emerge amongst the hedgerows of Normandy. To crack through that tight ring of fire, General Omar Bradley, in command of the American troops on the western end of the front, launched an operation "borrowed" by him from General George S. Patton, Jr. (and never accredited). Code-named Cobra, it began on the night of 24-25 July with the carpet-bombing of a 4-mile wide, 2-mile deep patch of land on the western end of the Allied front, what became known as the Avranches Gap. Waves of airplanes – more than 2000 fighters, fighter-bombers, medium bombers and heavy bombers – sacked the area relentlessly with showers of explosives, an array of bombs from incendiaries to 500- pounders. Half the German defenders were killed, the rest so dazed or wounded that resistance vanished. Once the flanks of the now undefended Gap were secured by the American First Army, there streamed through the American Third Army commanded by Patton, master of mobile warfare and the Allied general most feared by the German high command. In the clear beyond the Gap, Patton turned most of his armor and infantry eastward to join up with British forces commanded by Field Marshall Bernard Montgomery, moving westward from Caen. Montgomery's victory at El Alamein had prevented the German seizure of the mid-east oil fields and turned him into a national hero. The pincer closed near the village of Falaise with the almost complete annihilation of the German army in Normandy - 50,000 men killed, wounded or captured along with nearly all their armor and equipment. Twenty thousand Germans, who would later take part in the Battle of the Bulge, managed to escape, and only because Supreme Allied Commander Dwight D. Eisenhower ordered Patton to stop short of closing the gap. That allowed that "slow, little fart" Montgomery (in Patton's vernacular) to do so. Wrote Eisenhower in his book *Crusade in Europe*: The *battlefield at Falaise was unquestionably one of the greatest* killing grounds *of any of the war areas. Roads, highways, and fields were so choked with destroyed equipment and with dead men and animals that passage through the area was extremely difficult. Forty-eight hours after the closing of the gap I was conducted through it on foot, to encounter scenes that could be described only by Dante. It was literally possible to walk for hundreds of yards at a time, stepping on nothing but dead and decaying flesh* [as quoted in "Freedom From Fear: The American People in Depression and War, 1929-1945" by David M. Kennedy. This well-written book contains a wealth of information about the period. But, beware! Its economic philosophy is of the "absolute crap" variety].

The road to victory now appeared wide open. Employing the *blitzkrieg* tactics employed so successfully by the German military, Patton headed his columns east toward Germany, dashing more than 400 miles in the next twenty-six days. That brought him to the Meuse River between Verdun and Commercy, the site of the bloodiest battles of World War I. At this point, Patton was only seventy-five miles from the great Saar industrial and mining complex and less than 100 miles from the Rhine River. Almost all resistance to the Third Army's advance had collapsed, and the Siegfried West Wall, the German equivalent of the Maginot Line, was unmanned. So encompassing was Patton's drive that Army Chief-of-Staff General George C. Marshall could now envision an end to the war by 1 November and the redeployment of troops from the European to the Pacific Theater of Operations. And here it was that up reared *Mousie*.

Patton had shown the way, and one might think that all available resources should have been directed to him. Even an ant colony would have known what to do. But, unbelievably, just the opposite was to occur. Following the breakout from the Normandy beachhead, two main thrusts developed, one eastward by Patton's Third Army and the other northward by the 21st British Army Group commanded by Montgomery. For their campaigns, both Patton and Montgomery required huge supplies of equipment, gasoline, munitions and food, all of which had to be transported on a continuing basis hundreds of miles from limited port facilities in Normandy. Because the bombed out French railroads were of little use, delivery was necessarily by truck and airplane. Thus far, Eisenhower had managed to keep both Patton and Montgomery going by allocating half of all supplies and transport to each.

But Patton's successful drive through France contrasted sharply with Montgomery's snail-paced advance in Belgium. Impassably muddy fields and narrow causeways criss-crossed by rivers and canals bogged down the British offensive. But, as wrote Mark Twain, "No man can stand prosperity, somebody else's, that is." And that most certainly proved to be the case here. Begrudging the greater glory going to arch rival Patton, Montgomery now conjured up an "Operation Cobra" of his own, one as big as his ego. Code-named Operation Market- Garden, its objective was to spring his stagnated forces loose for an invasion of the German homeland. The plan envisioned a huge airborne drop of 35,000 men behind German lines, their objective being to secure eight bridges over the rivers and canals that barred the way to the German border and the Ruhr industrial complex beyond. The 21st Army Group would then advance rapidly along a 60-mile corridor in "one-tank fronts" and relieve the airborne forces before they could be eradicated by Panzer divisions stationed in Holland. The movie *A Bridge Too Far* vividly portrays the dumbfounded looks of dismay on the faces of Montgomery's field officers when briefed about the plan. To them, the intricacies of the operation rendered it a foolhardy gamble, its chances of success near zero. Their opinion mirrored precisely that of MacArthur's staff officers in Manila when they heard of it. Worse still, its logistics required the requisition of all available supplies, and that meant taking them away from Patton.

It was now up to Eisenhower to approve or disapprove. "… if Ike stops holding Monty's hand and gives me the supplies, I'll go through the Siegfried Line like "shit through a goose," bellowed an exasperated George Patton. But, somehow or other, and over Bradley's strong opposition, Montgomery bullied his boss into going along with him. It was opportunity lost. In Patton, Eisenhower had his "Stonewall Jackson," but he would now fail to exploit his unique talents to the full. No Robert E. Lee was he.

As is well known, Operation Market-Garden turned out a colossal blunder. Its human cost alone amounted to 17,000 casualties – killed, wounded and captured – among the airborne troops. But its unintended consequences extended far and wide. In Holland, 18,000 Dutch civilians starved to death that winter as all available food was requisitioned by the Germans. "My country can never again afford the luxury of another Montgomery success," lamented Prince Bernhard of the Netherlands. Furthermore, the cutoff of supplies halted Patton's advance and gave the Germans sufficient time to regroup, man the Siegfried Line and mount the Battle of the Bulge counterattack. That battle would result in 80,000 American casualties, more than in any other. The only winner was Josef Stalin. Russian armies were given the opportunity to sweep over eastern Europe and subjugate millions to Communist slavery. "This war is not as in the past," Stalin had said "Whoever occupies a territory also imposes his own social system. Everyone imposes his own system as far as his army can reach. It cannot be otherwise" [as quoted in David Kennedy's *Freedom From Fear*]. And that is exactly what he would do.

"Hell, get onto yourself, Ike. You didn't make Patton, he made you!" That caustic remark concluded a conversation between Dwight Eisenhower and General Albert C. Wedemeyer, commander of American forces on mainland Asia. It reflected the thinking of many high-ranking officers worldwide, including that of Douglas MacArthur and his staff in Manila. These men recognized Patton as one of the all-time great generals, the far-seeing man who had created the Army's Tank Corps way back in 1918. Of Eisenhower, MacArthur said only that "He was the best clerk I ever had." Unfortunately, Patton's genius was not recognized by the "small men by whom we are governed" in Washington. To the great detriment of the war effort and hundreds of thousands of unnecessary casualties, they regularly bypassed Patton and promoted officers over him who had never before exercised a combat command, Marshall, Eisenhower, Smith and Bradley among many others. A pipsqueak Harry Truman could write in his diary: "Don't see how a country can produce such men as Robert E. Lee, John J. Pershing, Eisenhower, and Bradley and at the same time produce Custers, Pattons, and MacArthurs." Imagine, this about Patton who saved the invasions of North Africa and Europe from turning into catastrophes. And MacArthur, who conducted a masterful retreat to Corregidor in Manila Bay when faced by overwhelming Japanese forces, who would conduct a brilliant campaign to save Korea from Communism in the coming Korean War (until sabotaged by Truman's no-win war policy) and who, as Supreme Allied Commander in the Pacific, would guide Japan into becoming a free-market economic powerhouse. It sounds like a little man with a big ego confronting a big man with a big ego. But what matter vanity and ego in the face of competence? Had Patton been used wisely instead of ignored by mediocre men of lesser ability, the war could have ended much sooner than it did and with the avoidance of future consequences. And if MacArthur had been heeded, the 50,000 American boys killed in the Korean War might have survived. But let me review General Wedemeyer's remark in context.

In late 1942 and in response to Stalin's urging, American and British forces under the command of General Eisenhower (recently raised to the four-star rank) opened a second front with the invasion of North Africa. Code-named Operation Torch, its objectives were 1) to expel the German and Italian armies occupying Tunisia and 2) and to attack General Erwin Rommel's *Afrika Corps* retreating to Tunisia after its defeat at El Alamein. But inexperienced leadership from Eisenhower on down threatened the whole expedition with disaster. The first battle between U. S. troops of the II Corps, commanded by Major General Lloyd Fredendall, and Rommel's *Panzer* units occurred on 15 February 1943 at Kasserine Pass in Tunisia and resulted in a disastrous and demoralizing defeat for the American forces. Fortunately, Rommel could not follow up his advantage because of Montgomery's entry into southern Tunisia. I myself took basic training later that year at Fort Hood, a tank destroyer camp in Texas that had seen many of its units simply wiped out. "Never have so few commanded so many from so far away," was how one recently returned survivor put it. Eisenhower had directed overall operations from his command bunker at Gibraltar, Fredendall from a large dugin headquarters seventy miles behind the lines. Eisenhower finally had the good sense to dismiss the incompetent Fredendall (the choice of both he and Chief of Staff George C. Marshall to command II Corps) and bring in a hands-on, combat seasoned Patton to revitalize the troops. Soon after, II Corps aided Montgomery's advance along the coast by routing a German advance near the oasis village of El-Guettar. Eisenhower received his fourth star and Patton a long overdue third star just before this first American victory of the war.

There then ensued "Operation Stop-Patton," a line of four orders from SHAEF (Supreme Headquarters of the Allied Expeditionary Force), the first two of which (at Falaise and the Meuse River) I have already covered. The third occurred just after the so-called Battle of the Bulge in the winter of 1944-5. "Bulge" was to be the greatest land battle ever fought by American soldiers. It would involve 600,000 Germans, 500,000 Americans, and 55,000 British and claimed 80,000 American casualties. And it should never have taken place.

The Market-Garden debacle had given the German commander in the west, Field Marshall Gerd von Runstedt, the time to establish a strong defense line extending some 120 miles southward from the border city of Aachen through the Ardennes Forest to Luxembourg. Along with torrential rains, a harsh terrain and the coldest winter in years, it stalemated American operations into the winter. Bradley's 12th Army Group, composed of Major General Courtney Hodges' First Army and Major General William Simpson's Ninth Army in the north and Patton's Third Army in the south, fronted the Germans. The area facing the Ardennes functioned as a rest and recuperation sanctuary and was thinly held by only six divisions of the First Army. It was from here that the German *Panzers* had broken out at the beginning of the hot war in May of 1940. But Eisenhower (just raised to the newly created five-star rank of General of the Army), Bradley and Hodges thought it unlikely that a major attack could be launched under the existing weather conditions. And even if one were to occur, flanking attacks from north and south would easily contain it. All of them ignored ominous intelligence reports from Colonel Oscar Koch, Third Army's G-2 (intelligence) officer, pointing to a huge buildup of men and equipment in the sector. The coming battle would catch them flat-footed.

On 16 December 1944 and in miserable weather conditions that grounded Allied air operations, twenty-eight German divisions stormed out of the Ardennes hoping for a repeat of the 1940 breakthrough. The main target was the Belgian port of Antwerp through which nearly all Allied supplies passed. Once secured, that would split Montgomery's 21st Army Group from Patton's Third Army and subject each in turn to annihilation by superior numbers of German troops. "We can still lose this damn war!" Patton exclaimed. When the magnitude of the attack became apparent, Eisenhower, over Bradley's vehement objections, placed the American First and Ninth Armies under Montgomery's command and ordered him to attack the northern shoulder of the developing salient in the Allied lines. Montgomery, however, delayed and did not attack until 3 January, by which time the Germans had reached nearly to the Meuse River. Only determined American resistance at the vital Belgian road center of Bastogne and other points slowed the advance sufficiently to prevent the immediate seizure of the huge American supply base at Liege. That city formed a vital part of the "Ardennes Offensive" because German tanks lacked adequate supplies of gasoline to reach Antwerp.

In desperation, Eisenhower called an emergency top command conference for 19 December at Verdun to see what could be done. Fortunately for Eisenhower and the war's outcome, however, Patton had anticipated the offensive. He believed Koch's intelligence reports and had prepared all the paperwork necessary to swivel the Third Army, 250,000 strong, 90 degrees from east to north. He informed the conferees that he could have three divisions headed for Bastogne in 48 hours. Colonel Charles Codman, his aide, writes of the reaction in the room: "There was a stir, a shuffling of feet, as those present straightened up in their chairs. In some faces, skepticism. But through the room the current of excitement leaped like a flame." Patton's army and logisticians would now "be responsible for a major effort to knife into the German southern flank." A forced march of 100 miles along icy, rutted roads brought the troops to besieged Bastogne, and on the day after Christmas the village was liberated. "Funny thing, George," Eisenhower had remarked after the conference, "every time I get a star I get attacked." "And every time you get attacked, Ike, I have to bail you out" retorted Patton.

The north-south pincer feared by the Germans now began to close. Dwindling supplies of gasoline and ammunition plus the return of fair weather Allied air operations turned a German retreat turned into a rout, and only Montgomery's delayed attack permitted the escape of a few divisions. But the Germans had lost upwards of 100,000 irreplaceable men and tons of equipment. Again, the road to Berlin appeared wide open. And once again, another stop-Patton order surfaced. From here to the end, the war would take on the aspects of a huge publicity campaign. Oh, yes: Both Bradley and Hodges received Distinguished Service Medals for their laxity in leadership and command; neither Patton nor his Third Army received a polite thank you for their monumental rescue.

Montgomery argued for, and Eisenhower approved Operation Plunder, a "single, full-blooded thrust" toward Berlin starting with a giant pincer movement to cut off the industrial Ruhr Valley. The plan called for the British 21st Army Group, along with Simpson's Ninth Army, to cross the Rhine between the German towns of Wesel and Rees. The American 1st Army, further up river to the south, would make its crossing *after* Montgomery and turn north to close the trap. Patton's Third Army (his "Eighth Wonder of the World") would be relegated to a defensive posture protecting the southern flank of the operation. As might be imagined, Patton, with Berlin again wide open, was furious when notified of his non-attack role on 10 February, so much so that Bradley had to threaten a cutoff of his gasoline supply to stop him from disobeying orders.

Montgomery, unnecessarily cautious as usual, waited until 23 March before beginning the Rhine crossing. It was accompanied by a huge publicity campaign and wide press coverage. Even Winston Churchill appeared to see the great event. But the Germans had been given time to recoup and fight from prepared defensive positions east of the Rhine, and the British attack bogged down once again. And to make matters more embarrassing for the British, the whole affair was anticlimactic. Two weeks earlier on 7 March, the Rhine had been crossed when the American First Army seized the bridge at Remagen intact and established a bridgehead east of the Rhine eighty miles to the south. And to further complicate British- American relations, Patton also crossed the Rhine at Oppenheim sixty miles further south a day before Montgomery. When a British staff officer complained that Remagen did not fit in with "the plan," Bradley, now thoroughly fed up with Montgomery, responded: "What in hell do you want us to do, pull back and blow it up?"

Freed at last of all restraints, the three American armies plunged eastward, encountering only token resistance. German soldiers were all too happy to be taken prisoner by the Americans and not the Russians. In a message to Roosevelt on 3 April, Stalin complained that "at the present moment, the Germans have ceased the war against England and the United States. At the same time, the Germans continue the war with Russia, the Ally of England and the United States." Obviously, the Germans knew very well that capture by the Russians would mean execution or slave labor camps.

Simpson's Ninth Army and Hodges' First Army reached the Elbe River in early April. Simultaneously, Patton's Third Army took the Czechoslovakian city of Pilsen, forty miles from the capital city of Prague. And at this point there precipitated another of the great blunders of the war, for another stop-Patton order surfaced, and this time it included Simpson and Hodges.

On 4 April, Eisenhower informed Patton that the First and Ninth Armies would be halted at the Elbe River and await the arrival of the Russians. He, Patton, would stop at Pilsen and allow the Russians to take most of Czechoslovakia including Prague. Patton was flabbergasted: "Ike, I don't see how you figure this one. We had better take Berlin quick and then on to the Oder." At the time the Russians were stopped at the Oder River 40 miles east of Berlin by fierce German resistance. Even Churchill and Montgomery were appalled. On learning of Eisenhower's decision, Churchill immediately wired Roosevelt his views: "The Russian armies will no doubt overrun all Austria and enter Vienna. If they also take Berlin, will not their impression that they have been the overwhelming contributor to our common victory be unduly imprinted in their minds, and may this not lead them into a mood which will raise grave and formidable difficulties in the future? I therefore consider that from a political stand point we should march as far east into Germany as possible." Patton and Churchill were fully cognizant that Stalin wanted real estate and would not give it up once he got it. The phrase "cold war" had not been invented as yet, but they knew it was coming.

Obviously, the decision to hand Eastern Europe over to the Communists must have come from Roosevelt. And he had obviously not even informed Churchill of his deliberations. It was just one of many secret agreements agreed to by him and Stalin at the Yalta Conference. Not for naught did a Franklin D. Roosevelt Boulevard suddenly appear in Yalta. When Eisenhower secretly communicated the stopping plan to Stalin, the latter replied: "Berlin has lost its former strategic importance. The Soviet High Command therefore plans to allot secondary forces in the direction of Berlin." But within moments after receiving the communication, Stalin ordered Marshall G. K. Zhukov to attack in force along the Oder. Berlin and half of Germany would in the future be in the Russian zone. The decision marked the beginning of the cold war that would last until the demise of the Soviet Empire forty years later.

Simpson was less than 40 miles from Berlin when told by Bradley to halt at the Elbe and was of the opinion that he could take it in less than 48 hours. "Where the hell did you get this?" Simpson raged when ordered to stop. "From Ike," replied Bradley. Simpson, a close friend and confidant of Patton, could only obey orders convinced that a terrible mistake had been made. In Prague, the Czech resistance movement, upon learning that Patton was in nearby Pilsen, rose up, but all too soon. "For God's sake, Brad, those patriots in the city need our help. We have no time to lose." But Bradley refused to countermand Eisenhower's orders, and the uprising was ruthlessly suppressed by the German SS.

Roosevelt died on 12 April 1945. He was succeeded as President by Vice-President Harry S. Truman who, at the Potsdam Conference in July, displayed to Stalin the same naïveté in foreign affairs as his predecessor. As a result of that meeting, Eastern Europe would remain in the Russian sphere of influence and Berlin would be divided into four zones – American, Russian, British and French – all located completely in the Russian half of Germany. Stalin would take advantage of Truman's timidity by unleashing Mao in China, by blockading "island" Berlin in 1948, and by sponsoring the Korean War in 1950.

Stalin violated most of the agreements made at Yalta and Potsdam. He had already annexed Estonia, Latvia and Lithuania and would soon establish puppet Communist governments in East Germany, Romania, Bulgaria, Czechoslovakia, Yugoslavia, Albania and Poland, all now occupied by Russian troops. And he was attempting to do so in Greece and Turkey. Roosevelt and Truman seemed like putty in his hands. They even referred to him as "Uncle Joe," taking little heed of the well-known fact that he was the greatest mass murderer of all time. Upwards of 50 million people died, either through execution or starvation, from the imposition of communism in Russia. Roosevelt and Truman – "Innocents Abroad," as Mark Twain might have characterized them – both ignored Averell Harriman's admonition that "We can't do business with Stalin." They were under the illusion that their years of political experience enabled them to size up a man merely by looking him in the eye. "Ah, humbug!" And again, "Ah, humbug!" Those are the first words that should come to mind when reading about or listening to politicians.

George Patton, warrior, military historian, scholar, writer, poet, raconteur, gourmet, opera lover, mystic, arch conservative and an unbridled anti-Communist, died on 20 December 1945. How unfortunate it was, for a far better world might have emerged from World War II had he lived. On 9 December – it was supposed to be his last day in Germany before returning to an uproarious hero's welcome in America – his limousine collided with an army truck in a suburb of Mannheim. Injured in the crash, he was taken to a hospital in nearby Heidelberg where he died. Shortly thereafter, messages began coming through the Manila code room alluding to the strange circumstances surrounding his demise. None of these are pictured in the movie *Patton* (one of the all-time great films, in my opinion). There is a scene in which Patton and Bradley are nearly crushed by a heavily laden cart that inextricably breaks free from its moorings, but there was no hint of any wrong-doing. All messages concerning Patton, however, stopped abruptly. Names had been mentioned – a Donovan and a Bazata among others, and even the Russian NKVD secret service and the U.S. Office of Strategic Services (OSS) – but these meant nothing to me at the time, and I forgot about Patton's death until 1969, twenty-five years later. That was the year I joined the Pratt Institute faculty as professor and chairman of the physics department. A James Donovan had recently become president of Pratt, and that brought back memories. Was it the same man mentioned in the top secret messages I had seen in Manila? When I looked into it, I realized it could not have been. This Donovan had served on the legal staff at the Nuremberg war crime trials. He also negotiated the exchange of U2 spy plane pilot Gary Powers for Russian spy Rudolph Abel. Powers had been shot down and imprisoned in Russia while Abel was serving a 30-year term for heading an espionage ring working out of an artist studio in Brooklyn. But James Donovan had also been legal counsel to Major General William "Wild Bill" Donovan (no relation) who was commissioned by Roosevelt to create the OSS during World War II, and that aroused my interest. OSS was a cloak-and-dagger organization designed to aid underground resistance fighters in German occupied countries, and it was the forerunner of the CIA. Donovan was very pleasant and communicative when I met him at a Pratt cocktail party, until I told him about the Patton messages I had seen in Manila. When I asked him if he knew anything more about Patton's death, he broke off all conversation and turned abruptly away from me. He died of a massive heart attack a few months later, and I never saw him again. Not until 2008 did I think back on the implications of that rebuff. That is when Robert K. Wilcox's excellent book *Target: Patton* (Regenery Publishing, 2008) appeared, and it raised the strong possibility that Patton had been assassinated. But let me summarize what "actually" happened as presented in the book. Always remember, however, that history, like beauty and truth, is in the eye of the beholder. And when there are two or more beholders, you never fail to get an argument.

Patton was completing a tenure as governor of Bavaria and commander of a non-existent Fifteenth Army. More than likely, he had been assigned these posts to keep him quiet and out of the way. On this next-to-last day in Germany, he and his aide, Major General Hobart "Hap" Gay, were being driven in a dark green Cadillac limousine to a hunting site in the woods near Mannheim for shooting pheasants. It was about 11:45 on a Sunday morning in a northern suburb of Mannheim, on a road lined with litter and war ruin but devoid of traffic, that the car was approached by an oncoming, standard issue 2½-ton General Motors truck. Of a sudden, the truck driver turned 90° squarely in front of the limo. The limo driver managed to avoid a head-on collision but hit the truck sidewise. Patton was thrown forward and hit the wall separating sections of the limo and suffered a broken neck, a gashed forehead and paralysis from the neck down. No one else was injured, not even the driver. Taken to the army hospital in Heidelberg, he made a remarkable recovery, to the point he was about to be discharged and returned to America. However, he suddenly took a turn for the worse and died. There was no autopsy.

In December 1979 the other name mentioned above, Douglas Bazata, gave a speech at the Hilton Hotel in Washington DC to 450 invited guests, nearly all high-ranking ex-members of the OSS: "For diverse political reasons, many extremely high-ranking persons hated Patton. I know who killed him because I was the one who was hired to do it. Ten thousand dollars! General William "Wild Bill" Donovan himself, director of the OSS, entrusted me with the mission. I set up the 'accident.' Since he didn't die in the accident, he was kept in isolation in the hospital where he was killed with a cyanide injection." Bazata maintained that a refined form of cyanide, a favorite tool of the NKVD that caused embolisms and heart attacks, was used to kill Patton.

There could be no doubt that Patton was hated and resented by some and a hero to millions. He had made it known that he intended to resign from the army rather than retire so that he could speak and write freely without regard to military rules and regulations. He would give his version of the war, the truth as he saw it. It would "make big headlines," he wrote in his diary. If "Wild Bill" had given the assassination job to Bazata, the order must have come from Roosevelt to whom Donovan reported, and that was reaching into the highest places. Suppose we take a look at some of the high-ranking people who could have been embarrassed by Patton's revelations.

First, I consider President Franklin Delano Roosevelt whose administration was permeated with "Russky-files" from the very top down and with outright Communists. Vice-President Henry A. Wallace had proved himself so much a Communist sympathizer that the Democratic Party leaders forced Roosevelt to dump him for the 1944 election. Wallace would oppose Truman by running on the Communist-supported Progressive Party ticket in 1948. He was backed by Albert Einstein and many other intellectuals (my I-squares). Einstein even appeared on the same platform with Wallace during the campaign. Obviously, being a genius in one's own field of endeavor does not preclude one from being stupid in others.

Alger Hiss, a high ranking State Department official and a Russian spy, served on the American delegation to the Yalta Conference. He briefed Stalin on all the top secret deliberations of the American contingent and undoubtedly supported Roosevelt in the stop-Patton orders and land giveaways. Whether Patton knew anything about the Conference is moot. A counterpart in the British delegation, the "Cambridge Five" spy group, did the same. Stalin knew everything that was going on beforehand, including the atomic bomb project. He had started a Russian "Manhattan Project" of his own in 1942 utilizing secrets stolen from Los Alamos by physicist and spy Klaus Fuchs.

Roosevelt's infatuation with Russia went back at least to 1933. That is when he granted full diplomatic recognition to the Soviet Union, the model killer-state of the 20th century. It was something that Presidents Woodrow Wilson, Warren Harding, Calvin Coolidge and Herbert Hoover refused to do. In the " Roosevelt-Litvinov Conversations," the latter the Commisar for Foreign Affairs, they agreed to discuss at some future time the repayment of Russia's outstanding debt of $800 million to the U. S. Government and "private citizens." "Private citizens?" That could only mean America's merchants of debt headed by J. P. Morgan & Company. Litvinov also agreed to end Russia's interference in American internal affairs, I.e., aiding America's Communist Party. Finally, Litvinov promised to grant certain legal and religious rights to American citizens living in Russia. Following the conclusion of the talks, Roosevelt appointed William C. Bullitt as the America's first ambassador to the Soviet Union.

As might be expected by anybody but an innocent fool, Russia never lived up to any of the so-called agreements. Moreover, there began the first of the "Great Purges" through which Stalin liquidated all potential critics of the government. Execution and imprisonment awaited millions of Soviet citizens. The wide scope and public nature of the purges horrified both American diplomatic personnel stationed in Russia and the world at large. Bullitt resigned.

Roosevelt, however, seemed unaffected. In the hope of improving relations, he replaced Bullitt with businessman Joseph E. Davies, a heavy contributor to the Democratic Party. But relations between the two countries continued to deteriorate, reaching their nadir in 1939 when the Soviets signed a non-aggression treaty with Nazi Germany, the Molotov-Ribbentrop Pact. That permitted Hitler to launch his attack on France without worrying about a two-front war.

Patton, of course, was well aware of Roosevelt's attitude toward Soviet atrocities and duplicity. There could be no doubt that his public statements would have exploited Washington's softness toward Communism and its complicity in the European land giveaways had he lived.

Roosevelt died in 1945. Historians continue to write "absolute crap" about him.

Chief of Staff General George C. Marshall, along with General Dwight D. Eisenhower and his chief of staff Walter Bedell Smith, feared that Patton's outspokenness would expose many of the cowardly, incompetent and corrupt things done by the Allied High Command during World War II. I might begin with the choice by Roosevelt and Marshall of a "clerky," inexperienced and inept Dwight Eisenhower over Patton as Supreme Allied Commander in Europe. Then there were the frequent stop-Patton orders that cost over a hundred thousand American lives, and a monstrous and shameful Operation Keelhaul (see below) rigidly enforced by Eisenhower and opposed by Patton.

Wrote Patton in his diary in 1943: "Ike is very querulous and keeps saying how hard it is to be so high and never to have heard a hostile shot. He could correct that situation very easily if he wanted to. I also think that he is timid." Another entry in 1945: "Ike is bitten with the Presidential Bug and is yellow." And in 1945 when planning his resignation from the Army: "I shall prove even more conclusively that he lacks moral fortitude. This lack has been evident to me since the first landing in Africa, but now that he has been bitten by the Presidential Bee, it is becoming even more pronounced."

On Marshall's orders, Major [sic] Walter Bedell Smith was transferred from a Washington desk job to London where he became Eisenhower's chief of staff. He was quickly promoted to Lieutenant General, attaining that rank even before Patton. He died in 1969, a full general in the regular Army. Patton's permanent rank on his death was Lieutenant General.

With his seizure of power in Russia, Vladimir Lenin and his two lieutenants, Stalin and Leon Trotsky, turned immediately to their primary goal – world revolution. They invited members of the socialist parties in all countries to join a new grouping called the Communist

International or Comintern, thus forming, among many others, the Communist Party of the United States. All were under the control of the mother party in Moscow. Their openly avowed claim was the overthrow of all "capitalist" governments and the establishment of a universal state under Red auspices. All parties were to use whatever means – legal or illegal, peaceful or violent – that might be appropriate at the time. Their most noble intention was to bestow the blessings of Communism on all the world's peoples.

After World War II, Stalin returned to the old agenda. He foresaw one very formidable obstacle to his plans in the United States, the possible Presidency of George S. Patton. He well understood he could not toy with Patton as he had with Roosevelt and Truman, that a Berlin blockade or Korean War type of initiative could result in the downfall of the whole Communist movement. He certainly had the motivation to involve himself in any assassination plot.

Stalin died in 1953. The Soviet "Evil Empire" would persist until 1989 when a tough-minded President Ronald Reagan brought about its end.

Operation Keelhaul is little known to most people. To put it into perspective, it would be analogous to indicting all Americans for their complicity in the genocidal slaughter of the Indian population during the 19th century. We have here an excellent example of how the news media can bury unpleasant or embarrassing stories by simply not reporting them.

Keelhaul emerged from another one of those secret agreements made at Yalta by Roosevelt and Stalin. It specified that all refugees from Communism – men, women, children, soldiers, civilians, male or female – be rounded up and shipped back to "their countries of origin." Also included were German prisoners of war in Allied hands. Since all of Eastern Europe was under Communist domination, this was literally a death sentence either by execution or slow extermination from overwork and malnutrition in Siberian slave labor camps.

Rigidly enforced by Eisenhower, these people were rounded up at bayonet point, loaded into cattle cars – the same as used for transporting Jews to German death camps – and shipped off. Numerical estimates of those repatriated vary from two million to five million. Some 12000 American prisoners of war captured by the Germans suffered the same fate. No Russian prisoners of war wanted to return because Stalin regarded them as traitors.

The father of my German son-in-law, a prisoner of war in American hands, was able to escape when he and several comrades jumped off a Russia-bound train. The American guards allowed them to run off by firing over their heads, for which he was ever grateful. A fifteen year old cousin escaped impressment into the army during the last days of the war when his mother hid him on the family farm. At the time SS agents were rounding up all boys twelve and over for military duty. In no sense could these people be considered Nazis.

This repatriation policy of the Roosevelt Administration violated the same laws for which German officials were prosecuted at the Nuremberg war crime trials, but neither Roosevelt nor Eisenhower were ever accused of wrong-doing. Patton, who favored a combined effort using Allied and German soldiers to force Russian troops back to their pre-War border, was outraged. What a great President Patton would have made!

In July of 1945, General MacArthur was informed that extremely powerful bombs of a new type would be dropped on Japan. Scant attention was paid to the message, however. Japanese cities had been all but burned out in mass incendiary attacks, and nobody thought that more bombing could make much of a difference. Preparations were well under way for the invasion of the southernmost Japanese island of Kyushu that October, and some estimates of casualties exceeded one million. That the Japanese military would defend their holy homeland soil as it had the islands of Tarawa, Okinawa and Iwo Jima went unquestioned. The Japanese survivors of the battle for Manila had taken refuge in the mountains east of the city, and there most chose death by starvation rather than capture by the American devils. Those that didn't infiltrated into the city nightly looking for food, only to be shot and mutilated for souvenirs.

The new atomic bomb was another triumph for deterministic physics. A pre-calculated device, it generated temperatures and pressures never before approached on earth. And it ended the war with Japan. Significantly, in talking later with Dutch soldiers imprisoned near Hiroshima, I learned that their captors simply vanished after the explosion. And so did their *kamikaze*-like fanaticism. Those soldiers knew at once that all was lost and that it was now time to pursue their own best interests as seen by them and not by their rulers. But it took another bomb drop, this time on Nagasaki, to end the war. In retrospect, one bomb targeting the politicians in Tokyo rather than the civilian populations of Hiroshima and Nagasaki would have proved sufficient. With the top government officials dead, the Japanese men and women in the armed forces would probably have acted in the same way as the prison guards. And Japanese families, like their American counterparts, would surely have been deliriously happy to welcome their men home. The German officers who in July of 1943 attempted the assassination of Adolf Hitler obviously had the same thoughts about politicians. To them, getting rid of those at the top was the only way of ending what had become a hopelessly lost war. In more recent times, the same formula was applied to Libya. Rather than going to war, President Ronald Reagan ordered the killing of dictator Moammar Qaddafi for his complicity in a terrorist attack on a Berlin discoteque, 5 April 1986. That episode had resulted in the death of three American soldiers and injury to 79. Although a number of his bodyguards died, Qaddafi managed to survive the "smart bomb" strike on his home in Tripoli. Unfortunately, he could then sponsor the attack on Pan Am Flight 103 that exploded over Lockerbie, Scotland, on 21 December 1988. The death toll there amounted to 259 on the airplane and eleven on the ground. I must note as well that the Revolutionary War would have proved unnecessary if the American colonists had been able to get at George III. Political power does indeed grow out of the barrel of a gun, as believed by Mao Tse-Tung, but take the gun away and that power quickly evaporates. Maximum Freedom is what people need, and that means first dispensing with Maximum Leader.

Pandemonium! It broke out in the last rows of the makeshift theater where those of us off duty were watching a movie. It soon reached the front rows in a mounting cascade of shouts, hugging, back-slapping, hand-shaking. The Japanese government had sued for peace. Instantaneously, we in Manila realized that we would not have to contend with *kamikaze* suicide pilots on the coming invasion, that we would not have to die on the beaches of Japan, that we would no longer have to endure a terribly low standard of living for years to come, that we could go home to make a life for ourselves "in the freest country in the universe."

The swift and unexpected capitulation of Japan soon brought forth the joyous news of a quick demobilization; all personnel with two or more years of service were to be discharged by 20 March 1946. Our joy was short-lived, however. Sometime in October, disturbing messages began coming through the Manila code room indicating a slowdown in demobilization. The Washington establishment had finally begun to recognize Josef Stalin for the Marxist monster he was and they hoped to forestall Communist takeovers in China and Europe by lengthening enlistment times. We in the Philippines were to occupy the Chinese port cities of Hong Kong, Tientsin, Shanghai and Canton and furnish support for Chiang Kai-Shek in his civil war against Mao Tse-Tung. In addition, several army divisions from Europe would be deployed to Asia. But the announcement of the change in demobilization plans was greeted with massive troop demonstrations in Manila, Tokyo, Seoul, Honolulu, Frankfort, Guam, Vienna, Paris, London and elsewhere. We were expendable, we were outraged, and we had guns. Was this to be a war without end? How many more years would we civilian soldiers have to serve now seemed to rest on the whims and stupidity of the same politicians who had conceded almost everything to Stalin at Yalta and Potsdam. Truman was acting as if America had no atomic bomb, just as Stalin thought he would from his behavior at Potsdam. If it were necessary to stop Mao, he should have targeted him with it. And Stalin, too, if he objected. Why pick on us? If Russia had been successful in developing the bomb, Stalin would have become the Great Dictator of the World. Facing a Chinese Communist army of perhaps a million men armed with American weapons furnished to Russia during the War was not a prospect we looked forward to. But it must have been exactly what Stalin hoped for. With American forces bogged down fighting on the Asian mainland, he would have been free to subjugate all of Europe in what Ambassador to Russia Averell Harriman called a "barbarian invasion." Fortunately, the American people knew better. Protest letters by the hundreds of thousands demanding that the troops be brought home deluged Congressmen. The hue and cry had its effect. It forced Truman to rescind the new orders and discharge the troops as rapidly as possible.

There could be little doubt that Chiang Kai-Shek's Nationalist government was in serious trouble. Chief of Staff George C. Marshall, dispatched to China in 1946 to evaluate the prospects, described situation as "hopeless." But China had been in economic turmoil ever since America's nationalization of silver in 1934, and it had led to a massive government regulatory buildup and uncontrollable inflation. (A harbinger of times to come for 21st-century America?) By 1946, living conditions in China had worsened to the point at which the people thought they might be better off under Mao Tse-Tung's Communist rather than Chiang's Nationalist government. The Communists finally assumed full control of mainland China in 1949. Chiang managed to escape to the island of Taiwan where he set up his Republic of China government consisting of all his old cronies. When he died in 1975, his much wiser son, Chiang Chung-Kuo, took over as President and established a free market economy. From that time on,

GDP growth proceeded at the high rate of 8% per year, and Taiwan became one of the four "Asian Tigers," the others being Hong Kong, Singapore and South Korea. Mainland China would suffer under Mao's terrorist rule until Deng Xiao-Ping appeared on the scene thirty years later.

CHAPTER XXXVIII

WORLD WAR II AND THE RETURN OF PROSPERITY II

In monetary matters, appearances are deceiving; the important relationships are often precisely the reverse of those that strike the eye.

Milton Friedman and Anna Schwartz, A *Monetary History of the United States 1960-1967*

The nation that will insist upon drawing a broad line of demarcation between the fighting man and the thinking man is liable to find its fighting done by fools and its thinking done by cowards.

William Francis Butler

The 1940s arrived accompanied by another plunge in the nation's standard of living. And for the usual reason: government intervention into the private economy. But, in this case, it was all too justifiable. Politicians running the big government dictatorships of Germany, Italy and Japan were on the prowl, subjugating nations around the world, and spending for war was mandatory to avoid far worse consequences. Undertaking the defense of the nation, in my opinion, is one of the few legitimate functions of government.

World War II cost in excess of $500 billion, the money supplied by taxes, war bond drives à la Jay Cooke, short-term Treasury borrowings, and money printing by the Federal Reserve. It was inefficient government spending on a grand scale. The private economy was now called on to furnish war goods and services in place of those formerly produced in peacetime. The civilian home front, as a result, suffered. It had to carry on without new automobiles, without new housing or construction, and without new appliances, without new radios and without about-to-be released television sets. Shortages of clothing, food, gas, oil, electricity and transportation prevailed. There was little in the way of business expansion or start-ups, and that caused economic growth to come to a halt. Not a very pretty picture of life in the '40s, to be sure. But for the 16 million young people who served in the armed forces, the standard of living plummeted even more. In compensation, however, anybody who wanted a job had one. America's war economy, then, mirrored those existing in Communist Russia and China and the Third World countries in Africa where inefficient government spending is the norm.

After the War, a truly extraordinary chain of events inaugurated a full-blown "let my people spend" economy. And, as we chaosticians might expect, a booming prosperity ensued. President Harry Truman and the Congress, ignoring all the dire warnings from New Deal Keynesian economists, slashed government spending from $83 billion to $30 billion during the 1945 and 1946 years. The move allowed $53 billion in government procurements to be replaced by private contracts for peacetime goods and services. And, fortunately, war profits, redemptions of government bonds and short-term securities, hoarded cash, bank deposits and loans were more than sufficient to finance a rapid transition from war to civilian production.

Congress now chimed in with a tax cut, the Revenue Act of 1945. It reduced the top income tax rate from 94% [sic] to 86.45%, the top corporate rate from 40% to 38%, and eliminated the "excess" profits tax on business. Although Truman rejected the bill believing that balancing the budget was of first priority, Congress passed it over his veto.

[I should mention at this point that later studies by the Internal Revenue Service indicated that high income taxpayers rarely paid at the confiscatory top rates. Because of the convoluted tax code and tax exempt state and municipal bonds, their highly paid lawyers and accountants easily managed to reduce their average rate of payment to about 28% of income. That rate became tops in the Reagan tax cut of the 1980s. And it brought more tax money into the Treasury! Paying taxes to government became less costly than paying fees to lawyers and accountants.]

But perhaps the biggest tax cut of all came from black market operations. Home after discharge from the army in March 1946, I found everybody engaged in cash dealings for the necessities and niceties of life, all in short supply. It was a binge of highly efficient black market dealings unfettered by income tax considerations. No one believed "It was an honor to pay taxes!" as one very rich acquaintance of mine told me. Of course, his family had hired a gang of highly paid lawyers and accountants to do everything possible to avoid payment of them. A sharp drop in the ratio of bank deposits to currency held by the public attested to massive cash dealings. As for myself, I could not even find a suit for sale in local stores, and only when my father directed me to an inconspicuous second-floor hole-in-the-wall store in New York City could I buy a fine suit and have it fitted – cash only. "Cash was King."

Inflation, of course, was rampant. The War still had to be paid for. But the Federal Reserve could do nothing to contain it. In 1942, to help finance the War by making short-term securities more marketable, it had acceded to Treasury's request to buy and sell bills and certificates in any amount necessary to maintain interest rates at 3/8% and 7/8% respectively. (Bills are IOU's sold at a discount with maturities up to one year. Certificates are IOU's sold at par with interest payable at maturity.) This action prevented the Fed from pulling money out of the private economy via open-market operations and made bills and certificates the equivalent of cash. Buyers were given the option of repurchasing the paper they held in the same amounts and at the same interest rates at maturity. Thus, banks, merchants of debt, corporations, businesses and individuals could help Treasury service its debt by buying government paper, receive interest on it, and then retrieve cash immediately when the need arose. In addition, the Fed lowered reserve requirements for its member banks making for much greater loan availability. The policy continued into 1947 and then, with modifications, until ended by the Treasury-Federal Reserve Accord of 1951. So vigorous had the economy become by then that not even the Korean War could inflict much damage on it.

A further tax reduction was included in the Revenue Act of 1948, which reduced individual income taxes by as much as 13%, raised the personal exemption from $500 to $600, allowed married couples to split their incomes to take advantage of lower brackets, and added an additional exemption for those over 65 years of age.

Strikes in almost every industry beset the economy during the post-War era. Union workers who had held off demanding wage increases during the War now wanted "catch-up." But the unions also demanded price freezes from business ("no price increases because of wage increases"). Truman, a liberal who had railed for years against big corporations on the Senate floor, who had never run a successful business and who could not even read a balance sheet, went along as part of his anti-inflation policy. In his eyes, the free market served as the scapegoat for inflation, not government spending. It was the ancient formula of Roman Emperor Diocletian applied anew: Blame the greedy businessmen, not the greedy politician, for inflation! Government spending had nothing to do with it! Ah humbug, again.

In January 1946, a protracted strike of 700,000 workers in the steel industry began and brought about Truman's intervention into it. The steel workers demanded a 19½¢ increase in hourly wages and no increase in steel prices. Company officers offered 15¢. On the basis of figures supplied to him by his equally ignorant bureaucrats, Truman proposed 18½¢. Again, the companies refused. Their officers were not about to jeopardize the industry's future prospects by conducting business at a loss. And who knew better than they what their companies could afford. Hadn't free market performance all through the 19th and early 20th centuries shown that company officials were the best determinants of pricing policies? Haven't we learned from our study of chaos that you can't fix free markets, that government intervention can only make them worse? Of course, that is not what politicians or economists want to believe because such notions are against their own selfish interests.

A tyrannical threat by Truman to draft railroad workers into the Army in order to stop a railroad strike did not come to fruition due to a fortuitous settlement between management and labor.

The steel strike and all the others, although unnecessarily prolonged by government intervention, were finally settled by allowing companies to raise prices as well. Inflation subsequently subsided when War costs were paid down sufficiently and government expenditures came into balance with receipts.

In 1952, the strike threats reappeared during the Korean War, and it was the same old story – Diocletion reincarnated. Truman, having learned nothing in his long tenure as President, again blamed businessmen for the inflation that had erupted. Once again he veered toward tyranny in his attempts to cope with it, just as he had in 1946 when he threatened to draft railroad workers into the Army to keep the trains running. The steelworkers demanded a 35¢

hourly wage increase; the companies refused to negotiate. Truman referred the dispute to bureaucrats on a Wage Stabilization Board, which recommended an hourly raise of 26¢. The companies agreed if it were accompanied by a $12 price increase in a ton of steel. And there, all negotiation ceased as Truman stubbornly rejected industry demands out of hand. Even Truman's own director of defense mobilization, Charles E. Wilson, agreed with the position of the steel companies and resigned when overridden.

Truman now decided that he had no alternative but government seizure of the steel mills. On 8 April, just hours before the scheduled strike, he signed Executive Order #10340. At 10:30 that night, he explained his action on a nationwide broadcast: "The plain fact of the matter is that the steel companies are recklessly forcing a shutdown. They are trying to get special, preferred treatment . . . And they are apparently willing to stop steel production to get it. As President of the United States it is my plain duty to keep this from happening . . . At midnight the Government will take over the steel plants."

The steel industry immediately sued to get its property back. A federal district court judge, David Pine, ruled the action illegal. "So, you contend that the Executive has unlimited power in time of emergency?" asked Judge Pine of Assistant Attorney-General Holmes Baldridge attempting to clarify Truman's position on the mills. Replied Baldridge: "He has the power to take such action as is necessary to meet the emergency." To which he added that it was for the President to determine whether such existed and the decision could not be challenged in court. The Supreme Court announced that it would hear the case. Truman maintained that he would, of course, abide by the Court's ruling. He had, he claimed, no ambition to be a dictator.

On 2 June, the Court declared the President's action unconstitutional by a 6 to 3 majority. Those in the majority were ardent New Dealers Hugo Black, Felix Frankfurter, Robert H. Jackson, William O. Douglas and Tom Clark. Even they recognized tyranny when it was shoved right under their noses.

The steel strike began right after the Court's decision and dragged on for seven weeks. It was finally settled with the workers receiving a 21¢ hourly raise and the steel price increased by $5.20 a ton.

In 1955, Republican Dwight Eisenhower realized his ambition to become President. He ended the Korean War by threatening the use of newly developed nuclear tactical weapons. During his administration, high government spending for the Korean War was slashed and expenditures remained in line with receipts through the John F. Kennedy years 1960-1964. When recession loomed in the early 1960s, Kennedy launched the Revenue Act of 1964 (the Kennedy tax cut). Individual rates were slashed to 14%-70% from 20%-91%, the top corporate rate from 52% to 48%. The Act also created a minimum standard deduction of $300 plus $100 per exemption. It was signed into law by successor President Lyndon Johnson. Prosperity continued until government spending zoomed once again, when Johnson decided to pursue simultaneously his "Great Society" initiative and the Vietnam War. From then on, balanced federal budgets vanished into a string of deficits that exploded exponentially to *$3 trillion* in the year 2009. America's "Let my people spend" society would vanish in favor of inefficient political spending on an enormous scale. And because of our new "barnyard" policy of penalizing producers and rewarding failed and non producers, we even in America now stand a good chance of living hungrily ever after.

On 9 February 1946, the consequences of the Roosevelt-Truman policy of Russian appeasement came into glaring reality. Stalin, in one of his rare public speeches, laid down the gauntlet of things to come. Communism and capitalism were incompatible, he declared, and another war was inevitable. He called for a new five-year plan to "guarantee our country against any eventuality." Production for national defense was to be tripled; consumer goods "must wait on rearmament." Confrontation with the capitalist west, he predicted, would come in the 1950s, when America would be in the depths of another depression. Ah, yes. Another foolish Marxist prediction as wrong as could be. But, for Russia and Eastern Europe and China, it meant continued inefficient government spending and poverty.

Nowhere was the dividing line between western wealth and eastern poverty more evident than across the political boundary of West and East Berlin. Half a million people daily crossed the border between the two from one part of the city to the other. East Berliners could go to cinemas, discos and even work in the West. Only there were tropical fruits available, and only there could women can get their first seamless panty hoses. So galling to Communist leaders this state of affairs must have been that Stalin in 1948 clamped a blockade on Allied traffic into and out of Berlin. His aim, obviously, was to lower the standard of living of 2½ million West Berliners down to the Communist level. Interestingly, another one of those secret Yalta agreements had given him the power to control ground and water but not air traffic. Truman took advantage of this omission to launch an air supply operation which, against all odds, succeeded in supplying West Berlin with all the supplies necessary to maintain its status quo. One year later, in 1949, Stalin backtracked and lifted the blockade. In 1961, a new Soviet regime constructed the Berlin Wall that blocked all traffic between the two parts of the city, including train, bus, and subway service. It would last until the demise of the "Evil Empire" in 1989.

In 1948, under the urging of the Truman administration, Congress got around to passing the Marshall Plan to save Europe from itself. It earmarked the huge sum of $17 billion dollars to aid countries ravished by war. It was once again the "barnyard" policy of confiscating the wealth of American producers to reward non-producers on an international scale. Our great politicians and bureaucrats –inefficient spenders nonpareil – would sprinkle the bonanza on their counterparts in all the countries of Europe including Russia and the Communist dominated states. It mattered little that these countries had gotten along for hundreds of years, through war, pestilence, famine and disease, without us. The Plan was named for General George C. Marshall, Secretary of State because his war reputation was most likely secure Congressional approval. Well, my readers are somewhat familiar with Marshall's record during the War, and subsequent events would not enhance it, except in accounts by statist historians. [See, for example, David McCullough's *Truman*, Simon & Shuster, 1992. One cannot read this very detailed, well written book without conjuring up a picture of *beaucoup de médiocrités* lurching hither and thither trying to cope with chaos, while at the same time despising great men like Patton and MacArthur who might have shown the way.]

The Marshall Plan was of dubious value. Economic recoveries in Belgium, Holland, Germany, France and Italy, countries that depended on free markets to solve their problems, predated aid. Belgium relied most heavily on free markets and recovered earliest after liberation. She experienced the fastest growth and even avoided severe food and housing shortages seen in the rest of Europe. After a stumbling start, Germany recovered next, due to a brilliant Minister for Economic Affairs, Ludwig Erhard. By disposing of numbing regulations and letting free markets operate untrammeled, Erhard is credited for Germany's strong economic revival. He looked on aid as wastefully used by self-serving politicians and bureaucrats. On the other hand, France and Italy used the American subsidies to adopt socialist measures that retarded their recoveries.

Following the War, England elected a socialist government headed by Prime Minister Clement Atlee and that brought the country almost to its knees by 1980. By then the British pound, once the strongest currency in the world, had fallen almost to parity with the dollar, from $2.50 to $1.05. At the time, I was considering the purchase of a house in the Royal Crescent in Bath for $40,000 both as an investment and as a home for my British in-laws, but decided there was too much chance of an English bankruptcy. That holding is today worth millions, but who could know that a Maggie Thatcher would epiphanize. Finally, I must note that Japan, required no aid whatsoever in her strong recovery under MacArthur's guidance. Nor did Singapore, Taiwan, Hong Kong and South Korea.

The Marshall Plan, however, set a precedent. Hundreds of billions of dollars confiscated from American taxpayers would soon be squandered through highly-paid, world-roaming economists, bankers and bureaucrats at the United Nations, the International Monetary Fund and the World Bank to rescue countries from the "brink of oblivion." It is the old Marxist syndrome of spreading the wealth to achieve equality of reward and put America into a "barnyard hen" type of society – take from the producers and give it to the non-producers.

Korea! And another political boundary line dividing wealth from poverty. Somehow, for reasons known only to the great political minds of the world, the Korean peninsula had been divided along the 38th parallel of latitude into a northern communist part and a southern capitalist part. As in Berlin, it proved an intolerable situation for communist leaders in Pyongyang, the capital of North Korea, and in Moscow and Beijing. Only this time, it led to war. In June 1950 the North Korean army, 230,000 strong, crossed the line in overwhelming force, driving back 65,000 South Koreans and the few American troops remaining in Korea into a small area around Pusan, a port in the southeast, six hundred miles from the border. Known as the "Pusan Perimeter," it managed a desperate holdout against fierce attacks.

Truman quickly decided that Communist aggression such as this had to be stopped, so he drove our country to war with one hand tied behind her back, the one holding the atomic bomb. He could drop two bombs on the civilian populations of Hiroshima and Nagasaki to end World War II, but not one bomb targeting the political and military leaders in Pyongyang that could have ended the invasion forthwith. Instead, 50,000 young Americans would die for the cause along with an estimated 2.5 million Chinese and Korean soldiers and civilians. What part the Communists in the State Department played in his decision is an interesting point. More likely, Stalin knew Truman for the "not much" he was and had gambled that the bomb would not be used.

MacArthur quickly poured troops, artillery, tanks and munitions into Pusan stabilizing the front. At the same time, he set in motion an over-arching military operation that could end the war in one fell swoop. An amphibious attack on Inchon, 500 miles to the north on the Yellow Sea, would cut off the North Korean army and subject it to annihilation and capture. Despite reluctance on the part of the Washington generals, Truman approved the attack, and we all know how tremendously successful if proved. The War appeared over, and MacArthur was given the go ahead to liberate all of Korea right up to the Chinese border, despite ominous warnings from the Chinese that they would intervene. Since Truman seemed to have no contingency plans if that should happen, MacArthur must naturally have assumed he would call the shots. The Chinese did enter Korea over the Yalu River border bridges and in overwhelming numbers, driving the American forces back. MacArthur called for atom bombing the approaches to the bridges and isolate the Chinese from their supplies, and Truman again refused to use the bomb. The bloodiest part of the War now ensued as the American forces were driven back almost to the 38th parallel. There, a stalemate developed, which ended when a new President, Dwight Eisenhower, threatened to use tactical nuclear weapons on the Chinese, as already mentioned. A peace treaty restored the Korean Peninsula to its pre-War status.

It was a no-win war. And today, fifty years later, we still suffer the consequences. A Communist North Korea is now in the process of developing nuclear and missile capabilities.

CHAPTER XXXIX

THE DECLINE
AND FALL OF THE AMERICAN REPUBLIC:
THE CHAPTER I HAD HOPED NOT TO WRITE

Change has come to America.

Barack Obama

April 2009 and the Obama administration now can and has fired CEO's of private companies. This administration now is in control of the automobile industry, the energy industry, the health industry, and the financial industry. They have spoken of new tax schemes, government run health care and a volunteer citizen defense force equipped as strongly as the military.

There is a fear of ever-increasing Obama Administration and Congressional intrusion into our private lives. Gun sales are sky-rocketing on fears of a ban on the right to bear arms. Will the Constitution be amended?

Unemployment is almost 10% and rising. The government has printed trillions of dollars for economic stimulus and plunging this country into debt levels never before seen. Foreign countries are concerned also and list goes on and on... Are we heading into Socialism? Communism? Dictatorship?

Burton P. Fabricand did not want to write this chapter... He started, but died May 5th, 2009 at age 85, one day after completing Chapter 38.